/

/74

ALSO BY ROBERT D. KAPLAN

The Ends of the Earth: A Journey at the Dawn of the 21st Century
The Arabists: The Romance of an American Elite
Balkan Ghosts: A Journey Through History
Soldiers of God: With the Mujahidin in Afghanistan
Surrender or Starve: The Wars Behind the Famine

AN EMPIRE WILDERNESS

AN
EMPIRE
WILDERNESS

TRAVELS INTO AMERICA'S FUTURE

ROBERT D. KAPLAN

RANDOM HOUSE

NEW YORK

Portions of this work were originally published
in *The Atlantic Monthly*

Grateful acknowledgment is made to the following for permission
to reprint previously published material:

Henry Holt and Company Inc.: Excerpt from *John Brown's Body* by Stephen Vincent
Benét. Copyright © 1927, 1928 by Stephen Vincent Benét. Reprinted by permission of
Henry Holt and Company, Inc.

Liveright Publishing Corporation: One line from "Powhatan's Daughter"
by Hart Crane and title usage of the same line from *Complete Poems
of Hart Crane* edited by Marc Simon. Copyright © 1933, 1958, 1966
by Liveright Publishing Corporation. Copyright © 1986 by Marc Simon.
Reprinted by permission of Liveright Publishing Corporation.

Library of Congress Cataloging-in-Publication Data
Kaplan, Robert D.
An empire wilderness: travels into America's future/Robert D. Kaplan.
p.   cm.
Includes bibliographical references and index.
ISBN 0-679-45190-0 (acid-free paper)
1. West (U.S.)—Description and travel.   2. West (U.S.)—Social conditions.   3. Kaplan,
Robert D.—Journeys—West (U.S.).   4. United States—Social conditions—
Forecasting.   I. Title.
F595.3.K36   1998
978—dc21   98-10179

Random House website address: www.randomhouse.com
Printed in the United States of America on acid-free paper
2   4   6   8   9   7   5   3
First Edition

To Jim Lewin and Mitchell Pilcer

The fact, then, that all existing things are subject to decay is a proposition which scarcely requires proof, since the inexorable course of nature is sufficient to impose it on us. Every kind of state, we may say, is liable to decline from two sources, the one being external, and the other due to its own internal evolution. . . . It is evident that under the influence of long-established prosperity life will become more luxurious, and among the citizens themselves rivalry for office and in other spheres of activity will become fiercer than it should. As these symptoms become more marked, the craving for office and the sense of humiliation which obscurity imposes, together with the spread of ostentation and extravagance, will usher in a period of general deterioration. The principal authors of this change will be the masses, who at some moments will believe that they have a grievance against the greed of other members of society, and at others are made conceited by the flattery of those who aspire to office. . . . They will no longer consent to obey or even to be the equals of their leaders, but will demand everything or by far the greatest share for themselves.

—Polybius,
The Rise of the Roman Empire
(translation by Ian Scott-Kilvert)

Rome . . . under the mild and generous influence of liberty [might] have remained invincible and immortal.

—Edward Gibbon,
*The History of the Decline and
Fall of the Roman Empire*

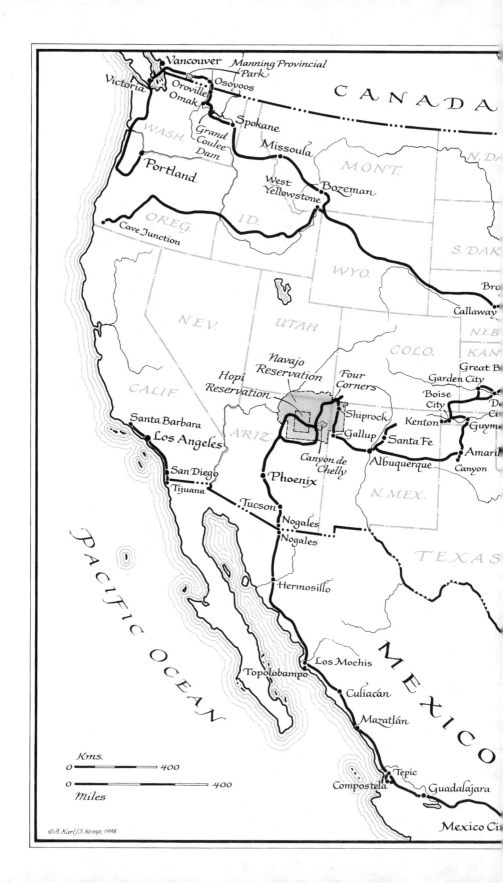

CANADA

Vancouver
Manning Provincial Park
Victoria
Oroville
Osoyoos
Omak
Spokane
WASH.
Grand Coulee Dam
Missoula
MONT.
N. DA
Portland
OREG.
West Yellowstone
Bozeman
ID.
Cave Junction
S. DAK.
WYO.
NEV.
UTAH
Bro
Callaway
NEB
Navajo Reservation
COLO.
KAN
Hopi Reservation
Four Corners
Great B
Garden City
CALIF.
Boise City
Kenton
Guym
Santa Barbara
Los Angeles
ARIZ.
Shiprock
Gallup
Santa Fe
Albuquerque
Amaril
San Diego
Tijuana
Canyon de Chelly
Phoenix
N. MEX.
Canyon
Tucson
Nogales
Nogales
TEXAS
Hermosillo
MEXICO
Los Mochis
Topolobampo
Culiacán
Mazatlán
Tepic
Compostela
Guadalajara
Mexico Ci

PACIFIC OCEAN

Kms.
0 — 400
0 — 400
Miles

©A. Karl/J. Kemp, 1998

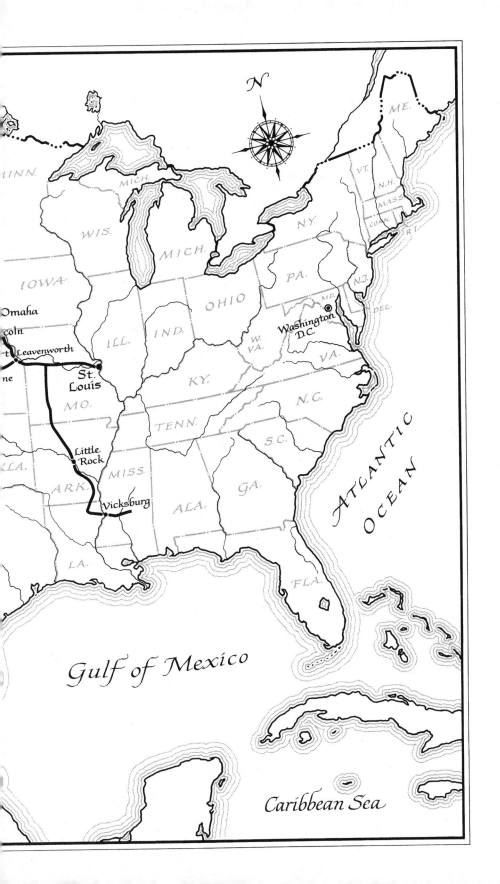

CONTENTS

PREFACE

THE WORLD IN the foreseeable future will depend more on the preferences of Americans than on any other single factor. Whether in preserving the balance of power in Europe, in Asia, or in the Middle East or in restructuring the United Nations, the wishes of the United States will be impossible to ignore. America's enormous technological advantages will sustain it as *the* military superpower for decades hence. But America's foreign policy, like that of any other country, is an extension of its domestic inclinations and conditions. Thus it is of the utmost importance to understand the direction American society is going in.

The continued existence of the United States should never be taken for granted. Democratic Athens led its allies in the victorious wars against Persia only to inherit a far-flung maritime empire that later crumbled as Athens gradually faded from history, leaving a vacuum eventually filled by the rise of Alexander's empire. In the wake of Rome's decline came the tribal configurations from which modern European states emerged. America's decline would leave a vacuum every bit as large as that left by Greece or Rome—to which America has often been compared—with immeasurable consequences for the human race. But this book is not about the decline of the United States; it is about its transformation.

*   *   *

MY PROBLEM IN writing about America at first hand was formidable, because it is my own country. The knowledge one accumulates of one's homeland, like the knowledge of oneself, is so varied and complex, so ambiguously objective and subjective at every turn, that each interpretation soon gives way to another: to write about one's own country is the most problematic form of autobiography. In the end, for all of the careful notes and no matter how much one has read and pondered, one is left with the problem of one's unconscious motivations. I have made no attempt here to be comprehensive, much less "definitive," but rather to offer an interpretation of our common future based on my best judgment after much travel. My travels were confined for the most part to the West, where it seems to me America's transformation is most transparent. Nine of the ten states whose populations are growing fastest are in the West.[1] It is in the West, particularly west of the Missouri, where the myth of American individualism—of pioneers taming a virgin continent—has been most clearly stated. I had yet another reason for choosing the West: I am from the East, and for me the West meant the chance to travel amid a relatively strange landscape, if not as strange as those abroad.

THIS IS NOT a specialist's book. It makes no claim to compete with books specifically about the military, urban transformation, the Mexican border area, race relations, the environment, and so on. Rather, my goal is to integrate all of these issues in the form of a travelogue. Like all travelers, I was subject to whim. I visited some cities but missed many more; I visited some wilderness communities but missed many more. Wherever I went, though, I tried to relate what I saw to larger meanings. I agree with Polybius, a Greek statesman who lived in the second century B.C., who believed that the "truth resides in a panoramic rather than a local view of events." This, at any rate, is what I have tried to achieve here.

My journey began at a holy, if rather obscure, place.

---

[1]According to the *Statistical Abstract of the United States 1996*, the fastest-growing states are, in the order of their population growth, Nevada, Idaho, Arizona, Colorado, Utah, Washington, New Mexico, Georgia (the only one in the East), Oregon, and Texas. (All books and articles mentioned in footnotes are cited in full in the Selected Bibliography.)

PART
I

LAST
REDOUBT
OF THE
NATION-STATE

1

—

Fort Leavenworth

WHEREAS EAST COAST monuments such as the Lincoln Memorial
and the Statue of Liberty speak specifically to ideals, the Protestant
memorial chapel at Fort Leavenworth, Kansas—overlooking the Missouri River at the edge of the Great Plains, with the rails of the Union
Pacific visible in the distance—invokes blood and soil. The chapel
was built from local limestone in 1878, two years after the massacre
of George Armstrong Custer's Seventh Cavalry. Six brass pack how-
itzers from the Indian Wars are embedded in the wall. In addition
to plaques commemorating the U.S. Army dead at Little Big Horn
and other frontier engagements, the walls are studded with the
names of heroes of every war since; Colonel Ollie Reed (July 30,
1944) and First Lieutenant Ollie Reed Jr. (July 5, 1944), for example,
a father and son killed weeks apart in France and Italy in the Second
World War. In early May 1995, on the fiftieth anniversary of V-E Day,
as I stood within this darkened holy of holies, my eyes struggling
to read the names in the gloom, I felt as if I were within the core of
nationhood.

The poignancy of the moment overwhelmed me, stretching beyond the deaths of those men. For after several weeks at Fort Leavenworth, freighted as it is with historical reference, and after heated
discussions with army officers about the failure of ancient Greece

and Rome, how could I not think about the future of the United States?

The officers and I did not assume that the United States was going to decline like those ancient empires. That is not the lesson of classical history. Rather, it is that change is inescapable and the more gradual and hidden the change, the more decisive: the great shifts in fortune for ancient empires were usually not apparent to those living at the time. At Fort Leavenworth I was intensely aware of such transformation—of history moving silently beneath our feet however much we deny it—and thus the memorial chapel affected me more intimately than any monumental ruin in Greece or Italy or Egypt.

THE SETTING IS fifteen miles northwest of Kansas City, where the Missouri flows swiftly, several hundred yards wide, encumbered with logs and other debris, the untamed signature of the New World. Here the river arcs before turning north. On July 2, 1804, the explorers Meriwether Lewis and William Clark camped nearby, en route to the Pacific. In May 1827, during the presidency of John Quincy Adams, Colonel Henry Leavenworth, sailing upriver from the direction of St. Louis, commenced construction here of what would become Fort Leavenworth: the advance post of European settlement within the western half of the American continent. Colonel Leavenworth's orders were to construct the fort on the east bank of the river. However, because the east bank was a floodplain, he built on the bluffs of the west bank, in what was officially "Indian territory" beyond the Union, in the future state of Kansas. By the time Washington bureaucrats learned of Leavenworth's decision, the colonel had already begun building.

As much as it is an army base or a war college, Fort Leavenworth is a living museum. French cannons, brought here before Thomas Jefferson purchased Louisiana from France, look out over the Missouri. Lining the parade ground are nineteenth-century redbrick Victorian houses, their facades framed by white porticoes. George Armstrong Custer lived in one, Douglas MacArthur in another. In 1926, when Fort Leavenworth was almost a hundred years old, Dwight D. Eisenhower lived with his family in nearby Otis Hall. It was at Fort Leavenworth that "Ike" learned to play golf. In another brick building, in the winter of 1917–1918, a young officer, F. Scott Fitzgerald, wrote the first draft of his first novel, *This Side of Paradise*. The post cemetery, designated by President Abraham Lincoln as one of our first twelve national military cemeteries, contains the graves of 19,000 soldiers who served from the War of 1812 through Desert Storm, including Shango Hango, an Indian soldier-guide, four officers from Little Big Horn, and a casualty from Fort Sumter. Fifteen hundred graves are unmarked.

The pièce de résistance is the Buffalo Soldier Monument, a sixteen-foot bronze statue of a black trooper mounted on his horse, rearing up before two reflecting pools. The "buffalo soldiers" were two African-American regiments, the Ninth and Tenth Cavalries, which, from the end of the Civil War through the closing of the western frontier, escorted cattle drives and wagon trains, installed telegraph lines, and fought Indians and Mexican revolutionaries. The monument was dedicated in 1992 and was the idea of Colin Powell when he was deputy commander here, in 1981–1982. The magnificent bronze horse and rider could have leapt out of a painting by Frederic Remington: a binding myth, true and necessary.

Inside the post buildings, the theatricality demanded by tradition deepens. The pictures lining the corridors range from a painting of Revolutionary War General Nathanael Greene to a giant photo of MacArthur striding ashore in the Philippines in 1944. For several days, army officials let me visit the varnished meeting rooms with plush red carpets, where I listened to officers in black boots and battle fatigues discuss future war scenarios in the Balkans, Central America, and Africa. The battle fatigues express the difference between Leavenworth and other war colleges, where dress greens and jackets and ties are required: Leavenworth is a frontier post still, and a nostalgic view of the United States is deliberately cultivated here, as if to bind the uncertain future to a reliable past.

Fort Leavenworth symbolizes the frontier. As the most important fort in the West, the place from which the first group of white settlers moved into Indian country, it was the starting point for what would one day be called Manifest Destiny. It was the main base for the exploration of the Great Salt Lake in Utah and of the Columbia River in Oregon. Eight miles west of Fort Leavenworth, the newly opened Oregon and Santa Fe Trails separated. Here a young man from Illinois, James "Wild Bill" Hickok, experienced the West for the first time, amid wagon trains as far as his eye could see. Fort Leavenworth was the base camp for building the transcontinental railroad. From here, troops marched off to the Mexican War and Custer's Seventh

Cavalry trekked to the Little Big Horn. In 1881, General William Tecumseh Sherman established a staff college at Fort Leavenworth, and when the frontier closed in 1890, Leavenworth began to train officers for fighting overseas—another territorial threshold—which they did in 1898, when U.S. troops carried the flag to Cuba and the Philippines. This has always been the place where the army prepares its commanders "to fight the next war." "Vinegar Joe" Stilwell, MacArthur, Eisenhower, and Powell, to name only a few generals, were indelibly marked by Leavenworth.

Almost every member of the army's top brass has spent at least several months, if not longer, at Fort Leavenworth. More than 90 percent of Army captains take a nine-week course here. More than 50 percent of all majors spend a year at Leavenworth before they are eligible for promotion to lieutenant colonel; of those majors who eventually make it to general, the percentage is much higher. Leavenworth is where military warfare doctrine is written. It was Leavenworth's School of Advanced Military Studies that, in 1990, outlined the strategy for Operation Desert Storm. When the United States intervenes overseas, the phones and computers at Leavenworth work overtime.

Leavenworth's Battle Command Training Program runs simulated war games—for example, "Prairie Warrior," an annual exercise in which computers link Leavenworth with other U.S. military installations around the world in a "virtual" war situation, with isolated command headquarters, battlefield observers, and so forth. During my visit, Prairie Warrior featured a scenario in an "imaginary Europe" menaced by a failing nation-state in the "north-central" sector near present-day Berlin. The state is both threatened by its neighbors and tearing itself apart through civil unrest and guerrilla insurgencies in densely populated urban areas. Because this scenario was set fifteen years in the future, the weaponry for the war game included "intelligent mines" that can distinguish among trucks, tanks, and people and identify the enemy. While other military institutions look "strategically" and thus more abstractly at the future, Leavenworth, because it concentrates on training captains and majors, the "middle ranks," is "where the rubber meets the road," explained Major Chris Devens.

Another exercise I looked in on involved a humanitarian emergency in Memphis and St. Louis after a major earthquake along the Mississippi Valley's "New Madrid" fault line, where a series of big quakes did in fact occur in 1811 and 1812. More earthquakes are expected, and buildings in Memphis and St. Louis have not generally been constructed to withstand major tremors. This exercise tested the army's ability to work with NGOs (nongovernmental organizations, or private relief agencies), as it has had to do in the Third World.

It was assumed that there would be civil disorder after the quake. "Martial law has rarely been declared in the United States," noted Lieutenant Colonel Marvin Chandler. "That's another thing we look at." Many times in the course of my visit to Leavenworth I heard discussion of the Posse Comitatus Act, which forbids the National Guard to act as a local police force once it has been federalized by the army in a civil emergency. The implication was that turbulence within the United States might one day require the act to be repealed. "The future is icky," said Lieutenant Colonel Chandler, showing me a cartoon of a cow, representing an awkward, slow-moving army, trying to negotiate a series of mud puddles that represent natural catastrophes, political breakdowns, riots, and nuclear blackmail, both foreign and domestic.

NOW THAT TECHNOLOGY has erased distances, Leavenworth stands on a new frontier, a global one. Its computers disgorge daily advice to field commanders in Haiti, Rwanda, the Balkans, and wherever else American troops happen to be. "The guy in a tent in Port-au-Prince can access the library here regarding lessons learned in Somalia," explained Major Devens. From Fort Leavenworth, officers fly to hot spots around the world every week. By planning for future conflicts, Fort Leavenworth is helping to transform the nation by redefining where its borders really are.

For example, a captain, looking at a map of a war game in Honduras, told me, "We know more about Honduras than about western Kansas during the Indian Wars. The intelligence on Honduras is more *dense*. Honduras is closer in time than western Kansas was, a few hours by plane rather than days on horseback. Communications are better, too." The Third World has become like the Old West. For the army, continental frontiers—of the kind that led to the building of Fort Leavenworth and of the nation—have grown dim.

What kind of continent will it be with Honduras this close and getting closer, I wondered? Could the dissolution of distances also dissolve the nation which this bastion of nationness overlooking the Missouri is meant to defend? The prairie surrounding Fort Leavenworth focused my mind on America's continental isolation, its debt to geography, while the tensions I encountered within the fort led me to wonder about the future status of traditional nation-state America in an age when oceanic distances matter increasingly less.

COLONEL JERRY MORELOCK'S walls are cluttered with U.S. military iconography: a dogged U. S. Grant, the father of total, unheroic war, leaning against a tree at City Point; Robert E. Lee after Appomattox; and so on. For a computer screen saver, Morelock uses a photo of Ike, George Patton, Omar Bradley, and other generals taken in May 1945 in Germany, after V-E Day. Morelock, who wears wire-rimmed glasses and whose gray hair has begun to recede, lives with his family in "The Rookery," the oldest house in Kansas, built in 1832. MacArthur lived here when he was on post in the early 1900s. A typical title on Morelock's bookshelf is *Frontier Regulars: The United States Army and the Indian Wars 1866–1891*. He salutes the flag every day at five o'clock, he told me.

"Fifty years after V-E Day, the U.S. has history's strongest military. But it has been eroded tremendously since 1991. And that is nothing new." Morelock then explained to me how following every conflict, including the Revolutionary War (after which the twenty-thousand-man Continental Army was disbanded and replaced by a "regiment" of seven hundred militiamen), military cutbacks ensued as memories faded. This was true of the periods following not just the First and Second World Wars, but also the War of 1812, the Mexican War, and the Spanish-American War. "After every war, everyone declared the end of war. Though now we talk about lots of smaller wars, what's to prevent a really big conflagration? The record of history indicates that a new and great threat is certain." The task for officers here is daunting: imagine being at Leavenworth after 1898, when the United States was flush with victory following its defeat of Spain, and trying to predict the rise of Hitler at a time when the words "totalitarianism" and "fascism" had yet to be coined. The horrors of the next century may not even have names yet.

Through most of our history, we have had a weak central government and a small volunteer army. The military draft has been strictly a wartime thing, a radical departure from most empires of the past, especially Rome's.[1] The United States, in fact, did not have an adequate standing army until the twentieth century. World War II, the Cold War, and the persistence of a military draft through 1973 masked the reality of a weakly governed, brawling, fractious society. Now two oceans may not seal us off from disintegrative forces elsewhere. As nation-states begin slowly, inexorably to melt into a transnational stew, army officers such as Morelock feel threatened. They think the military must do all it can to help America preserve some semblance of a blood-and-soil, continental identity. Morelock is not sure that this is possible.

"Just like at the end of the Indian Wars in 1890, the army finds it has no more territory left to conquer," Morelock said. "The answer a hundred years ago was imperialism." He meant the Philippines expedition, which, however misguided, primed the army to help Europe in both world wars. (In 1935, with the United States in an isolationist mode, Eisenhower honed his analytical skills by helping reorganize the Filipino Army, even if it was subsequently defeated by the Japanese.) "For now, we're the world's 911 force. The public screams 'Stop those images'—the ones on TV of kids starving. But that's not necessarily a national interest."

Such excursions are only a temporary raison d'être until a real threat appears. But the real threat could be so unconventional—chemical or biological bombs in domestic water or mass transit systems, for instance—that the "traditional" army of tanks and armored personnel carriers and what it has historically represented to the nation may seem quaint.

AT LEAVENWORTH I also saw how the acceleration of technology is driving the wedge deeper between military and civilian societies and bringing about, for the first time, a professional-caste elite, with serious implications for our national future. Today's volunteer army is different from all others in America's history. Soldiers are becoming like doctors and lawyers: a professional group we would like to need less but upon which we rely more. And just as health care reform

---

[1] Nor were the antiwar protests of the Cold War–Vietnam era unique. The Mexican War, for instance, caused dramatic protests whose pacifist rhetoric could be mistaken for that of 1960s demonstrators. Poet Robert Lowell opposed Vietnam, just as his great-granduncle James Russell Lowell, the first editor in chief of *The Atlantic Monthly*, opposed the Mexican War.

requires the consent of the medical community because doctors know things the rest of us cannot adequately understand, foreign policy will over the decades be increasingly influenced by the military, as war, peacekeeping, famine relief, and the like grow too technical and complex for civilian managers to control.

The most troubling break with the past, as I realized at Fort Leavenworth, is how abstract technological warfare is becoming. Though this tendency has been true for years, its continuation is having a powerful impact; a phrase I repeatedly heard at Leavenworth was "Attrition of the same adds up to big change." Colonel Thomas Suitt, an African American from North Carolina who runs a "command preparation" computer course for tank commanders, showed me how Information Age war will demand leaders, from lieutenants to presidents, who can sort through dense waves of data to make risky decisions rapidly and constantly. Suitt's course simulates tank battles for lieutenant colonels, who will lead three hundred to four hundred vehicles and five thousand troops against similar forces in a "combat window" where all will be decided in fifteen to thirty minutes. "Each of these engagements is bigger and faster than Waterloo," explained Suitt. "Commanding a tank brigade isn't brain surgery; it's tougher." When tank commanders saw only the narrow view from their own tanks, decisions, though often flawed and fatal, were easier to make, because there was less information to process. Now the commander in a M1A2 tank can map terrain over the horizon and know the amount of fuel and ammunition left in each of his hundreds of vehicles, the speed and timing of support helicopters, the location of each "dead zone" (an area between friendly vehicles that none of his tank drivers can see), wind and temperature patterns that affect how visibility will be obscured by the smoke from exploding shells, and so on. As Suitt ran me through the on-screen battle, displaying all the vehicles and terrain as combat progressed and asking me what I would do at each stage, I felt as if I were playing multidimensional chess at thirty seconds per move. The Roman empire lasted more than a thousand years, but during that entire period technology remained relatively unchanged. The acceleration of technology not only is working against America's calcification, it is adding a great degree of unpredictability, since the future is now far harder to discern than it was for any other great state in the past.

The professional-caste quality of the army is evident in other ways, too. The growing use here of technical jargon and acronyms to accompany the growth of military specialties has created an insider's jargon. Foreign territory is referred to as OCONUS (Outside the Continental United States), humanitarian and peacekeeping duties are called OOTW (Operations Other than War, pronounced "ootwa"), the technological revolution in the military is known as RMA (Revolution in Military Affairs), urban warfare is MOUT (Military Operations in Urban Terrain), and so on. Frequently, I had to stop a conversation to ask what those terms meant.

Significant, too, was the level of scholarship. At Leavenworth I encountered men and women, both whites and blacks, in their late twenties through early forties, who were on easy terms with ancient history and related subjects. In fact, at times army captains and majors seem immobilized by their knowledge of the past. To mention Haiti here is to elicit a detailed report on that country's troubles since independence from France in 1804. Mention Rwanda and Burundi, and you hear about ethnic violence from the late 1950s through the 1970s. The same with the Balkans. History, as these officers recount it, suggests that such places are hopeless, even as they provide the only work the army has at the moment.

Smaller wars with limited meaning for the rest of us may also widen the gap between the American military and society. Neither we nor the military wants this to happen. But late-twentieth-century life is driven by an unprecedented accumulation of knowledge that encourages the division of society into subgroups with their own journals, social networks, and obsessions. These subgroups are like lonely travelers who bump into other travelers—other subgroups—in superficial encounters. Why should the military be any different? Officers at Leavenworth read *The Economist* and *Foreign Affairs* and watch *The NewsHour with Jim Lehrer,* but that does not mean they interpret the information the way civilian policy makers and people in the media do. However sophisticated the reading lists, the people doing the reading here often come from rural, blue-collar America. As soldiers, they live in materially poor conditions, especially compared to people who spend their lives in affluent Washington suburbs. The fact that so many military bases are, like Leavenworth, in the Midwest or the South further isolates American soldiers from the sensibilities of coastal metropolitan elites. "It matters less what you read than where you live and where you come from, because that determines how you interpret knowledge," explained Major Susan P. Kellett-Forsyth, one of the first female graduates of West Point.

*   *   *

WHEREAS THE HISTORY-MINDED general public harks back to the Civil War and World War II, when secession, slavery, and fascism were the enemies, for this army drawn from the middle and lower classes, the defining moment was fighting the "Indians." The very location of army bases in the heartland is a legacy of the Indian Wars. Not only Fort Leavenworth but such other bases as Fort Riley and Fort Hays in Kansas, and Fort Sill in Oklahoma, were originally frontier posts. A popular book here is *Five Years a Dragoon* by Percival G. Lowe, a nostalgic memoir of Indian operations on the Great Plains between the Mexican and Civil Wars and of "the bivouac under the blue sky." (Lowe is buried at the military cemetery at Fort Leavenworth.) "The Indian plains beyond Fort Riley in central Kansas have been replicated in all the wars we've fought since: World War II, Desert Storm, Somalia," Morelock explained. "In our minds, we're still the cavalry. But that will end. We're not at the full *tech*-war stage yet, but we will be. All indications, demographic and otherwise, are that the future of war is urban. Patriotism, tied to a romantic vision of the land, will be harder to sustain."

The possibility of another great war in coming decades notwithstanding, the near term, according to the people here, offers the uninspiring prospect of small, increasingly urban wars and rescue details that will have increasingly little meaning for the nation. "In the future, the shelf life of victory will be short," said Roger Spiller, the George C. Marshall Professor of Military History at Leavenworth. "Military operations will proliferate but mean less." These smaller deployments will represent a departure from our history, which through World War II were driven by a major war every few decades. (If anyone believes that major wars have not been crucial to our sense of nationhood, consider how few patriotic songs and national holidays we would have without them. True, we might be happier from now on without great military struggles: but whatever it is we will become without them, it will not be the nation we once were.)

It was with such lugubrious thoughts in mind that I listened to a number of roundtable discussions at Leavenworth. In one a group of majors lamented the end of the draft. "People who want the draft back are hankering after a lost golden age," said Major Robert Everson. "The draft is obsolete because of the way warfare is changing. War has become so technological that it takes too long to train people who will serve for only a year or two." The talk switched to the 1995 bombing in Oklahoma City. A marine in the group, Major Craig Tucker, said, "The minute I heard about Oklahoma City, I knew who did it: rednecks, the kind of guys from southern Idaho." I had heard similar remarks. The initial assumption that Middle East Muslims were responsible reflected an East and West Coast media preoccupation with foreign policy, as well as an ignorance of social upheavals in the heartland, to which people in the military, many of whom are from blue-collar backgrounds, are sensitive. Tucker and another officer suggested that "a time may come when the military will have to go domestic," as when George Washington put down the Whiskey Rebellion in western Pennsylvania in 1794. During another discussion a visiting Canadian officer said, "The biggest threat to Canada is that the United States will collapse on itself. Canada's problems are out in the open, but the degree of turmoil in the U.S. is not admitted." Canadians have always sneered at the "disorderly" United States, but I noticed that protests from the American officers to the Canadian's remarks were muted.

These discussions were remarkable for their intensity. Quotes from books, pointed aphorisms, and Latin phrases came at me rapidly. "The Athenian oracle said the Persians would be defeated by 'wooden walls,' which meant the Athenian navy. That's the kind of riddle we have to solve." "Remember Heisenberg's rule: One who engages in foresight alters the future by the choices he makes." This technological and intellectual elite is poorly paid and lives in spartan, almost monastic, conditions. But here I was much less conscious of race: everyone, both white and black, wore fatigues, and the whites and blacks spoke the same arcane language, laden with technical and bureaucratic jargon. This is the way our nation—or at least our school system—should be, I thought. Here is the "Great Society" as Lyndon Johnson envisioned it.[2]

AS THESE NEW American centurions guard the frontier of a strange new world, the nation-state they are sworn to defend is undergoing a vast transformation, in which its continental geography—its abundance of sparsely inhabited space defined by two oceans—may prove to mean the inverse of what it once meant: While Europe has had too much history and not enough geography, America has had

[2]See Thomas E. Ricks, "The Great Society in Camouflage."

relatively little history and plenty of geography.[3] America happens to have been the last large, resource-rich part of the temperate zone uninhabited at the dawn of the European Enlightenment. In the sixteenth century, when 100 million people lived in Europe, the area of the current United States was empty except for a few million natives living in scattered settlements. On this exceptionally rich and unexploited landmass, with good soil and an abundance of minerals, some of the most ambitious Europeans reinvented themselves.[4]

Indeed, no continent has been as well suited to nation building as the temperate zone of North America. The Appalachians had provided a western boundary for a nascent community of states through the end of the eighteenth century, but river valleys cutting through these mountains, such as those of the Mohawk and the Ohio, later allowed for penetration of the West by settlers. Beyond the Appalachians the settlers found a flat panel of rich farmland without geographical impediments where, in the nineteenth century, wealth could be created and human differences could be ground down to form a distinctive American culture. By the time westering pioneers reached a truly daunting barrier—the Great American Desert, both east and west of the Rocky Mountains—the transcontinental railroad was at hand.

According to the historian Frederick Jackson Turner, at the turn of the twentieth century the western frontier—and free land in particular—was the guarantor of American democracy, since each westward migration produced an encounter with a new landscape that allowed the settlers to re-create local government, as continual economic opportunity drew newcomers. And because taming the land was an eminently practical task, ideology had a marginal effect on this emerging American life, compared to that of Europe. When the last interior tracts of the western frontier closed in the 1890s with the settling of Oklahoma and the Dakotas, Turner told a July 1893 Chicago symposium that there was nothing left to ensure America's dynamism.[5]

---

[3]Daniel Boorstin and Aldous Huxley have also made this observation.

[4]In his book on the origin of cultures, Columbia University anthropologist Marvin Harris notes, "The American colonial experience was an anomaly. The Americans took over a continent where no dense population previously existed. Even a bronze age people would have been able to eke out a hundred years of rising living standards from a wilderness so richly endowed with soils, forests, and minerals."

[5]See H. W. Brands, *The Reckless Decade: America in the 1890s*, for a fine account of Turner and his thesis, "The Significance of the Frontier in American History."

Turner's warning about decline was premature. Much frontier land remained cheap and underdeveloped, even if it had already been officially "settled." Through most of the twentieth century, oceanic distances were formidable enough to secure America's virtual monopoly over its large internal market in an age of industrial expansion and economies of scale. Oceans also protected the United States from the devastations of the First and Second World Wars, giving us a relative advantage over Europe and Asia that allowed for the "American Century." Our protected landmass with its abundance of natural resources was an ideal setting for the Industrial Age, whose passing has only recently begun. From the end of the Civil War to 1973, the U.S. economy, largely insulated from foreign competition, grew at an average rate of 3.4 percent annually, excluding inflation. The real wage nearly doubled from one generation to the next, so that the American Dream in these years came true and optimism was the official American religion.[6]

But now we face the loss of the protection that geography once provided. Because the United States has been so overwhelmingly a creature of geography, in the twenty-first century shrinking distances will affect us more than they will our competitors, whose economic development never depended on continental isolation. The region near Fort Leavenworth showed me how the vast stretches of land within our continent could become liabilities.

THE TOWN OF Leavenworth, the oldest in Kansas, is, like the fort, a museum piece. Influenced by an elite military institution, the town, with a population of 36,000, is harmoniously multiracial to a degree that few other places in the country are. A town council member I met told me happily that Leavenworth is "twenty years behind the curve in social change." Here is an older America of low brick buildings and sidewalks, and a succession of streets named for Native American tribes with which the army negotiated treaties: Cheyenne, Pawnee, Seneca, Dakota. But whereas thirty years ago, Leavenworth boasted a hundred mom-and-pop stores, the downtown is now failing, a victim of chain stores and the regional shopping mall. Crime, too, has risen: in the early 1990s the town saw a spate of murders.

[6]See Jeffrey Madrick, *The End of Affluence: The Causes and Consequences of America's Economic Decline.*

Mention Leavenworth and people think of a prison. The silver-domed federal penitentiary, with its white Doric pillars and large American flag near the Missouri River, is a building straight out of Washington, D.C. That is fitting, since prisons may define us to future generations, including archaeologists, as much as the buildings on the Capitol Mall. "Prisons are good business," a member of the Leavenworth city council told me. "They bring jobs, increase your tax base, and cause no pollution or traffic jams. There are no layoffs in the prison sector. It's a growth industry."

But as I drove beyond the town of Leavenworth, the deeper story emerged. Kansas City, Missouri, like other Americans metropolises, is slowly separating out into economic and racial enclaves that have little in common with one another even as some of these enclaves become increasingly like those in Asia and Europe. A new Kansas City is growing up to the west of the old one, around Overland Park and nearby towns in Johnson County, Kansas, a booming, predominantly white, high-income and high-technology area. While Johnson County's population grew by more than 15 percent from 1990 through 1996, according to the U.S. Census Bureau, the population of Kansas City itself—which dropped in the 1980s by 7 percent on the Kansas side and by 3 percent on the Missouri side—has not grown as much. Johnson County, in turn, is forming a cultural community with up-and-coming Lawrence, forty minutes further to the west, the site of the University of Kansas. Lawrence's main street features a succession of fashionable apparel stores. This new Kansas City region, with its cappuccinos, French pastries, and designer seafood in the midst of the formerly beef-eating prairie, where European-designed fashions manufactured in Asia are readily available, is yet another globalized settlement. One night I had dinner with two military historians from Fort Leavenworth at Yayas, a "Eurobistro" in Overland Park that offered nineteen kinds of single-malt whiskey and a "continental cuisine . . . embraced as an art form," one of many such restaurants within the mallscape.

True, the style is at the same time distinctively midwestern: big smiles, free drinks while you wait for a table, huge portions, a lack of subtlety in the interior design of new buildings and in clothing combinations. But such localisms are increasingly elusive, harder than ever to tease out of the people and places I saw in the vicinity of Fort Leavenworth. What was easier to notice was the growing similarity between this new Kansas City region and upstart Asian cities I had visited that have unapologetically embraced global materialism. If the comparison seems a bit forced, it will seem less so as the years and decades roll on.

America's geographical advantage—the vast empty tracts beyond the older suburbs with their low real estate values, especially compared to those of Europe and East Asia—allows the middle class to move further and further away from the disruptive poor and thus avoid, among other things, local taxes for social programs that may—or may not—work. For the citizens of the new Kansas City region, the traditional social contract that binds all citizens to the common good is gradually becoming an impediment to participation in the emerging global economy. The coming medievalization of the continent that I sensed in the western extension of Kansas City and in similar urban pods I would later visit brought to mind the period before the birth of the United States, when the land was peopled by isolated communities of Pilgrims, Spanish settlers, and Native Americans.

The same spirit of individualism that helped build the nation may henceforth deconstruct it, as new worldwide settlement patterns link similar communities by new computerized technologies and air travel while traditional states defined simply by geography wither. Nineteenth-century "print capitalism," with its local newspapers and manufacturing centers, once formed the basis of our nationhood. But in a computer-driven, knowledge-based world economy, educated Americans may have more in common with (and, ultimately, more loyalty to) their highly educated friends and counterparts in Europe, Latin America, and Asia than they do with less educated fellow Americans a few miles away. Such public infrastructure as airports and roads will still have to be built and maintained, if only to link places such as Johnson County and Lawrence; but in the future this might be done by private capital, both domestic and foreign, whatever "foreign" might eventually mean—perhaps no more than a fading memory of a time when cultures (and nations) were still distinct and colorful, as on today's map, rather than the free-floating aggregations they will have become at the upper end of the world economic spectrum and the unpromising sludge they will have become at the bottom.

As I traveled from one prairie enclave to another, I wondered if traditional patriotism may become a waning formality, as Earth Day becomes more significant for wealthier and more sophisticated citizens than Independence Day. (The Pledge of Allegiance may ultimately become a caricature of itself, as it already is among certain militia groups.) Perhaps one day the officers at Fort Leavenworth may sit around their wooden conference tables, as Nathanael Greene, Douglas MacArthur, and other ancient warriors look down from the walls, and argue about what—and whom—they are supposed to defend.

Jacksonian democracy, the Civil War, progressivism, and the New Deal were times in which America restructured itself. But as American society becomes more complex, more implicated in other societies, the odds for future reinventions of the nation-state get longer, especially as an aging population puts additional pressure on traditional institutions. By 2025, America's population will be as old as Florida's is now: one in five persons will be over sixty-five. By 2040, the number of Social Security beneficiaries will double.[7] While more than half of all Americans are now over forty, nearly half of Mexico's population is fifteen years old or younger, just as half the population of many places in Latin America and Asia is under age twenty-five. Large-scale immigration may have to continue if for no other reason than to provide an army of younger workers to support America's retirees.

Thus a vibrant America in the twenty-first century may become an America of "rooted cosmopolitans," reinventing itself in a larger world by becoming history's first international nation (and the home of a value-driven international constabulary hunting down war criminals, plutonium terrorists, and so on) where the best and the brightest of Mexico and the other continents come to live and pay taxes, if only for six or eight months a year.[8] The great historian Edward Gibbon believed that a decentralized, pluralistic society with a highly mobile citizenry might survive forever. The periodic reductions in military expenditures after each war are an example of how America renews itself by deliberately weakening the center in order to remain vibrant at the edges—as opposed to the Oriental and late-Roman models, characterized by despotism at the center and weakness at the extremities.

MATT NOWAK IS Fort Leavenworth's forester. "America is soil, geology, ecosystem. I teach the military, literally, what it is supposed to

---

[7]Figures from Peter G. Peterson, "Will America Grow Up Before It Grows Old?"
[8]The term "rooted cosmopolitanism" was coined by *Dissent* editor Mitchell Cohen. The concept is partially influenced by the writings of Randolph Bourne.

defend," he told me, holding in his hand a clump of loess (loamy soil kept in place since the last ice age by prairie grass) and pointing out some old-growth pecan trees that have lined the Missouri River since before the Lewis and Clark expedition. The nineteenth-century New England poet William Cullen Bryant wrote that "prairie"—suggestive as it is of an "encircling vastness," with that long, drawn-out first syllable—is a quintessential American word (albeit of French derivation) "for which the speech of England has no name."[9] More important, for Bryant it is a "vastness" signifying "union." Walking with Nowak, amid fields of tall grass, ragweed, and sunflowers, along the great curve of the river near the fort, lined by sycamores and cottonwoods, I wondered what, precisely, the sound of that word will signify for future inhabitants of the continent.

Will the prairie continue to signify "union"? Will the memorial chapel at Fort Leavenworth stir a future American traveler as it did me, the son of a World War II veteran for whom that receding Homeric age and the Cold War that followed are living history? Or will such a traveler see the chapel merely as an interesting archaeological site, the relic of a civilization whose passions—like those of Greece or Rome—can be studied, but never again be felt? How much longer, I wondered, will the patriotic marches of John Philip Sousa move America's inhabitants?

Europeans, with their intimate experience of occupation, annihilation, and the passing of one political order after another— monarchy, fascism, communism—know intuitively about historical change. They know how frighteningly adaptive human behavior can be and how some of a society's most cherished assumptions can shift—cruelly, if necessary—to accommodate new circumstances. They know that no society is permanent and, as D. H. Lawrence put it, that "Men live by lies."

Americans, however, because we have had no experience of violent upheaval since the Civil War, lack awareness of historic mutation and thus more easily imagine the future with optimism: a stable future of even greater wealth and, perhaps, even more fairness within a permanent nation. History shows that such permanence is most unlikely.

Racial divisions are greater in America than in most other democracies, and class divisions may also harden as such equalizing experiences as the settling of the West and the military draft fall behind us

[9]See Bryant's poem "The Prairies."

and private education continues to increase.[10] Meanwhile, such issues as race and class suggest that perhaps one of the greatest agents of change may be the northward migration from Mexico, which bears with it the cultural patterns of an Old World society as intractable as Egypt's or China's and influences us not only through its people, but also through drugs.

SUCH WERE THE preconceptions I formed at Fort Leavenworth, which supplied my journey with a purpose. My aim in traveling through North America was to stimulate my thinking about the future, which is what travel has always been about for me. My routes often lacked geographical logic. Unlike my travels through Africa, the Middle East, and Central Asia, I followed no river, mountain range, or compass direction. Nor is the ensuing account of my travels always given in the order in which I made them. What follows is more the story of an idea as it emerged.

[10]See Amitai Etzioni, *The Community of Communities.*

PART
II

THE
NEW
WILDERNESS

2

—

Fort Leavenworth
to St. Louis

THE POPULATION MAP of the United States is changing as Americans continue to migrate from both cities and struggling small towns into suburbs, so that the future United States will become increasingly a network of vast suburban blotches separated by empty space. Of the twenty-five largest cities in 1950, eighteen have lost population, while the suburban population has grown by more than 75 million.[1] By 1970, more people resided in suburbia than in major cities.[2] In 1990, the United States became the first nation in history to have more suburbanites than city and rural dwellers combined, and this trend goes on.[3] The travel writer in me wanted to avoid or downplay the new suburbs and office parks, whose architectural uniformity and lack of street life offered little to see. But America's open spaces contain less than a quarter of our population; the rest of us live in an urban-suburban setting. No portrait of the United States at the turn

[1]See Columbia University Professor Kenneth T. Jackson, "America's Rush to Suburbia." Jackson also notes in another *New York Times* article ("100 Years of Being Really Big," December 28, 1997) that since 1950, "the population of Chicago proper has dropped 25 percent, Baltimore 28 percent, Philadelphia 29 percent, Washington 32 percent, Cleveland 43 percent," and so on.
[2]See William F. Gayk, "The Taxpayers' Revolt" in *Postsuburban California*.
[3]See Jackson, "America's Rush to Suburbia."

of the twenty-first century would be accurate if it did not begin with this population shift.

The midwestern prairie, whose good water supplies and flat terrain encouraged suburban growth, seemed a likely place for me to learn more about the transformation of the traditional American city. So I left Fort Leavenworth and headed for St. Louis. It was from there that, in 1827, Colonel Henry Leavenworth had set out up the Missouri River to establish the fort named after him.

From Fort Leavenworth I crossed the Missouri River, barely half a mile to the east, into the state of Missouri. I could now see behind me the brown bluffs on the Kansas side of the river that mark the edge of the plateau that helps define the American West. Having crossed the river and entered the forested East, I had begun my journey through the continent.

Driving west to east across Missouri through a generic American landscape, I saw giant "center-pivot" sprinklers, like those I would later see throughout the arid plains states further west, but soon I entered the rolling emerald hills of eastern Missouri, which reminded me of Virginia and Maryland. Kansas City, Missouri, still a principal railhead for the cattle trade, has traditionally oriented its economy westward, while St. Louis has always been the first of the great eastern metropolises one encounters as one leaves the western plains. Northern Missouri belongs—along with Iowa, Illinois, Wisconsin, and Minnesota—to the midwestern prairie, while Missouri's southern half, especially the Ozark Plateau, is where (as I was repeatedly told) the South begins. The Civil War split Missouri wide open. Though a slave state that contributed thirty thousand men to the Confederate Army and a state where in the early 1950s Jim Crow laws segregated schools, theaters, restaurants, and hotels, Missouri also furnished more than one hundred thousand men to the Union Army. Many Missouri families had sons on both sides.

The restaurant with its cheap table and chairs just outside Jefferson City, the state capital located in the center of the state, featured a sign that said "All You Can Eat." The display included German pot roast, spareribs, fried chicken, gravy, mashed potatoes, iceberg lettuce, Russian dressing, pecan pie, and iced tea in red plastic glasses. Many of the waitresses as well as the customers were overweight, some grossly. The men wore feedlot caps as they ate. "This is a good place," one fellow said to another. "You don't see any stray hogs banging at the door." Like the setting and the food, the conversation was timeless.

Throughout the day I would encounter banal scenes like this. Accompanied by snatches of predictable chatter, they made it appear as though the demographic changes I knew had taken place in America were simply modifications to an immense, resilient landscape.

In downtown Jefferson City I listened as a group of happy schoolkids counted the cars on a Union Pacific freight train that was passing along the Missouri River. "One, two, three," they yelled, all the way up to "one hundred eleven." Later that afternoon I arrived in Fulton, which, like Jefferson City, gives the impression of an idyllic American town, whose centrality to the American experience is presupposed by *Reader's Digest*—a magazine I would see almost everywhere in small-town America. (If you stayed away from airports, throughout much of the countryside you would think that elite magazines such as *The New Yorker, The Atlantic Monthly, The New York Review of Books,* and so on, along with their concerns and obsessions, simply did not exist.) In Fulton I passed rows of frame houses with big manicured lawns and heavy-limbed trees on streets where only the sound of birds and children playing broke the silence. On one downtown street, a white boy on a bicycle was good-naturedly pulling a black friend on in-line skates. It was at Fulton's Westminster College on May 5, 1946, that Winston Churchill officially ushered in the Cold War with his famous "iron curtain" speech. Near the campus was a statue of Churchill along with eight sections of the Berlin Wall. From this memorial middle America extends for many miles, its serenity the ultimate rebuke to communism.

From Fulton I followed Route 94 along the Missouri River, a panoramic rampage as it neared the end of its 2,565-mile journey from southwestern Montana to St. Louis, where it merges with the Mississippi. After days of heavy rain the river was brown and swollen. The rain fell harder as I neared the confluence of the two great rivers and drove north, circling St. Louis on Route 94, to end up on a spit of farmland five miles wide between the converging rivers. Suddenly water surged across the road and a young man in a pickup truck yelled, "Follow me, I'll lead you out of here." Following his pickup across a small patch of field onto a series of dirt feeder roads, I made it safely back to Route 94 near the bridge over the Mississippi, where I crossed into Illinois: it was the first of many encounters I was to have with floods.

After a few miles I turned off the highway, onto a dirt road that led me to the eastern bank of the Mississippi at the spot where it joined the Missouri, where I found a sign announcing that a memorial to Lewis and Clark would be built here, near the site of Camp Dubois (Camp Wood), where the two explorers had spent the winter of 1803–1804 before beginning their journey up the Missouri into the Pacific Northwest.

The rain had stopped for a moment, but water still covered the thick undergrowth and was almost even with the road. A man was fishing a few inches from his car, the only other vehicle out here. Pointing to the water slowly creeping up to the road, he said, "You be careful, don't walk away from your car. If we get even so much as another drizzle, you and me have to get the hell out of here." I saw a log float by a few feet away. I looked out at the expanse of brown water welded to a dark gray sky. "Even on a clear day you can't see where the rivers meet," the fisherman said. "All you see is water, like the sea."

The confluence might as well have been a vast, misty lake, but the place where the two greatest rivers of the North American continent converge was no disappointment. If someone had told me that the outskirts of a great modern city, St. Louis, were ten miles to the south, I might not have believed him, for I saw nothing but water and a wilderness of towering cottonwoods and sycamores. "I never saw anything more terrific; a tangle of entire trees, of branches, of floating islands," wrote Jesuit Father Jacques Marquette, coming upon the meeting of these two rivers in June 1673, in his voyage down the Mississippi with Louis Joliet. Marquette called the great river flowing into the Mississippi the "Pekitanoui," Algonquian for "muddy waters." It was plied by what the Algonquians, who lived east of the Mississippi, called the "people of the wooden canoes," which to the French settlers sounded like *"Ou-missouris,"* hence the river's eventual name.

From this site in Illinois, America seemed still an untamed wilderness, especially given the leaden air and the floods, the tornados, and the hurricanes that regularly ransack the lower Mississippi Valley. Many inhabitants of the Mississippi and Missouri Basin have seen their houses flooded and their life's possessions destroyed not once, but several times. Geography and climate still rule, and the weather is anything but a frivolous topic here. Nature exacts a price from such instances of overdevelopment as the excess of paved streets, which inhibits drainage. Americans like to think that their opportunities are limitless, but the truth is that their contempt for natural limits has often been disastrous, whether for farmers on the Great Plains, whose overtilling helped precipitate the Dust Bowl; for homeowners in California or the Pacific Northwest, whose houses, built on unstable hill-sides, wash away in floods; or for residents of the Mississippi Valley, liv-ing too close to a river made even more unstable by dams and concrete spillways.

I would confront these environmental issues later in my journey, but now St. Louis beckoned.

3

—

The Average American City

THE WORD "ST. LOUIS" conjured up for me a sepia image of lost glories.

It was the North American waterway system that made St. Louis great, the pivot of Spanish, French, British, and American ambitions in the interior continent. From St. Louis northward the Mississippi is navigable for 800 miles, connecting with other rivers to the Great Lakes and Canada. It flows southward for 1,345 miles to the Gulf of Mexico. The Missouri, meanwhile, is navigable for 2,000 miles beyond St. Louis to the western Dakotas, while 200 miles south of the city the great Ohio River—navigable from Pittsburgh—empties into the Mississippi at Cairo, Illinois. Thus, St. Louis became the commercial entrepôt at the head of the Santa Fe Trail, shipping manufactured goods in exchange for raw materials by wagon train to Spanish outposts in Mexico. In 1867, a long article in *The Atlantic Monthly* predicted that "fair St. Louis" was destined to become "the future capital of the United States" and a "greater and more imperial city than Rome."

When railroads edged out steamboats and Conestoga wagons in the decades after the Civil War, Chicago, whose business community had wisely invested in feeder rails, switching yards, and grain elevators to take advantage of its location on the Great Lakes and its proximity to the farm region, eclipsed St. Louis as the principal city of the Midwest. Then, in 1904, St. Louis had a last fling at glory when it became the first American city to host a modern Olympics. In the same year the Louisiana Purchase Exposition—a world's fair to celebrate the centenary of Lewis and Clark's journey—drew 20 million visitors to "the most cosmopolitan city on earth."[1] The exposition was where the "hot dog," the "ice cream cone," and the song "Meet Me in St. Louis"—later immortalized by Judy Garland—all debuted. In his autobiography, Henry Adams, a normally dour New Englander with limited enthusiasm for the Middle West, wrote about the exposition:

> The world had never witnessed so marvellous a phantasm; by night Arabia's crimson sands had never returned a glow half so astonishing, as one wandered among long lines of white palaces, exquisitely lighted by thousands on thousands of electric candles.

On May 21, 1927, Charles Lindbergh flew solo over the Atlantic in the single-engine *Spirit of St. Louis,* named for Lindbergh's St. Louis backers, who had paid $10,580 to build the plane. Between 1926 and 1934, the St. Louis Cardinals won five pennants and three World Series. But thereafter the city seemed to fade. As a local public relations executive, Al Kerth, told me, "We spent most of the twentieth century remembering the past."

IN NORTH AMERICA, unlike in Europe, each new layer of civilization and development erases rather than builds upon the previous ones, so that while the history of St. Louis can be told, it cannot be seen.

A thousand years ago, the St. Louis area was the center of the "Mississippi culture." Forty thousand Mississippians lived in a city across the river from present-day St. Louis, where they erected great public works, including a ceremonial mound 100 feet high and 1,000 feet long. When this Mississippian culture disintegrated, Sioux-speaking Missouris and Osages, along with other tribes from the Great Lakes region, migrated here. Then came French explorers and fur trappers, who throughout the seventeenth century had been filtering down

---

[1]The phrase in quotes is from an article by Stephen Raiche, quoted in James Neal Primm, *Lion of the Valley: St. Louis, Missouri.*

the St. Lawrence River, through the Great Lakes, and then down the Mississippi Valley, building a chain of forts as they went. In 1682, Robert Cavelier, Sieur de La Salle, made his way by sailboat down the Mississippi to present-day New Orleans, thus securing for the French a riverine empire that arced behind the Appalachians from the freezing Atlantic coast of Quebec to the muggy wetlands of the Gulf of Mexico. On February 14, 1764, thirty Frenchmen led by the tough, young, and charismatic Auguste Chouteau established a trading post near the junction of the Mississippi and Missouri Rivers in the heart of this empire. To honor the reigning sovereign, Louis XV, the site was named after Louis IX, Saint Louis.

Elsewhere the French empire in the New World was in decline. Quebec had fallen to the British in 1759, and in 1763, the year before St. Louis was founded, the Seven Years' War ended with France's defeat. Soon St. Louis's Creole population—a mixture of French, Spanish, and Africans from the West Indies—came under Spanish rule, while the English threatened the French on the eastern shore of the Mississippi River in present-day Illinois. In 1800, Napoleon, at the height of his power, reclaimed the French empire in western North America, called the Louisiana Territory in honor of Louis XV. But in 1803, Napoleon, who was in the midst of a worldwide strategic retreat precipitated in part by the costly loss of Santo Domingo, sold his North American empire to the United States. St. Louis was now in American hands, the remnants of its French culture to be memorialized in the mispronounced names of streets and suburban townships.

Between 1830 and 1844, St. Louis tripled in size as the Santa Fe Trail trade boomed. The European political troubles of 1848 and the Irish potato famine of 1845–1846 brought many German and Irish immigrants to the city (the innate conservatism of the Germans helped keep the city in Union hands during the Civil War), accompanied by a great influx of blacks, both slaves and freemen. In 1870, central St. Louis had 310,000 inhabitants, more than Boston and exceeded only by New York, Philadelphia, and Brooklyn. In 1996, when I visited, the city was down to only 350,000 inhabitants from the more than 800,000 after World War II. By the end of the twentieth century, St. Louis was no longer among the top three dozen cities in the United States, its population having fled to the suburbs faster and in larger numbers than in most other metropolitan areas. Austin, Texas, now has more people than St. Louis.

"*Ah,* St. Louis," a Chicago-based French diplomat had told me.

"The clink of fine glassware at a country club—in St. Louis I found a real elite: genteel, undynamic, truly refined. There was something almost southern about those people, a lassitude amidst their lawns and mansions, hanging on while all around them the city disintegrated."

It was this conversation that brought me to St. Louis, the largest metropolitan area close to the geographical as well as the statistical middle of the country. "St. Louis tends to be very average," Don Phares, a local urban economist, told me. "Whether it's industry, unemployment, per capita growth rates, whatever, this is the mean-level American metropolis. You cannot judge what's going on in urban America by New York, Boston, or Los Angeles. St. Louis, though, except for its rapid-fire suburbanization, which is even greater than the national average, is unexceptional."

WHAT I DISCOVERED, however, was that St. Louis no longer exists. After days spent looking for it, I never quite found it.

To begin with, there was Clayton, where I stayed: a predominantly white, upper-middle-class center of finance and high technology strategically located beside an interstate, with sharp-angled chrome-alloy buildings and restaurants whose decor and cuisine were so eclectic as to be placeless—at one restaurant I was served a Greek salad, "Costa Rican–prepared" fish, and pasta. Despite its gleaming office towers, Clayton lacks a coherent skyline. Like a vast chessboard with many missing pieces and lonely, windy spaces, Clayton is indistinguishable from Overland Park, Kansas; Bethesda, Maryland; Tysons Corner, Virginia; and a host of other high-technology suburbs with which I was familiar: with repetitive vistas of wide, treeless streets, multistory parking facilities, and fancy shopping plazas. Two thirds of America's new office space is in such cities.[2] I felt as if I had arrived nowhere.

In my hotel room I looked at several maps of the St. Louis area drawn during the last few decades. Each resembled a comet, with its urban head on the Mississippi burning up as the trail of suburbs extending westward grew longer and longer as it approached the western prairie. From head to tail I could trace in the following order, from east to west, urban streets, then so-called edge cities such as Clayton, then old wealth, and finally new wealth. The most recent

[2]See Joel Garreau, *Edge Cities: Life on the New Urban Frontier.*

map showed extreme fragmentation. St. Louis, it turns out, is a mis-
nomer. In fact, there are ninety-two incorporated cities—some with
only a dozen or so inhabitants—in greater St. Louis (there were five
in 1876), with a combined population of 2.3 million. Though St.
Louis proper remains the largest, it continues to lose inhabitants.

From Clayton I drove slowly westward for two hours through winding residential streets until I reached the end of the St. Louis suburbs
thirty miles away, where the repetition of fitness centers, shopping
malls, mountain bike stores, and green lawns finally ended. As I drove
I crossed a border every few minutes or so:

"Welcome to the City of Ladue. Drive Carefully." "Welcome to the
City of Chesterfield. Population 42,000." "Welcome to the City of
Frontenac." "You Are Entering Ellisville City Limits." . . .

Because some of these signs were of hand-carved wood and painted
in tasteful earthen hues, I mistook them for antique shop shingles, of
which there were also many. When I saw the sign for the "City of Town
& Country," with its stylish black script against a whitewashed background, I thought of a J. Crew catalog. The design consciousness extended to the houses, too. The entrance to one community of luxury
homes appeared guarded by Tudor-style ramparts and turrets. Many
of these townships had their own schools, policemen, and firemen,
and their own way of painting lane dividers.

The townships also had rigorous zoning restrictions concerning
acreage per unit and building materials that made it impossible for
people beneath a certain income to move in. One incorporated
township, Country Life Acres, seemed to consist of just one opulent
street with only a few inhabitants. "If you don't incorporate, you
might be annexed by a slightly poorer suburb. So there has been a lot
of defensive incorporation," one area resident told me. It was easy to
tell by the types of houses and signs that while almost all of these suburbs were prosperous, there were gradations of income within the sea
of affluence: these borders were real.[3]

Such unabashed suburban autonomy did not quite obtain in other
American metropolitan areas I had seen. Several residents told me
that this was partly because of St. Louis's "southern" aspect. Describ-

[3]In a study of 240 metropolitan areas by Paul Jargowsky of the University of Texas
at Dallas, it was confirmed that American neighborhoods have become increasingly class-segregated, a trend apparent among both blacks and whites. See Paul
Glastris and Dorian Friedman, "A Tale of Two Suburbias."

ing a journey from Springfield, Illinois, to St. Louis, *The Atlantic Monthly* in 1867 reported:

> It is strange to be at 9 A.M. at Abraham Lincoln's tomb and see pilgrims approach it with uncovered head, and at 12 P.m. to find yourself surrounded by people who affect to hold in contempt all that he represented.

Indeed, from St. Louis it was only a two-hour drive to the Missouri "boot heel" (the southeastern corner of the state enclosed by Arkansas and Tennessee), or "Little Dixie," as it is known. One local historian told me that the St. Louis suburbs "represent an unreflective, nouveau-riche South that never suffered the humiliation and guilt associated with desegregation in the Deep South in the 1950s and 1960s." Suburbanization here does not mean decentralization as much as it does jurisdictional sovereignty for well-off whites so they can isolate themselves from the problems of predominantly black inner cities.

This was the culmination of a historical process. In the nineteenth century, American cities evolved mainly as centers for commerce, rather than as religious, military, and cultural centers as well, as in Europe. Suspicion of newly arrived urban lawyers and bankers and other middlemen by rural inhabitants ran deep, because for rural inhabitants the city was all about money and thus alien to their values. The turn-of-the-century populism of William Jennings Bryan and the Prohibition Act of 1919 were rural-based movements directed against another aspect of city life: immigrants. Beginning in the 1940s, when 5 million blacks began their great migration north as mechanical cotton picking brought an end to their agricultural servitude in the South, a new factor was added: race, which led to race- and class-based suburbs that cordoned off the city. Frederick Jackson Turner's frontier, with its new opportunities and emphasis on practicality, worked against racial and class distinctions. These suburbs suggest that, in St. Louis at least, the frontier may, at last, be closed.

THE NUMBER OF American communities built by single developers and surrounded by defensive perimeters grew from a thousand in the early 1960s to more than eighty thousand by the mid-1980s, with further increases in the 1990s (as I had seen for myself in the predominantly white Washington, D.C., area suburbs that abut a large inner-city black population). "Gated communities" are not an American invention; they are an import from Latin America, where deep social divisions in such places as Rio de Janeiro and Mexico City make them popular—indeed, necessary—among the middle class. On a visit to São Paulo, for instance, I noticed that almost every apartment building resembled a diplomatic compound surrounded by high fences and surveillance apparatus. Should such fortress architecture eventually predominate in the United States, how would it alter our society, with its fluid class distinctions so different from those of Latin America?

Then, of course, there are the malls, with their own rules and security forces, replacing public streets; private health clubs rather than public playgrounds; and other aspects of daily life in which—perhaps without realizing it, because these changes have been so gradual—we have opted out of the public sphere and dissolved the social contract in order to protect ourselves from the old central cities.

"It's nonsense to think that Americans are individualists," Dennis Judd, an urban affairs professor at the University of Missouri's St. Louis campus, told me. "Deep down, we are a nation of herd animals: mouselike conformists who will lay at the doorstep all our rights—*if* you tell us that we won't have to worry about crime and that our property values will be protected." Americans, he explained, willingly put up with restrictions inside a corporation that they would never put up with in the public sphere. Then he added that life within some sort of corporation is what the future will increasingly be like. "Just look at our suburbs," he said. "We are going to depend less and less on the public sphere."[4]

Alexis de Tocqueville and others warned that material prosperity in America might ultimately breed withdrawal. As material wealth accumulates within a society along with technological conveniences, people's personal lives become more complex, with new choices and stresses, leaving them with less time and energy for communal concerns. As I drove through the St. Louis suburbs, I was struck by the in-

---

[4]Consider Westlake, a planned California community built by the American-Hawaiian Land Company. Westlake had no old people and no blacks. Visiting Westlake in the early 1970s, British writer Michael Davie wrote that the inhabitants of Westlake "did not want, any longer, their ambience to be interesting or stimulating: they wanted it perfect: a safe and beautiful rest-home, cut out from the pain of the world, for healthy people"; see Davie, *In the Future Now: A Report from California.*

verse relationship between material possessions and conveniences on the one hand and social unity on the other. Are we, I wondered, increasingly a nation of overworked, lonely people? What struck me here was the high number of cars in the office parks late in the evening. In *The Time Bind: When Work Becomes Home and Home Becomes Work,* sociologist Arlie Russell Hochschild claims that many women are actually fleeing their disorderly and tense home lives for the "reliable orderliness" of work. In the 1980s and 1990s, the American worker's work year increased by a month—164 hours.[5] The link between overwork and the decline of the family seems obvious to me. While in 1960 there was roughly one divorce for every four marriages, in 1994 there were two for every four marriages; and in 1995 only a quarter of all American households were couples with children: only half of all children now live in such conventional households, and each year that number declines.[6]

MY NEXT FORAY from Clayton was into University City, which despite its name is in fact a splatter of repair shops, low-end stores with signs in Korean, empty lots, middle- and lower-middle-class subdivisions, and some ugly yellow-brick garden apartments. As the income gap widens, the American middle class continues to split into an increasingly rarified upper middle class and an increasingly downtrodden lower middle class, as the middle middle slowly fades into one or the other. During the 1980s, a third of American suburbs saw income rises of 10 percent or more, while another third—represented by the older suburbs closer to downtown areas—saw steep declines.[7] University City is a suburb of the latter kind.

On a noisy thoroughfare in University City congested with trucks, I saw a dark brick building with Hebrew lettering on its door that announced a synagogue. The path of synagogue development in St. Louis has followed the lines of suburban migration out of the city, which in turn followed the highways that had once been Indian trails. The doors of the synagogue were locked. I noticed an alarm system and rang the buzzer. An electronic signal allowed me in.

Behind Rabbi Aaron Borow, with his gray beard and sad expres-

---

[5]See Juliet B. Schor, *The Overworked American: The Unexpected Decline of Leisure.*
[6]See Hochschild; Andrew Hacker, "The War over the Family"; and Stephanie Coontz, *The Way We Really Are: Coming to Terms with America's Changing Families;* and *Statistical Abstract of the United States* for studies on the American family.
[7]See Glastris and Friedman, "A Tale of Two Suburbias."

sion, was a statue of Moses and a wall of books in dark bindings. "I've been at this synagogue for thirty years. My first pulpit was in Montgomery, Alabama, from 1959 to 1964. Yes, I remember the whites with baseball bats hitting prointegration blacks. I am a Jew, so I spoke out morally for integration. But I was in a quandary: if I spoke too loudly I might endanger my congregation, which was my first responsibility. . . . Thirty years ago, when I came here, University City was a center for St. Louis Jewry. But the Jews went west to the new suburbs, to get away from the blacks: that was the mood. When the blacks arrived here, the Jews who stayed did not want integration. So they sent their children to Jewish day schools. But recently more Jews have moved back to the neighborhood, and it is heavily Jewish again. The new arrivals are more Orthodox. They live here, but they don't send their kids to school here. So social unity is not what it used to be. Still, without the Jews there would be no whites at all in University City.

"I see a lot of movement and turbulence," Rabbi Borow continued. "The idea that the children follow the religious traditions of their parents is not so anymore in America. At this synagogue we're centrist Orthodox. But the children of many of our members have moved to more liberal synagogues out in the western suburbs, while children whose parents are from more liberal branches of Judaism have come to us. But the fastest-growing branch of Judaism in St. Louis is the Orthodox Agudat, who are the most fundamentalist of all. Ten years ago the Agudat couldn't get a *minyan* [the ten males or more above the age of thirteen, required for Jewish public worship]; now they have a hundred families. The Agudat has very good networking." Rabbi Borow winced as he pronounced this new, fashionable word. "Fear motivates some of the drift to this old-time religion." By fear, Rabbi Borow meant the difficulty of coping with late-twentieth-century life, with its tidal wave of technological and cultural change. I had seen this phenomenon before in my travels in the Middle East and elsewhere: technological innovations and the cultural turmoil they foment, rather than diluting religious feeling, seem to lead many people to build a fortress around their beliefs. An interconnected, globalized world seems to be encouraging the spread of Orthodox Judaism, as well as more extreme forms of Christianity, Islam, and other religions.

"It's harder now," he lamented. "The problem is that people have so many other interests and financial pressures these days. The wives work. Everyone has less time for the community. Though, if we get a local TV personality to talk at the synagogue, we draw a big crowd. I try to give my congregation an idea of Jerusalem, of its sights and smells, of what Jerusalem means." Trucks whined outside the window. I sensed that for Rabbi Borow Jerusalem was not only a place but an oasis removed from the superficiality of the mass culture that Americans in general—not just Jews—depend on to maintain their equilibrium. But even Rabbi Borow knew that to attract people to his synagogue he needed the vehicles of mass culture themselves, in the form of TV personalities.

THE CITY OF St. Louis proper is divided between a northern half, which is black, and a southern half, which is still predominantly white.

In the past, north St. Louis was heavily Italian and Irish and the south German. Then, in the 1950s, the Irish and other whites began fleeing to German neighborhoods in the southern half of the city as blacks took over the north, leaving an Irish stronghold in the extreme northern tip of the metropolitan area called Florissant, an incorporated township and thus "protected." I wanted to see for myself what the Irish needed to be protected from. Because I preferred not to wander these unfamiliar streets alone and wanted a guide who knew the neighborhood well to help interpret it for me, I explored black north St. Louis with Major Gregory Hawkins of the St. Louis Police Department.

The twenty square miles of north St. Louis that Hawkins showed me, containing more than a third of the city's population, are dangerous, and Hawkins, a forty-year-old black who has lived here since he was two, has bullet wounds to prove it. Hawkins, with short, graying hair and aviator glasses, spoke, like many people in St. Louis, with a slight southern accent. Diplomas, award citations, and his children's graduation photos decorated his office in the new Area 3 police station.

"When I grew up, if you so much as broke a window, by the time you arrived home your parents would know about it. Now there are no home owners, they're all renters, and it takes days to locate the parents of a delinquent child—if you're lucky. When you do find the parents, they're not really *parents:* they're just kids who've had kids. The very term 'parenting skills' "—Hawkins said the words with disgust—"indicates the breakdown of the family in places like this.

Being a parent is something that can't be taught: if you're raised properly, you just know how to do it! Without real parents in the area, we've resorted to curfews: eleven P.M. on weekdays and 12 A.M. on weekends for children sixteen years old and younger. . . .

"The only thing you can do with high-rise housing projects," Hawkins went on, "is tear them down and disperse the inhabitants. In Cabanne Courts [a project that once stood in Hawkins's area], even in a police car, I was running the gauntlet. You attract fire. I was shot at close range near there in a stakeout. The guy who shot me went to prison. Days after he got out of jail, he brutally raped a woman. A few years ago the city bulldozed the project. . . .

"The war on drugs is unrealistic. A unit of substance that costs $2,500 in Turkey sells for $250,000 on the streets of an American city. With such profit levels the incentive is too great not to sell—unless, of course, you can stop the demand. I often ask myself: What would happen if we legalized drugs at safely diluted levels and regulated them out of the hands of organized criminals? I can't help thinking about such ideas because from what I see on the street, the reality is that this so-called war is just not working. Come on, let's get in the car and wander around."

Hawkins turned the unmarked car south down Union Boulevard into the heart of north St. Louis. One thing I did not see was a crowded urban slum. I saw something worse: a once solid residential area with stately brick houses topped by mansard roofs and intermittent knots of retail stores that resembled an archaeological site, sparsely inhabited by squatters and other scavengers and strewn with refuse. Weeds grew high from cracks in the sidewalk. Not a lawn was mowed. Plywood was nailed over window spaces that vines had grown over. Shops that were not boarded up were protected by heavy iron grilles over their doors and windows. "I can remember when all of this was nice, well kept," Hawkins said. I saw only one well-maintained building without iron grilles: a funeral home. The red brick was a link to the Mississippian period, when great earthworks were built from the high-quality clay here. Because there were no high-rise projects or many crowded tenements in sight, it was hard to blame urban planners or architects for this blight.

A crude hand-painted sign announced the "St. Mark's Free Will Baptist Church," which used to be a movie theater, Hawkins told me. "I'll never forget when I was a kid, my mother tried to explain to me why I couldn't see a movie. The theater was closed to blacks. St. Louis is the northern tip of the South. I will never forget how confused and hurt I was. You can't walk around here now. There's a lot of violence."

On a street with brick houses along both sides, Hawkins said, "That's where I lived until I was thirteen years old, 5173 Maple Street. We were the first of two black families on what was a well-established block. The white families eventually left for south St. Louis and the suburbs. Many of the people around here are junkies. The cleaner's, the confectionery, they're gone. You see that building," Hawkins said, pointing to a four-story brick building that was boarded up, "that used to be the Will Rogers Thee-ater. If you were black, you couldn't go inside. Now I'm going to show you something you won't believe."

He turned the car to the right and drove for about forty-five seconds at average speed through a nondescript street. Then, suddenly, it was as if I were back in Country Life Acres, except that here it was old wealth on view, the kind of mansions the French diplomat had talked about. This was St. Louis's Central West End, all white. I saw mowed lawns and polished stone villas with attached carriage houses, baroque sculptures and fountains, trimmed hedges, pollarded trees, little hexagonal signs proclaiming electronic security systems, and speed bumps in the road. "The average home here is about $500,000," Hawkins said, adding that the residents have their own private security patrols in addition to the electronic systems.

Hawkins again swerved the car, and in less than a minute we were back in the poor area, where skeletal roofs reminded me of scenes from war-torn Bosnia and groups of homeless people squatted in weedy fields against a panorama of vacated buildings. Then came a liquor store covered with black grilles and bullet-proof glass surrounded by young black men holding beer cans and staring fearlessly at Major Hawkins. One young man without a shirt had a mobile phone in his hand. "That used to be a real drugstore, with a nice soda fountain," Hawkins said.

The juxtaposition of the Central West End with a wasteland of wrecked buildings and streets as ominous as any I had seen in the war-torn Third World had come about when working-class whites fled and wealthy whites in luxury homes hired private security services to protect their investments. It made me shout the phrase "policy vacuum" at Hawkins. "It's as if the government were never here," I said. "What you are showing me through this car window are cruel social and economic forces that have overrun urban policy." Cultures rooted in Europe had moved out and a culture deformed by slavery and the sharecropper system had moved in, a transformation too great to be controlled by traditional democratic government, with its limited powers and halfway measures. A day ago, economist Don Phares had told me that there is too little historical proof that public policy can greatly improve the overwhelming majority of inner-city areas: The success stories tend to be small and specialized.

Ultimately, many inner cities may simply burn themselves out to conclude the vast movement away from urban cores. But that is no excuse for leaving inner cities to their fate. Though the facts are undeniable, it is also undeniable that civil societies are hollow if they do not care for their most needy citizens. Aristotle wrote that the real difference between democracy and oligarchy is that democracy is to the advantage of the populace at large, while oligarchy is to the advantage of the rich. Throughout modern history, enlightened conservatives have worked to soften the blows of great social and technological changes on people, to alleviate suffering and prevent revolution. The destruction of inner cities is precisely the kind of upheaval that Edmund Burke, for example, would have humanely attended to, rather than brutally ignored. He would have known that simply because government has no overall solution to the problem does not mean that it cannot continue to help in many ways. No true descendant of the Enlightenment could justify leaving inner cities as they are.

Hawkins remarked, "My mother worked all her life for Washington University [in St. Louis], and my father worked for General Motors. They are old people with small pensions. They cannot afford to relocate. The government should either help people like my parents relocate or build up the neighborhood." He said that anybody who could manage to leave north St. Louis was doing so.

Yet black flight to the suburbs was not speeding integration. Studies of St. Louis and other cities show that racial segregation at upper income levels is only marginally less severe than in poor urban areas. The majority of neighborhoods in greater St. Louis are either less than 2 percent African American or more than 84 percent African American.[8] Moreover, one third of the area's incorporated townships

[8]See John E. Farley, "Race Still Matters," for data about segregation in St. Louis. For a more general discussion of urban and suburban segregation in America, see Dennis R. Judd and Todd Swanstrom, *City Politics: Private Power and Public Policy*.

are black-controlled, and there is substantial black resistance (not to mention white resistance) to the black-dominated city of St. Louis rejoining the wealthier, white-dominated St. Louis County, because blacks do not want to lose political influence even if they might benefit financially. Like it or not, the record is clear: on a local level, blacks want to govern themselves; they want the power and the patronage that come with self-governance, just as whites have had. Nobody, either black or white, is pushing integration in St. Louis.[9]

The tour continued.

Hawkins pointed out the ruined hulk of the United Clothing store. "It was Jewish-owned. The store was a real community anchor. It's gone." Hawkins pointed to a nearby abandoned house. "In 1980, I found a dead twenty-three-month-old baby on that roof. The boyfriend was high on drugs and slapped the girlfriend's baby until the baby died. Then he put the baby in a plastic bag and laid it on the roof. The people who live here have absolutely no perspective on how the outside world behaves. For them, these streets are the entire earth. So how can they have anything resembling ambition?

"For example, on that street over there, we carried out a drug raid. In the midst of the chaos, with police officers chasing down junkies, I saw a little girl walk out of a house without a coat in the cold weather. An old women ran after the kid. Now, I thought that the woman was going to throw a coat over the kid. But no—the woman slapped the child hard and shouted, 'Git your fucking ass inside!' How is a child who hears such language supposed to grow up, be normal, and properly raise children of her own? . . .

"This was once a prominent area. When the Irish lived here, you could fall asleep on the sidewalk and people would bring you lemonade."

Hawkins told me about ten guns that had been confiscated from one house within a block of a primary school and about how twelve people from another house had been arrested on drug charges. Meanwhile, the grainy war-zone look did not change. I was witnessing the brutal human by-product of a passing Industrial Age. The unskilled manufacturing jobs held by the parents and grandparents of many of these inhabitants no longer exist. The frontier Turner wrote

[9]My observations are based partly on interviews with two urban sociologists in St. Louis: Robert Salisbury at Washington University and Andrew J. Theising at the University of Missouri.

about is dying in yet another way: the job market for physical labor—
a twentieth-century substitute for the raw opportunity offered by the
burgeoning western towns—no longer offers a living wage.

Hawkins drove me back to the police station, where we said
good-bye.

LATER THAT DAY I parked in a monitored underground garage beneath a tall building, rode an elevator to an upper story, and stepped
into a quartz-and-steel lobby, like a mini-atrium, brightly lit by halo-
gen lamps. A series of clocks showed the time in Atlanta, Belfast, Brus-
sels, Beijing, and other places. On a table were foreign newspapers.
The silken-voiced receptionist from Fleischman Hillard International Communications, a public relations firm, ignored me for a few
minutes while she transferred voice mail messages and took calls.
Then she apologized and escorted me into a room decorated in gray
leather and marble with a panoramic view of the Gateway Arch, a
short distance away. The Gateway Arch, completed in 1965 to com-
memorate the "Opening of the West" by Lewis and Clark, is St. Louis's
totem, a shimmering steel rainbow sixty stories high (632 feet from
base to apex) rising beside the muddy, reddish Mississippi River. On
the eastern side of the river I saw cement silos and frayed brown buildings barely rising above the greenery. Since the late eighteenth century, those lowlands have been known as the "American Bottoms";
today, partly hidden behind a screen of foliage, East St. Louis, Illinois,
one of the worst inner-city slums in the United States, worse than
north St. Louis where I had just been with Major Hawkins, lies there.
But next door to this building on the western side of the river were
luxury hotels.

"Mr. Kerth will be in shortly," a secretary told me. "Feel free to
phone anywhere."

Al Kerth gave me a hearty "Hello," then immediately sat down in
one of the leather swivel chairs, leaned back, cupped his hands behind his head, and called me by my first name in a booming voice, as
if we were old friends. We could have been in Manhattan, Paris, or
Milan. Kerth wore a wide bright yellow tie, suspenders made of
braided leather, and glasses with fashionable frames. He represented
St. Louis 2004, a nonprofit organization marking the centennial of
the 1904 World's Fair and Olympics and the bicentennial of both the
Louisiana Purchase and the Lewis and Clark expedition. Kerth told
me that his organization wants to channel "forward-thinking energy

for the future." He handed me a glossy folder with fact sheets enclosed, then walked over to a blackboard, where he wrote:

REGION-WIDE VISIONARY PROCESS. THIS VISIONARY PROCESS WILL CONSIST OF REGIONAL GOALS IN KEY AREAS: WORK, LEARNING, HEALTH, THE ENVIRONMENT, AND GOVERNANCE.

"Income-sustaining jobs, for instance," said Kerth, lowering his voice as he walked back to the leather chair. "Bio and nanotech jobs. How do we attract them? That is the question St. Louis 2004 must answer." Will anyone in north St. Louis, or East St. Louis for that matter, be qualified for nanotech jobs? I wondered. "Of course, it helps if we construct a positive environment within which firms can operate. That means good housing, infrastructure, cleaning up poverty-stricken areas, and so on."

Kerth continued, "We are in a race with cities around the world. For instance, there may be airports in every city, but there won't be spaceports. But we plan to have the mid-American spaceport. We believe that private corporations will be regularly sending people into space on orbital and suborbital flights in the twenty-first century. Low-cost, reusable-launch technology will get people from St. Louis to Beijing, for example, in forty-five minutes. Our public relations battle to host the spaceport for mid-America is already on. Lindbergh flew across the Atlantic to win a $25,000 prize. Well, we're supporting a multimillion-dollar international space prize series for advances in aviation technology. We even have an idea for an orbital hotel charging $50,000 for a gravityless weekend honeymoon in space, reached from the St. Louis spaceport."

I was flabbergastered by Kerth's boosterism. He seemed to me a typical American type of a sort now found in cities around the world, at once successful and naive. He was so optimistic that all argument seemed pointless. So I just took notes as he spoke. But the very wealth and efficiency of the surroundings—with men and women dressed as expensively as Kerth himself moving quickly and quietly through the corridor—suggested that I not dismiss his futuristic vision out of hand. In fact, reusable-launch technology is already being developed, and corporations are already playing a big role in the space program with their own satellites and space shuttle payloads. And given the consumer excess already here, how excessive in a few years or decades will a gravityless honeymoon in space seem?

Fleishman Hillard's office and other corporate offices nearby suggested that the policy vacuum I had noticed in north St. Louis would likely be filled by corporations and their needs rather than by government. As I walked across the street after my session with Kerth to the Museum of Westward Expansion beneath the Gateway Arch, in the heart of "historic St. Louis"—where the museum gift shop was stacked with souvenirs of St. Louis manufactured in Asia—I wondered whether, as upwardly mobile whites and blacks continue to flee into their own suburban enclaves, caring increasingly less about the neighborhoods beyond their township borders, corporations such as Fleischman Hillard might inherit the hollowed-out shells of cities, where the only salable assets would be the names of the cities themselves and the historical associations that accompany them, which these firms can then exploit in their marketing campaigns. As political power fragments—as one city becomes ninety-two municipalities—civic decisions reached behind the closed doors of corporate boardrooms become increasingly probable.

In our own frontier society driven by private enterprise, big business has often decided America's future, despite intermittent bouts of countervailing government pressure. From the 1870s through the 1890s, such Gilded Age millionaires as John D. Rockefeller, Andrew Carnegie, and J. P. Morgan developed an economy of scale to fit the landscape of scale that Abraham Lincoln had secured by unifying the nation in the 1860s. These millionaires built libraries, museums, and universities and founded symphony orchestras and historical societies to consolidate their own civilization in the making, which happened to be a specifically American one. Yet, to a much greater degree than a hundred years ago, today's fortunes are being made in a global economic environment, in which an affluent global civilization arising in places such as Johnson County, Kansas, the western St. Louis suburbs, and high-technology centers such as Bangalore in India is being forged even as strata of our own society are left behind, rooted in place.

Perhaps a few decades hence there will no longer be a specifically "American" city if the revitalization of our urban areas takes the form of Singapore, with protected suburbs and corporate fortresses devoted to international trade and the accumulation of personal wealth, even as security precautions fed by the fear of crime lead to the loss of some individual rights and inner cities, like failed Third World states, continue to stagnate or recover only marginally. (New York may retain its identity because it has never really been an American city but rather a global entrepôt of goods, ideas, and fashions.)

Urban fragmentation is sometimes obscured by white-lie facades. At the 1996 Olympic Games in Atlanta, for example, racial harmony was proclaimed ad nauseam as an Olympic theme, even though whites and blacks in Atlanta live in separate enclaves and the downtown has been transformed into a corporate fortress whose streets are empty at dusk. The murder rate in metropolitan Atlanta, a hollow shell with 411,000 inhabitants amid a suburban pod of 2.7 million, is among the nation's highest.

I continued my walk, up Market Street away from the Gateway Arch and the museum, into the heart of the business district, where I saw a bleak vista of office buildings along wide avenues and only a few pedestrians. I counted more joggers than strollers. There was an "Irish pub," a café offering espresso and bagels, and a few other restaurants, along with another bank whose clocks showed the time in London, Beijing, and so on. In New York, whose streets are crowded at all hours with people from all over the world, such establishments help create a cosmopolitan milieu. Here I was disoriented: I still had no idea what, or even where, St. Louis was. The closest I got to "St. Louis" was on its Metrolink transit system that is partly responsible for the empty streets in the downtown areas. On the Metrolink I saw crowds of people and for the first time felt the *buzz* of a great city.

The problem was me. The cities of the future—as I would understand more fully when I visited Omaha, Nebraska, and Orange County, California—will not be distinctive as cities have always been. Instead of reflecting a unique culture, each future city seems likely to consist of the same borrowed fragments: standardized corporate fortresses, privately guarded housing developments, Disneyfied tourist bubbles, restaurants serving the same eclectic food, and so on. The loss of architectural and cultural distinction does not mean that the inhabitants of these cities will necessarily be unhappy, but to my late-twentieth-century way of thinking, such cities are jarring. In *On Native Grounds* literary critic Alfred Kazin wrote that America at the end of the nineteenth century "stood suddenly, as it were, between one society and another, one moral order and another, and the sense of impending change became almost oppressive in its vividness."

I looked back at the Gateway Arch and imagined a corporate logo, accompanied by a corporate flag, rather than a monument to what Thomas Jefferson and Lewis and Clark had wrought. I thought it fitting that T. S. Eliot, whose poetry betrays little trace of nationality, had been born in St. Louis.

4

—

The "American Bottoms"

"DON'T CROSS THE bridge into East St. Louis." That's the advice
that people in St. Louis's western suburbs give tourists. Even when it
was white, East St. Louis had a bad reputation.

By the 1780s, Spanish-ruled Creoles and Indians in St. Louis were
referring to the lowlands across the Mississippi River as the "American Bottoms," the place where Virginia ruffians under the command
of George Rogers Clark made life hell for French-speaking half-
castes. In 1797, Revolutionary War officer James Piggot established a
ferry service connecting St. Louis and East St. Louis, then called "Illi-
noistown," a place "where the law did not reach." By the 1870s, steel
plants, railroad switching yards, and factories making railroad equipment were going up in East St. Louis, attracting Irish, Eastern Europeans, and blacks to low-wage, low-skill, dangerous work. At the turn
of the century came aluminum and chemical plants, and East St.
Louis confirmed its reputation for pollution, poverty, prostitution,
corruption, and violence. The factories created their own incorporated towns, legal fictions with few or no residents, to avoid paying
taxes to East St. Louis. Sherwood Anderson called East St. Louis
"nobody's home." When the factories recruited southern blacks
as strikebreakers, race riots flared there in July 1917. Eight whites
and thirty-nine blacks died, and three hundred buildings occupied

mainly by blacks were set afire by white rioters. Roger Baldwin, a local white activist, disgusted by the assault on black homes, moved to New York City and in 1920 founded the American Civil Liberties Union.

The industrial plants in East St. Louis went into overdrive during World War II, but by the 1960s the obsolete plants began to close and whites fled across the river to the western St. Louis suburbs. By 1971, blacks accounted for nearly 70 percent of East St. Louis's population, and the election of the first black mayor signaled the end of the white political machine. At first the black machine lacked the organizational skills of the white one, but the level of corruption remained high. Whites and blacks who were able to leave did so. By the 1980s, East St. Louis was more than 95 percent black. Forty-five percent of its population lived in poverty, and 25 percent were unemployed. The median income was under $10,000. A third of East St. Louis families lived on less than $7,500 a year, and 75 percent of the population was on some form of public assistance. Four out of five births were to single mothers. East St. Louis could not even afford to collect its trash. The sewers were broken, and the city, located in a floodplain, could not afford to pump water out after heavy rains. The traffic lights seldom worked, and police cars lacked gasoline and radios. In 1992, the state of Illinois was forced to take control of the city's finances and many of its operations. For those who remained, there was not even a bowling alley or a movie theater.

By the 1990s, East St. Louis was 99 percent black. The Daughters of Charity, whose humanitarian operations are mainly in the Third World, opened a mission there.

"EAST ST. LOUIS was like a Third World country when I went there in 1991. I remember taking bathroom tissue over here," said H. C. Milford, a white Republican from the prosperous St. Louis suburb of Webster Groves. Milford, a wealthy insurance executive, sat behind his desk in the East St. Louis city hall, where he is now the economic director for the municipality and experiences daily the huge gulf between the vibrant international city to the west and the Third World disaster across the river. Milford is a conservative who has not given up on black inner cities and genuinely enjoys working in them. His East St. Louis office explains that apparent contradiction.

The office is in a quiet part of the building, behind several antechambers. His desk is enormous and supports many stacks of papers arranged in neat rows, each the same number of inches apart from the other. The sixty-four-year-old Milford has gray hair, gold-framed glasses, and a square face. His clothes are rumpled. Pens clutter his breast pocket. He looks down at his feet as he talks, as though thinking out loud. When I visited him, he counted off the points he made on his fingertips. Milford was organized, work-driven, and without a scintilla of pretense. Inner cities were just another challenge for him. He is among the most valuable members of American society at the turn of the twenty-first century, because he grasps at a deep level that the very definition of civil democracy rests on its willingness to help those who seem the most hopeless; that his wealthy neighbors had given up on poor blacks did not mean that he or the country as a whole should; and that just because poor blacks may not matter in the larger economic scheme of things, that is no moral justification for abandoning them.

"Five years ago there was municipal debt but no income. There was no money for fire trucks. It was tough on morale when city paychecks bounced. Now things are better but not good. The debt has been re-structured, but we have insufficient income [from taxes]. East St. Louis remains a dependent population, where the overwhelming majority of jobs are in the public sector." Milford convinced white businessmen to invest $43 million in the Casino Queen, a gambling palace in the East St. Louis harbor, which, in addition to creating 1,250 new jobs, has added $10 million in revenue to the municipal treasury. This has paid for new fire trucks, police equipment, and a property tax cut of 25 percent to curb middle-class flight and encourage investment. "We're now thinking about a 315-room hotel with a golf course by the river, near the casino. I'm a connector," he said, "a conduit. I bring white businessmen together with blacks. I meet this guy and say he ought to meet that guy."

Milford admitted that he was providing the equivalent of foreign aid through a casino. When I asked him what it was beside the poverty that made East St. Louis like a Third World country, he thought for a moment and said, "Nobody keeps records here. The filing system in city hall is a mess. It's hard to get phone calls or messages returned. I can't explain why, but people here just don't see the importance of returning calls. A lot of officials here are related by family, so it is hard to criticize people since you don't know who else in the office you might be offending. The main thing that's needed is basic literacy."

Much of what Milford told me would no doubt offend black residents, even as many of his suburban white neighbors may think he's crazy for doing what he does.

"Come on, I'll take you around." He led me out of the office. In the elevator we encountered a tall youth restrained by handcuffs, accompanied by a policeman. What I saw as we walked through East St. Louis and drove through its outlying areas was much worse than what I had seen in black north St. Louis with Major Hawkins the day before.

As in north St. Louis, there were few high-rises here. Instead, I saw a city of boarded-up storefronts and simple brick houses in ruins. Uncut grass and weeds were taller here than in north St. Louis, so that the term "lawn" was meaningless. Windows were boarded up and houses covered by vines, as in north St. Louis. Many roofs had collapsed. A tree had grown through the open rooftop of one home. I passed a baroque fountain and a public swimming pool, both dry and caked with greenish mold. Manhole covers were missing, which made driving at night particularly dangerous. Milford told me that the manhole covers had been stolen and sold for scrap metal. East St. Louis was largely a ghost town. The fountain, the pool, and most of the brick houses, all built by Irish and eastern European immigrants, were the remains of a bygone civilization, surrounded by a wilderness of oaks, sycamores, and cottonwoods.

Here and there I saw groups of menacing young men hanging out, but mainly I saw no one. Milford said there was now one supermarket for this city of 40,000. He pointed out an abandoned movie theater, where, it was said, Mel Torme's first wife had once worked as a ticket collector.

"Even when you have the money to level abandoned houses and rebuild, you can't always do it," Milford told me. "You can't get title insurance on many of these places because they were abandoned and the legal ownership is in question. You can't find records in city hall. People are apathetic; they don't demand action. When money is appropriated from the state or some other outside source to build or repair something here, fights break out over who will get the contract, and, of course, they feel the contractor has to be black and has to be a friend of someone in the local government. That often means that the contractor is not the best-qualified person for the job, nor the one with the best price. The problems go on."

He mentioned the school system, which several experts had told

me was rife with nepotism: there were more administrators and teachers than children. When I told him I planned to see Lillian Parks, the
former superintendent of schools, Milford replied, "Yes, you see"—
his voice was hesitant, and he chose his words carefully—"she's one of
the nicest women in the world. But, I don't know, I've worked here
for five years and I can't explain it, many things just don't change."

Milford and I walked into an old building that housed an after-
school program for young people. "Hello, Debra," Milford said to the
woman in the reception office. I saw old typewriters but no computers; old, fraying wires hung from the ceiling. The furniture was old,
and the fluorescent lights were cracked. The paint was peeling. There
was no air-conditioning, though it was humid and ninety degrees outside. The thick, damp heat seemed to have melted the walls. I thought
of the offices I had seen throughout many parts of southern Asia and
Africa that looked like this one.

Milford led me into the building's auditorium, which was even hot-
ter than the office. Chessboards were lined up in rows, as if for a large
competition. "They teach chess here after school. You see, sports
aren't for everybody. People here need more chess heroes and fewer
sports heroes. Chess is about math and reasoning. By learning to
think several moves in advance, you train children to plan for the future. I'm trying to fund this chess program," he continued, still making his points on his fingertips, his eyes on the floor.

MORRIS HUNT WAS a middle-class black whose home and office
were at the edge of East St. Louis, where there was less crime. Hunt
was tall, with an extremely dark complexion and a Bic pen stuck behind his right ear. His insurance business was in a down-at-heel building that was missing some door bolts and sections of carpeting. On
the second floor was an office for "Foster Care Youth at Risk." Hunt
and his secretary worked on old-model computers with grimy moni-
tors and keyboards. The place seemed a half century removed from
Al Kerth's office in downtown St. Louis's corporate enclave. Hunt's
office was busy with customers, though, and the fax machine was
working nonstop. Hunt's manner was both paternal and efficient
with his black clientele, as if he knew something not only about insurance but about the ways of the outside world that they did not.

"When I was growing up in the early 1960s, the south side of State
Street was all black and the north side white. On the way to the ball
field we had to hit State Street running, since it was white neighbor-

hoods we had to pass through. My kids can't fathom this, because now East St. Louis is all black. We were adolescent kids with differences, and the main difference happened to be race. If it hadn't been race, we would have found something else to fight over."

Hunt said that white migration left East St. Louis desolate. Urban flight brought property prices down; then white realtors bought cheaply. The city did not enforce building codes, and there was no screening of tenants. Because the owners did not live there, they didn't care. Nobody got fined for not cutting the grass, or for not having derelict cars and appliances taken away. Then even the absentee landlords abandoned the houses. "These little things add up," Hunt said. "I've always believed that the single most effective thing we can do to improve the slums is to turn people into owners, not renters. If people work and own houses where they live, no matter how ignorant they are, they will take care of their neighborhoods. For years now, people have used decent city salaries to buy homes elsewhere— blacks, I mean."

He continued, "I insure a lot of black policemen and firemen. The blacks that the city hires are now, finally, required to live here, but not the whites. There is an implicit recognition by the authorities that whites and blacks cannot live together."

I asked, "How can the city legally force black employees to live here and not the whites?"

"Oh, it can't. It's unofficial intimidation applied to blacks only."

A man walked into Hunt's office, a light-skinned black in a blue shirt, a lightweight leather jacket, and with a gold medallion around his neck. He was an off-duty police officer in East St. Louis with an insurance matter to discuss. Joining our conversation, he said in a slow drawl, "Even with intimidation, it's still hard to enforce residency for black city employees. You see"—shaking his head—"it's all a can of worms. We're an underdeveloped colony ruled by a class of administrators—teachers, bureaucrats—who drive to work here each morning from the outer world. Burglary escalates, and it's costing me more and more just to live here because the value of my property goes down. My kids are badly educated. I never intended my kids to get used to uncollected trash, burglaries, and so on. I've learned that there is only one strategy for realizing the American Dream: *You make it by leaving others behind.*"

The off-duty policeman asked me what I did. I said I was a journalist.

"In that case, I have a question," he said matter-of-factly. "How come these political scientists did not foresee the social problems in the cities and have plans in place to avoid them?" He was a streetwise cop, but he was naive enough to assume that academics and politicians were as straightforward and practical in their jobs as he was in his. What was I to tell him?

"I REMEMBER EAST St. Louis as a beautiful town. Did you know that *Look* magazine [in 1960] named us an All-American city? We were second only to Chicago in packinghouses and railroads. Did you know that Miles Davis and Jackie Joyner-Kersee are from East St. Louis? We were ninety thousand people then, and we were integrated. Of course, the schools and the movie theaters were not integrated. We were not equal, but we interacted, unlike now."

Lillian Parks, the retired East. St. Louis superintendent of schools, told me this wistfully, as though under hypnosis and far away. It was midafternoon of another hot day, even more oppressively humid. In the wealthier white areas of greater St. Louis the air-conditioning separates you from the climate. Here you are immersed in it, conscious of the heavy moisture generated by the two great rivers nearby. Your shirt is always stuck to your chair.

Parks's home was at the edge of East St. Louis, on a suburban street called Les Pleins Drive. We sat in the white wicker chairs in her solarium. Birds chirped. When she had told me how to get there, she pronounced the French name perfectly.

"We're now ninety-nine percent black. We've been left with all the people on welfare. There are some Koreans and Indian immigrants who own stores, but they live elsewhere. Our kids don't know that streets elsewhere aren't lined with garbage and weeds; that there are actually streets in this country where everyone mows their lawns. Our kids grow up with no aesthetic sensibility. Because a human being's outlook is formed so early, many of our kids are already lost."

Leaning over the kitchen table toward me, she began to plead, not so much to me as to herself: "When do you start to come back? When do you take down that shack without waiting for some authority to do it for you? Why haven't we organized ourselves to sweep the streets? Why do we need a government merely to make the streets beautiful, the way they used to be, the way they are in other neighborhoods? Why can't we do it ourselves? Now that the casino gambling has given us some money, we have no excuse." She laughed delicately, like a flower opening.

"I guess we're just set in our ways, that's all," she went on. "I'm just hoping that things will come back the way they were in the fifties. I did the best I could as superintendent, but the school system is in chaos now and people are still leaving if they can afford homes elsewhere. Most of our teachers don't live here. They don't see their students in the supermarket or in church. In the age of segregation our children learned because their teachers were esteemed; now they don't learn. Nevertheless, most of our kids go to college."

"What percentage?" I asked.

"Well, it used to be sixty percent. It's not so high anymore. Now it's thirty-five percent, maybe. But we still have students who go to college," she said a bit defensively. "A few years ago we had a [National] Merit Scholar. . . .

"As a teacher, I never had to tolerate a smart-alecky kid. I'd call a parent, and they'd respond. . . . Yes, we would walk through the park late at night without fear. We all went to church. You always said, 'Yes, ma'am' and 'No, ma'am.' Parents were in charge. Our children didn't wear baseball hats indoors, and they didn't wear them backwards! Don't our people know that the way you dress helps determine how you act; that to succeed you have to modify your dress and behavior to match the environment; that if you want a good job you shouldn't wear a stupid hat? We need uniforms in every black school across America, no exceptions!"

Now almost in tears, she said, "I want our children just to walk down a sidewalk where weeds have never grown through the cracks and there have never been broken bottles or trash or discarded mattresses or *stuff*. Why can't we do that? Why do you need a government to do that? Why can't we have a schedule: this group of neighbors will cut the weeds this week, and that group will cut them next week? I scream at people, 'Doesn't this rubble disturb you?' But people answer, 'Well, you know . . .' "

"What about Louis Farrakhan, the Nation of Islam leader?" I wondered. "Does his group have a presence here? After all, his group has a reputation for getting things done."

"I'll tell you something," she said, almost whispering. "They do have a growing presence in East St. Louis because, well, they're clean, well disciplined, and their facilities are spotless. Where they live there is no *stuff* lying around, and they don't wear baseball hats either. The Muslims promote their paper, *Final Call*, on the street. When you tell them that you're not interested, they never cuss you out. They always say, 'Yes, ma'am,' or 'No, ma'am.' That impresses me. They can go into a housing project and"—she snapped her fingers loudly in front of my face—"end crime. They put the fear of God into people."

As she talked, the solutions seemed to hang in the air in front of us, just out of reach.

Her husband, who had been into and out of the kitchen during our conversation, suddenly stammered, "The problem is that all these idiots are allowed to vote! When ignorant people are allowed to vote, they elect leaders like [Marion] Barry in Washington! The leadership in our cities merely reflects the culture of the inhabitants!"

I THOUGHT OF the failed places I had seen in the Third World that the United States—so I had often been told—felt obligated to assist, even to save. I wondered whether the thirty square miles of East St. Louis, close enough to Al Kerth's office that he could see it from his window, could be saved. According to demographers, the failure of places such as East St. Louis and north St. Louis—of many such inner cities, in fact—will not seriously jeopardize the economic future of the United States. Partly because of the projected influx of Hispanics and Asians over the coming decades, the percentage of blacks in the population will rise only slightly.[1] Moreover, a significant number of blacks will continue to desert places such as East St. Louis for better neighborhoods as they pry their way into the middle class. Migration, the desertion of poorer settlements for richer ones, is, after all, what history has always been about.

America is supposed to be an exception to such unsentimental historical forces, but the legacy of slavery and the relative intractability of black poverty and social disintegration suggests that American exceptionalism—the advantage of having had a largely empty and mineral-rich swath of the temperate zone at the time of the European Enlightenment—has its limits. America has always been an intensely competitive environment for individuals, groups, and cultures, and as our postindustrial transformation continues to generate an economy in which a worker's ability to process and analyze information is paramount, competition for places will reach gale force and the myth of group equality will be further exposed.

[1]In 2050, blacks will constitute 15.4 percent of the population, as opposed to 12.6 percent today; see Samuel H. Preston, "Children Will Pay." The growth of the Asian and Hispanic populations and the leveling off of the number of blacks is something that demographers generally agree upon.

To wit, in 1997, the on-line service Prodigy announced that unless the United States imports software engineers from overseas, the domestic computer industry will suffer. In Silicon Valley and Orange County, California, computer companies have been founded by immigrants from India, Pakistan, and Hong Kong employing immigrant workforces from Asia and Latin America; one in four people with a science degree in America was born abroad. India, in particular, sends 15,000 of its 50,000 information technology graduates to the United States annually.[2] The nanotech and other high-technology workers that Al Kerth wants to attract here in the twenty-first century will probably be not specially trained residents of East St. Louis or north St. Louis but more likely young people now in Asia and Latin America who have yet to immigrate here.

[2]See "Silicon Valley: The Valley of Money's Delight" and Nathan Gardels's interview with Ryzsard Kapuscinski about California immigrants.

5

—

Omaha: Plugged In

THE DESTRUCTION IN our lifetime of such American cities as St. Louis "could not have been otherwise," writes John Keegan, the British traveler and military historian.[1] Because of the automobile and America's vast continental space, sooner or later American cities were bound to lose their human scale and cultural identity as people sped along interstate highways to far-flung workplaces and malls, while standardized architecture and speech patterns—reflecting the compression of distance—diluted local character. But how will such vast, low-density cities affect nationhood, which as Tocqueville among others observed, was created from vibrant local associations? A country whose inner cities become wastelands, whose citizens are segregated by both race and class and guarded by private police forces, whose corporations take over public spaces (as in St. Louis) may be economically efficient but socially ephemeral.

This question shaped my itinerary. I headed next for Omaha, whose urban fragmentation, I had been told by experts, was less severe than that of St. Louis. It was in Omaha that I first began (how-

---

[1] See "One Englishman's America" in Keegan's book *Fields of Battle: The Wars for North America*.

ever tentatively) to sense a future that was not so bleak: a future that might, in its own way, be as wondrous as our past.

I LEFT ST. LOUIS in the morning and sped west along Interstate 70 back toward Kansas City, then north on Interstate 29 to Council Bluffs, Iowa, which faced Omaha, Nebraska, on the far side of the Missouri. I arrived there in the evening.

I had last been in the Council Bluffs–Omaha area in August 1970, when I had hitchhiked across America and slept in a field near the Missouri on the Iowa side, near where a Nevada-based casino gambling complex and its vast parking lot are located today. The following morning I had caught a ride across the bridge into south Omaha and then wandered through downtown. I was eighteen and had never been away from the East before. I found Omaha magical, the real West. South Omaha was a dusty, windblown grid of low brick buildings and meatpacking houses; I remember vividly men in cowboy hats. The downtown was a hodgepodge of similar brick stores interspersed with Romanesque and classical revival edifices maybe ten stories high. I grew up near New York City, and Omaha looked quaint and miniature to me, especially since, just beyond it, I was soon to find only cornfields.

Like many cities in middle America born, in essence, after the Civil War, Omaha has had roughly two conspicuous periods of urban growth: from the 1870s through World War I, and from the 1970s through the present. The Omaha I had seen in 1970 had still been an architectural creation of the Gilded Age, before the burst of building activity toward the end of the twentieth century that would turn it into a city of the New Gilded Age, operating in an international economy rather than a national one.

Omaha and similar cities of the late nineteenth century reflected America's nostalgia for its European roots, just as many of the new "old towns" of today, and new baseball parks such as Baltimore's Camden Yards, reflect our nostalgia for the America of the 1890s. Though Gilded Age architecture was not indigenous to America, at least it was borrowed from belle epoque Europe, from which much of America's late-nineteenth-century culture evolved. But much of today's new architecture has no specific geographical or cultural origins. Its spare, standardized forms evoke a missile launch pad more than a city. The myths and other associations that this new architecture summons forth, though dynamic, are not specifically American. Perhaps America is just growing into what it was always meant to be: not a single national community at all but an international mosaic of nations, where all peoples, not only Europeans, can take root.

Omaha's skyline as I drove west from Council Bluffs was a mixture of what I remembered from 1970 and the tinted glass of the 1980s and 1990s. The city still appeared to be gazing out toward the blankness of the western plains, as though the flatiron vastness of the inner continent represented not just the world beyond Omaha but the future, too.

While St. Louis owes its existence to rivers, Omaha owes its to railways. In 1859, the Illinois presidential aspirant, Abraham Lincoln, gazed over the Missouri from the bustling town of Council Bluffs toward the saloon town of Omaha, named for a local Indian tribe. Later Lincoln would choose Omaha as the eastern terminus of the transcontinental railroad because of its proximity to the point at which the Platte River, a major artery of western settlement, flows into the Missouri. It was the citizens of Omaha who conceived the name "Union Pacific," thinking it might appeal to Lincoln by linking the Union Army's struggle with America's destiny as an Atlantic-to-Pacific nation. The ground was broken for what would become America's principal transcontinental railroad in 1863, in Omaha.[2]

Omaha, like so many successful American frontier towns, was a business venture that happened to work. "Community" had nothing to do with it. In the 1860s, when Omaha was still a risky proposition, the buildings were hastily constructed of wood, and collapsed or were torn down by the 1870s and the 1880s, much as substandard housing from the quick-growth 1950s and 1960s is being torn down today. By the 1880s, the brick homes and neoclassical and Romanesque structures that I saw in 1970 began to appear. By the end of the century, a sewage system, electric lighting, six streetcar services, and the meat-packing industry had come to Omaha, as had many of the city's Czech, Croatian, German, Irish, Jewish, Italian, Polish, and other immigrants. In the 1880s alone, Omaha's population rose from 30,500 to 140,000: a substantial if not a spectacular rise, given the even greater expansion during that period of many other American cities, such as Birmingham, El Paso, and Kansas City.[3] The Industrial Revo-

---

[2]In 1872, a bridge across the Missouri here united the East and West Coasts by rail for the first time.

[3]See Carl N. Degler, *Out of Our Past: The Forces That Shaped Modern America.*

lution ignited an exodus from rural areas to cities and led in Europe to population growth and political unrest, which, in turn, led to emigration to America.

If St. Louis typifies urban America statistically, Omaha is typical in a more elusive and anecdotal sense. Its history reveals the crass commercialism, the blunt meat-and-potatoes aggressiveness and masculinity, as well as the military power that helped define twentieth-century America. Swanson Foods invented the TV dinner in downtown Omaha. A few blocks away, in the kitchen of the World War I–era Blackstone Hotel, the Reuben sandwich was invented. In Omaha a Russian Jewish immigrant family founded Omaha Steaks. The Strategic Air Command (SAC) with its underground nuclear nerve center is based here. SAC's vast telephone linkage fans out throughout the country, providing the infrastructure for the nation's telemarketing and credit card authorization industries, both born in Omaha in the 1980s. Many of the unsolicited and obnoxious calls that Americans get at dinnertime come from Omaha, and almost every time a credit card is swiped through a machine for authorization, that machine is communicating with a computer in Omaha.[4] Johnny Carson got his start in Omaha on WOW-TV in 1949. Henry Fonda and Marlon Brando began their careers here. Malcolm X was born Malcolm Little in west Omaha. Warren Buffett, the second richest man in America after Bill Gates, still lives and works in Omaha. The college baseball world series is held every year in Omaha. Omaha could hardly be more American.

But the Omaha I visited in 1996 had a distinctly international flavor. At breakfast I read in the *Omaha World-Herald* that area farmers had imported llamas from South America to protect their calves from coyotes. The lead editorial was about how high death rates in eastern Europe had influenced the downward trend in the rate of world population growth. The first person I met in Omaha was Susan Leonovicz, who worked in a nondescript suburban office and handed me a business card with English on one side and Chinese on the other.

---

[4]There are other reasons why Omaha is the nation's telemarketing center: midwestern accents are considered neutral and therefore not offensive to anyone—unlike a New York or southern accent, for example. And because of its Central Time Zone location, Omaha-based telemarketers can start calling the East Coast in the morning, work their way across the country, and dial the West Coast in the late afternoon.

Leonovicz is a vice president of Mangelsen's, an Omaha firm that imports thread, feathers, porcelain eggs, dolls, and other items from China and other Pacific Rim countries, in addition to wedding ornaments from South Korea, for resale throughout America and Canada. I had wanted to see several other Omaha businesspeople involved in international trade, but they were out of town: in St. Petersburg, Tokyo, and other foreign cities negotiating deals. "Can't some of these items be made in America?" I asked. "Sure," Leonovicz answered, "but Americans won't pay more than, say, $1.99 for a feather, so we import feathers and many other things from places where wages are much lower."

She told me that the Japanese and South Koreans were opening *maquilladora* factories in China, much like ours in Mexico, using cheap labor to make products for re-export back home, which is partly why Mangelsen's and other businesses with factories in Asia were lobbying for permanent "most favored nation" trade status for China. A foreign policy dominated by human rights would mean job cuts in Omaha, she told me emphatically. What struck me about this discussion was its ordinariness. Foreign trade is a normal subject for the business elite not only in Omaha and St. Louis but, as I would later learn, in Wichita, Tulsa, Des Moines, and other heartland cities, too, all of which had formed their own "foreign policy committees." Intermediaries in New York and Washington were no longer necessary. The foreign policies pursued by these heartland cities were, ironically, more like those of European countries than of the East and West Coast elites, dominated by the concerns of trade and realpolitik rather than by human rights and spreading democracy.

My next encounter was with a dozen Japanese interested in trade and other opportunities here. From Leonovicz's suburban office I had driven downtown along wide, treeless, right-angled streets named after such nineteenth-century army officers as Henry Leavenworth and Henry Dodge, streets lined with homely old liver-hued storefronts. Downtown Omaha seemed at first glance a grid of parking garages. I saw few pedestrians on streets that seemed even bleaker than those of St. Louis and much windier. Martin Shukert, a local architect and former director of the Omaha City Planning Department, was going to give these Japanese visitors a guided tour in a renovated turn-of-the-century trolleybus. I tagged along.

Shukert led us to a city center that, like America itself, was in transition. The lively streets of the manufacturing era were gone, particularly in the northern part of downtown. But here First National Bank of Omaha, the *Omaha World-Herald,* and the Union Pacific Railroad were building a new office park that could mean $1 billion in new construction. Union Pacific had recently acquired the Southern Pacific Railroad, and one thousand jobs were being transferred from Denver and San Francisco to Omaha and St. Louis. As in the late nineteenth century, when a surge in railroad construction and manufacturing had forced a Darwinian competition for survival among cities, a similar process was again under way; and the Union Pacific—which handles a massive amount of freight even though the passenger era is over—is, at the end of the twentieth century, helping to save the city it created at the end of the nineteenth. Shukert drove us to the former Union Station, an art deco pile built by Union Pacific from 1929 to 1931, and to the new Harriman Dispatching Center, from which Union Pacific now controls its freight trains across America electronically.5 The jarring architectural distance between the massive old station and the slick new dispatching center spoke for the difference between the monumental Industrial Age and our own computer age of miniaturization and abstract standardization.

The former Union Station, now the city's Western Heritage Museum, is a five-hundred-foot-long colossus of cream-colored glazed terra-cotta on a hill overlooking the Missouri. Its echoing waiting hall is of rich, marblelike surfaces with terrazzo floors beneath a lofty ceiling of sculpted plaster trimmed with gold and silver leaf. The chandeliers are magnificent. The schedules are displayed as they were in the 1930s, with "The Corn King Limited," "The Portland Rose," and "The Hawkeye" about to depart for points west. The adjacent Harriman Dispatching Center is a diminutive two-story brick shed, easily ignored and filled with computers that control a rail network as complex as that of the 1930s. Omaha's Amtrak station was the size of a rural post office.

Though the day was mild for November, when Shukert stopped the trolleybus and we began to walk, the wind was strong and steady. Omaha had once been a pedestrian city because people had no choice. Now, with cars and malls, I wondered why anybody would choose to face this harsh climate. How can you revive a "downtown"

5The dispatching center is named after Edward Henry Harriman, the head of Union Pacific during its 1890s expansion phase and the father of the late diplomat and New York governor W. Averell Harriman.

where winters are so long and cold and summers are so stifling—
unless, of course, you enclose it?

The cityscape I walked through was an architectural time line: the
red stucco Campbell's Soup building from the 1970s, looking like
an old warehouse; a new park with Henry Moore–like sculptures;
vacant lots about to be acquired, as Shukert told us, by credit card
firms; a U.S. West office whose tinted chrome facade was indistinguishable from buildings I had seen in the wealthy quarters of Berlin,
Bangkok, and other foreign cities; the classical revival edifices of
the U.S. National Bank building, raised in 1887 in Romanesque style
with Ohio blue stone; and the Orpheum Theater, a 1920s confection
of gold leaf, veiny black-and-white marble, and a rococo interior.
Shukert led us into a community children's theater so baroque that
its style could, he said, "only be labeled as Tuscan-Moorish revival."
Nearby was another vacant lot, on which the architect I. M. Pei was
about to construct a federal courthouse. Next came the Jocelyn Art
Museum, a sleek marble fortress with an entrance hall in "Egyptian
art deco," whose tony café—and its customers, too—were indistinguishable from well-dressed crowds on the East or West Coast. Back
on the sidewalk, I noticed that the streetlamps were orange plastic
bubbles, a generic design I had seen three years before in Samarkand,
Uzbekistan.

As we walked down to the riverbank, I could see the downtown
"campus" of the Omaha-based ConAgra corporation, a food conglomerate that by some accounts plays a role in the production of half
of all the items in American supermarkets. Beside the corporate campus was a waterfront park, built by the city with help from ConAgra.
In the other direction I saw a giant lead smelter, the sprawling Union
Pacific switching yard, and two highway overpasses leading to cross-
country interstates: a beautiful panorama of gray and charcoal curves
despite the contamination wrought by decades of diesel fuel soaking
into the earth. Shukert told me that the lead smelter would soon
close, the soil beneath the railroad tracks would be "remediated" at a
cost of tens of millions of dollars, and the switching yards would be
moved outside the city, as America, unlike Rome, continues to evolve
technologically. It is this very technological and economic change
that clearly separates us from Rome and other fallen ancient empires,
creating more risks but more chances for renewal, too.

Our single, halting translator provided little interaction with the
Japanese. Later, over lunch at a restaurant serving Persian food in

Omaha's restored Old Market, I asked Shukert what Omaha's downtown would be like in twenty years. He answered, "One thing I've learned in urban planning and community development over the years is that you can always point to a successful project and say, 'The trend in such-and-such a place is, therefore, positive.' For example, how many upbeat newspaper stories have you read about this American city, or that poor country, framed around some fine development project? But you can easily have several successfully executed schemes in place while the quality of life deteriorates. Take north Omaha, which is predominantly black. There are several good projects under way there. But is life improving for the average resident of north Omaha? I'm not so sure. For years now, unemployment in black Omaha has hovered around twenty percent, with little fluctuation. Regarding the downtown, there are two thousand new housing units near here occupied by middle- and upper-income people—yuppie types who hate the suburbs and like living in a city, with real sidewalks. That's good, and you could write a nice feature story about that, but the overall trend in Omaha is still toward fragmentation: isolated suburban pods and enclaves of races and classes unrelated to each other. While you read about 'downtowns coming back,' the overwhelming majority of construction in Omaha and other metropolitan areas—suburban supermarkets, restaurants, and so on—is automobile-oriented. You will be even less comfortable outside of your car in the future than you are now."

Shukert made another point: that all big redevelopment projects are, by definition, high risk, because no one really knows how they will affect city life. Thus, the truly worthwhile urban renewals are always those that happen gradually and by themselves—by accident, almost. "Take the Old Market," Shukert said. "Even at night you'll see people strolling here. The Old Market works because it was never really planned. A few people took a risk and started opening foreign restaurants and retail stores, and then more did. It was an organic process, not a grand scheme."

But the park by the Missouri River built by the ConAgra corporation is, according to Shukert and everyone else I interviewed, a big success. When weather permits, large groups of people stroll along its paths by the Missouri, because, as he said, "ConAgra is a hometown firm that understands the city and what its people need, because it is so much a part of it. ConAgra began as a struggling grain elevator company, grew into a big multinational, and stayed loyal to Omaha.

The same with Mutual of Omaha. Because these corporations are well rooted in the community, they feel accountable and do not behave wantonly. The problem, of course, is that mergers and acquisitions mean this situation will not obtain forever. Omaha and other cities will face more out-of-town corporate ownership: you know, the kind of firm that donates $75,000 to an arts project and then, in effect, tells a city not to complain about anything else it does."

As in St. Louis, I learned that corporations are truly affecting Omaha's destiny. Here is a story.

The University of Nebraska's Omaha branch is a campus on the make, with big business behind it. "In an age of suburbanization and the death of small farming, our campus is stealing the land grant function from the main campus in the state capital of Lincoln," Del Weber, the chancellor of the Omaha branch, told me. Omaha branch professors are the principal foreign consultants for urban redevelopment in eastern Romania and Moldova, and they are involved at the highest levels in negotiations among ethnic factions in Afghanistan.[6] But the real accomplishments of this branch—with 15,200 students compared with Lincoln's 23,000—appeared just over the horizon.

In 1994, the president of the University of Nebraska, L. Dennis Smith, and the Board of Regents did not approve a request by the Omaha branch to build a college of engineering. Weber and others saw this as a move by the main campus to prevent the growing Omaha branch from challenging Lincoln's prestige. Weber then met with First Data Resources, an Omaha corporation, the largest processor of credit cards in the world. The Aksarben horse-racing track, built in the 1920s, had recently closed, and its large tract just west of downtown Omaha was up for sale.[7] First Data effectively vetoed the University of Nebraska's decision to keep engineering studies in Lincoln. Working with the university's Omaha branch, First Data and other companies raised the funds to build the Omaha Institute of Information Science and Engineering, a corporate/educational complex. First Data and the Omaha branch now work together on issues such as curriculum and student jobs.

[6]Omaha professor Thomas E. Gouttierre was in Afghanistan at the time of my visit, on loan to the State Department as an adviser. In fact, at many a seemingly obscure college far from America's main metropolitan regions, I would often discover impressive contacts with foreign countries. This trend appears to be increasing as trade and other direct contacts grow between the American continent's newly emergent suburban city-states and the outside world.

[7]Aksarben, if the reader hasn't noticed, is "Nebraska" spelled backward.

"The future of the American university," Weber told me, "is as an entrepreneur working with corporations. Otherwise many universities will die. The curriculum, therefore, will lean increasingly toward applied subjects, subjects that lead to real jobs. Because Omaha has more corporations than Lincoln, in the coming decades we may become the state's main campus."

OMAHA'S URBAN GEOGRAPHY is, it turned out on further inspection, eerily like St. Louis's and Kansas City's. The differences are of degree, not of kind. All are river cities in the flat middle of the continent. Omaha on the western bank of the Missouri, and St. Louis, on the western bank of the Mississippi, originated on the eastern banks of those rivers—in Council Bluffs, Iowa, and East St. Louis, Illinois. East St. Louis is in much worse shape than Council Bluffs, but both are decayed manufacturing cities. In the 1950s, at the peak of the Industrial Age, when the mortgage interest tax deduction and the G.I. Bill allowed for rapid suburbanization, Omaha, Kansas City, and St. Louis all expanded westward, away from the river and beyond the tall buildings. Cornfields were turned into suburbs with winding streets and few sidewalks, but with a lawn and driveway for every house. Sixty percent of Omaha's population of 336,000 now lives in the western suburbs, like most inhabitants of greater St. Louis and greater Kansas City.

Seventy percent of Nebraskans live in the emerging Omaha-Lincoln suburban region in the southeast of the state. Not only will that percentage increase, but much of the remainder of the state's population will reside in yet another emerging suburban "pod," the tri-cities area of Kearny, Hastings, and Grand Island.[8]

The downtowns of Omaha and St. Louis (and, to a lesser extent, Kansas City) are similar. North Omaha and north St. Louis are both black. In north Omaha and north St. Louis, Jews left for the western suburbs as blacks moved in, while many other whites fled south. (In south Omaha, though, unlike in south St. Louis, Mexicans are establishing a base, working in the packinghouses where I saw Anglos in the summer of 1970.) But, unlike St. Louis, Omaha has been able to annex its emerging suburbs in order to prevent their separate

[8]These figures were supplied by Professor B. J. Reed, chair of the University of Nebraska at Omaha's Department of Public Administration.

incorporation. So while St. Louis is a feudal assemblage of ninety-two separately incorporated cities, Omaha is overwhelmingly *Omaha*. Only four southern suburbs are beyond its grasp, and everyone, not simply poor blacks and Mexicans, attends Omaha's public schools. Thus, Omaha's downtown and immediate surroundings are less depressed than St. Louis's, while its suburbs are less opulent, so that the border between the two is blurred. Thus, on the face of it, Omaha reflects a victory for public policy over the social and economic disintegration that in St. Louis seemed overwhelming to me.

But has it really been a victory for public policy? Peter Suzuki, an urban affairs expert at the university's Omaha branch, told me that, except for the Old Market, downtown Omaha is strictly eight to five. "That's because the perception in the suburbs is that downtown is not safe. There have been carjackings, drive-bys. The L.A. gang culture of the Crips and Bloods now plagues Omaha. The incidence of downtown crime, of course, is highly exaggerated. Still, that's the suburban perception, strengthened by the tabloid style of local TV news. The downtown renovation is not keeping up with the expansion of the suburbs, which, in turn, are either predominantly white or predominantly black."

In other words, public policy here may simply be softening the effect of deep social and economic forces, rather than seriously altering them. Is the effort to "sell" downtown simply another futile attempt to restore the unrecoverable past? Not necessarily. It seemed to me that, as at Fort Leavenworth, it was an effort to rein in the future by reaffirming tradition.

6

—

Against the Current

BECAUSE IN AMERICA the state has generally let people alone in their scramble for wealth on a mineral-rich continent, social and economic forces, particularly the advance of technology, have shaped America far more than the exertions of elected governments have. This is not to say that Americans are driven by blind forces over which they have no control, for these same forces are shaped by Americans themselves, by the daily efforts of millions of ambitious individuals—individuals such as John and Karen Bluvas and Joe Edmonson.

I sought out both the Bluvases and Edmonson because they were working against the very trends that seemed overwhelming to me: the disintegration of old downtown neighborhoods and of families not able to escape to the suburbs.

First, the Bluvases.

DAHLMAN, LOCATED JUST south of downtown, is one of Omaha's oldest neighborhoods. Its population, like its worn brick and frame houses with their bleak yards, is old: the remnant of the turn-of-the-century European immigration that created modern Omaha. It was a rainy, cold afternoon, but as I walked through the front door of a day care center I was greeted by John and Karen Bluvas, a late-middle-aged couple booming with optimism, and my spirits picked up.

John's Czech forebears immigrated to Dahlman from Central Europe in 1908. Karen's family has been in the neighborhood even longer, so that the couple's teenage daughter is the seventh generation to live here. In the late 1970s, John and Karen saw their friends desert Dahlman for the western suburbs, but they themselves refused to accept their community's deterioration. When John retired after twenty-five years at the Enron Corporation—which manufactures, among other things, oil pipelines for the Middle East—he and Karen worked full-time as neighborhood volunteers. When the Bluvases began their project to renew Dahlman, the average house was worth $9,500; twenty years later, in the late 1990s, the average house was worth $160,000. Inflation accounts for only about half of that increase.

"How did you do it?" I asked.

"Well," John replied, "one thing we tried was to mail pictures of houses with sad faces on them to people who did not keep the fronts of their houses neat. When they tidied up, we'd mail pictures of houses with happy faces. That sort of thing."

Of course, it was more than that. As I learned, it was Sisyphean persistence, in which activity by itself became a strategy. John and Karen drove me to a hill graced with new town houses overlooking downtown Omaha, whose driveways were filled with late-model Jeeps and other upscale cars. John told me the recent history of this hill: "Eight years ago this hill was vacant, a dump for soil contaminated with battery fluid. We negotiated back and forth for a year with the city and a developer to replace the soil. Afterwards, the developer, who helped pay for the environmental cleanup, built these town houses. They've tripled in price since—look at the view."

I knew from my own experience how costly and legally complex an environmental cleanup for even a single house yard can be. When an underground oil tank leaks, tests have to be run, the contaminated soil has to be incinerated, and the state bureaucracy becomes involved. The process can delay the purchase of a residential property by six months or longer and run into tens of thousands of dollars. Organizing a cleanup for a big property and then managing to construct two dozen town houses on the site seemed impossible to me.

"Oh," Karen said, "we just kept repeating to the city and to the developers what a beautiful view there is from this abandoned hill, and how people would pay good money to enjoy it every morning from their living rooms, if only the site was cleaned and built upon. John and I are always working on a property somewhere that has a soil contamination problem. We get them all resolved eventually. If you can't find a donor to pay for the cleanup, then the lot is abandoned. And spaces that are dark and abandoned become hangouts for drug dealers. So we don't concede even one property. One vacant lot can destroy a whole neighborhood."

The more I drove around Dahlman with the Bluvases, the less depressed the neighborhood looked. Here and there I saw a refurbished house, a renovated school, or a new restaurant. "Yes, now we have French Vietnamese food in Dahlman," said John. "Small investors are willing to take a chance on us.

"The way you control the destiny of your neighborhood," he continued, "is to have a relationship with the city planning staff, so that you don't get blindsided by some awful highway project, for instance. And you bother people to death." John drove us past the Great Lakes Chemical plant. "We got Great Lakes to stop their toxic emissions."

"Now we have a new challenge," Karen explained. "Mexicans, Hondurans, and other Central Americans are moving here to work in the packinghouses. They've got social problems. We're pressing for day care expansion, special school programs, and so on."

Whenever I mentioned the "historical movement" to the western suburbs, John or Karen responded by talking about "saving this vacant lot," "saving that community program," or "getting that homeowner to remove the old appliances from his porch." At first I thought they were not listening to me. But it was I who had not listened to them: John and Karen were pioneers of a sort, nuts-and-bolts doers. "Our goal is to rescue and restore our neighborhood in order to anchor it against the ravages of the future," John told me. "But I don't walk around alone at night here. I know the limits of what we can accomplish."

I SCANNED THE paperback books: Charles Darwin's *Voyage of the Beagle*, Goethe's *Elective Affinities, Beowulf,* and similar titles. I saw several sets of encyclopedias and many "How to . . ." and "I Can . . ." manuals.

"Do the kids read this stuff?" I asked.

"Not all of it, but some of it. At least it's here. They see these titles every day, and they wonder about them," said Joe Edmonson, the executive director of Edmonson Youth Outreach, a club for 265 underprivileged kids in black north Omaha.

I saw a poster advertising a dance for fourteen-to-eighteen-year-olds. "No Team Gear, No Saggin', No Ball Caps" would be allowed, the poster warned. Spray-painted on the wall were these words: "Hard work and determination are the keys to success, for fatigue can make cowards of us all." Joe shrugged and said, "They're my words; you never know when a simple saying may help you out."

Joe went on in his baritone voice, "The center is open from one to nine during the school year. The kids do their homework and studying here. It's a home for them. In the summer, we open first thing in the morning. We serve lunches and organize frequent educational excursions."

Pigeon, in his twenties, clean-cut and soft-spoken, explained the computers the kids use. When I mentioned to Joe that Pigeon's grammar was impeccable, Joe replied, "For all intents and purposes, Pigeon is homeless. His mother's a crack addict, his father's a drifter. I let him sleep at the center. I'm working on getting Pigeon into a vocational program at a radio station. You can see that he has great technical gifts and makes a good impression on people. But with a childhood like his, he'll need constant attention for years."

"I can't imagine the memories Pigeon must have," I said lamely.

"No, you can't," said Joe sternly. "Neither can most of the people Pigeon is likely to encounter if he is to be successful. So he'll bury his memories, that's all." He went on, "The mentality in north Omaha is how to be the top piece of trash in your garbage dump. My generation grew up with Captain Midnight, who told you how to make your bed. But Bart Simpson cusses his father; that's why I don't allow anyone at the center to watch *The Simpsons*. I don't allow baseball caps either, and when a girl walks by, the boys are *required* to open the door for her or offer her a place to sit."

Joe's wife, Jean, drove the van as Joe and I talked. Joe is handicapped and gets around in a wheelchair. He and Jean have been married for more than a quarter century. Their house is in a predominantly middle- and lower-middle-class black section of north Omaha. The house was neat, frugal, and full of rich memories. Some of the light fixtures had no bulbs, and Jean gave me a cup of coffee in a paper cup. But the plants and books were all in order, and family photos were everywhere, including a photo of Joe with President Bush. In 1991, the White House chose Joe as one of 535 community "Points of Light" in America.

Joe Edmonson was born in 1947 in Kansas City and came to Omaha when he was six months old, the son of an unwed mother, raised by his grandparents in black north Omaha. Joe's grandfather held two jobs, as a packinghouse worker and a janitor; his grand-mother ran a Sunday school. "I couldn't stay out of trouble. I stole cars, many of the kids were doing it. I was kicked out of junior high school. Because I loved attention, I acted in Shakespeare, too. That sounds illogical, doesn't it—a black kid who steals cars and recites lines from *Julius Caesar*? Well, a lot of troubled kids have hidden talents. Whenever I see a kid walk through that door at the outreach center, I see me.

"I ended up in juvenile court and in late 1962 was sent to the Nebraska Boys Training School in Kearny" in south-central Nebraska. "Reform schools then were not like they are now. Then, there really was a possibility that a boy like me could be reformed.

"Yeah," he continued in his booming voice, looking out at the bare trees and asphalt roofs through his living room window as though looking into the past, "there was an old, kindly-looking gentlemen at the school, a Mr. Thurmond. Mr. Bill Thurmond smoked a pipe and had a Pekinese dog in his lap.

" 'Sir,' I said to this kindly-looking gentleman with a dog in his lap, 'I understand that you can get out of this place in three months?' He was silent for a moment; then he said to me softly, 'You should have thought of that shit when you were running down those dark alleys. Son, I'm going to challenge you every chance I get.' So began my relationship with Mr. Bill, as everyone called Mr. Thurmond.

"Mr. Bill was white. Of the 435 boys at the school, ninety were black and many of the rest were Hispanic or Native American. 'What was in the newspaper today?' Mr. Bill would always taunt me. That's when I started reading papers. Mr. Bill ran the reform school the way I run Edmonson Youth Outreach. He and his staff never let up on you. We received the level of adult supervision that privileged kids in the best private schools get. I came home after fifteen months, truly changed.

"It was spring, and I planned to return to high school in the fall. I had wrestled competitively at reform school and wanted to join the high school wrestling team. So I began working out. I started a band, too, afraid that if I did not put structure immediately into my life I would slip back into my old ways. I was seventeen. One morning during a workout I decided to try a double somersault on the trampoline. I went into the air and came back to earth and my whole life changed—I was paralyzed from the waist down."

In the hospital Joe read self-help books; later he attended the University of Nebraska at Omaha, from which he went on to get a master's degree in criminology. He became a scoutmaster and wrestling coach. Edmonson Youth Outreach evolved from his wrestling team. "I believe in long-term, low-number mentoring programs," Joe explained. "More than two or three hundred kids cannot be handled by any group of adults at any one time. Unless a kid receives a high degree of individual adult attention over a long period of time, he or she is gone."

"You're trying to reestablish a culture," I said.

"Something like that," Joe replied. "But it's hard. Because my organization survives on donations, I can only help a fraction of those who need help. I live in an area where there is no movie theater. Thirty miles to the west a complex of twenty movie theaters is being built. This part of Omaha is dying. Omaha may not be as fractured as St. Louis, but it's getting there. Public school busing still holds the community together. But you'll see, busing will go, and it will just be a matter of economics."

FROM BLACK NORTH Omaha I drove to the Garden Café, amid the glitter of the western Omaha suburbs and its many corporate campuses. Not only did I see no black faces here, but the whites I saw looked different from the whites I had seen downtown. Downtown Omaha, as its skyline had suggested, was in transition. Despite the foreign cuisine of the Old Market, I had also noticed downtown many slow-moving, overweight people, poorly dressed, eating in old-fashioned restaurants with zinc counters and plastic squeeze containers for ketchup and mustard, being served by overweight waitresses in orthopedic shoes who said, "Eggs over easy, you bet, *hun*." But at the Garden Café in western Omaha health food was the item of choice: here I was back in the rushed, cell phone global culture I knew from the Washington suburbs and dozens of similar prosperous areas around the world. The waitresses were lithe and fetching, fit and dressed in the latest styles.

At night, I would soon see, western Omaha meant miles upon yawning miles of pulsing neon and packed shopping centers and parking lots. The city's two Borders bookstores are both located in the western suburbs. This was the new Omaha, just as western St. Louis is the new St. Louis and Johnson County, Kansas, is the new Kansas City. Omaha's downtown, even if it does "come back," will probably remain a sideshow in the twenty-first century, because no one here needs to go there to shop, see a movie, or go to a fancy restaurant. And the residents can be hooked up to the world from their homes. By 1994, two out of five Omaha residents already had computers and two thirds of them had modems.[1] These percentages have risen steadily.

People in suburban pods such as Omaha's western suburbs—each as similar to the other as oases in the wilderness—are creating an international civilization influenced by the impersonal, bottom-line values of the corporations for which these people work. Both Joe Edmonson's and John and Karen Bluvas's neighborhoods belong to another century compared to the affluence I saw in western Omaha, just as the heroic efforts of such people appeared increasingly less significant the further I went in the suburbs. Joe Edmonson and John and Karen Bluvas were relief workers, administering aid to those left behind.

These pods, some of which, as Al Kerth had told me, might become wealthy and aggressive enough to host a spaceport, were becoming neither cities nor towns nor even suburbs in the known sense; they were emerging slowly as a vast conglomeration of minifortresses hooked up to satellites above as much as they were to similar pods a few hours away. Americans are increasingly living in these large, urbanized areas that are not dominated—or even very much controlled—by central municipal administrations. Whatever happens in such economically marginal places as East St. Louis will not shape America's future. The future, it seemed to me, was this new urban phenomenon whose outlines I was just beginning to grasp.

At the Garden Café I talked with Russell Smith, another urban affairs expert from the Omaha campus. Smith agreed with Joe Edmonson that school busing was on the way out and that when it went Omaha would become increasingly fragmented, like St. Louis. "What you see may look cosmopolitan," Smith said, glancing at the crowd in the café, "but this is just a sprawling conglomeration of many small-town people. Historically, the suburbs have always been everybody's version of a small town, though denser, where each little lawn is symbolic of a rural field. Many of the inhabitants of the Omaha, St. Louis, and Kansas City suburbs grew up in small towns where there were no blacks. They are just not comfortable around blacks. It may be that simple.

"My church group recently held a joint service with a black church

---

[1] The figures are from the Omaha Conditions Survey conducted by the University of Nebraska at Omaha.

group. Everyone on both sides went out of their way to be friendly. But it was clear we represented different cultures. The black pastor talked about the title match between Mike Tyson and Evander Holyfield. He said that Holyfield won because he was a good Christian, and that God had given him strength. Almost none of the suburban whites related to that, almost none of us follow boxing anymore. The terms of reference for the two races are different."

"PEOPLE ARE APATHETIC," explained Ed Jaksha, a retiree and political activist who organizes petition drives in the western Omaha suburbs. We were in another suburban restaurant a few miles away. "When people here are not working," Jaksha said, "they are hooked on tennis, health clubs, cyberspace. But if any issue consistently grabs them, it's taxes: government eating up their paychecks. Whenever I organize a petition drive against taxes, I get an impressive response. It never fails."

If Jaksha's experience was typical, the idea that people in poor neighborhoods such as north Omaha might get substantial help from anyone other than themselves was essentially nonsense.

"What about busing?" I asked.

"It'll be gone. Sure. Private schools will increase. Each class and neighborhood will take care of itself."[2]

The future of America may be like the present of Jerusalem, I thought: Jews and Arabs do not like to live together, but that does not mean that they cannot coexist. Instead of a melting pot, former mayor Teddy Kollek once said, there can be a mosaic of separate communities in the same city. Perhaps, as America becomes increasingly a transnational mélange—becoming more like the rest of the world as the rest of the world becomes more like us—we will come to resemble some Old World societies in this respect: instead of a

---

[2]In fact, researchers at the Harvard Graduate School of Education found that desegregation had been a temporary phenomenon lasting one generation only. When busing was enforced by the courts, the white middle class simply moved far enough away from blacks to make busing impractical. The largest backward movement toward resegregation since the Supreme Court declared it unconstitutional in 1954 was between 1991 and 1994. According to the Harvard report, the ten largest inner-city school districts in the United States are mostly black and Hispanic. The Harvard study was reported by the Associated Press on April 5, 1997.

nation, we will become as the sociologist Amitai Etzioni suggests, a "community of communities" on the same continent.

Jaksha, retired, with white hair and a red-checked shirt, paused and then changed the subject. "I'm of Slovenian descent. If I were young again, I'd go back to Slovenia—that's a country with a future now that communism is dead. I spent much of my life in the telephone business in Fremont, about forty-five minutes northwest of here. I raised kids there in the fifties. *Boy*, it was another world," he said with a wistful shake of his head. I knew what he meant. I had grown up in a New York City suburb in the late 1950s and 1960s but then lived for several years in the 1990s in a Washington, D.C., suburban town house, where in the morning, from my study window, I could see working mothers rush out to their cars, their hands filled with briefcases and cups of coffee, yelling instructions to their children. Many of the children in our development lived in single-parent homes. Almost all the traditional families with children in my neighborhood were those of Asian immigrants. Whereas in 1976 there were 1.6 million "latchkey" children in America—kids left alone during the day without parental supervision—in 1994 there were 12 million.[3]

But as Jaksha reminisced about the 1950s and expressed a deep fear of the future, I took comfort in history. In the 1880s and 1890s, industrialization and urbanization shook the roots of America's religious and family life. Sects sprouted, racist populists ranted, and single women like Theodore Dreiser's Sister Carrie worked in filthy factories. Racial tensions hardened as the Jim Crow system spread across the South. Americans confronted a "new and disturbingly altered world" as pastoral life was replaced by the desperate search for values amid the "bleak table-lands of materialism."[4] "Gadgets" such as the lightbulb and the automobile brought an array of new choices and stresses. "The city was so big now, that people disappeared into it unnoticed," lamented Booth Tarkington in *The Magnificent Ambersons*. A hundred years ago, millionaires' mansions arose within sight of spreading slums. By 1912, 2 percent of all Americans controlled 60 percent of personal wealth, while close to half the nation lived in poverty or so close to it that illness could push them over the

---

[3]Sources: U.S. Departments of Commerce and Labor. See also Arlie Russell Hochschild, *The Time Bind: When Work Becomes Home and Home Becomes Work.*
[4]See Paul A. Carter, *The Spiritual Crisis of the Gilded Age,* and Vernon Louis Parrington, *Main Currents in American Thought.*

edge into destitution. Meanwhile, America was being transformed by millions of new immigrants. When America became a global power after its victory in the Spanish-American War of 1898, it soon encountered an unstable world, including a tottering Russia that would be shaken by the disastrous war with Japan in 1904 and a revolutionary upheaval in 1905, to say nothing of what would come a decade later. It is so familiar: America undergoing wrenching change while the world outside draws nearer and becomes ever more volatile.

America is now changing along similar lines, but the outer world is reaching a critical mass of intimacy with us. While we may not be heading for a cataclysm on the scale of World War I, in many other ways this outer world is increasingly unstable precisely because it is developing economically and changing socially so fast (as well as growing in absolute population at greater numbers than ever). For example, many previously poor and oppressed places are now generating middle classes of their own. Jaksha's Slovenia, for instance: Would anyone as well established as Jaksha have talked of going back to the "old country," in central eastern Europe a hundred years ago? Thus, the international context of our transformation is different from before. When foreign correspondent John Gunther returned full-time to the United States after World War II to write a comprehensive sociopolitical travel book, *Inside U.S.A.,* he could think of the United States in isolation. Now we are on increasingly intimate terms not only with Mexico and Canada but with much of the rest of the world too.

PERHAPS, RATHER THAN culminations, the spanking new urban regions of the Midwest that I had seen were actually crude beginnings, just as the grainy war-zone images of the black ghettos were crude endings, revealing only part of a larger picture of an emerging world civilization. Because I was in the continental interior, where immigration was least noticeable, I had seen only a typical black-versus-white divide. Moreover, the cultural conservatism of the Midwest meant that such pods as Johnson County and western Omaha would be less daring versions of what I would find on the West Coast and in the Sunbelt.

PART III

IN THE FUTURE NOW

7

—

Like Teheran and
São Paulo

JOHNSON COUNTY, KANSAS, and the western suburbs of St. Louis and Omaha, with their immense networks of malls and office parks reachable only by car, prepared me somewhat for Los Angeles. But Teheran and São Paulo—to both of which I had traveled as a foreign correspondent—prepared me more. Teheran, which takes ninety minutes to traverse even in light traffic, has, like Los Angeles, an increasingly vague center and mile after mile of chalk-colored houses hidden by high walls. In São Paulo, I stood in a farm field and saw a different skyline in almost every direction. São Paulo is both a sprawling megacity of 25 million people and a compact, urbanized region-state of 50 million that produces half of Brazil's manufactured goods and is increasingly independent of the Brazilian central government. The middle-class apartment houses in São Paulo look like foreign embassies with their high gates and private security guards; that could be one future for L.A., I thought.

On the other hand, East Coast cities such as New York and Boston, which I have known all my life, did not prepare me at all for Los Angeles. Great metropolises before the invention of the automobile, New York and Boston radiate from central cores along fixed rail lines; thus, their suburbs are easily connected by mass transit, unlike Los Angeles and most Third World cities, which experienced their growth after the auto was invented and have no central cores but rather a dense webwork of townships for which mass transit is a far more costly option. Neither had New York or Boston, or any midwestern city for that matter, prepared me for the problem of race in Los Angeles to the degree that São Paulo did—or Houston or Miami certainly would have. But I'll get to that later. . . .

I FLEW TO southern California from my Massachusetts home in the spring of 1997. Sandstone cliffs, a peacock-blue ocean, and an endless bar of cream-colored sand supplied my first view of greater Los Angeles as I drove south from the Santa Barbara airport on the Pacific Coast Highway and entered Los Angeles County. With the 10,000-foot-high San Gabriel Mountains tripping down to the sea, L.A. seemed too beautiful to be real. Ulysses S. Grant, that solemn, humdrum businessman of war, would have lived on the warm California coast after falling in love with it in the 1850s, had the Civil War not "blasted my last hope of ever becoming a citizen of the further West."

No wonder such landscapes encumbered by relatively little history often give the inhabitants the illusion that human beings face no spiritual or economic limits here. California was not seriously explored until the second half of the eighteenth century, when the Spanish, based in Mexico, surveyed likely sites for Christian missions. In 1848, on the eve of the Gold Rush, California's population was only 14,000. Today one out of eight Americans, approximately 32 million people, lives there. I saw a line of flimsy dwellings off the highway, built of violet-painted wall board. Because of the warm, breezy climate, little heating or air-conditioning is necessary in southern California, so it doesn't cost much to make a house livable. Nor does it rain often. Such a climate lures the homeless and those who can barely keep a roof over their heads.

From north to south, greater Los Angeles spans close to one hundred miles of seacoast. I stopped at Santa Monica, an incorporated beach suburb of more than 100,000 inhabitants just to the north of the city. I checked into a hotel, looked at a map, and saw that the Third Street pedestrian promenade was only half a mile away. My decision to walk there was a mistake I did not repeat in Los Angeles. The scrawny palms provided no relief from the sun-blasted asphalt. Except for a bag lady, a black woman pushing her child in a pram, and a young man with tattoos who passed me at high speed on in-line skates, the street was empty for that half mile, a half mile that took me past the Civic Center and Auditorium, where the Academy Awards ceremonies were held, the art deco town hall, and the Rand Corporation. Rather than people, I saw only cars and enormous parking lots.

Cars could not enter Third Street, which was roped off for pedestrians, filled with food and jewelry carts, and packed with shops and restaurants. The result was hordes of people strolling—whereas just across the street and all the way back to my hotel, there had been nobody. The crowd here was young, heavily Oriental, and fiercely middle-class, in fashionable leisure and beach gear like the crowds I had seen in Brazilian cities. I sat down at an outdoor Thai-Chinese restaurant for an early dinner. The manager was Japanese, the hostess Iranian, and the other help Mexican immigrants. The Iranian hostess, who wore many rings and mint-green fingernails, was telling a friend that as a graduation present, her father was going to drive her cross-country to see Elvis's grave at Graceland. On the sidewalk beside my table a large crowd watched a black youth tap-dance to Brazilian music. The shops and office facades were familiar from the globalized architecture of upmarket malls I had seen in the Midwest. Also on Third Street, I saw more homeless people than I had ever seen before in a similar-sized venue in New York City or Washington, D.C. They were doing crossword puzzles, talking to themselves, or trying to enter the restrooms of pricy restaurants without being stopped by waiters. They were overwhelmingly white and male. I saw one man with long gray hair wearing an army jacket and a woolen hat despite the eighty-degree weather. He banged his hand against a bench and shouted disconnectedly. People moved away. The homeless barely threaten the panorama of prosperity created by a burgeoning multimedia and software industry in Santa Monica, which the well-dressed, thirtyish crowd reflected.

Over the next few days I drove through the suburban San Fernando Valley, bordering Santa Monica to the northeast, which is equally prosperous. Unlike Santa Monica, the San Fernando Valley is part of the city of Los Angeles. But now its business and political leadership wants to secede.[1] With its 1.3 million inhabitants, the San Fernando Valley would constitute the nation's sixth largest city and one of its richest. This is not just white flight. Forty percent of the valley's

[1] See Joel Kotkin, "Make Way for the Urban Confederates."

population is Latino and Asian, and among the white population Jews are the largest ethnic group. These people want to duplicate the prosperity of such incorporated posturban dynamos in north Los Angeles as Burbank—now the home of Walt Disney, Warner Bros., and NBC—and Glendale, 45 percent of whose population are foreign-born Latinos, Asians, and Armenians. Joel Kotkin, a Los Angeles–based urban affairs specialist, calls the secessionist trend that has already balkanized St. Louis and similar places the "urban confederacy movement." Unlike the original secessionists, they will win, he thinks, because cities are now too big to work anymore; they can function only as a league of smaller, incorporated pieces.

A third of all U.S.-born Latinos and more than a quarter of all U.S.-born Asians in the five-county greater Los Angeles region intermarry with other races. Almost one out of ten blacks in greater Los Angeles intermarries, a percentage high enough to create significant changes in black racial identity in years to come.[2] With Latinos constituting 38 percent of the greater Los Angeles population, Asians 10 percent, and blacks only 8 percent, the racial polarization that divides Washington, D.C., for example, where white suburbs surround what is, in effect, a black urban "homeland," is far less apparent in L.A. Even within Los Angeles's city limits, blacks make up only 12 percent of the population, compared to 27.1 percent in New York City. For ten days I drove throughout greater Los Angeles, stopping every fifteen minutes or so to walk in a different neighborhood. The media image of the L.A. riots and the O. J. Simpson trial had prepared me for a city as divided as Washington, D.C. But in L.A., where eighty-one languages are spoken, that's not what I found.

TAKE ZAHEER VIRJI (an alias), a twenty-seven-year-old ethnic Indian immigrant from the East African nation of Tanzania. Zaheer wore a blue velvet baseball cap, a white T-shirt, jeans, and running shoes when I met him and his American wife, Heather, in a Santa Monica hotel lobby. Zaheer's family, which imports goods from Hong Kong to Tanzania, is part of a merchant community from the Indian subcontinent that forms the middle class in Tanzania and several other African countries. Zaheer remembers police thugs of the former Tanzanian

---

[2]See *The Emerging Latino Middle Class* by Gregory Rodriguez, with help from UCLA professor David E. Hayes-Bautista, Aizita Magana, and Paul Smilanick, for intermarriage tables and other charts comparing the assimilation of Latinos with that of other groups in greater Los Angeles.

president Julius Nyerere harassing his relatives and arresting his parents.[3] He told me that race relations are "so much better" in southern California than in Africa, where Indians and Africans completely stereotype each other. "I came here to escape not just Africans but Indians, too." He went first to England, then to Canada, where there are large Indian communities. But he didn't feel free. "In those places, the community is what is happening. Here in the U.S., it's *you* that is happening. There is less of system here, fewer laws to restrict you."

Zaheer came to the United States six years ago and has no college degree or green card yet. In the previous six months he had earned more investing in the stock market than his wife had made at her job, a reflection not only of his skill but of an economy where the prices of stocks and other assets have risen but wages have not. With this money, along with funds from his family in Tanzania, he was looking to a buy a business: a flower shop, a gas station, whatever he can get the best deal on. He is using a broker. If he buys a gas station, he told me, he needs to know about the underground tanks and the environmental regulations. He wants to be partners with the current owner for a three-year transition period; that way he will still keep some of his money even if the business does not turn out as advertised. Ten years from now, he explained, he wants to be the owner of a small business with good employees so he can spend his time investing the profits in the stock market. "Everything is a risk. A few years ago, to make some money, I bought a hundred and fifty tons of rice in Tanzania and sold it in Zaire. That was more risky than buying a business in Los Angeles, I can tell you."

Los Angeles is full of Asian and Latino immigrants creating their own civilization, just as European immigrants did a hundred years ago. Because these new immigrants bring a different historical and cultural experience and are integrating under more advanced technological conditions than immigrants in the past, they will further erode the distance between America and the rest of the world, especially as immigrants such as Zaheer are bent on increasing the wealth of family networks abroad through maintaining a strategic base in the United States, something that was not possible before computer links and jet planes. This international civilization of entrepreneurs that includes Zaheer suits perfectly the office parks

---

[3]Since Nyerere left office in 1990, conditions for the Indian community in Tanzania have improved dramatically, unleashing the economic dynamism of these people and contributing substantially to Tanzania's improved fortunes in this decade.

and knowledge economy that have replaced the muscle labor of the Industrial Age, because it is increasingly based on the ability to make the complex decisions necessary for establishing a business and investing in the stock market and less on the ability to work physically hard.

I DROVE EAST from Santa Monica across the northern tier of the city of Los Angeles to the incorporated suburb of Monterey Park. On the way I saw a sprawling metropolis in transition. The official, ceremonial downtown, composed of the Convention Center, courts, government offices, and the *Los Angeles Times* building, looked less vibrant than the new, pedestrian-packed downtown further west, in Westwood and Beverly Hills, dominated by the office buildings of Northrop Grumman Corporation, City National Bank, Occidental Petroleum, and other corporations, adjoining a Korean church, a Mexican-American realtor, and one of the largest English-language schools in the country. Several real estate agents told me that the 1992 riots in heavily black South Central Los Angeles had quickened the exodus of corporations toward the wealthier western part of the city.

Driving from the new downtown to the old one, I passed through West Hollywood, an area of gays, elderly Jews, and Russian immigrants; Koreatown; and the "Banana Republic," a neighborhood populated by Central American immigrants. Watts and South Central were one-story encampments of poor blacks encroached upon by Latino immigrants, who now make up two thirds of the population of those areas as upwardly mobile blacks move to the Moreno Valley and other inexpensive suburbs east of greater Los Angeles, in the "Inland Empire." Watts and South Central are, in ethnic-racial terms, being annexed to Mexican East Los Angeles. Demographers say that in coming years Latinos will, in relative terms, reduce the presence of blacks in Los Angeles as they already have in Miami. Latinos now make up the majority of the region's industrial workforce. The number of Latino- and Asian-owned businesses in greater Los Angeles has increased from 70,000 to 220,000 since the early 1980s, while the number of black-owned businesses has remained static at 20,000.[4]

[4]See Joel Kotkin, "Rebuilding Blocks: A Boom in Latin and Asian Businesses Shape the City," *The Washington Post*, April 20, 1997.

I parked in Mexican East Los Angeles and walked about a mile past small stores selling furniture and other household goods. I noticed many bridal shops, suggestive of the strong family ties among Latinos, and many pedestrians, too. Los Angeles, I had begun to realize, was very much a vibrant pedestrian city. For example, it has the largest garment district in North America, whose narrow alleys—which I visted on another day—are packed with Latins and Asians, a throwback to early-twentieth-century New York. This vast posturban confederation teems with successful communal venues such as the Third Street Promenade and Mexican East Los Angeles. But you need a car to get from one to the other.

From "Mexico" I crossed into Monterey Park and San Gabriel, which had once been gray and run-down. Now it is booming, with glittering nearby banks supported by Hong Kong Chinese and Chinese-American immigrant money, and many new malls, too, particularly the Great Mall of China.

Here I entered the 99 Ranch Market, part of a Californian Chinese supermarket chain that at first seemed like any other enormous American supermarket with forty aisles of food products and too much air-conditioning. But nearly every product in the store was an Asian specialty item, either imported or grown in the Los Angeles or Houston area. Chinese food stores are common in the nation's various Chinatowns; so, increasingly, are supermarkets like this one. But never before had I seen one with forty aisles, each a hundred yards long, devoted to noodles, pork, taro, tofu, pea sprouts, dried shrimp, soybean paste, spicy bean cabbage, dried seaweed, rice spirits, and so on. I could have been in Hong Kong or Taiwan. Next door was a Chinese restaurant with a red dance floor, an overabundance of employees, women pushing food carts serving stewed chicken feet, and an absence of Western cutlery and Caucasian customers, except for myself and a friend. Southern California has enough middle-class Chinese to support an entire consumer civilization, with giant supermarkets and restaurants aimed at Chinese diners only; but the supermarket also carried Thai, Korean, and Japanese items. An all-new Asian-American civilization is forming here, and flourishing, too: Pacific Rim cultures that were antagonistic for centuries are cooperating in the California marketplace, specifically here in this mall decorated with Spanish colonnades. Traditionally nations rise and fall; but at the 99 Ranch Market I wondered yet again if America might escape that fate by shedding its skin as a nation altogether and revealing an international civilization based on a single continent.

While I sat with my coffee and sweet bun in a Japanese pastry shop decorated in colorful marble next to the Chinese supermarket, I wondered, too, to what extent such an international community requires continued government protection, given that many shops in the mall relied on private security agencies, as did countless homes I had seen in greater Los Angeles. It is such mundane, gradual changes, so easily overlooked, that shape the future. Was the future here to be an international civilization grafted onto a corporate culture that hired its own police: police forces that are cheaper to maintain than official ones because their members are not necessarily unionized? In 1970, there were more public than private police in the United States, but in the 1990s there were three times as many private as public police and in California four times as many, a development triggered partly by the replacement of public spaces—downtowns, neighborhoods, and playgrounds—by private spaces open to the public, such as malls, gated communities, and health clubs.[5] The privatization of space and the increasing urban character of the United States are driving the growth of the surveillance industry. Indeed, the etymology of the world "police" is *polis,* Greek for "city." Crime is down, but our society is more heavily patrolled than ever. Yet one wonders about a future in which the official government no longer has a monopoly on the use of such force.

I visited another Pan-Asian supermarket, this one to the south, in Cerritos, once a dairy farming district but now a planned, separately incorporated community 45 percent of whose inhabitants are Asian. The checkout counters are manned by Latinos; the customers are mainly Chinese. A few blocks away I called on Vincent Diau, a forty-four-year-old Chinese immigrant from Taiwan who came here in 1981. In Los Angeles such top hotels as the Beverly Wilshire and the Los Angeles Biltmore are Chinese-owned, while one in five home buyers in Los Angeles County is ethnic Chinese, though they account for only 2.7 percent of the county's population.[6] Diau, wearing expensive glasses and leisure clothes and sporting two cars in his driveway, is one such home buyer. His household appliances were new. Everything was in perfect order, almost as though nobody lived there, though Diau and his Chinese-American wife, Alice, a schoolteacher, have two chil-

[5]See "Welcome to the New World of Private Security," *The Economist,* April 19, 1997.
[6]See Joel Kotkin, "Will the Chinese Save L.A.?"

dren, whose academic awards are framed near a violin and piano. The schedule for music lessons along with other after-school activities is posted on the wall along with illustrations of the English and Chinese alphabets. The Diaus own several computers, as do 72.1 percent of Chinese Americans who own at least one computer. Fifty-three percent of Chinese-American families are linked to the Internet, compared to 11 percent of all families.[7] Forty percent of Asian-American adults hold university degrees, twice the percentage as Caucasians. Almost 40 percent of Chinese in America have home security systems. "I moved to Cerritos for the same reason that many Chinese and Korean immigrants have," Diau told me, "because Whitney High School is one of the best public high schools in the state."

Diau has law and political science degrees from universities in Taiwan and a law degree from Tulane. He is a consultant on Asia with the Hughes Corporation. People complain about the American legal system, he told me, but compared to those of Asia the American legal system "is straightforward. If you have discipline and determination and a strategic goal, this country is simple; only the language and alphabet are hard." Because Americans are clear and informal, you can cut through issues quickly and "accomplish your plan," he told me. "In Taiwan, everyone wants to control you; there is so much social pressure. Here, among people who are not Chinese, I can truly be myself." Diau told me that he mixes with all kinds of people: Spanish, Middle Eastern, Indians, but unfortunately not blacks. Chinese families favor intermarriage with whites but not with blacks, he noted, adding, "I hope that changes."

Why, I asked myself, worry about the Asian threat? The best way to contain Asian economic dynamism (such as it still exists) is to absorb it, which is exactly what the United States is doing by attracting and Americanizing so many Asian immigrants.

AS I DROVE through greater Los Angeles, the term "city-state" was foremost in my mind, not because L.A. resembled ancient Athens or Sparta but because of the very size and eye-popping variety of this

---

[7]These and other statistics about Chinese and Asian habits in America come from the Asian American Survey Center in El Monte, California. There are approximately 12 million Asians in America, accounting for 4 percent of the population, according to the Asian American Survey Center. Almost a quarter of them are Chinese.

thriving urban confederation with its hinterland of oil refineries and agricultural valleys. Santa Monica has the ambience of a beach resort, but East Los Angeles is like Mexico and Monterey Park is like Asia, while Cerritos is an Orientalized Levittown for the nineties. The winding streets near Dodger Stadium north of downtown—were it not for the prevalence of home security systems—has almost a rustic southern European aspect, with their vine-clothed houses and steep hills. Going from one township to another in Los Angeles, I often felt as if I had journeyed far and wide; such are the stunning differences in urban setting. The freeway system made this compression of distance possible, and freeway growth is partly abetted by climate: because Los Angeles gets little rain or frost, road surfaces are easily and cheaply maintained.

"I'm middle-class," explained researcher Gregory Rodriguez, who lives on a steep hillside street near the stadium. "But there are also working-class and poor people a block away, and some wealthy entrepreneurs: Jews, Anglos, Mexicans, Chinese, you name it. It's an Old World neighborhood of immigrants, like those of Manhattan." I had sought out Rodriguez, a thirty-one-year-old third-generation Mexican American, to learn more about ethnicity in southern California and particularly about "Latinos," a word Rodriguez prefers to "Hispanics," which he calls "a cold and generic government term. 'Hispanic' is a term people in the East use, but here no one does." Had I never set foot in southern California and relied merely on my East Coast impressions, Rodriguez's figures would have startled me. In the Northeast, "Hispanics" are often Puerto Ricans and Dominicans, who have not integrated as successfully as Mexicans, yet it is Mexicans who make up 70.1 percent of all Latinos in America.[8]

According to the U.S. Census, Rodriguez told me, 78.4 percent of Latinos are completely bilingual in English and Spanish, and most of them favor English over Spanish.[9] In the United States as a whole, four times as many Latinos are in the middle class as are beneath the poverty line. A quarter of all middle-class families in southern California are Latinos, and U.S.-born Latinos in greater Los Angeles are not far behind whites and Asians in economic performance: about

---

[8]Unless otherwise stated, the statistics here are from my interview with Rodriguez and his monograph *The Emerging Latino Middle Class*.
[9]In California, 76.9 percent of Latinos speak English exclusively or are bilingual.

half of Latinos here are in the middle class, compared to 58 percent of white and Asian households. Among black households in the area, 37.6 percent are in the middle class—significantly higher than the national average, which is 26 percent of black households. Perhaps the most telling distinction among Latinos, Asians, and blacks is in the percentage who are government workers in an increasingly entrepreneurial economy: while 27.73 percent of blacks in greater Los Angeles work for the federal, state, or municipal governments, only about 14 percent of Asians and Latinos do.[10]

Latinos often intermarry and welcome U.S. citizenship, yet they believe fervently in retaining some degree of bilinguality, rather than *melting* into America. Rodriguez calls this "mestizo-izing" it.[11] David E. Hayes-Bautista, a UCLA sociologist, told me that the Latino experience suggests that "being American simply means buying a house with a mortgage and getting ahead. There is no agreement anymore on culture, only on economics." Seventy-five years ago, D. H. Lawrence called America a homeland of "the pocket. Not of the blood."

Immigrant dynamism coupled with Asian-mestizo-ization are the central facts of late-twentieth-century Los Angeles. The reality is richer still, as Indian immigrants buy up Artesia (next to Cerritos) and Iranian immigrants buy many properties in Beverly Hills. "I know children who are Jewish Filipinos with Iranian cousins who are married to Guatamalans," observes Mexican-American writer Richard Rodriguez.[12] "South Central is no longer a burnt-out core, and that is partly because of Latino immigrants," Gregory Rodriguez explained. "Because Latinos came in at the bottom, a pool of home buyers existed for upwardly mobile blacks who needed to sell their properties and escape South Central and Watts for racially mixed middle-class areas. Leftists talk of blacks being 'displaced,' but that disparages the very blacks who have succeeded. Is it 'displacement' to climb your way out of the ghetto?"

---

[10]See George M. Frederickson, "Land of Opportunity?"; Jennifer L. Hochschild, *Facing Up to the American Dream: Race, Class, and the Soul of the Nation;* and G. Rodriguez, *The Emerging Latino Middle Class.*

[11]A third of Latinos in greater Los Angeles intermarry, and increasingly more are applying for U.S. citizenship in the wake of the 1994 Proposition 187 scare. For information on bilinguality, see Aida Hurtado, et al., *Redefining California: Latino Social Engagement in a Multicultural Society.*

[12]See R. Rodriguez, "Letter from 2042, an L.A. Memory," *Los Angeles Times,* April 27, 1997.

*   *   *

JUST AS EUROPEAN immigration—a result of the upheavals that
accompanied the Industrial Revolution in Europe—was responsible
for much of New York's turn-of-the-century dynamism, L.A.'s late-
twentieth-century dynamism is mainly a product of immigration from
Asia and Latin America, as those regions approach the peak of their
own industrial revolutions. Los Angeles, with 15 million people, is the
second largest metropolitan area in the United States after New York.
It is not much further from Asia than Seattle and Vancouver are and
much closer to Latin America than those two cities.

But as I would soon learn in both the Southwest and the Pacific
Northwest, the mestizo-ization of greater Los Angeles holds implications for the entire continent. For it is another instance of "decon-
centration," the dilution of the urban core by smaller, incorporated
townships and the replacement of concentrated heavy manufacturing and muscle labor by service and high-tech information industries
that require a brainy, driven workforce that prefers protected, engineered landscapes. Since this process began in southern California
decades earlier than in Kansas City, St. Louis, or Omaha, such aspects
of life as the mall and high-tech Evangelical churches have evolved
further here. So I headed for the apex of this posturban phenomenon, Orange County, which forms the southern part of greater Los
Angeles.

8

—

One of the World's
Biggest Economies

ORANGE COUNTY IS, along with Westchester, Marin, and Dade, among the few counties in America that have become household names. Orange County is America's most fully evolved urban pod, in which classic definitions of city and suburb no longer apply. Perhaps the county—larger and less dense than the largest cities but smaller than the smallest states—will be the civic cement of the future, replacing the city. Already locals refer to the western Kansas City suburbs as "Johnson County" and the prosperous Maryland suburbs of greater Washington, D.C., as "Montgomery County."

Orange County stands for what everybody hates about the suburbs with their "crass affluence" and neither-nor landscape. It is often described as 798 square miles of dull residential streets, malls, and office parks without a downtown; as a major airport in search of a city—notorious for its bankrupt county treasury, the result of trying to fund its operations not through high taxes but through risky investments. I was prepared to hate Orange County. I came away respecting it, more stimulated than I had been by many "exotic" and "romantic" cities that I had seen throughout the world. Parts of Orange County seemed beautiful to me.

Orange County works. If it were a state, its economy would be roughly equal to Arizona's; if it were a country, it would rank among the top thirty or so world economies. About a third of county-based firms are involved in international trade in a range of high-technology products. Orange County now is what Johnson County and other suburban pods I had visited in the Midwest are becoming: multiracial, mini–world trade centers to be linked by frequent direct flights overseas: Omaha–Beijing, Kansas City–Paris, and so forth. (Since the late 1980s, the export sectors of local economies in America have grown dramatically: there was a 200 percent increase from 1987 to 1995 in California, 260 percent in Utah, 375 percent in Idaho . . .[1])

The received impression that Orange County's population of 2.6 million is "white bread" is false. Almost a quarter of the county's population is Latino, two and a half times the national average; 11 percent is Asian, nearly three times the national average. Only 2 percent of the population is black, one-sixth the national average.[2]

Another false perception of Orange County is that "there is no *there* there." In fact, there are many *theres* there. Orange County comprises twenty-eight separate municipalities, many with their own centers. The term "suburb" does not properly describe this most advanced, polycentric urban pod. Because these centers do not resemble traditional downtowns, they are missed by people whose eyes have yet to adjust to the postindustrial age.

Unlike such less evolved pods as Johnson County and western Omaha, Orange County seemed coherent to me. I recognized its many centers easily. For me, Orange County was a more refined and sophisticated version of what I had seen elsewhere.

I drove first to Newport Beach, one of Orange County's twenty-eight municipalities, to see real estate consultant Dennis Macheski, who worked in a well-appointed two-story office complex beside the Pacific. "The myth that people in places like Orange County spend an inordinate amount of time in their cars is wrong," Macheski began. "The average commute in the United States is twenty-two minutes. In the city of Los Angeles it is twenty-four minutes, but in greater L.A., including Orange County, it's only fifteen minutes. That's because almost everyone in the area works close to home. The jobs are no

---

[1]These statistics were supplied by the Pacific Council on International Policy in Los Angeles.
[2]See Dennis Macheski and Shais Khan, *Demographic and Economic Trends: Their Implications for Real Estate in Orange County, California* for data on ethnic and racial groups.

longer in the city; they're right here, in postsuburbia or whatever you want to call it. Even in the Inland Empire [the eastern, desert extension of greater L.A., around San Bernardino and Riverside], whose suburbs are the least developed and attractive, 70 percent of the residents work locally. Nobody in the suburbs needs to drive more than thirty minutes to a great restaurant or a theater." (In fact, established postsuburban regions such as Orange County and northern New Jersey rank high nationally on the availability of cultural venues, nineteenth and twenty-second among major urban areas.[3]) "We're no longer a suburb. Affluent New York City bedroom communities average fifteen hundred persons per square mile. Orange County's average density is six thousand. So we're far more urban in many respects than parts of New York."

I asked him to tell me about the future of greater Los Angeles, and of America, in terms of real estate patterns.

"Fifteen years hence we will be bigger. Nothing will stop us. Instead of fifteen million in greater Los Angeles, we'll be eighteen million. Two thirds of the new people will be in outlying areas as the urban region spreads further. The same will be true for Las Vegas, Phoenix, Portland, Sacramento, cities in Colorado, and elsewhere. Two thirds will be home owners, but only one quarter will be married with children. There will be more and more nontraditional families and singles."

By that he meant more gays, lesbians, and unmarried heterosexual couples. Perhaps the further acceleration of postindustrialization, by creating more independence and alienation, will lead to a greater experimentation with lifestyles. But beyond that, what is a nontraditional family? I wondered. American women began joining the workforce after the Civil War. By 1900, three quarters of all teachers in the United States were women.[4] For 150 years now, American families have had to adapt to social and economic change. The explosive growth of two-wage-earner families in recent decades is not as unusual as we imagine, for the advance of women into law, medicine, and the corporate world is not so much a historical departure as the closing of a circle that began in the mid–nineteenth century, when, because of the growth of manufacturing, the job functions of men

[3]See Rob Kling, "Beyond the Edge: The Dynamism of Postsuburban Regions" in Kling et al., eds., *Postsuburban California: The Transformation of Orange County Since World War II.*
[4]See Carl N. Degler, *Out of Our Past: The Forces That Shaped Modern America.*

and women first became sharply differentiated and spatially separated. In previous agricultural ages, while men and women had performed different tasks, families had worked in close proximity at
chores that were as tedious for men as for women. Now, finally, men
and women are working together again. Moreover, it was only after
World War II that the nuclear family became typical. Before then, extended families were the norm. To say that the demise of the nuclear
family implies the decline of American society is, I realized, to ignore
the record of our history, in which our social structures have often
adapted successfuly to economic change. The extended family—this
time via divorce and stepchildren—may in fact be returning; thus, the
closing of another circle.[5]

Macheski went on, "The number who work at home and telecommute through their computers may double from two to three percent
of home owners to six percent. But so what? It's still just six percent.
Because media people travel in the same circles as telecommuters,
they exaggerate their importance, but in the real estate business
we know that most people—no matter what wonders technology
brings—want to be reasonably close to the action in urban regions.

"Otherwise, the two big immigrations will continue because the
economy requires highly educated Asians [including Indians and
Pakistanis] and low-skilled Latinos to be the housekeepers and gardeners for the high-tech people. These are the people who will
largely account for the increased growth of urban regions across
America. In greater Los Angeles, the black population grows at one
percent a year, but the Asian-Latino population grows at three percent. Even in California, politicians have proven that they lack the will
and the ability to stop immigration. Proposition 187 [an effort to
deny public welfare benefits to noncitizens] was directed against the
poor—nobody wanted to punish Asians or middle-class Latinos. The
result, of course, was merely to encourage more Latinos to apply for
citizenship." Apparently Proposition 187 is as nasty as it gets. As
Macheski said, "Corporations will determine immigration: if they
need highly skilled workers in defense and software industries, they
will recruit them in one form or another from Asia and other places."

[5]But for poor whites and blacks, the breakdown of the nuclear family is obviously
a cause for alarm. According to the *Statistical Abstract of the United States,* between
1980 and 1995 the number of married couples living under the same roof with
their own children declined from 42.9 percent of all white families to 37.7 percent, and from 31.2 percent of all black families to 23.8 percent.

As I had been told over and over again by businesspeople and other experts, it is far more cost-efficient to import the rest of the world's talent than to train citizens at home, especially as weak or nonexistent national education standards and insufficient tax revenues make a mockery of many local American schools.[6] For the low-skilled, American citizenship confers less advantage in the job market than it used to, since those who are better skilled will get the good jobs anyway and become citizens in the process.

Macheski's analysis, by the way, does not contradict Gregory Rodriguez's: the housekeepers and gardeners that Macheski mentioned are first-generation Mexican Americans; the skilled Latino middle class that Rodriguez documents are usually from the second and third generations.

"BEFORE YOU LEAVE Newport Beach, go see the Fashion Island Mall," Macheski suggested.

"But I've seen malls before," I told him.

"See this one, it's really affluent and evolved. Believe me, it's worth it."

It was.

From Macheski's office I drove past two more office campuses, then into a large parking lot. I ascended a wide stairway and entered the mall, an outdoor labyrinth of crowded pedestrian streets punctuated with large clay pots full of flowering, bright red geraniums, with storefronts that combined neoclassical and baroque styles with red-tiled roofs. There was a fountain that shot pellets of ice and jewelry carts made of hand-tooled wood painted in rich earthen shades in the middle of the sidewalk, which was laid with brilliant tiles. Looking at the geometric sweep of marble, of sea-green wrought iron, and of terra-cotta partially obscured by bougainvillea—a brilliant mixture of late-twentieth-century abstractions with nineteenth-century intimacy and rusticity—I was as impressed as I had been when I had seen the great squares of medieval Bukhara and Samarkand. An atrium was made of pink and cream stones, veiny marble, terra-cotta, what looked like malachite, and chrome alloys. Postmodernism (an

---

[6]University of Toronto expert Thomas F. Homer-Dixon will soon publish a book on "human ingenuity" that will deal, in part, with how the North American economy is stripping the developing world of many of its most talented citizens.

architectural style highlighted by eclectic juxtapositions) was fully articulated. Malls in affluent pods of the Midwest might soon be like this.

Of course, the year-round warmth of southern California helped: it allowed for the outdoor setting as well as for the flowers that softened the industrial aspects of the architecture. Still, I thought about what Joel Garreau had suggested in *Edge City: Life on the New Urban Frontier:* that beautiful urban settings like Venice had seemed crass, too, at first, to the sophisticated inhabitants of the age; and that malls and office parks were only early phases of an architecture that might become equally lovely as it developed. Were the souks of Damascus or Fez truly more beautiful than the Fashion Island Mall? I did not think so. But the Damascus and Fez souks did have one feature that they shared with ancient and medieval marketplaces, though not with this one: they bustled with activity and chatter. The shoppers at Fashion Island, unlike the less wealthy crowd at Santa Monica's Third Street Promenade, were quiet. Conversations were so few as to be memorable: I recall a group of men and women in business attire at a café table with open account books and spreadsheets, talking softly about a building plan. Otherwise, smooth elevator music was all I heard.

Private security was noticeable, as were stores devoted to physical fitness and "health management." In superaffluent Orange County (where household wealth is much higher than the national average and poverty far below) we have clearly moved to a stage of economic development that encourages an obsession with oneself.[7] Macheski had told me that despite Orange County's wealth, "there is almost no philanthropy here." Tocqueville saw religion and patriotism, but primarily religion, as the adhesive in a democratic society no longer kept together by external authority.[8] Noting the deathly silence, the absence of public police, the prevalence of private security, I wondered if perhaps Tocqueville had been too optimistic, for these people were surely patriotic and many of them must have been religious. But Tocqueville also wrote, "Despotism is more particularly to be feared in democratic ages" because it thrives on self-absorption and

[7]Relative to the national average, Orange County has 37 percent more households earning between $50,000 and $75,000 annually, 95 percent more households earning more than $75,000, and 35 percent fewer households below the poverty line. See Macheski and Khan, *Demographic and Economic Trends . . . Orange County, California.*
[8]See Michael Davie, *In the Future Now: A Report from California.*

the desire for personal security that equality fosters. Indeed, the Fashion Island Mall reminded me of the rigidly controlled interiors imagined by science fiction writers of the 1950s.

Self-absorption also encourages fantasy. Alladi Venkatesh, of the Management School at the University of California, Irvine, describes the Nordstrom store at nearby South Coast Plaza as "both a shopping complex and a fantasy land," where a shopper can try on a pair of Italian shoes while a live pianist plays Chopin. I saw similar scenes at the mall here. The pursuit of physical comfort and high fashion, now so much more widely available than in the past, means that the threatening and unsightly poor are kept out of sight; hence the growth of social- and income-exclusive residential areas, just as I had seen in the Midwest. The pursuit of style, whether in art, architecture, or the flesh, may be the ultimate goal of the good life as these people conceive it. But its side effect is social fragmentation.

Libertarianism, which largely describes the politics of many Orange County residents, is the ideological counterpart to such fragmentation, favoring individual choice on such social issues as abortion and marijuana use, along with fiscal conservativism and lower taxes. Libertarians say, "Leave me alone to live my life and don't bother me with the cost of helping less fortunate citizens." Fashion Island Mall suggested how the urban pods I had seen in Johnson County, western St. Louis, and western Omaha could one day be as aesthetically agreeable as they already were economically efficient, but I wondered whether the new urban civilization evinced by this mall could foster traditional patriotism or civic virtue.

I DROVE INLAND from Newport Beach to visit Orange County's John Wayne Airport in Irvine, a monumental arrangement of towering palms and cylindrical spans of glass, stone, and concrete. Inside were miles of pale cream-colored carpeting and an electronic voice announcing flight departures to destinations throughout North America. Through sheets of glass I saw a gleaming corporate skyline: Apple Computer, Texas Instruments, Transamerica, and several banks. This was economic clout. Five sixths of the world's countries are less significant in international trade than are Orange County–based corporations. And what made all this possible—these corporations, this power statement of an airport—was the car! For two weeks now I had been going here and there in L.A. effortlessly by rented car, soon learning that even at rush hour, if I planned ahead, studied a map, and used side streets, I could travel seamlessly. Greater Los Angeles was not intimidating at all for the out-of-town driver. Except for the outlying foothills, most areas had grid street patterns and were connected with one another by interstate highways, called "freeways" in the Pacific West. Without the car, Orange County, a network of malls, office parks, and subdivisions, would collapse overnight. A mass transit system that would truly be convenient for most of the population here is nearly unthinkable. Even the best-equipped buses are uncomfortable, and rail transport is prohibitive where suburban centers fan out from each other in every direction. The malls and office parks are designed for cars, with vast parking lots everywhere. Martin Shukert in Omaha had told me that the car would be even more important in the early twenty-first century than in the twentieth. Orange County and the pods I visited in the Midwest suggest that many of us now prefer the solitude of automobiles to the intimacy of public transport. Many people seem not to want urban life. Great cities, as we have known them, are products of the industrial and typewriter-and-paper age, and now they are in the midst of transformation.

Of course, it would be fashionable to argue that the end of the oil age spells doom for America's auto-driven culture. But new oil discoveries in the Caspian basin, the South China Sea, Saudi Arabia, and many other places, as well as new energy technology applicable to the car, suggest that the automobile will remain practical for decades to come. The issue in the American West, as I would learn later in my journey, is water, not oil.

NEAR THE AIRPORT in Irvine, in another office park, was the *Orange County Business Journal.* When I had phoned for an appointment, the editor, Rick Reiff, had offered to take me to lunch. I assumed he preferred to talk over lunch rather than in his office. I was wrong. Reiff took me to lunch to show me what Orange County is all about.

Reiff, a Pulitzer Prize recipient for local reporting in Akron, Ohio, has run the editorial wing of the *Business Journal* since the late 1980s. He wore no tie but a stylish, collarless shirt and blazer as he ushered me toward his car and then from his own office park to one just like it, where he led me to a restaurant, called Bistango, next to a

Japanese bank. Inside, amid sculptures, tinted glass, metal alloys, spotlights, canopies, and a black see-through pyramid stacked with expensive wines that reached almost to the ceiling, I heard the hum of conversation that had been absent at the Fashion Island Mall. The place was packed. The men and women at the tables were flashily dressed in dazzling ties, with much jewelry. I saw brown and yellow faces everywhere and noticed many more glasses of iced tea and coffee than alcohol. "That's because real business is occurring here," Reiff said in a warm, rough Chicago accent as we sat down to eat. "Millions of dollars are being transacted all around you." It had been the same in the 1880s, when Rudyard Kipling observed America's extraordinary urban growth and complained that "men were babbling about money, town lots, and again money."[9]

"Where's the power?" was the question John Gunther always asked in his travelogue of mid-twentieth-century America, *Inside U.S.A.* In the late 1940s, the answer was often the local party machine. Power now was here, in this restaurant, dispersed among many more people and much less accountable, for the issue was simply profit, disconnected from political promises or even geography. Orange County's global corporations were merely home bases—which could be removed in an instant in response, for example, to tax increases.

"What kind of business is being transacted?" I asked.

"Biomedical, pharmaceutical, genetic engineering, chips for fax machines, and all kinds of software-multimedia," Reiff told me. "Then there are firms, big firms, that specialize in teaching English to Vietnamese, Chinese, and other Asians and Latinos. Global trade and workforces are everything for us. Orange County is roughly one percent of the U.S. population, but it has three percent of *Fortune* 500 companies. Every time there is a conflation of the publishing and multimedia industries, power shifts slightly to California from New York, because the future will favor multimedia over mere books."

Later, back at Reiff's office, I leafed through more than a hundred editions of the *Business Journal* and found stories about this group of Iranians or that group of Taiwanese or Pakistanis or Mexicans from Sonora buying this or that technology company. Ethnic Indians and Chinese predominated. Seeing Vietnamese, Cambodian, Laotian, and Mexican faces in an Orange County computer factory owned by

[9]Kipling, *From Sea to Sea and Other Sketches;* see also Carlos Arnaldo Schwantes, *The Pacific Northwest: An Interpretive History.*

a Pakistani and two Chinese some years ago, Polish journalist Ryzsard Kapuscinski noted that the culture of the new workforce here "is a mix of Hispanic-Catholic family values and Asian-Confucian group loyalty," with hiring done through family networks.[10]

"Mexico has become both our poor labor force and our export platform," Reiff went on. "Companies that are moving factories to Mexico would have left the U.S. anyway, to Malaysia, for instance. The nation-state cannot keep them here if cheap, competent labor exists abroad. With NAFTA [the North American Free Trade Agreement], at least we can keep much of the work in North America."

I asked about the credit collapse in the early 1990s, after Orange County officials had made bad investments with public money. "A blip on the screen, in historical terms just a rainy day," Reiff said. "Roads are still being paved. No police have been fired. Only some social service cuts, which affect the relatively few poor people here. What I'm saying is that *the Orange County phenomenon* is intact: imagine the effect on Cleveland, for instance, if it lost two billion dollars in bad investments. If in twenty years all this glitter around you fades, historians will look back on the 1980s and 1990s as a golden age here, with the credit crash a minor theme.

"I'm originally a city kid," Reiff continued. "I played baseball in the alleys in Chicago. I know what is urban and suburban, and *this*"—his eyes wandered around the room—"is neither: it's something new."

But precisely because of its dynamism, Orange County and places like it, despite the likelihood of an abundance of oil for a few decades yet, are a bubble. Reiff admitted that the reason for so many malls—particularly the auto malls that have burgeoned throughout southern California—"is that with income tax a dirty word, the only way for municipalities to raise revenue is through sales taxes, so they encourage mall building and build too many. A lot of these malls will go bust."

"Will this place fight for its country? Are these people loyal to anything except themselves?" I asked.

"Loyalty is a problem," Reiff said. "Only about half the baseball fans in Orange County root for the California Angels [whose stadium is in Anaheim, a county municipality]. I root for the Chicago White Sox. So many people here are from somewhere else, whether from the U.S. or the world. People came here to make money. In the future,

[10]See Nathan Gardels, "*La Raza Cosmica* in America."

patriotism will be more purely and transparently economic. Perhaps patriotism will survive in the form of prestige, if America remains the world economic leader."

Rather than citizens, the inhabitants of these prosperous pods are, in truth, resident expatriates, even if they were born in America, with their foreign cuisines, eclectic tastes, exposure to foreign languages, and friends throughout the world.

FROM IRVINE, WHERE the airport and a branch of the University of California are located, I drove through the county municipalities of Santa Ana, with its largely Latino population; Garden Grove, with its many signs in Korean and Vietnamese; and Anaheim, home of the California Angels, a convention center, and Disneyland. Near Disneyland is the Crystal Cathedral; the proximity may not be an accident. The cathedral is an $18.5 million, skyscraper-proportioned, geometric cutout with 70,000 windows, an electronic organ, multimedia shows, greeting card sayings etched into adjoining sidewalks, and a corporate ambience in which religion is an enormous infomercial. The cathedral's "combination of religious magnificence and material grandeur resembles Nordstrom's mix of high culture with consumerism," writes the urban scholar Alladi Venkatesh. That remark is actually unfair to Nordstrom, as well as to the Bistango restaurant and Fashion Island Mall, all of which I found more authentic than this glitzy, evangelical cathedral. Whatever the homilies etched in the sidewalk, the architecture itself shrieked materialism.

I reentered the car and headed to the northeasternmost township of Orange County: Yorba Linda, birthplace of Richard Nixon. The little wooden house that Nixon's father, Francis, built himself in 1912, with materials from a mail-order catalog, still stands. The president and his wife, Pat, are buried a few steps away. The memorial, which includes a museum and library, was packed with visitors the day I went, more crowded than the presidential memorial sites of Harry Truman in Independence, Missouri, and of Dwight Eisenhower in Abilene, Kansas, on the days I visited those. The multiracial crowd at the site, like the residents of Yorba Linda itself in the late 1990s, appeared to represent Nixon's "silent majority." Yorba Linda is a place of clean, spanking new malls, gated communities, restaurants, fitness centers, and so forth, with sizable Latino and Asian minorities.

When Nixon's father built the house, there was nothing around it

for miles but orange and avocado groves watered by the Santa Ana
River. Yorba Linda is a bit too far inland to be truly part of coastal California, and the conservative culture in which Nixon grew up has not
really changed. The malls and restaurants here looked midwestern
compared to those in Irvine and Newport Beach. Yorba Linda is the
original sepia-toned California—Iowa in the Sun Belt. The Latinos
and Asians in Yorba Linda looked wholesome and self-assured; they
looked American, lacking the worldly ethnic flair of their compatri-
ots at the Bistango restaurant. Still, I looked in all directions from the
Nixon family house at the network of crowds and streets and shopping centers where farm fields had once been and was struck by the
magnitude of change in less than a century. I shuddered at what
might evolve over the next nine decades, as change becomes more
compressed and economic growth all, it seemed to me, that keeps society together here.

I headed southwest, back through Anaheim and Garden Grove,
into the heavily Vietnamese Orange County municipality of Westminster. Amid miles of one-story tract homes, I pulled into a shingle-
and-Sheetrock strip mall named Saigon Plaza to look for a place to eat
dinner. I entered a run-down café, where the men were playing cards
and listening to Vietnamese music. The atmosphere was thick with
unfiltered cigarette smoke. I felt as if I were back in Southeast Asia.
Then somebody switched off the Vietnamese music video and put on
the NBA play-offs.

9

—

Low-End Cosmopolitanism

WHEN ONE THINKS about southern California, train travel does not spring to mind. But the rail journey from Los Angeles south to the Mexican border was more pleasant than any I had taken on the East Coast. L.A.'s Spanish art deco Union Station looked like a backdrop for a Claudette Colbert movie, clean and safe and filled with people of all classes and ages, including, as usual in greater Los Angeles, many multiracial couples.

The trip by rail south to San Diego and Tijuana took me through a medley of typical southern California scenery: oil refineries and industrial zones, vast tracts of mobile homes and Sheetrock subdivisions with bougainvillea climbing up walls and oil pumps nearby; fancy suburbs with golf courses and engineered landscapes; auto sales malls; avocado groves by the desert; steep, lawned hills followed by the spectacular blue seascape at San Clemente, where Nixon had his summer White House. Two Spanish-speaking women sitting behind me talked quietly the whole way about relatives in Idaho. Three hours after I left Los Angeles, the office park of Lockheed Martin came into view, heralding San Diego, whose Spanish mission–style train station was as clean and handsome as the one in Los Angeles.

San Diego is the ultimate urban success story, with more Ph.D.s per capita than any other American city, eight thousand software jobs and

forty telecommunications firms added in the 1990s, and more bio-
tech firms than either greater New York or greater Los Angeles. As
usual in such cases, the number of Asians, Latinos, and other immigrants is abnormally high and the number of blacks low—5 percent of the city's population compared to the 12.6 percent national
average—and most blacks here work for the military. (San Diego is a
base for the navy's Pacific fleet.) This unfortunate fact need not be
a future reality, though. For the most successful societies devote
money and effort to their weakest aspects.

It was Sunday. The colorful, tiled downtown sidewalks were deserted except for tourists and the homeless. I walked back to the train
station and took a trolleybus on the thirty-minute ride to the Mexican
border town of Tijuana. En route a white woman with frosted, bluish-
blond hair talked to a woman who looked Latino: "You work for the
government. Well, I'm losing my Social Security and Medicare, and
do you know why? Because the government is sending all the money
to foreign countries. Explain that to me!" The Latino women did not
answer.

IF EVER A border was designed to display distrust, it was at Tijuana:
not ideological distrust as between North and South Korea or the former West and East Germany, but something deeper and harder to
eradicate: the distrust of race and class. Throngs of Mexicans and a
smaller number of tourists walked in both directions between high
gray concrete walls topped by wire grates and razor-sharp corrugated
iron. The Mexican authorities did not bother to check those entering
or leaving Mexico; the U.S. authorities searched belongings and
asked for proof of citizenship or residence upon my return from Tijuana a few hours later.

For decades Tijuana had meant sleaze and tackiness: that I expected. But I was not prepared for the city's eclectic composition.
The Fashion Island Mall and the other shopping plazas of Orange
County and the Midwest reflected the high-end cosmopolitanism
of the global marketplace. Tijuana reflected low-end cosmopolitanism; for it would be inaccurate to label Tijuana's shopping area
"Mexican."

On sale along with the brass knuckles, the switchblades, and the
bleeding plastic Jesuses were molds of the dogs in *101 Dalmatians* and
other Disney characters. The signs for Indian blankets and Aztec sun

masks were in Korean. Indian women sold beads outside a store filled with Dior and Estée Lauder products that was protected by private security guards, ever present here. I heard street hustlers speaking Japanese and Hebrew in addition to Spanish. Against a cacophony of canned mariachi music, a black woman called out in English the pleasures of a topless bar featuring margaritas for ninety-nine cents. There were karaoke bars, too. The ceramic tiles, stonework, and steel tubing were similar to the materials I had seen in upscale malls, but their arrangement and loose fittings, along with the plastic, the neon, the corrugated ironwork, the violet-and-mint-painted concrete, and the graffiti made for an unremitting ugliness and an aura of violence. Many American tourists here were clownish caricatures of faddishness: tattooed and overweight, with "hip-hop" baggy clothes and loud sports shoes. They looked more threatening than the hustlers.

Tijuana showed how multicultural compositions can be bad as well as good; how a globalized world need not necessarily be peaceful or pretty; how with so much cultural grafting the important distinctions will be not racial but between classes. Tijuana is a "city on a hill" for the world's underclass: white, yellow, and black.

Tijuana also illustrates the jarring divide between the United States, a society governed through flexible and interlocking jurisdictions, and Mexico, an oligarchal tyranny that does not really govern at all. In Mexico the distinction between tyranny and anarchy is ambiguous. Indeed, Tijuana offered a pageant of child labor, unsafe vehicles, bridges without safety rails, drugstores selling unregulated drugs, buildings without doors. . . . While the flood spillway on the American side of the border was empty and clean, the one on the Mexican side was cracked and filled with trash. The cactus-bearded orange hills on the American side were empty, those on the Mexican side crowded with flimsy dwellings.

Mexico's population, increasing at two and a half times the rate of America's, will continue to seep across the border, as Mexico increasingly colors America's new posturban culture. Because Tijuana is a distorted, diluted version of Mexico, let me describe an earlier journey: one that took me by bus and car from Mexico City into the American Southwest a year before my trip to southern California.

THE

AGENT

OF

HISTORY

10

History Moves North

HOW IS MEXICAN society merging with our own?

I began in Mexico City's Church of Jesus of Nazareth, where the remains of the sixteenth-century Spanish conqueror of Mexico, Hernando Cortez,[1] are buried inside the wall to the side of the altar. I stood there on a Sunday morning—my first day in Mexico—amid a crowd of worshipers: each pressed against the other, damp with sweat, chanting a Christian hymn to the tune of "Shalom Aleichem" groaned out by three accordion players. The worshipers were clapping hands and banging feet on the flagstones, their faces full of laughter. Children ran wild. Some adults were filming their families with handheld video cameras, oblivious to the mass in progress. There was none of the sad dignity I knew from church services in Spain and Portugal, where I had once lived; none of the shyness or the intense reserve and educational films I would experience in evangelical churches later in my odyssey through America. Here were spontaneity and the crude sensation of dirt beneath the fingernails. When I mentioned that the music was Jewish, the worshiper next to me shrugged and said, "Whatever it is, it sounds good."[2]

---

[1]The correct Spanish name is Hernán Cortés. But Hernando Cortez is also accurate and is more familiar to English speakers.

[2]In fact, many of the Spanish conquistadors who first settled Mexico and the American Southwest lit candles on Friday night and did not eat pork, partial evi-

That same morning I went to the Basilica of Our Lady of Guadalupe, the country's patron saint.[3] Amid the sleek modern contours of this Mexico City basilica, built in 1976, Mexicans, both old and young, middle-class and working-class—some in stylish leisure garments, others in the soiled, baggy clothes of workers—wailed in ecstasy on a moving electric walkway that took them past a glass-framed image of the Virgin. They left the basilica wiping away tears. Many streamed into a nearby McDonald's for lunch.

It was a naive, premodern landscape I encountered, filled with emotional theatrics, despite the contemporary architecture and Big Macs, where human beings stood in rapturous awe of a cosmos that the West assumed it had mastered long ago.

On my second morning in Mexico I saw this premodern world in turmoil: Fifteen miles south of Mexico City in the shadow of volcanoes, Xochimilco is "ecologically fragile" terrain where people are legally forbidden to live.[4] Yet here I saw thousands of squatters, packs of growling dogs, hills of garbage, pots of flowers, and rickety stands offering liquid sour chocolate—the *chocolātl* that the Aztec king Moctezuma was drinking when Cortez found him—and listened to stories of robberies, glue sniffing, alcoholism, and cocaine addiction. Every day a thousand migrants from the Mexican countryside drift into Xochimilco and similar shantytowns.

"No Mexican will ever go to the police for help," a migrant from the state of Guerrero, southwest of Mexico City, told me. Another told me he had been robbed twice by the police. Yet another told me that after his car had been stolen, the police had wanted to take his wife back to the station to fill out a report. "I wouldn't let them, they would have raped her."

Gracialla Branca Castillo, an attractive woman with dark hair, tasteful makeup, a track suit, and Adidas shoes, directed a group of men in straw hats paving a road. She belonged to a local council that had organized the work and obtained the materials. "One of the condi-

---

dence that they were descended from Jewish families who had converted to Catholicism before the Inquisition. Judaism, like Islam, tinctured Spanish culture in the New World.

[3]In December 1531, an Indian peasant named Juan Diego saw a vision of the Virgin Mary, which was later emblazoned on his cloak. The original church was built on the spot.

[4]I refer to the southern part of Xochimilco: the northern part is a lacework of canals and floating gardens, popular among tourists, that was settled by Indians in the thirteenth century.

tions of council membership," she told me, "is never to have worked for the central government."

I caught the sickly sweet odor of guavas and the dampness of jungle greenery as I climbed through another muddy, caved-in hillside toward hundreds of other shacks, these made of cardboard, black plastic, and rusted black iron sheeting—a step down from the cinder-block hovels at lower levels—where another woman told me, "We have no guarantees concerning our ownership or permission to stay here, except for bribes to police and officials, and the grace of God." A middle-aged man in one house confirmed that he had eight children, eight grandchildren, and "many more coming." None had finished school. The churned-up soil was filled with tiny shards of obsidian, remnants of Aztec utensils and cooking pots.

These slums were familiar to me: the spray paint, breeze blocks, corrugated iron, exploding demographics, distrust of central authority, and crime rotting the base, to say nothing of the peak, of an ancient pyramidal power structure. Here was everything I had found in the poor and overcrowded countries of the Eastern Hemisphere where I had traveled for many years. The differences between Mexico and the United States are basic: we, despite our inequalities, are a civil society in which citizens feel reasonably secure under a rule of law; Mexico is not.

Indeed, many of the faces I saw throughout Mexico City looked as if etched in bas-relief, the downcast expressions numbed by centuries of oligarchy and absolutism, so much like the faces I had seen in Central Asia and China. Crumpled Indian women, draped in scarlet robes like medieval Madonnas, sat begging on the pavement. The vast plazas of black and red volcanic stone, Catholic and baroque in appearance, evoked the distant Orient: ceremonial spaces that ended in towering, multitiered cathedrals, pyramids by another name, meant to intimidate through their supernatural associations. The monumentality and slithery terror of the Aztec stonework, beside the gilded, intricately carved birds and other animals of eighteenth-century churches, reminded me, as they did the nineteenth-century American historian William Prescott, of the ancient art "of Egypt and Hindostan." The cratered streets spotted with mud puddles, the unfinished, weather-stained overpasses, the gritty air, the crowds, all recalled Cairo or Bangkok without the minarets or Buddhist temples. This was an Old World culture, despite the baseball hats and the lumbering American cars.

The United States of America, that "great, metallic beast,"[5] that east-west middle-class machine and the principal focus of my search, seemed far, far away to the north. But is it really that far removed? Does Mexico suggest something deeper than northward population drifts and immigration disputes? Does it imply something called "history," that fate which eventually catches up with every nation and which Americans have traditionally preferred to deny, believing history is a misfortune that happens to other people?[6] Is it Mexico's destiny to reveal something "final" about the United States, or will Mexico remain that perennial problem—and diversion—*down there?*

FROM XOCHIMILCO I went to the home of a former top government minister in the fashionable Zona Rosa section of Mexico City. The back wall of his split-level study was glass, revealing a hanging tropical garden illuminated by spotlights. Everywhere I saw shelves filled with well-bound historical works in Spanish and English. This was old wealth that advertised its accomplishments through the size and quality of a library rather than by a display of cars, expensive gadgets, or soulless decor. Among the volumes I noticed Fernand Braudel's great work *The Mediterranean and the Mediterranean World in the Age of Philip II,* about the second half of the sixteenth century, when the Mediterranean had begun to lose its primacy in favor of northern Europe and North America. Braudel emphasized the north-south orientation of the Mediterranean. He showed how historical agents are shaped by the economies and institutions in which they operate and how all of them, in turn, are shaped by climate and geography: mountains, not rulers, come first. Observe a landscape well enough, in other words, and you will see the past, present, and future of its inhabitants unfold.[7]

When I mentioned this to the minister, he nodded, as though familiar with Braudel. Then he told me, "Mexico is reverting back to

[5]From the conclusion of Stephen Vincent Benét's epic poem *John Brown's Body*. Benét's point is that the South's defeat meant an end to aristocracy and the nation's north-south orientation in favor of an egalitarian, industrial, east-west destiny.

[6]See Arnold J. Toynbee's remark about how some nations believe themselves to be outside history, discussed in C. Vann Woodward, "The Irony of Southern History."

[7]See also Octavio Paz, *The Labyrinth of Solitude.*

weakly governed Indian-style fiefdoms, a balkanized tributary state as in the time of the Aztecs. . . . History is migration and settlement patterns. Borders are ultimately uncontrollable. Northern Mexico will gradually merge with the southwestern United States. Monterrey and Houston will be linked to a degree that neither is linked to cities in their own countries. Southern Mexico has profound Indian roots. Its ties with Guatemala may become more developed than with Mexico City."

In fact, geographical Mexico is, not unlike the Balkans, a myriad of mountainous indentations that divide the population, particularly in the south. The paucity of navigable rivers further contributes to disunity. The Aztecs in Tenochtitlán (modern-day Mexico City) did not constitute a centralized tyranny over pre-Hispanic Mexico: they dominated a triple alliance composed of themselves and the Texoco and Tacuba Indian groups. This alliance administered a loose tributary state system around Tenochtitlán, while in much of the northwest the Tarascan Indians were a law unto themselves. The northern desert near the U.S. border—a barely inhabitable region from which all these tribes had once migrated—was always unstable. Aztec Mexico, implied the ex-minister, could become a model for twenty-first-century Mexico, as the five-hundred-year period of the formal state (beginning with Spanish colonization under Cortez in 1519) gradually ends.

He added, somewhat coyly, that the state is being undone by "modernization." He meant that the corrupt, drug-infested, and rigidly hierarchal power structure is under siege. Millions of rural migrants like those I had met in Xochimilco were reinventing community, drawing strength from a credible God in their struggle against a discredited government. I had also seen an increasingly sophisticated middle class whose demands were becoming harder to satisfy. Driving from Xochimilco to the ex-minister's home, I had passed miles of banal districts with crowded Wal-Marts, Price Clubs, Blockbuster Videos, and ATM machines. This, I soon learned, was not a narrow petite bourgeoisie, the nationalistic kind that had emerged in nineteenth-century Central Europe and in Greece in the 1950s, the kind that strengthens state identity. Mexico's is a postmodern middle class connected to the outside world by fax, mobile phones, and satellite dishes, which I saw everywhere, even in poor areas such as Xochimilco.

As in so many societies faced with social transformation and decaying power structures, crime was high. The ex-minister's book-lined home was protected by high walls and an electronic security system. So were others I visited over the next few days. "We have to build a wire fence, our wall is too low," said another former government official. Every house in this ex-official's wealthy neighborhood had a guard dog—a German shepherd or a rottweiler. He told me how off-duty police are behind much of the crime, including carjackings in which the victim is forced to drive to a secluded ATM machine and withdraw large amounts of cash before giving up his car, too. Yet another well-off Mexican, an analyst at a think tank, told me, "I used to say, 'I know there is crime.' Then it got to a point where I said, 'I know a friend of a friend who was a victim of a crime.' Now I have friends who have been attacked. Even me, I was carjacked recently." He told me that when he had described the guns of the carjackers to a friend in the presidential security guard, the friend had advised him to report only that the car had been stolen during the night, when it was parked—since the guns belonged to either off-duty or former policemen and to make accusations might be dangerous.

The police in Mexico are not merely corrupt, they *are* criminals—and thus the symbol of Mexico's decaying political system, whatever democratic trappings it may claim. The resulting insecurity expresses itself visually: the new pink stucco town house developments going up in Mexico City have sliding security gates and armed private guards at the entrances. I had once visited Leon Trotsky's villa in a southern suburb of Mexico City, where in the late 1930s he had lived in exile behind high walls in an unsuccessful attempt to hide from Stalin's agents: it is now just another house with fortress architecture.

Unlike the former Soviet Union, Mexico's party despotism has never been guided by an ideology or the pretense of one. It exists for crime, whether in the form of patronage and nepotism at the top or armed robbery at the lower reaches. One of my hosts said, "Even the opposition figures are weak, with many violent people in their ranks whom they cannot control. So a multiparty system will not necessarily change the way things are done." Perhaps as the civilian power structure weakens and divides, the army will play a larger role. Given the pervasiveness of narcotics money throughout the economy, the Mexican Army, with its airplanes and its high-tech communications gear, may become the world's most formidable drug dealer.

Meanwhile, the population increases in a manner that favors the breakup of central power. Though Mexico's rate of population growth has been steadily dropping, the annual growth for years to come will add almost 2 million new Mexicans a year to today's 92 million. Forty percent of Mexicans are so poor that they spend more on condoms than on clothes.[8] Future population growth, added to the extremely high birthrates of the 1970s and 1980s, means that millions of new Mexicans will reach employment age each year through 2020—with far fewer retiring—in a country where real unemployment is already 25 percent. With 40 percent of the population under the age of fifteen, Mexico's economy must grow by 6 percent annually to create enough menial jobs. To create good jobs for these new workers and move the country into the "First World," the economy will have to grow by 9 to 10 percent annually for about a decade. That is unlikely.[9] Either Mexico will gradually become poorer and meaner than it already is, or more Mexicans will migrate to the United States. Immigration limits on Mexicans are, in the long run, probably unsustainable. I would learn more about this as I traveled northward.

Nor is this population growth spread evenly. While women in southern Mexican states such as Guerrero, Oaxaca, and Chiapas have four or more children over their lifetime, those in northern Mexico are having between two and three. Southern Mexico suggests a Third World, Central American–type growth pattern, while northern Mexico follows a First World, U.S.-type pattern. In the center is Mexico City, where roughly a third of the population—nobody knows exactly how many—are rural migrants living in shantytowns. Yet Mexico City is increasingly assuming the character of a middle-class city-state. With more and more poor to placate even as the middle class becomes better educated and informed about the outside world, the central government is finding it increasingly difficult to satisfy its citizens.

Mexico's slippage into quasi anarchy should not be surprising. The strong, stable civilian-led state of the 1940s through the mid-1990s, dominated by the Institutional Revolutionary Party, is a rarity in Mexico's otherwise turbulent history. Mexico's War of Independence from Spain lasted eleven years (from 1810 through 1821) and cost 600,000 lives. The first three decades of independence saw fifty governments tumbling over one another. Then came the wars between the Indians and the mestizos and *criollos*—Spanish families who had

---

[8]In addition to published statistics, I was aided in this section by a leading Mexican demographer, Antonio Alonso Concheiro.

[9]For comparison, the U.S. economy, which accounts for almost three quarters of Mexico's imports and exports, has grown at a rate of less than three percent per year on average since 1973.

settled in Mexico—over land, as well as war with the United States from 1846 to 1848. The chaos of the Mexican Revolution, which pitted northern guerrillas led by Francisco "Pancho" Villa, Álvaro Obregón, and Pablo Gonzáles, and southern rebels led by Emiliano Zapata, against each other and the waning dictatorship of Porfirio Díaz in Mexico City, went on for a decade, until 1917, with no conclusive result. In 1920, rebels assassinated President Venustiano Carranza in southeastern Mexico. The erratic route to stability in the mid-1940s broke this violent pattern. But success brought development and a new category of problems that has now attained critical mass. Since 1940, Mexico's population has risen almost fivefold. Between 1970 and 1995, it nearly doubled. From 1985 until the end of the century, it will rise by over a third. In the Valley of Mexico, the great lake that once held the two Aztec Venices of Tenochtitlán and Tlatelolco has been sucked dry. Rivers are now underground sewers, with water pumped from further and further away. "This city, founded by water, will die from the lack of it," poet Homero Aridjis told me. Mexico is due for another round of roiling, decades-long *history* at a time of dissolving borders and distances, with a population more than a third that of the United States, rather than the mere 15 percent it represented in 1940, when the Institutional Revolutionary Party first assumed power and ended the earlier chaos.

In addition, the working-age population of Mexico, Central America, and the Caribbean basin is, relative to that of the United States, exploding. In 1995, there were 13 million new members of the working-age population in the countries immediately south of the U.S. border, as opposed to more than 9 million new job seekers in the United States.[10] In 2020, there will be 14 million new job seekers each year south of the border but only about half a million new job seekers in the United States. In the former countries, where the well off have servants, private security guards, and Miami bank accounts, the poor masses just want a place where they can work hard, earn real currency, and not be judged by their fathers' names; in such places the most lucrative racket, after drugs and money laundering, is forging U.S. visas.[11] Over the next few decades, the Hispanic component

[10]These figures derive from adding the new twenty- to twenty-four-year-olds, then subtracting the sixty-five- to sixty-nine-year-olds who are leaving the workforce; see Leon F. Bouvier and Lindsey Grant, *How Many Americans?: Population, Immigration, and the Environment.*

[11]The Dominican Republic, which I visited in 1997, is a quintessential example of all of this.

of the U.S. population will more than double, from 10 to 22 percent. Latin history is moving north.

FRITZ MONSON IS an American advance man for this cultural merger. Rather than fear it, he welcomes it. Originally from central Michigan, then El Paso and Mexico City, Fritz strode into the lobby of my Mexico City hotel one afternoon, a Mexican assistant at each side, bellowing a hearty "Hello, Robert—you look like a Robert!" He had never met me (we had spoken once on the phone), yet he picked me out of a crowd. Fritz wore an off-the-rack checkered sports jacket. His wide, pink, friendly, Fuller Brush–man face was pure Main Street. Fritz handed me a business card with three phone numbers and a fax number. His Motorola cell phone beeped, and before Fritz and I had fully introduced ourselves, I overheard him talk about letters of credit worth "$26 million."

I had heard that Fritz was involved in tourist development in the scenic Copper Canyon area of northern Mexico. "*Sí*," he replied, nodding his head. Spanish worlds such as *sí* and *nada* dotted his conversation, but he readily admitted that after five years in Mexico, his Spanish vocabulary barely exceeded a hundred words—the ones he kept repeating.

"I want to help develop the canyon and protect the Indians there. If the wealthy Mexicans develop the canyon, they'll ruin it. I'm not interested in big hotels; just simple, clean, third-class establishments linked by hiking trails. I want tourists who appreciate the environment, upmarket backpackers . . ."

The Motorola beeped again: a conversation about buying a bank.

Fritz's was raw, unreflective energy: supertankers full of it. His two Mexican assistants seemed amazed by him.

Fritz was involved in charitable clothing drives, a record company (he gave me some cassettes), bankrolling a race car driver, setting up a clinic, buying an eight-hundred-acre cattle ranch in Durango, buying turbocharged Cessnas, improving a private telecommunications system with dishes and transponders, helping Taiwanese investors find a Mexican home for their money, and so on. If the planes and the communications gear suggest something untoward about Fritz's activities, that would be wrong. Two hours with Fritz over lunch (he paid) convinced me he was genuine, an honest, garrulous hustler. "I'm a little guy who fits between the cracks and cements things together. I'm involved in a thousand things," including long lunches and several marriages. He showed me a picture of himself in a safari shirt crossing a footbridge at the jungly bottom of the Copper Canyon: a Sinclair Lewis optimist who had stumbled into a Conrad novel, throwing the grim plot off course.

As I told Fritz, it seemed to me that the entire autocratic Mexican power structure was dissolving under the weight not just of population growth and social change but of multinational business and people like him, who were circumventing the system with cellular phones and an energy with which the government ministries could not cope.

"That's it," he said, smiling.

"For instance," he said, "you take Topolobampo. It's a pretty little port right on the Sea of Cortez, less than half an hour across the desert from Los Mochis, a terminal of the Copper Canyon Railway, a day's drive from the U.S. border. The water there is great. You buy some shrimp, you sit and eat with some of the old folks, and it's paradise. You've got to see it! You'll love it! And here—here's the best part, Robert—there's nothing there! You could develop the place, make it a tourist resort for American families, create jobs, clean it up. I can see it in my mind in a few years. . . . They'll all be speaking English. We'll all be speaking Spanish. . . ."

I never met Fritz again, but, intrigued by his description of Topolobampo, I stopped there in the course of my journey north and found a leaden green bay, like a tub of bathwater, stretched out before me, the desert at my back. Stony hillsides glinted like broken glass in the midday sunlight. Sweat ran from my forehead into my eyes. Even my watchband felt oppressively hot. Where the desert met the bay was the potholed main street of a small, wrecked town: Topolobampo.

I walked a few feet to what, from the sun-blinded street, looked like a deep and invitingly cool, coffin-black shop of some kind. Inside I found blocky men lathered in sweat, with ponytails hanging from their L.A. Raiders caps, some with tattoos on their arms, pacing silently around pool tables, lining up their shots. I walked back out into the street in time to see a wide-wheeled pickup truck, its body low to the ground, rumbling by, full of Mexican policemen who looked like criminals, with white T-shirts, black baseball hats facing backward, sunglasses, and AK-47 assault rifles. One had a gold chain around his neck. As I walked further in the hundred-degree heat, I noticed skeletal dogs, their gums exposed, hiding from the sun beneath rusted car bodies.

The houses were made of unfinished cement, corrugated asbestos, some brick, a lot of black plastic wrapping, and rotting wood. The hillside overlooking the small harbor had eroded so that I could see a rusted gridwork of water pipes that had once been underground. I bought some fried shrimp, whose aroma blended with that of the sewage, the urine puddles, and the salt water. As I sat and ate on a metal kitchen chair, a young woman passed me. Her expression was melodramatic; her posture heroic, disdainful. Her shiny black hair reached nearly to her waist—that was one thing Fritz had right. I remember him saying, "Isn't Mexico a great country! Even the poor women are beautiful!"

Yes, there was real artistry in her walk. In Mexico, as a Mexican friend had told me, "the past weighs three thousand pounds and the future is nonexistent," so appearances were everything: a way to maintain dignity in the face of death. Looking at a few young men hanging out—and thinking of the men in the pool hall—I could picture them all slipping into crime across the U.S. border only a day's ride away, stripped of the inhibitions imposed by family and culture: four fifths of the outdoor cannabis fields that law enforcement agents discover in California are cultivated by Mexicans.[12] (The Mexican influence in the United States is enormous and encompasses both the middle-class dynamism that Gregory Rodriguez in Los Angeles spoke of and the crime that is undeniable.)

The tepid bay that opened onto the Sea of Cortez, with its dozens of small fishing boats crowding the squiggly limestone outcroppings, seemed full of possibilities: commerce, contraband. . . . Topolobampo is a deepwater Pacific port in the Mexican state of Sinaloa. Spanish explorers passed through here in the sixteenth century en route to what would one day be the western United States; through here passes 70 percent of the cocaine destined for Los Angeles and points north and east.

The transshipment of cocaine along these age-old trade and migration routes is worth more than twice the annual profits of the Mexican petroleum industry.[13] Sinaloa, it is said, is an emerging, semi-independent principality of the new North America, a "brown zone" where the police cooperate with drug smugglers and the decomposing state, as in the time of the Aztecs, barely exists. Here

---

[12] See "Mexico's Drug Menace," *The Economist,* November 15, 1997.
[13] See Eduardo Valle, "Narco-Power and the Subterranean NAFTA."

capitalism is real, unrestrained: a market is served, talent rises to the top, and incompetence is often punished by death. Here you find instinctive, blood-and-soil patriotism. Sinaloans, according to narcotics experts, had never allowed Colombians, Nicaraguans, or other outsiders to muscle in on the local drug trade. Wealthy government officials in Mexico City with foreign bank accounts desert their country in an instant when the political wind changes, but Sinaloan drug dealers stay put.

Yet Fritz had come here, seen what I saw, and his optimism was confirmed. I had met energetic businessmen all over the world, but, like the Germans I had run across in eastern Europe, they were often a dour lot, lacking humor and openness. They appeared invulnerable. And vulnerability, I suspected—the willingness to believe despite much evidence to the contrary, the willingness to be fooled—was Fritz's and, of course, America's secret strength. ("Americans love so much to be fooled," wrote Charles Baudelaire in the April 20, 1855, issue of the Parisian journal *Le Pays*.) Fritz was a counterpoint to the notion that America was merely about economics; merely about getting a mortgage and getting ahead. America, Fritz implied, would always be about *possibilities*, and therein lies the bedrock of its patriotism, even as a new urban civilization threatens the traditional national community. Still, for all its exceptionalism, the United States does inhabit a world of tragic intractability, as the history thus far of both Mexico and American blacks so well reveals.

So I headed north to see how a history so tragic was blending with one that has been replete with potentialities, at least for most of its citizens.

11

In Search of the Nonexistent

IN AN AGE of collapsing distances, when escape from problems overseas becomes harder, I wanted to see the United States as a contiguous extension of the Old World. To travel from the Old World to the
New World—from a developing country such as Mexico to a post-
modern one such as the United States—merely by walking through a
gate rather than by crossing an ocean might provide the kind of
shock I was looking for.

The route I followed was the one taken by Francisco Vázquez de
Coronado, a thirty-year-old Spanish nobleman who had come to
Mexico in the wake of Cortez's conquest. That conquest, from 1519
to 1521, had been an ordeal of fighting through mangrove thickets,
eating moldy cassava bread, witnessing daily human sacrifices, and
encountering a macabre tropical grandeur. According to historian
William Prescott, "it was as if" Cortez and his fellow Spaniards
"had alighted on another planet." But they comprehended little of
it, nor were these crude zealots especially curious. The Spaniards
massacred Indians, built Christian altars where they had smashed
idols, and went mad at the sight of the gold that covered the walls
of Moctezuma's palace and that Cortez and his men melted down
to enrich themselves and for shipment to Spain. Unlike the Europeans who would later come to the East Coast of the United States—

children of the Enlightenment and of the Protestant Reformation—Cortez and his men had come to steal; not to work and build cities. Religious dogmatists who combined the worst of Spanish and Moorish culture, these Spaniards lacked the habit of *process:* of investing years of labor to achieve material gain; in other words, the bourgeois mentality. Rather, they were the sons of El Cid, whose crier had announced:

> Those who would no longer be poor but rich, let them come and join My Cid, who plans to take the field and lay siege to Valencia and win her for Christendom.[1]

Mexico, like Valencia and the other Moorish cities of Spain, offered booty aplenty. The Spaniards were in a fever of greed and delusion. If so much gold was to be had in Tenochtitlán—present-day Mexico City—only 250 miles inland from where Cortez had landed near Veracruz, what about further north? Driven by rumors, exaggerations, and their own fancies, Coronado and others raided the great northern beyond, which they naturally assumed was much like Mexico, since mapmakers of the period gave the Western Hemisphere two isthmuses, one to the south of Mexico and one to the north.

The battle cry was "another Mexico" further north, where a quick route to Cathay was waiting to be discovered. "Romantic, histrionic, cruel, and trance-bound, they marched in rusty medieval armor toward the nonexistent," writes Bernard De Voto in *The Course of Empire.*

The first European to have the vaguest idea of what actually lay to the north of Mexico was Álvar Núñez Cabeza de Vaca. In 1528, twelve years before Coronado's exploration, Cabeza de Vaca's company had marched north from Tampa Bay but had soon been attacked by Indians. Two hundred fifty survivors retreated to the Gulf of Mexico, where they built boats out of horsehide and ate the rest of the animals' remains. They then set sail back to Mexico. But a storm wrecked their ships near Galveston Bay. Only four men were left alive, including Cabeza de Vaca and his Moorish slave, Esteván. They survived for almost six years, naked and starving, among the local Indians before

---

[1] *The Poem of the Cid* [*My Lord*] is based on the exploits of Rodrigo Díaz de Vivar, an eleventh-century Christian adventurer who fought the Moors.

wandering back home across present-day Texas, New Mexico, and eastern Arizona, then south along Mexico's Pacific coast. Coronado's later expedition, from Mexico north to Kansas, where he gave up his search for Indian cities of gold, occurred against the backdrop of Cabeza de Vaca's and Esteván's confused accounts of where they thought they had been.

As a boy, I came across a book that included a heroic portrait executed by Frederic Remington of the bearded, half-starved Cabeza de Vaca resting atop a bare rock with two Indian braves, looking out over a mesa-strewn emptiness of what would one day be called "Texas." He had wandered through this landscape in the 1530s. I recalled that portrait while traveling through the war-ravaged desert of Afghanistan in the 1980s, moving, like Cabeza de Vaca, on foot from village to village, scavenging for maize off the stalk, and, when I found none, living on boiled turnips and rice. Cabeza de Vaca's world no longer seemed so distant to me since I had experienced it in Afghanistan. Consequently, I would be mindful of the fragility of much of the economic development I would see in the American Southwest.

AT THE START of my land journey northwest from Mexico City to Topolobampo and beyond, I met a tough-looking young man with a cheaply made sports coat, a bad complexion, and callused hands. He was sitting beside me on the bus, reading a book. On its cover were pasted photographs of several nude blond women. I peeked over his shoulder: it was a guide to learning basic English. "Where are you going?" I asked. "To the United States, to look for work," he replied. He said he had no visa or green card. When I queried him further he became silent—suspicious, perhaps, of me. His eyes shifted between the road ahead and his language book. He never looked in my direction. I thought of the radio broadcasts I had heard about here, paid for by American companies, advertising for Mexicans to work on southwestern and midwestern pig farms.

It was the late-summer rainy season; iron-gray clouds hung low over a high, rolling, green plateau as I glanced through the window. Though Mexico did not share the poisoned ugliness of the environmentally ravaged ex–Soviet Union, or the bleak underdevelopment and deforestation of sub-Saharan Africa, it offered a familiar Third World prospect: cratered dirt roads leading off the main highway, overgrown and scruffy greenery, mounds of rotting garbage at the roadsides, elevated gas pipes covered with black tape, houses made of cinder block with rocks holding down corrugated iron roofs, and clothes drying on sagging lines. Puddles were everywhere: the effects of a poor drainage system or none at all.

After eight hours the bus reached Guadalajara, and I was grateful for the opportunity to take a walk. Beyond Guadalajara's historic center I saw what a European might notice on his or her first visit to America: the flattening out of the urban landscape, with wide streets creating intimidating distances between buildings. There were many fast-food outlets, each with its own large parking lot. I felt stranded without a car. Even in the vastnesses of Central Asia where I had traveled, the roads were narrow and people traveled by public bus; and because many of the towns were walkable, there was a vivid sense of huddled-together community. Guadalajara was different. The private American car dealerships and service stations were not gritty, marginalized places on the city's edge but modern emporia with snack bars and waiting rooms. Men with guns guarded the American Express office, as well as other banks on the yawning boulevards. Black graffiti were scrawled on new pink adobe houses. The empty, alienating vistas I had seen in parts of St. Louis and Omaha I saw here too in the heart of Mexico, whose civilization was under attack by our automobiles and our appetite for drugs.

"SON OF A bitch."

"Jesus Christ."

"Shit."

"Fuck."

On went the casual, matter-of-fact dialogue of an American-made karate film in the darkened bus. The passengers read the Spanish subtitles. The bus had left Guadalajara and was continuing northwest. When it slowed to a crawl in the town of Ixtlán del Río, I opened the curtains and saw dusty streets, broken sidewalks, windows protected by metal bars, a man slowly cutting sugarcane in worn and filthy clothes, women waiting in line with plastic buckets for water, peeling posters advertising a bullfight, and men wearing parts of uniforms and carrying AK-47 assault rifles. At one corner, there was a shrine covered in white tiles with busts of three early-twentieth-century revolutionaries: Francisco Madero, Venustiano Carranza, and Emiliano

Zapata. I knew that each had fought the other; that each had been assassinated.

Several hours later, I got off at Tepic, a city of 400,000 people, and checked into the Hotel Fray Junipero Serra. American rock music blared from the lobby and the corridors leading to my room. Later in the restaurant, half a dozen young men wearing jeans, T-shirts, and Nike Air track shoes entered. Two of the men carried magnum revolvers, which they carefully placed on the chair cushions and then sat on. They ate a three-course meal without the slightest show of discomfort. Except for me, no one gave them a glance.

The baroque cathedral across the street was all that seemed to remain of traditional Mexico. Beyond it, stretching in a grid pattern all the way to the surrounding volcanoes, were boxy two- and three-story, spray-painted buildings, many of them marred by graffiti. This was a treeless wilderness of broken signs, drooping electric wires, and hard right angles. The Old World had disappeared over the horizon—perhaps in the historic part of Guadalajara, with its mustard-yellow walls and dignified archways—with nothing but this architectural vacuum to replace it. Tepic was a town of the new Third World Sun Belt, sprinkled with the worst refuse of American capitalism.

"Compostela, Francisco Vázquez de Coronado?" I inquired at the hotel reception desk. One employee knew of Compostela; none of Coronado. At the municipal tourist office, too, Coronado was unheard of. When I told officials there that the little town of Compostela, forty minutes south of Tepic, was where Coronado (having arrived from Mexico City and Guadalajara) had mustered his troops for the exploration of the north, they stared at me uncomprehendingly. "Who was he?" one woman asked. She fished out a dusty, faded brochure with a paragraph about Compostela. It did not mention the Spanish explorer.[2] The past here seemed as blank as the urban landscape. Because so many Mexicans are of mixed Spanish *and* Indian origin and the rest mostly Indian, the attitude toward the Spanish conquerors who massacred Indians is highly ambivalent; yet they—like it or not—are also among Spanish America's "founding fathers." Few Mexican streets are named for Cortez, Coronado, and the like, and relatively little is taught about them in Mexican schools. This

[2]Coronado's muster in Compostela was held on February 22, 1540, 192 years to the day before George Washington was born. His was an army of three hundred Spaniards in mail coats on horseback, assisted by several hundred Indians. Coronado wore a "gilded suit with helmet and crested plume" on the day he set out.

denial of an important part of Mexico's past, in which one line of forebears murdered the other, both complicates and dilutes the meaning of a state that, while officially founded in 1821, ultimately grew from the Spanish conquest and the oligarchy it begot; an oligarchy that to a great degree still rules, as suggested by the light skins of Mexico's ruling class and the brown skins of Mexico's poor.[3]

I took a taxi to Compostela. The farmers in the sugarcane and avocado fields carried shotguns—"against thieves," the driver told me, since "the police provide no protection." Compostela was a mess of flooded streets, distempered walls and curbsides, mangy dogs, beeping video game machines, and a few satellite dishes. The potholes were as deep and numerous as any I had seen in sub-Saharan Africa. Opposite the sixteenth-century ocher-hued cathedral with a green dome—the only remnant of Spanish glory—were a few amusement park rides where a boom box blared heavy metal music. In the pouring rain, a few men in palm-leafed cowboy hats had taken refuge under the gazebo. I walked into a bar where a mariachi band performed for a few customers seated on broken-backed chairs. Rainwater dripped through the ceiling cracks into a few plastic pails behind the bar. At 3 P.M., the place smelled of beer, cigarettes, and mildew. The customers looked groggy.

Carlos had greasy black hair patched with gray; his shiny, coppery skin was pockmarked. He said he had lived for twenty-seven years in California and Nevada, but he spoke English badly. He had a green card, a girlfriend in California, and a wife in Compostela, he claimed. "The government here is good for shit. There is no money for roads. No police anywhere: Tell me, do you see police around here? But guns, yes, many guns. And no economy. The money goes into the politicians' pockets. Many little towns in Mexico are like this: dead, with no work for anyone. No matter. I can go to the States for work. In the States there are benefits for kids, welfare, food stamps. . . ."

CULIACÁN, THE CAPITAL of the drug-rich coastal state of Sinaloa (which includes the town of Topolobampo), lies three hundred miles

---

[3]Ulysses S. Grant, in his memoirs of the Mexican War, wrote that after the Mexican Revolution the Mexicans merely adopted Spain's former tyranny. Carlos Fuentes, in *The Old Gringo*, likens Mexico to a "child" forever trying to be born from a "dead womb." See also Nathan Gardels's interview with Octavio Paz in the Winter 1991 issue of *New Perspectives Quarterly*.

north of Tepic, through jungly mountain ranges and pine-clothed canyons. At Culiacán, Coronado resupplied his army before continuing north, and Cabeza de Vaca and his slave, Estevan, ended their horrific wanderings and reentered "New Spain." Stepping off the bus in Culiacán, the other passengers and I passed through a metal detector to enter the station hall. But the policeman on duty was sipping coffee, not paying attention. In the station hall I saw more armed police, hanging about like many of the young males, who wore silver-toed boots.

The temperature must have been 100 degrees on the sidewalks: they *baked*. The smells of frying tortillas, salsa, and urine were sharp and overpowering. Many of the men sported tattoos and baseball hats facing backward. Then there were the pickups: Chevy and Dodge Rams with oversized wheels and high suspensions, sporting fins, silver guardrails, and silver hood ornaments in the shape of bulls and horses. The pickups were all freshly painted. According to the published reports on the narcotics trade, it was obvious where the money for these vehicles had come from. The food stands were filthy, but in their midst I saw a new hotel, the Executivo, full of shiny marble and credit card stickers. The gift shop in the lobby sold only key chains, baseball hats, and cheap plastic toys.

Culiacán, nearby Topolobampo, and the rest of Sinaloa constitute a principal route of migration, trade, and cocaine headed for the United States. Culiacán is the Mexican version of Cali, Colombia. Nicknamed "Little Chicago" in Mexican news reports, Culiacán, a city of 600,000, averages several drug-related murders daily. Folk ballads such as "White Load" and "Death of a Snitch" glorify drug kingpins. Nowhere in the developing world had I seen so many handguns carried by men in civilian clothes.

The most popular religious site in Culiacán is a shrine dedicated to Jesús Malverde, a common criminal hanged in 1909 and now known as "El Narcosantón," the Big Narco Saint. Here drug lords come to pray for good fortune. The shrine is built of plate glass, white bathroom tiles, and corrugated sheet metal. It is covered with blue spray paint, tar, and cheap wallpaper. The walls don't quite fit the sheet-metal roof. The first time I walked past the shrine, I mistook it for a gas station or an auto parts shed, sandwiched as it was between two dusty lots and obscured by a taco stand. When I saw it a second time, I noticed three young men in tight jeans praying before the painted plastic doll of Jesús Malverde, while behind the makeshift shrine two other men played a sad tune on a bass fiddle and a wheezing accordion. The plastic statue was surrounded by red drinking glasses filled with burning wax. I bought an amulet containing a photograph of the Narco Saint from an old woman. She dipped it into a sink of holy water and rubbed it over the face and black-painted hair of the statue before handing it to me for the equivalent of five dollars. Meanwhile, a stream of people—young toughs, old women, and children— stopped to pray. The local newspapers said that among the drug traffickers who prayed here was Rafael Caro Quintero, who allegedly ordered the 1985 slaying of the American undercover agent Enrique Camarena.

But as crass and brutal as the shrine was, it was *real:* the poor had built it with their bare hands from scraps of junk, without planning or authorization from the authorities, and now they were filling it with their emotions. It was a true holy place. With its spray paint and gas station decor, the shrine rebukes established aesthetics: another sign of revolt. A hundred yards away is the massive ceramic-and-stone Government Palace of Sinaloa, with its manicured lawns and hundreds of white-collar workers. But I saw less energy and spontaneity in that giant building than in the shrine that could have fit inside one of the palace's offices.

As I closed in on the U.S. border, the architecture became increasingly oppressive. Even the newest poured concrete and tinted glass structures in Culiacán looked temporary: disconnected from any known past or imaginable future. This was *America,* a land without limits and of chronic impermanence, unprotected and unhindered by tradition.

Nobody with whom I spoke at the tourist office in Culiacán knew who Coronado or Cabeza de Vaca was. Here too, history was irrelevant. As the new buildings suggested, from such a vacuum wealth is easily—if too quickly and unequally—created, and drugs are only partly the reason. Sinaloa produces three quarters of Mexico's soybeans and a third of its sesame seeds. Its hotels are crowded with American businesspeople such as Fritz Monson opening factories. Employment opportunities here draw migrants from poorer Mexican provinces. The drug trade is just another business: another opportunity for those with ambition.

I was struck by the pervasiveness of uniformed schoolchildren with backpacks. While I walked along a sun-blasted street suffused with pink, dusty light—the cardboard of my notebook damp with sweat inside my pants pocket—I noticed a classroom of children through the rusted grillwork of a window set in the brick schoolhouse wall. There was no air-conditioning in the powdery heat, yet I saw some of these children raising their hands to answer the teacher's questions while others wrote quietly in their exercise books. In a nearby candy store, locals of several generations gathered to buy knickknacks, exchange gossip, and, in the case of the children, play games. This community was far from devastated. Its children seemed to have the advantages of family life that many Americans of their age in inner cities do not have. In a transnational North America, would these children in Culiacán end up in ten or twenty years competing with less competent, less determined Americans of their own generation? While the sleazy aspect of Mexico's border culture is obvious to Americans, Americans may be less aware that an aggressive middle class is burgeoning in such cities as Culiacán, Guadalajara, and Mexico City; as more of its members decide to head north if central authority continues to break down, they will not face the same racial barriers that blacks do. In the municipal park, not fifty feet from where hoodlums with tattoos and beepers were having their silver-toed boots shined while they talked on cellular phones, I saw several neatly dressed teenage couples, holding hands, who looked straight out of Orange County.

To pigeonhole Culiacán as a drug depot would be to miss the point. The multibillion-dollar narcotics trade in Mexico is simply too vast to be dismissed as "illegal." It is the heart of the Mexican economy and constitutes the principal economic fact of life for the southern part of North America at the turn of the twenty-first century: the subterranean aspect of North American free trade that does not require treaties or congressional approval.[4] The narcotics trade indicates as much about the social fiber of the United States (where the market is) as about Mexico, where young men on the make are responding to consumer demand in ways that both challenge and further corrupt an already imploding political power structure. I walked around frequently at night in Culiacán, when the candles burned bright amid the crowds at the shrine of El Narcosantón. As dangerous as Culiacán was by Mexican standards, it was safe by those of some American cities. For me, Mexico's "Cali" was also a civil society, whose growing

[4]Former president Carlos Salinas de Gortari says that Mexico's drug cartels net $30 billion annually, more than the 1995 U.S. bailout of Mexico's economy. Mexico expert Charles Bowden writes in "While You Were Sleeping," "The dimensions of the dope business are simple: without it the Mexican economy would totally collapse."

middle class will increasingly be pursuing opportunities in the United States.

THE BUS PLIED north into the Sonora Desert, a cindery wasteland stubbled with thorns, where I came upon more towns with block-house architecture and little evidence of tradition, as if you could see right through these buildings, as you could though the gaunt, spindly creosote bushes. In these fast-buck towns, I heard gunfire and obscenities issuing from loud video game machines. But along with the young men wearing dark glasses and tight jeans bulging with pistols, and the policemen with white T-shirts and black chinos carrying assault weapons—who conducted useless, cursory inspections of bus passengers—I also saw throngs of neatly dressed children and teenagers with schoolbooks. And as the bus stopped at a succession of stations featuring broken fluorescent lights, zinc kitchen tables, greasy food, and heavily thumbed comic books for sale, places where the word *Caballeros* (Men) was scrawled in crayon on peeling restroom doors and where I washed my hands in an open oil drum while mosquitoes whined and an old man politely acknowledged the peso I gave him, I encountered a steady stream of people heading north. Many were young, humbly dressed, and perhaps humbly educated, like the fellow learning English from the book covered with photos of nude women. At the close of the twentieth century there were evidently cities of gold on the other side of this bleak desert terrain, which new Spanish-speaking adventurers, now millions of them—creatures of a medieval faith like that of Coronado and his soldiers but sustained by a work ethic now driven by global materialism—might conquer and, in so doing, subtly transform.

12

Upheavals and Transformations

THE BUS CONTINUED north. Thick-columned saguaro cacti began to appear, like giant totem poles. For the first time since I had left Mexico City for Guadalajara, the bus was filled. But the passengers were now of a rougher sort. There were fewer families and more individual young men: more tattoos and gold chains. The seedy ambience, with its hint of violence, hinted also of opportunity. The beggars at the bus stations were no longer passive. They cursed and complained if you refused them money, as the homeless in the United States sometimes do. Here I saw no crowded kiosks and candy stores. Everyone seemed busy doing something. Women rushed here and there in tight shorts with rollers in their hair. I saw more children with knapsacks bulging with books; even in playgrounds they were relatively quiet and focused, requiring little supervision.

Rome had been transformed by the migration of millions of determined people from northern Europe, Asia, and North Africa: Visigoths, Huns, Vandals, and so on. Even had Rome possessed the vibrant, flexible institutions we do, it would still have given way to a jigsaw of smaller polities—though the transformation would have been more peaceful and gradual. Success, like failure, breeds its own instability. Rome's very culture and economic dynamism had attracted the "barbarians" who toppled it. Would America's effect on Mexicans and other Third World citizens have similar consequences?

*   *   *

NORTHERN MEXICO, ESPECIALLY Sonora, is *"más gringo,"* Rosa Delia Caudillo, a Hermosillo psychologist and relief worker, told me. "It is more developed, more middle-class, and more rootless—like the U.S.A. There is greater individuality and less community life here. Divorce rates are greater." These trends have been rapidly intensifying in the 1980s and 1990s. Because of the growth of *maquilladoras*—American-owned factories where American component parts are assembled as finished products for re-export back to the United States—cheap labor is replacing settled agriculture as the backbone of the local economy.

What we call "the border" has always been a wild, unstable swath of desert, hundreds of miles wide, where culture was always as thin as the vegetation: a region that the Aztecs, cruel as they were, could not control; that the Apaches brutalized in eighteenth- and nineteenth-century raids; and in which U.S. soldiers unsuccessfully chased the bandit revolutionary Pancho Villa. "The greatest obstacles to colonial expansion into this region were almost all 'natural,' " writes scholar Daniel Nugent, "a harsh climate, scarcity of water, great physical distances separating the region from the center and each 'civilized' settlement from the next."[1]

The bus came around a low rise, and a long, narrow belt of factories and shanties stretched out almost to the horizon between brown hills studded with juniper and sagebrush. This was the border town of Nogales: a crowded warren of distempered stucco facades spray-painted with swastikas and commercial graffiti; broken plastic and neon signs; garish wall drawings of the Flintstones and other television icons. Among these images were the industrial *maquilladora* plants that Rosa Caudillo had told me about that attract blue-collar workers from throughout Mexico.

The migration has spawned shantytowns and violent crime, drug and alcohol abuse, class conflict, the breakup of families, and unemployment, since not all of the immigrants find jobs. Rape and car accidents are more common in the north than in the rest of Mexico. From 1968 through 1995, more than two thousand companies lo-

---

[1]Nugent, *Spent Cartridges of Revolution: An Anthropological History of Namiquipa, Chihuahua.* Though it focuses on Chihuahua, the border province to the east of Sonora, a subtext of Nugent's work is the historic thinness of civilization in northern and northwestern Mexico.

cated in this region, causing what the American Medical Association calls a "cesspool" of polluted air, contaminated groundwater and surface water, unsanitary waste dumps, and other health and environmental problems associated with uncontrolled urban growth.[2] It is a latter-day gold rush—with its ugly upheaval and bright promise—but on a vaster scale and more likely to be permanent.

Many of our microwaves, televisions, VCRs, toasters, toys, and everyday clothes are made by Mexican laborers along this border, who earn between three and five dollars a day—not an hour, but a day!—often in dangerous conditions. American consumers are now in a tight political-economic relationship with Third World workers. But the relationship is oligarchal, like that between the citizens of ancient Athens or Rome and their slaves.

I also saw evidence of easy money: bars, nightclubs, cheap hotels, and souvenir stores; too many pool halls, "happy hour" signs, and heavily armed police in shiny Dodge Ram pickups; too many men in designer jeans with beepers or holding cellular phones and other light communications gear. Instead of rusted bicycles without locks, for the first time in Mexico I saw expensive mountain bikes double-chained to metal posts. In one window display a cellular phone stuck out of a cowboy boot with a black alligator design and a white leather, pointed tip. Nogales, Sonora, was the compressed summation of the aesthetic and communal abyss that I had seen expanding since Guadalajara.[3]

I checked into a hotel and then walked toward the international border, where I watched two boys kick a soccer ball made of rags until one of them kicked the ball onto a scrap-iron roof. When the ball failed to roll back down, the boys walked away. I saw a group of teenagers with punk haircuts dyed in primary colors, wearing expensive leather belts, winter ski hats, and summer shorts—anything they could get their hands on. Their expressions were untamed. A hundred yards from the border there began a final concentration of scrap-iron storefronts offering every manner of souvenir and after-hours activity, including off-track betting, where I saw crowds of destitute people reeking of alcohol. Edward Gibbon, in *The History of the*

---

[2]See Robert G. Varady et al., "The Sonoran Pimeria Alta: Shared Environmental Problems and Challenges."

[3]I agree with what William Langewiesche wrote in *Cutting for Sign*, a travelogue of the Mexican-U.S. frontier: "The border is transient. The border is dangerous. The border is crass. It is not the place to visit on your next vacation."

Decline and Fall of the Roman Empire, writes that the fifth-century Goths "imbibed the vices, without imitating the arts and institutions, of civilised [Roman] society." What I saw at the border is nothing new.

The actual border on "International Street," as it is called, is a twelve-foot-high, darkly rusted "iron curtain," constructed by the American authorities from scraps of sheet iron that the U.S. Army had brought back from Vietnam and the Persian Gulf.[4] Standing back from this wall a bit, I could make out the neat squares and rectangular roofs of the houses high on the hills of the American side, where it was obvious that every joint fit and every part was standardized, in contrast to the amateurish, inspired godowns all around me.

From the "iron curtain" I walked back into this Mexican border town. Nogales, Sonora, officially has 108,000 inhabitants and unofficially more than 200,000. Its population growth rate—because of a high birthrate and persistent migration from the south—has been an astounding 4.2 percent yearly. This means that Nogales's population doubles every sixteen and a half years. In 1980, there were about half as many people in Nogales as at the end of 1995. Many of the migrants come from Sinaloa and the southern part of Sonora to work in the city's eighty *maquilladoras,* which employ 40 percent of the city's labor force. Areas further south in Mexico are emptying out, while the population and social problems along the border continue to mount. Whole sections of Nogales have no running water or sewage lines. "Crime has jumped off the charts," a social worker told me. Still, Nogales is less violent, less dilapidated, and smaller than Ciudad Juárez three hundred miles to the east, opposite El Paso, Texas, where civil order has to a large extent broken down, where all the homes other than those of the poor have electronic surveillance systems, and where a U.S. drug enforcement agent was shot on sight by a thirteen-year-old Mexican in 1995.

"The border used to be for entrepreneurs, people of high incomes," Francisco Lara Valencia, a local economist, told me. "But now the local reality is driven by people from the bottom of the social ladder. We used to have just migrants here; now we have a whole generation who are the children of migrants. At the end of the twentieth century we have what we never had before: not just a border, but a whole border culture of poverty and unemployment."

Though, here, in the midst of a city, the border looked forbidding,

---

[4]A more architecturally attractive fence was constructed in 1997, after my visit.

out in the desert it would ebb to a few strands of barbed wire, which work only to keep cattle from migrating. Along the narrow Rio Grande in Texas, there is no fence at all, nor any natural obstruction—no mountain range or wide, surging river—and the border is easily penetrable. The military radar used by U.S. border guards is like a penlight in a dark forest. An artificial, purely legal construct, the border will one day revert to what it always has been: an unruly, politically ambiguous "brown zone" of desert, several hundred miles wide, where civilizations (Spanish and Anglo, Athapaskan-speaking Indians from the Arctic, and Aztecán Indians from southern Mexico) once mingled. "No one has ever really been stopped at the border," the saying goes, "only delayed."[5]

The factors that have kept Mexico at bay so far—drug profits and the sent-home wages of illegal aliens—are the very ones Washington claims it wants to stop. But without drugs and illegals, the United States might face what it has always feared, a real revolution in Mexico and true chaos on the border. To deprive Mexico of its largest sources of income would threaten the collapse of the country's central authority. Given the porous nature of the border, people in the American Southwest would, as I would later be told, sacrifice almost any principle to avoid such a catastrophe. Indeed, America's appetite for marijuana and cocaine, by artificially supporting and disfiguring the Mexican economy, now provides strategic protection against a further flood of immigrants from a contiguous, troubled, and ever more populous Third World country.

The unpalatable truth about Mexico is its intractability: the intractability of an ancient and populous "hydraulic" civilization, like Egypt's, China's, and India's, in which the need to build great water- and earthworks (Mexico has experienced the building of both canal systems and pyramids) led to vast, bureaucratic tyrannies, which have existed in one form or another for so many centuries that the political culture, even with multiparty democracy, is well embedded, despite the influence of the great civilization to the north. Nor is it clear

---

[5]This, in fact, was starting to happen. The border was being assaulted by hordes of migrants who crossed at night and even in broad daylight, in the desert not far from the "iron curtain" in Nogales. In 1994, despite a general amnesty granted eight years before, Texas still had more than 550,000 illegal Mexican aliens, and California Governor Pete Wilson had declared California "under siege" by illegal aliens. In fact, an estimated 10 percent of Mexico's population— 9 to 10 million people—actually live in the United States. See Douglas Payne, "Mexico and Its Discontents."

that our influence on Mexico is more beneficial than not. Our great appetite for drugs may be turning this ancient non-Western civilization into an amoral, yet dynamic beast of the twenty-first century.

Meanwhile, integration proceeds irreversibly. Vectors of binationhood have emerged between Phoenix and Guaymas, Tucson and Los Mochis, Dallas and Chihuahua City, and so on, in which prosperous Mexicans and Americans commute back and forth by air. While California's hostility to more Mexican immigration was widely reported in the mid-1990s, such Texas politicians as Governor George Bush Jr. and Senator Phil Gramm have sought more links with Mexico. The different responses of California and Texas to the Mexican challenge are geographically determined: while major urban attractors such as Los Angeles are close to the Mexican border, which makes California vulnerable to illegal immigrants, Texas is not quite in the same situation (El Paso's population is only 515,000, compared to 3.5 million for only Los Angeles). Moreover, Mexico's Pacific coast, adjoining California, has always been a route of trade and migration. And while northwestern Mexico lacks an urban attractor to compete with Los Angeles, in northeastern Mexico, Monterrey, the country's third largest city with 2.2 million inhabitants, is booming and industrialized and retains many migrants who would otherwise threaten Texas.[6] Thus, despite the noisy political war over immigration in California in the mid-1990s, the remelding of Texas and northeastern Mexico is history, quietly in the making.

There is, too, a burgeoning network of binational business and relief organizations, like the new Arizona-Sonora Chamber of Commerce, and the Sonoran Institute in Tucson, an environmental organization whose purpose, according to what one of its officials, Wendy Laird, told me, "is to blow the border apart and link communities on each side." Rosa Caudillo had said in Hermosillo, "A progressive person today is binational, because there is globalization not just from above," with these new cross-border organizations, "but from below, too," with the press of legal and illegal immigrants.[7] I wondered

---

[6]Of course, the Tijuana area, with a population recently estimated at 1.9 million, is adjacent to San Diego and nearly as populous as Monterrey. But Tijuana retains the character of an overgrown border settlement rather than of a more stable, urban community such as Monterrey. Therefore, a Mexican is much more likely to want to escape Tijuana than Monterrey.

[7]The Colorado, Santa Cruz, and San Pedro river systems, as well as numerous tributary washes, also disregard the border. The same underground aquifers supply both Mexico and the United States. In 1989, when a drought stopped

whether the two Indian tribes, the Cocopah and the Kikapu, who slip back and forth across the border and have dual Mexican-American citizenship, were a model for the future, as the sheer volume of trade and humanity to and fro erodes nationalist resistance in both countries.

The French historian Fernand Braudel—whose book I had seen in the ex-minister's study in Mexico City—believed that geography ultimately determines everything. North America's geographical destiny may be not east to west but one in which the arbitrary lines separating us from Mexico and Canada will disappear, even as relations between the East Coast and Europe, the West Coast and Asia, and the Southwest and Mexico all intensify. Two other French thinkers, Michel Foucault and Claude Lévi-Strauss, believe that there may be no end, or beginning, to history: only continual upheavals and transformations beyond the reach of moral or political purpose.

Mexico's evolution suggests as much. In the early sixteenth century, settled Indian nomads, the Aztecs, whose distant ancestors had come from the eastern rim of Asia, were conquered by men from the western rim of Europe, Spanish soldiers of fortune, who had negated the ocean through a revolution in shipbuilding. Neither the Indians nor these Spanish conquerors had experienced anything like the European Enlightenment, upon whose principles of free inquiry, opportunity, and justice the United States was founded. But now Mexico's Old World mestizo society is blending in unpredictable ways with our own Enlightened one. Not just Mexico but the United States, too, may be developing a new, highly ambiguous culture.

Is our border with Mexico like the Great Wall of China: an artificial barrier in the desert built to keep out nomadic Turkic tribesmen but which, as Gibbon writes, while holding "a conspicuous place in the map of the world . . . never contributed to the safety" of the Chinese?

It was time to cross the scrap-iron fence.

---

the flow of water into the homes of Nogales, Sonora, officials in Nogales, Arizona, allowed water to be pumped at no cost across the frontier into waiting trucks. Sewage and pollution from Mexico cross the border to the United States, contaminating the groundwater and the air, leading to complaints from Americans, but also to aid. See Varady et al., "The Sonoran Pimeria Alta."

13

Across the Great Wall of China

I HAD CROSSED the Berlin Wall several times during the Communist era. I had crossed the border from Iraq to Iran illegally with Kurdish rebels. I had crossed from Jordan to Israel and from Pakistan to India in the 1970s, and from Greek Cyprus to Turkish Cyprus in the 1980s. In 1983, coming from Damascus, Syria, I had walked up to within a few yards of the first Israeli soldier in the demilitarized zone on the Golan Heights. But never in my life had I experienced such a sudden transition as when I crossed from Nogales, Sonora, to Nogales, Arizona, on November 1, 1995. It would help me understand America's urban transformation.

SURROUNDED BY BEGGARS on the broken sidewalk of Mexican Nogales, I stared at "Old Glory" snapping in the breeze over two white McDonald's-like arches, which marked the international crossing point. Cars waited in the inspection lanes. The pedestrian crossing point was in a small building constructed by the U.S. government to the left of the car lanes. The building's glass doors were the actual border; by merely touching the door handle, one entered a new physical world.

The solidly constructed handle with its high-quality metal, the clean glass, and the precise manner in which the room's ceramic tiles were fitted—each the same millimetric distance from the other—seemed a revelation to me after the chaos of Mexican construction. There were only two people in the room: an immigration official, who checked identification documents before one passed through a metal detector, and a customs official, who stood by the luggage X-ray machine. Both were quiet; neither talked to the other. In government enclosures of that size in Mexico and other places in the Third World, I remembered crowds of officials and hangers-on lost in animated discussion while sipping tea or coffee. Looking through the window at the car lanes, I saw how few people there were to garrison the border station, yet how efficiently it ran.

I gave the immigration official, a woman, my U.S. passport. She looked up at me and asked how long I had been in Mexico. I told her several weeks. She asked, "Why so long?" I explained that I was a journalist. She handed me back my passport. With her eyes, she motioned me through the metal detector. The customs official did not ask me to put my rucksack through the machine. The U.S. Customs Service works on "profiles"; evidently I did not look suspect. Less than sixty seconds after walking through the glass doors on the Mexico side, I entered the United States.

The billboards, sidewalks, traffic markers, telephone and electric cables, and so on all appeared straight, all their curves and angles uniform. The perfect standardization made for a cold, alienating landscape after what I had grown used to in Mexico. The store logos were made of expensive, tony polymers rather than cheap plastic. I heard no metal rattling in the wind. The cars were the same makes I had seen in Mexico, but *oh,* were they different: no more chewed-up, rusted bodies; no more cracked windshields held together by black tape; no more crosses and other good-luck charms hanging inside the windshields; no more noise from broken mufflers.

The taxi I entered had shock absorbers. The neutral gray upholstery was not ripped or shredded. The meter printed out receipts. As I sunk into the soft upholstery for the ride to the hotel, I felt as though I had entered a protective, ordered bubble. I do not mean only that the taxi was a bubble; rather, this whole new place was one.

The Plaza Hotel in Nogales, Sonora, and the Americana Hotel in Nogales, Arizona, both charged $50 for a single room. But while the Mexican hotel was only two years old, it was already falling apart: the doors did not close properly, the paint was cracking, the walls were beginning to stain. The Americana Hotel in Nogales, Arizona, was a quarter century old and in excellent condition, from the fresh paint to the latest fixtures. The air-conditioning in the Americana Hotel was quiet, unlike the loud clanking across the border. There was no mold or peeling paint in the swimming pool outside my window. Here there was potable tap water. Was the developed world, I wondered, defined not by its riches or a lighter skin color but by maintenance? Maintenance indicates settlement rather than nomadism; faith in—and thus planning for—the future, rather than the expectation that what is here today might be gone tomorrow. Maintenance indicates organization, frugality, and responsibility: you don't build what you lack the money, the time, and the determination to maintain. Maintenance manifests a community and a system of obligation, without which substantial development is unlikely. Maintenance reflects the prudent use of capital.

As I walked around Nogales, Arizona, what I saw was a way of doing things differently from Mexico's that, in turn, had created material wealth. This was not a matter of Anglo culture per se, since 96 percent of the population of Nogales, Arizona, is of Mexican descent and Spanish speaking. I mean the national culture of the United States, which seemed to me in Nogales that day sufficiently robust to absorb other peoples and other languages without losing its distinctiveness.

The people I saw on the street were, in most instances, speaking Spanish, but to me they might as well have been speaking English. Whether it was the high quality of their leisure clothes, their purposeful stride—indicating that they were going somewhere, rather than just hanging out—the absence of hand movements when they talked, or the impersonal and mechanical friendliness of their voices when I asked directions, they seemed to me thoroughly *modern* compared to the Spanish speakers over in Sonora.

Mario Soares, the former prime minister and president of Portugal, once said that the language you speak determines what you are. Now I was not so sure. Perhaps English was not so important to the United States after all. Henry James, after reconciling himself to the fact of immigration, noted, "The accent of the very ultimate future, in the States, may be destined to become the most beautiful on the globe and the very music of humanity . . . but whatever we shall know it for, certainly, we shall not know it for English." A state of mind, rather than a religious denomination or a linguistic style, is what defines America. (Here was what the author Michael Lind calls the "Trans-American cultural nation," even if the tie of language was missing. Elsewhere, though, my experience did not generally bear out Lind's vision of a nation as solid and identifiable as in the past.)

Though the expression *"ambos Nogales"* (both Nogaleses) asserts a common identity, the differences between the two towns are basic, physical. Nogales, Arizona, covers somewhat less land area than Nogales, Sonora, but has only 21,000 residents, a fairly precise figure, while nobody in Nogales, Sonora, has any idea how many people reside there. (The official figure is 108,000, but I heard unofficial ones as high as 300,000.[1]) Here the streets were quiet and spotless, with far fewer people and cars than in Mexico. Distances, as a consequence, seemed vast. Taxis did not prowl the streets, and thus I was truly stranded without a car of my own. I had reached a part of the earth where business was not conducted in public and thus street life was sparse. There was much less to catch the eye, since American civilization is driven largely by economic and technological progress rather than by tradition and ideology. The posturban pods I had seen in southern California and the Midwest showed how such progress and technology are shaping habitation patterns.

When the English and other northern European settlers swept across this mainly uninhabited land with their bourgeois values, then and there the past was left behind; technology and the use of capital have determined nearly everything since. Because subsequent immigrants sought opportunity, the effect of periodic waves of immigration has been to erase the past again and again, replacing one technology with another. In America economic efficiency, as these streets in Nogales, Arizona, proclaimed, is everything. Liberals may warn against social Darwinism, but the replacement of obsolete technology and the jobs and social patterns that go with it is what our history has always been about, because immigrants—like Zaheer Virji and Vincent Diau in Los Angeles and the Mexican Americans here (as I would learn)—want it that way. For them it means liberation: the chance to succeed or fail and to be judged purely by their own talents, energies, and good fortune.

In Mexico, the dusty post offices had looked as if they had just been vacated, with papers askew and furniture missing. In Nogales, Arizona, the Spanish voices in the post office were the last thing I noticed; what struck me immediately was the neat piles of printed forms,

---

[1]Nobody really keeps figures about the populations of the other Mexican border towns either. Ciudad Juárez, for example, reportedly has 2 million inhabitants, but the real number is anybody's guess.

the big wall clock that worked, the bulletin board with community advertisements in neat columns, the people waiting quietly in line, and a policeman standing slightly hunched over in the corner, carefully going through his paperwork, so unlike the leering, swaggering police I had seen in Mexico.

I noticed a park nearby where some kids were kicking a new soccer ball on a landscaped field, with a baseball diamond and a plastic castle. I thought of the two boys kicking the rag ball in the street a mile away, on the other side of the frontier.

The silent streets of Nogales, Arizona, with their display of non-coercive order and industriousness, cast the United States in a different light not only from Mexico but from the other countries I had seen in my travels. Nogales, Arizona, demonstrated just how wonderfully unique and insulated America has been—thus far at least. In America, a travel writer has no exotic props at his disposal.[2]

"WE IN NOGALES, Arizona, pay taxes to Uncle Sam, but what happens in Mexico affects us more than what happens in the United States. Eight of ten shoppers in this town are Mexicans from over the border. Because of the latest peso devaluation, their buying power is down, so now they don't shop. Unemployment here is twenty-five percent. The reason the streets are quiet is not only because it's the orderly U.S., but because this part of Arizona is in a recession caused by the Mexican economy."

Louie Valdez, whose great-granduncle was a Mexican guerrilla in Pancho Villa's army, looked like a bond trader with his wire-framed glasses, neutral green shirt, and paisley tie. Seeing me glance at the square yellow stickers all over his desk, he noted, "Yeah, I'm from the Post-it generation." He continued, "When I was ten years old, I went on a trip all the way across the country to Washington, D.C. It was my first time away from Arizona. We went to the National Archives and saw the Constitution and Declaration of Independence framed under spotlights. I was a little kid. The documents looked bigger than I was.

[2]Nathaniel Hawthorne wrote in *The Marble Faun,* "No author, without a trial, can conceive of the difficulty of writing a romance about a country where there is no shadow, no antiquity, no mystery, no picturesque and gloomy wrong, nor anything but a commonplace prosperity, in broad and simple daylight, as is happily the case with my dear native land. . . . Romance and poetry, ivy, lichens, and wallflowers need ruin to make them grow." Slavery, of course, was the "gloomy wrong" Hawthorne overlooked.

I was awed. It's corny, but that trip was the highlight of my youth. All I ever wanted to do afterwards was go into politics." At twenty-one, Valdez was elected to the local school board. In January 1995, at age twenty-four, he was elected the youngest currently serving mayor of an incorporated city in the United States.

"NAFTA [the North American Free Trade Agreement] is a charade," Valdez told me. "Quite a few Mexican Americans here will tell you that [Pat] Buchanan and [Ross] Perot are right. Of course, I understand the macro, geopolitical need for NAFTA. I know that the Berlin Wall fell, that we're in a global village and all that. But we in Nogales fall through the cracks when the border eventually dissolves." Valdez handed me a doleful letter from a Tennessee-based company, informing him that it would be closing its plant in Nogales, perhaps to open a new one in Mexico, where wages are lower.

"We don't want an open border where all of Mexico's problems come here. People were happy to see that corrugated iron wall go up along the border; it has reduced crime, because poor Mexicans have a harder time sneaking across. We don't want a free flow of truck traffic through the border that congests our streets and pollutes our air. I agree, in fifty years we may be at the center of a prosperous, bi-national region. But between now and then, we will not be able to handle Mexico's problems. . . . We're Americans, which means that we have rights. In Mexico, human rights are a farce. That's why we're ultranationalist. Many people here think, 'Why does someone in Sonora come over to our side? He comes to have kids, to go on welfare.' This infuriates people. The public here does not want people who cannot make it on their own."

Valdez added, "I live a mile from the border. At night I hear sirens, gunfire, the rumble of the border patrol vehicles in the hills."

"What's going to happen in Mexico at the turn of the century?" I asked Valdez.

"Forget the poor. It will be the growing middle class in Mexico that will make a truly great political upheaval within the next ten or twelve years. But it could be an upheaval without resolution, like in Mexico's past. Then watch out: nobody in Washington will be able to help us down here."

NEXT I SAW Brendan FitzSimons, the Irish immigrant editor of the *Nogales International.* He told me, "The war on drugs is a joke."

FitzSimons wondered if in a few decades "you'll find cocaine and marijuana on Safeway shelves, taxed to the hilt like cigarettes. At the moment, Nogales, Arizona, and McAllen, Texas, are the main entry points for cocaine in the U.S. The people in New York and Boston are getting cocaine through our streets. If the small-plane traffic is lighter in the surrounding desert, it is only because the Mexicans are now flying the cocaine on 707s and 737s direct from big Mexican airports."

Over the coming weeks I heard this again and again. At the border issues such as drugs and illegal immigration are not moral and political abstractions as they are elsewhere in America, particularly in Washington, D.C. Listening to county sheriffs, city officials, young professionals, economists, and journalists such as FitzSimons who live close to Mexico talk about drugs was to see the problem in terms of actual shades of gray rather than in black-and-white absolutes. Only when I was several hundred miles north of the border did people talk about the war on drugs as a serious endeavor.

A few weeks later, to investigate the drug problem further, I drove back southeast from Tucson to meet John E. Pintek, sheriff of Cochise County, along the border just east of Nogales. In the lobby of the Cochise County jail I saw photos of Pintek's predecessors, including "Texas John" Slaughter and C. S. Fly, who had run a photography shop next door to the O.K. Corral in nearby Tombstone, at the time of the famous 1881 gunfight. Pintek was in his midfifties, with gray hair turning white. He was the first sheriff in the county's history whose official picture showed him without the customary sheriff's badge and cowboy hat. Nevertheless, his deep twang and blunt talk were typical of western lawmen. Pintek was the son of a late-nineteenth-century Croatian immigrant. When I asked what he thought about the current Balkan crisis, he shrugged: "Just a bunch of crazy people *killin'* each other."

Cochise County, named after the famous Apache warrior who battled settlers here in the 1860s, is 6,300 square miles of desert, larger than Connecticut. Because almost every phone call within the county is a toll call, Pintek has a toll-free number. As for the war on drugs, Pintek said, "Cochise County comprises eighty-two miles of Mexico's border with the U.S. The BAG [Border Alliance Group] has eleven people from seven different agencies to patrol these eighty-two miles. There's a [radar] balloon that has more or less stopped small-plane traffic here. But the stuff enters by land all the time. When you catch someone, he'll say to you in Spanish, 'You caught me, but nine others got through.' That's about accurate: for dopers, a ten percent merchandise loss because of drug busts is just the price of doing business. Now, think about that. Think about the fact that your average quickservice convenience store in the Southwest loses maybe thirteen percent of its merchandise through shoplifting and still does okay. Unlike the convenience stores, the dopers have no overhead: no insurance costs or pensions they have to pay. And you know what happens when you confiscate their cars in the course of a bust: they just buy them back at auction. The border towns of Douglas and Nogales—I'd say about sixty percent of their economies are drug-driven; the figure for the retail economy in Tucson would be twenty-five percent, I'd guess."

A Tucson economist explained to me how "drugs cushion the retail trade" throughout the Southwest. "Where else are these people from Sonora getting their money to buy six-foot TVs, Dodge trucks, Chevy pickups, Estes homes, and other expensive consumer goods? Have you been into Sonora? There's nothing there except for low-wage *maquilladora* jobs. A guy will bring his grandmother up to a Tucson hospital for a gallbladder operation and pay for it in cash. He'll say he's a rancher in Sonora. More likely, he's got an airstrip on his ranch that's used for you-know-what." The conventional wisdom in southern Arizona is that *drugs are the substitute economy that helped Mexico survive the 1994–95 peso crisis without violence.*

Pintek agreed that Mexico needs the income from both drugs and illegal immigration to remain economically stable. "Of course," he said, "few people here in Cochise County use drugs. They can't afford it! The dopers sell the stuff for so much more in Phoenix. The stuff just passes through."

The real issue concerning drug use was not how to stop it: that was probably impossible and, perhaps, not even completely desirable given the risks to Mexican stability. Rather, drug use interested me because of what it said about American society and where it might be headed. Writing in 1921 in *The Atlantic Monthly,* philosopher Bertrand Russell explained that because modern life is often "a life against instinct," many people lead lives that are "listless and trivial, in constant search of excitement." In the twenty-first century, with its additional conveniences and simulation, life will be lived even further "against instinct." Will the use of consciousness-altering drugs increase, perhaps legally by means of substances promoted by the pharmaceutical lobby?

PART
V

SEPARATE NATIONS

14

The First Oasis

INTERSTATE 19 FROM Nogales to Tucson was a typical American four-lane highway with luminous metallic signs and landscaped roadsides, unlike the mud puddles and trails of garbage that began an inch from the road in Mexico. The bus passed through Green Valley, a high-income retirement community with Spanish archways and upscale minimalls. Still fresh from Mexico, I gawked at the prosperity: people with coppery tans, expensive sunglasses, and golf shirts carrying groceries to late-model cars. I thought of the tens of millions of poor people just over the "iron curtain" thirty minutes to the south—so much younger than the population on this side of the border. While the median age in Mexico is seventeen, in this part of Arizona it is thirty-three and rising quickly. If the history of migration is a guide, borders like this one, not based on geographical barriers, may slow and interrupt great movements of humanity; ultimately, they will not stop them.

A cluster of dramatic, sun-beaten escarpments a pitiless gray in color—the Santa Catalina Mountains in the north, the Tucson Mountains to the west, the Rincon Mountains to the east—announced Tucson. Greater Tucson, with a population of 779,000, is larger than Atlanta, Miami, St. Louis, Minneapolis, Pittsburgh, or Cincinnati.[1]

---

[1] This figure includes incorporated suburban townships; otherwise the population is 450,000.

The recent settlement of the arid Southwest is an even more intense result of the flight to the suburbs than I saw on the midwestern
prairie. Eighty-five percent of Arizonans live in either greater Tucson
or Phoenix. By the middle of the next century, 98 percent of them
will live in those metropolitan areas.[2] The Arizonan pattern suggests
what is happening throughout the arid West, as small towns die and
suburbs around big cities grow by an acre an hour.[3] The West, despite
its mythic grandeur, is actually the most crowded, urbanized part of
the United States.[4]

THOUGH THE TUCSON region has been continuously inhabited for
more than 12,000 years, the first European to see it was the Spanish
missionary Fray Marcos de Niza, a barefoot friar-adventurer, who
passed through here in 1539, a year before Coronado. His highly
exaggerated accounts of "cities of gold" helped precipitate Coronado's doomed odyssey. The Spaniards named the town they eventually founded "Tucson," a Spanish corruption of a Pima Indian word
meaning "foot of a dark mountain." Control of Tucson went from
Spain to Mexico after the 1821 Mexican War of Independence. The
1846–48 war between Mexico and the United States did not affect
Tucson. But in 1854, a weakened Mexican leader, Antonio López de
Santa Anna, sold the Arizona territory south of the Gila River, including Tucson, as well as several thousand acres of southwestern
New Mexico, to the United States for less than a dollar an acre. Sec-
retary of War Jefferson Davis had ordered army General James Gads-
den to close the deal, which became known as the Gadsden Purchase.
Though in the 1860s Davis would be vilified for his leadership of
the Confederacy, during the administration of President Franklin
Pierce, Davis was a staunch advocate of "Manifest Destiny," and he
considered a low-elevation rail link to California through southern
New Mexico and Arizona (what would later be called the Southern
Pacific) essential to that enterprise.

During the Civil War, Arizona was a territorial member of the Confederate Congress and the Tucson area was a rebel hotbed. A period

[2]These figures were supplied by David K. Taylor, a Tucson demographer.
[3]See Timothy Egan, "Urban Sprawl Strains Western States."
[4]Ibid. Whereas less than 80 percent of the inhabitants of the "crowded" Northeast live in urban settings, the figure for the West is close to 90 percent. The
figure for the Midwest is 70 percent; for the South, 67 percent.

of Wild West lawlessness followed in the late 1860s and 1870s. Only with the arrival of the first railroad in 1880 did U.S. sovereignty and the rule of law extend in fact, as well as in theory, over Tucson, and the city's economy begin to expand. Tucson then got a further boost from the U.S. military. Thousands of troops were based in Tucson in the 1880s to round up Geronimo and other renegade Apaches. Adventurers, bootleggers, and similar types rushed in, staked out claims on what, in many cases, was Indian land, even as merchants and traders followed to service the new population and the army. Tucson's was a classic settler economy, where wealth was a matter of who got there first. In 1947, John Gunther wrote in *Inside U.S.A.*, "In Tucson and Phoenix . . . people claim seniority over others if they arrived at the railway station twenty minutes earlier."

After World War II, the Sun Belt phenomenon, made possible by the spread of air-conditioning, gave new life to the Tucson land boom. The city's population grew from 40,000 in 1940 to 200,000 in 1960.[5] In the 1980s and 1990s, as the communications revolution took off, with more people able to operate their businesses from anywhere via computer, Tucson's warm desert location became an additional advantage. The population, which had grown by 55 percent in the 1970s, has risen an additional 30 percent since, according to city officials. Many who came here to live do not rely on Tucson for their businesses, whose clientele is regional or even global, while other newcomers are prosperous retirees with independent incomes. The local economy has thus not grown commensurately with the population. Aside from the University of Arizona—something of a social and economic island—and boom-and-bust military aircraft industries, there is little here except low-paying service jobs and a millionaire elite that acquired its wealth by sitting on real estate, rather than by producing anything. On the whole, Tucson is a century-old speculative bubble that has yet to burst.

THE BUS ENTERED a gridwork of dead space: miles upon yawning miles of strip malls with no edifice more than two stories high, each with a parking lot: Arby's, Yokohama Rice Bowl, Lube Pit, Jack-in-the-Box, Denny's, Southgate Shopping Center, Exxon, Discount Tire, Quik Mart, McDonald's, Whataburger!, Foodmart, Midway Manor,

[5]See *Tucson: The People and the Place: Highlights from the 1990 Census.*

Dunkin' Donuts, Bank One, Taco Bell, and on and on. There was an ordered repetition: every few miles there was yet another Yokohama Rice Bowl and another Arby's and Bank One. What seemed an unending sameness was a series of interconnected shopping centers serving individual neighborhoods, often single-level, cookie-cutter subdivisions of cheaply framed Sheetrock houses: "Three houses to an acre, ticky-tacky junk," according to a local planner.

I tried to remember the sequence of the bus's ninety-degree turns but soon lost any directional sense, since nothing seemed to change, as if I were inside the circuitry of a computer chip. Later, when I picked up a rental car and looked briefly at a city map, I saw that except for the hilly northern suburbs, there are no winding streets to confuse one. Tucson is a military-style, two-hundred-square-mile cantonment whose central thoroughfare, Speedway, is a multilane highway lined with one-story, flat-roofed stores and restaurants defined to a large extent by the sizes of their parking lots. Tucson appeared truly futuristic: a deliberate pod.

But the fact that Tucson resembles a military encampment with wide, angular boulevards and little communal ambience makes historical sense. In 1776, the Spanish built the first town here, modeled, like many Spanish colonial towns, on Roman garrisons: the houses had no windows, and their backs faced the street; the focus was on the interior, not the exterior. Indeed, the city's main bookstore, Bookmart, on Speedway, is a nondescript shed whose main entrance is in the rear, by the parking lot. Many people would tell me that partly because of the clean air and surrounding mountains, Tucson still evinces a Wild West quaintness. Nearby Phoenix, on the other hand, is four times as large. Its growth faces no natural limits, and its air is among the dirtiest in the nation.

Though 25 percent of Tucson's population is Mexican American and 2.9 percent African American,[6] almost everyone in the bus station when I arrived seemed either black or Spanish speaking and poor. I asked several people where the Congress Hotel was. No one knew. The Congress is among Tucson's most famous historical landmarks, the last of the old downtown hotels still in operation. It was in the Congress, in late 1933, that local police arrested America's most famous bank robber, John Dillinger. The hotel, it turned out, was just down the street, thirty yards from the station.

---

[6]These figures are from the 1990 census and have probably risen since then, albeit slightly.

What little there was to Tucson's downtown was here: a few empty streets with brick-fronted stores selling T-shirts and Native American and Indian-subcontinent fabrics, "heavy leather"–and–chain apparel, some traditional clothes, and trite western landscape paintings. Much of the merchandise had a faded hippie look. There were few customers, and some of the stores were closed. They open only on weekend nights, when the streets fill with students from the University of Arizona, who have little disposable income. Roy Drachman, who has lived in Tucson all of his ninety years and has been the city's leading real estate developer since World War II, told me that while he leads an active life, he has not been downtown in years. "There are no good restaurants or anything worthwhile, and I wouldn't feel safe there at night."

"Downtown," began a senior official in the city administration, "it's a place for ex-hippie entrepreneurs to go broke. Your average store owner is . . . oh, say, thirty-seven. Some have tried just about every chemical substance and think that because they have nostalgia for certain items, so do other people. Your average downtown store changes owners and merchandise about every five years. The rationale is certainly not economic, but maybe—as far as some store owners are concerned—therapeutic. Ultimately, after the last ex-hippie goes broke, the city may try a major renovation, with potted plants on the sidewalks and stores that sell more things that people want. But the record in the Southwest suggests that even when this type of thing is done right, the nearest mall still beats it to shit."

It was this downtown, however, that helped give Tucson the romantic ambience that Phoenix lacked.

OF COURSE, THE decline of Tucson's downtown may mean only upheaval and transformation, constants in American history. America's ideology has been the creation of wealth and permanent experimentation: a never-completed construction site of torn-down, temporary schemes. Constructed beauty does not accumulate here to the degree it has in the Old World. Thus an observer requires both a new aesthetic and a new approach to history, in which the creation of wealth itself becomes a liberating ideal. The Founding Fathers, it is often forgotten, basically rejected the ancient Greek "republic of virtue" in favor of a utilitarian, Hobbesian approach to humankind.[7] "Man,"

[7]Paul A. Rahe, *Republics Ancient and Modern.*

Benjamin Franklin once remarked, "is a tool-making animal." Prosperity, not beauty, was what Franklin and the other Founders clearly had in mind.

But what were sprawl and the decline of the downtown doing to Tucson's citizenry? After all, Tocqueville stressed that American patriotism grows out of "free and strong," public-spirited communities, where "the characteristic features of his [the American's] country are" not abstract but "distinctly marked" around him. It is this concrete sense of community, wrote Tocqueville, that engenders such an "instinctive love of country" even in a newly arrived immigrant. But in middle America I had seen fracturing metropolises in which a global middle class was emerging in affluent suburbs that had increasingly less to do with neighborhoods inhabited by the working poor. So how are classes and ethnic groups divided in Tucson? Does a single community still exist here in any sense?

"THERE MAY BE so little holding these western cities together that a basketball team is all there is: it's a sports team, a symphony orchestra, and a church rolled into one," said a Tucson sociologist. "Since neither Tucson, nor any other city with a big state university, can find the talent locally, community self-esteem becomes a matter of which southwestern city can hire the largest number of talented blacks from far away to represent it."

My first night in Tucson, I went to a varsity basketball scrimmage at the University of Arizona's indoor stadium. The game was part of neither the regular season nor the preseason but a scrimmage in which the varsity players split into two groups, put on dark- and light-colored jerseys, and played each other for a while. Yet thousands of spectators had paid several dollars each to pack the stands and scream, encouraged by not one but three groups of cheerleaders: two of college age and one a troupe of high schoolers. Not only is each regular-season game sold out, but a pair of season tickets can, in effect, require a $10,000 to $15,000 donation or more to the university. With a pair comes social prestige that has no equivalent on the East Coast. Who gets the pair can be among the most contentious issues in Tucson divorce cases. At the game I overheard two women—in their seventies, I presumed—feverishly discussing the strengths and weaknesses of the varsity team. I saw an attractive middle-aged woman wearing varsity sweats under her glittering necklaces and other gold jewelry. There seemed to be more at stake here than just a game.

"Any civilization," writes the Nobel laureate Czeslaw Milosz, "if one looks at it from an assumption of naive simplicity (as Swift looked at the England of his day), will present a number of bizarre features which men accept as perfectly natural because they are familiar." The bizarre yet utterly familiar feature I observed was this: the entire crowd, as well as every cheerleader and nearly every coach and official, was white, in many cases with honey-blond hair, while almost everyone playing on the court was black. Wasn't this a bit like ancient Rome, in which the gladiators were often from "barbarian," that is, subject races? While these stars of the colosseum sometimes garner fame and the attention of beautiful women, they are definitely not seen as equals. This inequality mirrors the inequality that ultimately contributed to Rome's downfall through "barbarian" infiltrations. Race has been America's historic tragedy, but the crowd in Tucson was not Roman. It did not scream for blood but roared with admiration for the players. Basketball, because it features almost constant physical movement, provides the simulated excitement that mass existence "against instinct"—as the philosopher Bertrand Russell labeled it—requires. And because basketball is even more fluid than football and the shorts and tank tops of the players so vividly reveal their muscularity, basketball *excites* the populace without exposing it to the unwholesome violence associated with boxing. Basketball is a sanitized colosseum sport. The blunt racial fact—that the audience was white and most of the players black—went either unnoticed, disregarded, or channeled into positive feelings. The shrieking blond crowd and the sweating black players may indicate a society's way of coping with racial tensions rather than dramatizing them, as in ancient Rome.

TUCSON IS AN oasis culture located in the desert along the Rillito River, a shallow, dry gulch that fills with brown, gushing water after a heavy rain. It is a city of nomads, both rich and poor, in which much of the local population struggles at subsistence level. "Tucson is generally a minimum-wage town," Charles Bowden, the author of nine books about the Southwest, told me. "It has the American equivalent of a *maquilladora* economy," like that in Nogales, Sonora.

It is said that most of the people who live in Tucson have come here from somewhere else just to be left alone. Involvement in local politics is abysmally low, with 25 to 30 percent voter turnouts in off-year elections: the lowest turnouts in the United States. You see relatively few people in the streets. There are few sidewalks and almost no taxis. It is a city of beepers, cellular car phones, and private security systems. The local business elite is disappearing as an increasing number of Tucson's retail outlets give way to chain stores. Wages are stagnant. The crime index is the eighth highest among large U.S. cities, after those of Tampa, Miami, St. Louis, Atlanta, Baton Rouge, Newark, Baltimore, and Kansas City.[8] There is almost no urban planning.

"There are many neighborhoods where people don't stay long enough to build community ties," explained Tom Sheridan, an anthropologist at the University of Arizona. "It is a Sun Belt phenomenon of people in transit. Still, neighborhood associations are more vibrant in Tucson than in Phoenix, where seven out of ten newcomers leave sooner or later."[9]

"Since 1980, there has been a real decline in community life," Molly McKasson, a Tucson city councilwoman, told me. "Despite the massive growth and development of the 1980s, the median household income declined by eight percent, the unemployment rate rose by twenty-eight percent, the number of people living in poverty increased by sixty-eight percent, and for the first time we are close to being a renter economy: almost fifty percent of people here rent rather than own their homes."[10]

The average household income in Tucson is $21,748, compared to $25,500 in 1972 (in the same dollars). The average income for a single woman with children is $14,595. More than a third of all Tucson households earn less than $15,000. "Do you realize how low these numbers are?" McKasson said. "These women can't afford day care, their kids are left alone during the day. And these are the people above poverty! All the stress indicators are up. There is an increase in

[8]The crimes included in this index are murder, rape, robbery, assault, burglary, and car theft; see *Statistical Abstract of the United States 1996.*

[9]The West is the most mobile region in the nation, with a quarter of all households having moved in the previous year. In Tucson, almost 30 percent of all households have lived in their homes less than fifteen months; about 60 percent, less than five years.

[10]Tucson renters have increased nearly four times as fast as home owners since 1980, according to the census. According to *Statistical Abstract of the United States 1996,* 68.6 percent of white households in the United States own their own homes, while 41.9 percent of blacks do.

transiency, in single motherhood, in renters, in child abuse, in juvenile crime." Most of McKasson's figures represent only slight exaggerations of the national average. The social crisis affects the black, white, and Mexican communities to similar degrees.

The Southwest is full of such oases: low-wage, one-story encampments with a high proportion of drifters and broken families. The drug arrest rate is higher in the West than anywhere else in the country.

WHEREAS NORTH TUCSON is mainly white, Tucson's "south side" is mainly Mexican (with both legal and illegal immigrants)—and crime-ridden. Sixty-six-year-old Arturo Carillo Strong, a retired Tucson policeman and federal undercover agent, gave me a tour of the Mexican south side one morning.

"Over there," Arturo said, pointing to some stately brick ranch houses with iron fences, "you see your drug money at work. Just look at that fancy wrought-iron fence; you know it was paid for by drugs by the amount of wrought iron in the construction." Arturo's tour began in Barrio Centro and continued into Barrio Hollywood and Barrio Sobaco ("Armpit Quarter"). I was struck by the sterility of the south side. Nothing indicated that this was a dangerous area where most of Tucson's seventy-five known gangs operate. When Arturo told me about the drive-by shootings and the crack houses, I was truly surprised: I saw only well-maintained tract homes with metal or asphalt roofs and white-painted brick; some even had gardens of bougainvillea and oleanders despite the niggardly desert soil. The only hints of working-class poverty were the old pickups and the occasional sagging clothesline (though, in this dry climate, machine dryers are not really necessary). "The parents or the grandparents are okay, but the kids are bad," Arturo explained. "Because of peer pressure in the schools, the parents or grandparents can't control them. And it's common for one of the parents to be jailed or the parents separated. The grandparents tend the garden and make repairs, that's why it looks nice. But in this strange new country with so many temptations and powerful, destructive forces, the old folks can only watch as the kids become monsters."

Arturo went on, "In the old days, an arrest always meant a trip to the police station by way of the hospital for the offender. Once we caught these two guys, beat them up bad, and threw them down a gulch into a briar patch before we booked them. For a long time you couldn't do that. Now the rough stuff is coming back. The rules have loosened. There's an atmosphere among police which says, whatever it takes, get crime down." Arturo said that the emerging function of the U.S. police near the Mexican border is to apply as much countervailing violence as it takes to keep drug-related crimes at acceptable levels. Arturo worried that falling murder rates in the Southwest may actually be a bad development, since they indicate that "druggies are no longer killing each other as much" and "the herd," therefore, "is not being thinned."

An old, rust-stained car made a sharp turn at high speed in front of ours. In the ninety-degree heat the car's windows were rolled down: evidently it had no air-conditioning. Eyeing the driver, Arturo said, "Short hair, baggy T-shirt, mean eyes, he's a gang member. I'll bet he's wearing hip-hop shorts [baggy trousers cut off below the knee]."

We passed a lovely landscaped park with cypress trees. "It's full of drug dealers at night. If they see a white face even a block away, they'll shoot. They have whistlers, guys who hang out at the corner and whistle if they see someone strange approaching."

We came to a lovely Mexican church. Its whitewashed walls glittering in the sun, its bell tower and courtyard reminded me of the grace and purity of religious buildings in Spain and North Africa. The church conjured up tradition, sensuality, nostalgia. If only this church were more relevant to the social forces roiling the southern half of Tucson. I knew that to gauge the present and future here, I should focus on the tract houses.

In another park Arturo pointed to the homeless: "The police provide a number of one-way bus tickets to these people to get them to San Diego, where they will be San Diego's problem. Police and social service departments do that sort of thing: forget solutions; just keep the level of criminal activity at a reasonable level in your jurisdiction."

We passed through a section of town with restored adobe houses undergoing gentrification by yuppies. I noticed a handmade sign:

WE NEED AFFORDABLE HOUSING—
NOT $1,800-A-MONTH RENTS.
IF YOU PEOPLE WANT NEW YORK–STYLE LOFTS,
WHY DON'T YOU MOVE [BACK] TO NEW YORK?

I had seen more than enough evidence of class resentment, violence, and a social vacuum. Yet Arturo's cynicism had not convinced me that Tucson was in danger. For the inhabitants of the prosperous Catalina foothills north of here, where I was staying, I had already discovered the south side simply did not exist.

We passed a town house development painted in garish pink that Arturo called "a government-subsidized, low-rent hellhole for drugs and crime" and entered a section of town composed of tire shops, auto transmission stores, and Mexican restaurants. "Tire shops have traditionally been fronts for drug deals, or for laundering illegal cash. Arrest all the drug dealers, and the retail economy of Tucson's south side [composed mainly of the working poor] goes bust."

Because of the clumsy architecture and graffiti, I felt I was back in northern Mexico, a perception strengthened when Arturo and I entered the El Indio restaurant, a local hangout, formerly a beauty salon. Here Arturo introduced me to Alex Villa, a "semiretired" local gang leader.

Alex said that he was "semiretired" now that his younger brother had taken over the leadership of his old gang from him. "But two rival gangs still want my head as a trophy on the wall." Alex looked like a Mexican-American version of a sumo wrestler. He weighed nearly three hundred pounds, I thought. His head was completely shaven, and he had a black goatee. His sunglasses rested on a bulge above the back of his neck, as if he had two faces. Around Alex's neck was a gold necklace of Jesus Christ the Fisherman of Souls. "Who else is going to keep me alive?" Alex asked.

"What's a gang?" I asked him.

Alex stared at me very hard. After a moment of silence, he said, "A gang enforces order from chaos. A gang is about pride and respect, while mafias are all about business. Only if a gang achieves a certain level of organization can it become a mafia. In Tucson, gangs are more territorial than ethnic. For instance, there are often some blacks and whites in Mexican gangs. Black-dominated gangs tend to be more fluid, though, with less loyalty and more shirt flippers [different gangs sport different T-shirts]. The Phoenix gangs are allied with the [Los Angeles–based] Crips and Bloods, while the gangs here are independent of—yet still influenced by—the L.A. gangs.

"The schools have made things worse. In high school, in the Mexican areas, we were taught about Latino history and pride, while the blacks were taught about black history and pride. What the teachers never emphasized was respect for each other's cultures or how to think like an American. My sophomore year, blacks and Mexicans had a full-fledged riot."

"What about your old gang?"

"It's a subcell of what had been a larger gang." Alex went on, talking about gang "empires" and "territories," including one controlled by Yaqui Indians, "tough little guys whose territory was surrounded, yet they were able to hold off other groups." It reminded me of parts of the Third World where official order has broken down.

"You don't look like how you talk," I remarked. Alex again stared at me hard, then said, "You cannot believe how easy it is to be trapped by your surroundings, how the world beyond the south side of Tucson is not real. When I was in criminal court, I listened—really, for the first time—to how educated people speak. That's when I realized how dumb I sounded. Thanks for the compliment; I'm still working on myself."

Alex told me that he often reads in libraries. "I've learned to start sentences without saying, 'You know . . .' " Nor was Alex's expression mean and predatory, like that of the fellow Arturo and I had seen driving the car. Alex had arrived on time for lunch; for gang members it is a matter of pride to arrive late, to let the other fellow wait. I suspected that Alex was truly retired.

Alex had served a total of sixteen months in a juvenile prison and in an "adult facility for assault and battery. In the adult facility I learned how to hot-wire cars, get through home alarm systems, and make silencers." Alex taught me about "night crawlers," gang lookouts who flash Bic cigarette lighters to indicate Tucson street corners where cocaine is for sale. I also heard from others how cops are protected by gang members if "they let a certain amount of crime happen."

Alex is a third-generation Mexican American, born December 30, 1969. "I was a tax deduction," he joked. His deceased father was a roofer, his mother a medical assistant. "Because of my size, I was a natural leader in junior high school. Gangs are the most copycat of subcultures. It used to be zoot suits, now it's tattoos. When I was thirteen, I got a tattoo"—Alex pulled up his T-shirt and showed me a big tattoo that read "Chicano"—"so the other kids had to get a tattoo also. . . . If you were to chicken out when it came to committing a murder, all your friends from your entire life in the neighborhood would reject you: it's like excommunication. Tell me, what law or punishment could be worse than that, especially since none of the hardcore gang members expect to live beyond twenty-one?"

According to Alex, the real Mexican-U.S. border runs between south and north Tucson. "The south side is the Old World. In the Old

World, if a car passed by floating on air, people would fear it, then worship it. In the New World, they would dissect it to see how it works. In the Old World, even with the worst poverty there is an extended family that provides stability. But in the New World, if there is no economy there is no culture either, no family, nothing to hold people together: just look at the poor whites and blacks. For south side Mexicans to go into north Tucson for work is a death march. They hate north Tucson and envy it at the same time. South side Mexicans have no idea of gradually accumulating wealth. What they know from their own experience is 'If I could only sell a bunch of keys [of cocaine], I could move to north Tucson.' To think in terms of education and hard work as a way into north Tucson is, in fact, to buy into America. I know almost nobody in south Tucson who has bought into America."

Of course, Alex himself had. He counsels teenagers who perform below grade level as part of a city program called "Second Chance." One afternoon, I spent an hour in a Second Chance classroom, where I lectured children about reading. (I told the kids that they do not need money to travel beyond their poor neighborhoods, just a library card. Reading good books, I told them, is the key to success and adventure.) Some of the kids had punk haircuts. Some daydreamed, but the rest paid close attention. They asked me questions about what books they should read, what countries I had found the most interesting, and why. Of course, if only a few of these kids climb out of poverty, this school will have served its purpose. Arturo, the retired undercover cop, was right: forget "solutions." Ignorance, poverty, and crime have existed throughout history. Keeping crime and poverty at reasonable levels is the only realistic goal, and that requires tremendous effort.

"What about the war against drugs?" I asked Alex.

"There's no sign of it in south Tucson. Coke and heroin are on the rise, weed's the staple diet. I see more guys with exotic cars and beepers, whispering on cellular phones while the cops do nothing. Maybe the only way to cut the power of the gangs is to legalize drugs, at least marijuana. Then the gangs would have much less money to buy guns."

TUCSON'S CRIME-PLAGUED SOUTH side is composed of the "working poor." The official poverty levels are meaningless: between a fifth and a quarter of all Americans depend on incomes that cannot realistically provide for the basic necessities; and it is white males who make up the largest group of employed heads of households living in or near poverty, a fact that partially explains the resurgence of militias.[11] Bruce and Corinna Chadwick, who live on Tucson's south side in a predominantly black and Mexican area, epitomize the part of the white population of the U.S. that along with other races makes up the working poor. Bruce, who did not finish high school, is a supervisor in an automobile parts store, Corinna a cashier in a retail outlet. In their late twenties with three children, their combined gross income is $35,000 a year. While that is still higher than the Tucson household average of $21,748, the Chadwicks barely tread economic water, and even that is thanks to interest-free mortgage payments of $223 per month (including home owner's insurance) provided by Habitat for Humanity. Founded by a devout Christian businessman, Millard Fuller, and often associated with Jimmy and Rosalynn Carter, Habitat is part of a community-based housing movement across America that is beginning to fill some of the vacuum created by the failure of public housing.

I pulled my car up to Bruce and Corinna's tract house with its bare dirt yard, enclosed by a gate and protected by a loud buzzer and two guard dogs. Bruce came to greet me. I noticed that a black iron grille door had been installed over the original one. Inside I saw a spotlessly clean, frugal house, with flowers stuck in a plastic 7-Eleven cup on the kitchen table. Bruce and Corinna were both heavyset. Bruce had normal-length dark hair, a neat mustache, and wire-rimmed glasses; Corinna had long red hair and red fingernails. It was midmorning, and they were sipping Cokes. Their three children were at school—a magnet school in a better neighborhood, where Corinna had managed to enroll them. "I attended school in this neighborhood, and I don't want my kids exposed to the same things I was." Bruce and Corinna were intelligent people who had made, economically speaking, one mistake: they had married before finishing high school and quickly had children.

To get this house, valued at $48,000, the Chadwicks had had to

[11]See John E. Schwarz and Thomas J. Volgy, *The Forgotten Americans,* as well as figures provided by the U.S. Census Bureau in its graph "Barely Getting By." According to this graph, President Lyndon Johnson's much-derided War on Poverty actually worked: from 1964 to 1969 the percentage of workers at the poverty level dropped from 24.1 percent to 14.4 percent. President Richard Nixon continued the War on Poverty, and in 1974 the working poor were at an all-time low: 12 percent. Since then their numbers have crept back to 1964 levels.

invest several hundred "sweat equity hours" building other Habitat houses, go through a battery of long interviews and a credit check, and provide a $600 down payment. "It's taken me eight years," said Bruce, "to get a job that is somewhat decent. I'm not stupid, but I'm not the smartest guy in the world, and this house is a big step up from where we lived before."

Before moving here, Bruce and Corinna spent six years in a mobile home park in the south side of Tucson near the airport. "What was the mobile home park like?" I asked.

They smiled knowingly. Bruce said, "It was a real interesting experience, I can tell you. By the time we left, all of the people living there when we moved in had gone." Corinna added, "We saw the place gradually change, and always for the worse. The place was full of children without guidance."

"Before moving here seven months ago," Bruce told me, "we sold our trailer for fifteen hundred dollars in cash. We learned afterwards that it was confiscated from the new owners in the course of a drug bust." Here are some of the stories Bruce and Corinna told me about the trailer park:

- A child tried repeatedly to stab one of the Chadwicks' children with a screwdriver. Corinna phoned the police, who told her that they "could do nothing because the perpetrator was underage." Nevertheless, the police lectured the mother of the offending child. "It went in one ear and out the other," Bruce said.

- Another child was left alone in the driver's seat of a truck with the engine on. The child shifted gears and rammed a trailer home.

- One night, Corinna saw a group of men with automatic rifles outside their trailer. One of them said, "Okay, guys, let's hit it." Then they assaulted another trailer. The men were undercover Drug Enforcement Administration agents. Frequently, Bruce and Corinna saw helicopters shining spotlights on one or another of the trailers at night. "There was a lot of drug activity," Bruce explained.

- A next-door neighbor, six months behind in rent, rigged the wiring system to blow up his trailer. His attempt failed. After he was evicted, an electrician discovered the plot in the course of an inspection.

- Another trailer, where three families lived, was so roach-infested that it had to be condemned.

"The insides of many of these trailers were unspeakable," Bruce told me. "The park was full of people who were constantly drunk and dirty. There were single men with sons and girlfriends: few real families. There were single moms on welfare even though their men lived with them: a lot of welfare scams, yes. And there were always the loud arguments. I'll never forget the night that a man and a woman screamed at each other until dawn, when they started breaking windows. Once a neighbor became so drunk that he crawled up into a fetal position. The police took him away, and he had to have his stomach pumped."

"Do most poor people," I asked Bruce and Corinna, "fail because they are stupid and don't have their act together, while the few who are intelligent—like both of you—find ways, whether through Habitat or another means, to escape poverty? Or is it just that many poor people never get a financial break, which then leads to other problems?"

Bruce and Corinna had different answers. Bruce thought that the social dysfunction he had described could have been reduced by government aid. Corinna shook her head "no" and said, "A lot of people we've encountered can't be helped."

According to a land-use map I saw, the whole of Tucson is dotted with mobile home parks.

TUCSON'S PROSPEROUS CITIZENS live in the Catalina foothills, which look down upon the city from the north. The foothills are covered by winding streets with "Neighborhood Watch" signs and comfortable villas, often with red-tiled roofs, electronic security systems, and extensive gardens of wiry mesquite; lanky, fuzzy-limbed yucca; and cholla cacti, with their networks of right-angled arms with "shooting" needles. Towering over this vegetation and providing many a villa with a distinctive character are saguaro cacti, often as tall as thirty feet and weighing up to ten tons, some even older than the American Republic.[12]

Stuart Hameroff, a medical scientist at the University of Arizona, lives in the Catalina foothills. He told me, "I never could have come as far as I have in my research had I lived on the East Coast, or even

---

[12]It takes seventy years for the arms of the cactus to emerge from the main column.

in a place like San Francisco. Those places are too cluttered, too vertical, with too many physical and cultural distractions. I need the desert and the absence of anything to look at in order to think clearly and, more important, to think abstractly about the brain." In his nondescript little office with a weedy garden on the University of Arizona campus, Hameroff has created a Web site for scientists from several continents to exchange information about the biochemistry of consciousness. The office was as forgettable as the tract houses of the working poor. No imposing ivy-covered walls and neoclassical buildings were required for this ongoing, worldwide scientific work, nothing to suggest urbanity: just a computer and a telephone jack.

David K. Taylor, the planning program coordinator for the city of Tucson, also lives in the foothills. Taylor is a demographer who helped me understand the past and future social geography of Tucson—and of the United States, too.

I sat beside Taylor's grand piano under high white ceilings. "Where you are now could be Santa Fe, Palm Beach, or Long Island," he explained. "My neighbors are Pakistani doctors, Silicon Valley types, ingenious local entrepreneurs, wealthy Lebanese, Chinese. . . . They have their computers, their links with friends throughout the globe, and a patina of Spanish culture via the street names of this neighborhood and the villa architecture, and they call it a 'lifestyle.' Of course, these people are the only future Tucson has. You lure high-tech firms to relocate here with those high-paying jobs in order to attract more people like my neighbors to Tucson: because experience indicates that most of the poor, even with training, will never be qualified for such jobs"—exactly what I heard in St. Louis and Orange County.

Taylor continued, "The local government's promotion of tourism and the Tucson convention site will bring mainly low-paying service jobs to the area.[13] Tourist promotion is usually necessary to generate corporate moves; so if we want those high-tech firms, we will have to emphasize tourism."

Taylor showed me two graphs that point to a bifurcated future for Pima County, which includes Tucson. The 1979 graph showed, as Taylor put it, a "one-hump camel," with the rich and poor at the far right and left and the middle class forming the hump in the middle. The

[13]Between 1984 and 1995, the city of Tucson spent almost $48 million on tourist-related programs, compared to $17.4 million on economic development; see Molly McKasson and Dave Devine, "The Growth of Tucson's Working Poor."

1989 graph showed a "two-humped camel," with the rich and poor forming humps at the edges, at the expense of middle-income groups. In that year, nationally, 22.8 percent of the population lived in households whose income could not "realistically" provide for basic necessities, even as the numbers of the rich and upper middle class had grown, a trend that has continued throughout the 1990s.

"In Tucson," Taylor went on, "there are a large number of inexpensive tract houses thrown up hastily in the fifties, sixties, and early seventies which are now falling apart. Soon their repair costs will not make economic sense. Some of their owners will be able to afford more expensive homes in neighborhoods with good schools, further out in the desert; while many more will slip through the cracks, going broke on repairs or drifting to bad sections of town." Throughout the country, Taylor notes, the decay of cheap housing from the first decades after World War II is causing the same problem: further eroding the "middle middle" class, even as the working poor and the upper middle class become increasingly isolated from each other geographically. In Tucson, the high cost of bringing water and other services to the edge of the desert abets this trend, since only the well-off can afford to live in the new outlying suburbs.

Taylor summed up Tucson's history: "Two hundred and fifty years ago, the population here was one hundred percent Native American. Next, it became ninety-five percent Spanish. When Santa Anna sold southern Arizona cheap to Jefferson Davis, you saw the first and only integration of cultures here, because the Anglo males who came west had to marry Spanish women, or at the very least partially assimilate with the reigning Spanish culture, in order to do business. But the coming of the railroad and the automobile three decades afterward redivided the city into a poor Spanish-speaking section, with some blacks, south of the railroad tracks, and a wealthier Anglo one to the north. Now class barriers are further deepening cultural and racial ones." So instead of a unified, Spanish-built, Roman-style garrison as in the eighteenth century, Tucson is becoming several garrisons, where each house is more isolated than ever before. "Tucson has only twenty-five hundred persons per square mile; we're less dense than at any moment in the past two hundred years. And who knows what the limits of growth here are? Of course, we're not as bad as Phoenix, where the motto seems to be 'More development is better, and too much is just right.'

"Meanwhile," Taylor said, "the Anglo population keeps dropping.

Anglos are 68.2 percent of the Tucson area's population; in 2050 we'll be 40 percent, while the percentage of Hispanics will rise from 24.5 percent to 40 percent. The future means integration with Sonora. Why, Sonora will just be southern Arizona, and Chihuahua south Texas! Guaymas will be Tucson's main port. Tucson's economy already extends a thousand miles into Mexico."

"Will the American Southwest merge completely with northern Mexico?" I asked.

"Not completely. There will be a big Asian element here, too," Taylor said. "The Southwest will move toward both Latin America and the Pacific, in terms of trade and people. The young workforce that will subsidize the Social Security payments for our aging baby boomers will have to come not just from south of the border, but also from the densely populated, industrializing, low-crime societies of the Third World, places like East and Southeast Asia, and the Indian subcontinent, where life is much worse than in America but where talent and individual initiative are high. Racially, we'll look like a combination of Mexico and Hawaii. Tucson will reflect that trend." In other words, greater Los Angeles is not alone.

1 5

Individualists

LEAVING TAYLOR'S VILLA in the Catalina foothills, I thought: Tucson is American history on fast forward. A century ago there was little here but desert and a few dusty streets. Now there is a vast pod of suburbs differentiated by income, on the verge of becoming the hub of a transitional region extending deep into Mexico, even as drugs from Mexico feed the lawlessness that plagues the south side of the city. While Tucson becomes increasingly connected to the outside world thanks to immigration and the Internet, its people are increasingly isolated from one another: the houses further and further apart, the public spaces empty.

To me, the city's terrain seemed to say, "Leave me alone."

I wanted to sample true American loneliness, the extremes of individualism. So I left Tucson and headed back south, toward the Mexican border.

AFTER DRIVING MORE than a mile on dirt tracks in the desert, I descended a steep, rutted hillside before arriving at Jeff Smith's house, where I was met by a growling dog. Smith came out in his wheelchair. "Don't worry, I'll tow your car with my pickup if you can't make it back up that hill."

I was now only fifteen miles from the border, far from the nearest paved road, between the towns of Sonoita and Patagonia. Smith's closest neighbor was almost a mile away, and Smith himself, paralyzed from the waist down by a motorcycle accident, was feuding with him. Smith led me into his two-story adobe house, fitted with a specially designed elevator for his wheelchair, which he had built with the help of a few Mexican illegals. Smith was around fifty, in jeans and with gray hair: "a screaming liberal," his friend in Tucson, Emil Franzy, had told me.

"Unfortunately," Smith said, "while my fellow liberals on the East and West Coasts are very good on the First and Fourth Amendments— free speech and worship, and protection against 'unreasonable searches and seizures'—liberals look down on those rights and amendments that they don't use, like the Second Amendment, the right to bear arms." Smith put deliberate stress on the numbers "First," "Fourth," and "Second." The Constitution and Bill of Rights were clearly living, religious documents to him, as the Old Testament is to Orthodox Jews and evangelical Christians. Rather than a liberal, Smith, who owns thirty guns, was like many others I met in the Southwest: a spirited libertarian who felt the government had no right to ban abortions, semiautomatic assault rifles, or perhaps even marijuana. It was in the southwest desert, among such libertarians, that I felt that the traditional liberal-conservative dichotomy that still governs Washington politics had become completely irrelevant.

In Tucson, Smith's Republican friend, Emil Franzi, had asked me, "Do you know why marijuana is illegal and many depressants and stimulants are not? It is because we have built this mammoth social service machine of courts, prosecutors, rehab folks, and the like, whose jobs now depend partly on the criminalization of pot, while there is also a massive pharmaceutical lobby that protects the distribution of drugs, some of which may be more harmful than marijuana." Smith's view was that "the Mexican border is a semipermeable membrane. Sure, the war on drugs is a joke. Eventually, the American Southwest will be more influenced by Mexican values than by New England ones."

I changed the subject to guns: "Do we really need semiautomatics?"

Smith responded, "Chechnya proves that you need semis to prevent tyranny, because with an armed populace a tyrannical, central government will be forced to fight door to door."

"But the United States government is not like the Russian one."

"One day, it could become just as tyrannical. It would happen gradually, by stealth. Don't say it can't happen! Would you rather be free or merely safe? That's the question Americans have to answer. [President] Bill Clinton and [Attorney General] Janet Reno need to understand the natural state of human freedom."

"But you will always need a strong federal government," I said. "Just look at the land dispute between the Hopis and Navajos in northern Arizona. It is the federal government that to this day keeps the peace between many Indian tribes."

"If the federal government collapsed," Smith responded, "the Navajos might just kill the Hopis. Then, after an unstable period, the Navajos would assimilate into the general society. The world wouldn't come to an end. We think we need a federal government, but do we really?"

The morning wore on. Smith made more coffee, and talked about "large, bloody cataclysms" that could "bring down the electoral college"; about how "the south side of Tucson might make war on the Catalina foothills, an idea that might originate from some TV show." Smith, like many Democrat environmentalists but unlike Republican business types, was against further growth. "I almost hope for an environmental catastrophe, so people will start leaving Tucson and stop building more homes. If it takes thirty years for the area to recover, what's the harm in the long run, from an historical perspective?"

I liked Smith. His views seemed appropriate to the surroundings. Smith and I were sitting amid the mathematical purity of his white-walled adobe home. From his living room window I could see brilliant sunlight and a panoramic hillside of gama grass and mesquite trees (a North African species whose seedlings had come to the Southwest in the cow manure aboard the conquistadors' ships). Smith lived alone amid this meditative, prismatic beauty. His house was in a valley where radio transmissions were problematic. Like many people in rural America who live far from a big town, he had his own water well. He went only twice a week to his mailbox, more than a mile away on the nearest paved road. It occurred to me that Smith's political absolutes and abstractions regarding issues such as semiautomatic rifles and the power of the federal government were driven, to no small degree, by sheer physical isolation. The continent's very emptiness, along with its overpowering natural forces—twisters, hurricanes, extremes of heat and cold, for which Europe offers no equivalent—confers a pioneer spirit that, in an age of advanced technology, fast loses relevance; so that the last frontiersmen like Smith are, perforce, somewhat absurd.

I remember what Sheriff Pintek in Cochise County had said about militamen: "These are people who can barely speak without profanities: like, 'Why the fuck should I vote?' Besides being uneducated, they often have records of petty crime which prevent them from getting decent jobs. If they are not on welfare or unemployment insurance, they work as night clerks at convenience stores and, as they will tell you, 'defend the U.S.A. on weekends.' With social change so dramatic, there are just more and more losers out there." (What Pintek said reminded me of the officers at Fort Leavenworth who had sunk their heads in shame at the sight of grossly overweight men marching in camouflage suits on television one night, in a program about militias.)

Jeff Smith, of course, was no militiaman. He was far too well educated and cosmopolitan for that. He made a living as a writer for a weekly alternative newspaper. But just imagine, if you will, the state of mind of an uneducated, or badly educated, white male, someone full of resentment and without social graces—"a fat lard-ass with pimples," as Sheriff Pintek had put it to me—living in Smith's kind of isolation.

As Smith's friend Franzi had told me in Tucson, "Look, I'm a First Amendment guy, and a gun nut. I'm a member of the NRA [National Rifle Association], I go to gun shows on weekends, and I don't know any of these militia people! Where are they? These guys must live in the middle of nowhere: they don't vote, they're completely beyond the 'process.' They think the NRA is too left wing. . . . In the days of the military draft, when there was no mystique attached to carrying a gun and wearing a uniform, these guys didn't exist."

EMIL FRANZI RUNS election campaigns, mainly for Republicans, at the state legislature and county sheriff level. He is a small-time Ed Rollins, who happens to own sixty guns and three thousand opera records. Franzi supports both the NRA and National Public Radio. His motto might well be Jeff Smith's: "The less the government is able to accomplish, the better. Thank God for gridlock; James Madison spent his life inventing it."

I first met Franzi in the cramped cubicle of a Tucson AM station on election night, November 7, 1995. The station had that low-rent, fly-by-night quality of local radio stations throughout America: the furniture and equipment looked as though they had been dumped there by the moving company the day before and might be repossessed the next morning if the ratings dropped. Franzi's voice was loud, conspiratorial, friendly, as if we had known each other all our lives. Like the shorts and T-shirts people wore in fancy restaurants, formalities were not necessary in the Southwest. Because so many people who settle here come without friends or family and live in widely separated housing, when people do meet they connect quickly.

"Have you noticed something about this place, about Tucson and Arizona, I mean? Have you looked around?" Franzi shouted a few inches from my face, his voice now decelerated into a low, exasperated hiss: "It's a fucking desert—over seven hundred thousand people surrounded by a desert! And they still want to build, build. Where's the water going to come from? You tell me!"

Franzi was not exaggerating. Any place with less than twenty inches of yearly rainfall—a category that includes almost all the American West—will sustain a human population only with difficulty, and a place like Tucson, Phoenix, or El Paso in the Southwest, with sometimes less than eight inches of rain per year, is perhaps no place to inhabit at all.[1] Tucson is the largest city in the United States that is entirely dependent on groundwater, so that its underground aquifer is being steadily depleted. Not coincidentally, the most contentious issue on the November 1995 ballot in Tucson had to do with water. The dispute centered around Colorado River water transported here in a zigzagging, man-made river uphill from the California border, across the bleakest patch of the Sonora Desert, at a cost of billions of dollars in a scheme called the Central Arizona Project (CAP). But after all this expense, CAP river water turned out to be substandard. CAP water was hard, looked brownish, and reportedly caused illness. Many people wanted to ban CAP water from Tucson and continue to use only water from underground aquifers. Proponents argued, however, that CAP water was more affordable, that its quality could be improved by treatment with chemicals, and that it would ensure Tucson enough water for the next century.

"Who's really supporting CAP water, and who is against it?" I asked Franzi.

"Basically, a vote in favor of CAP water is a vote that says 'Don't fuck

[1] See Marc Reisner, *Cadillac Desert: The American West and Its Disappearing Water.*

with development'—since if we're forced to depend on aquifer water, there's just not going to be enough water for Tucson to keep expanding. Me, I'm a no-growther. I don't want the dirt road leading to my house ever to be paved. I don't want one more building to be built in Tucson. We're already too big. We're in a desert!"

The no-growthers won that night. CAP water lost. But that did not satisfy Franzi. On the air live in the studio, he told talk-show host John C. Scott that "Tucson voters are the stupidest voters in the country," because they had defeated CAP water but reelected the same Democratic Party politicians who had promoted it. Scott agreed. Earlier that day, Scott had told his audience that he himself had voted "down the line" Republican. Tucson's most popular radio commentators were trashing both the voters and the politicians that election night. Yet the voters phoned in and had their say, too. Sitting inside the dark, ten-foot-by-ten-foot recording room, lined with foam and stacked to the ceiling with dusty equipment, listening to callers scream at Scott and Franzi and hearing Scott and Franzi answer back, I knew that such places had become high altars of American democracy. This was local politics, and the issue at hand was water: life and death.

Yet only one out of four eligible voters had voted: a lower turnout than in the Haitian election held the following month. The voices crackling over the speakers represented only a minute subculture obsessed with politics. (According to *The Washington Post,* fewer than 5 percent of adult Americans engage in any kind of political activity, voting aside.[2]) I walked out of the dark, pulsing studio and into the open-air hallway, where I looked out over Tucson's lonely, nighttime silhouettes of blocky one- and two-story buildings separated by parking lots. And I thought.

THE UNITED STATES—aside from the policy and media types in Washington, the state capitals, and town halls—is politically apathetic. After spending much of my life amid traditional and highly politicized cultures in the Third World and the Balkans, sundered by ideological and ethnic obsessions and boasting, by the way, high voter turnouts, I found such apathy refreshing: at first, that is.

The seventeenth-century British philosopher James Harrington

[2]See Richard Harwood, "All-Pro Politics," *The Washington Post,* March 23, 1996.

declared that in a prosperous society it is the very indifference of most people that allows for a calm, healthy political climate, a view refreshed by the Founding Fathers' attempt to limit the franchise. The last thing America needs, I thought, is more voters—especially badly educated and alienated ones—with a passion for politics. Apathy, after all, can mean that things are fine; apathy is testimony to the fact that in America the basic questions (What should the system of government be? Where should the borders be? Which ethnic groups, if any, should control what regions?) have been more or less agreed upon, so that what is often argued about—gun control, abortion—is of secondary importance. (Despite what some believe, ethnic identity has yet to destabilize American politics because, with the exception of Native Americans, ethnicity is largely divorced from territory, unlike in the former Yugoslavia and Soviet Union.) And because what is argued about is often secondary, rather than something to fight or die for, democracy has evolved as the lowest common denominator of practical wisdom for a nation of individuals, most of whom prefer to be left alone to make money. America—the Civil War aside—has never been, for example, like 1930s Spain, where George Orwell could write about Communists, anarchists, democrats, and nationalists vying for hearts, minds, and power.

And not only politics has been secondary for most Americans; so for the most part has leadership. From the early nineteenth century onward, the nation prospered despite long sequences of mediocre presidents. Such periods of great growth as the second half of the nineteenth century were accompanied often by mediocre administrations. Only during wartime did it truly matter who the president was. (Indeed, in peacetime, the chairman of the Federal Reserve may now affect the lives of many more citizens than the president does.)

But this relative political vacuum—a sort of peaceful, productive anarchy—always presumed, among other things, abundant prosperity and resources, so that little governing authority was necessary to organize the scramble for wealth. The large-scale settlement of the West following the Civil War cramped this freedom a bit. Because the lands west of the 100th meridian (an imaginary line running through the Dakotas, Nebraska, Kansas, Oklahoma, and Texas) receive, for the most part, less than twenty inches of rain annually, the minimum required for agriculture without irrigation, government help and supervision were ordained by nature. Land had to be surveyed, parceled out, and regulated, and great water projects begun, which required vast bureaucratic institutions (the Reclamation Service, the Geological Survey, the Forest Service, and so forth) that, together with the great increase in both the population and the economy in the latter part of the nineteenth century, contributed to the big federal government that people such as Smith and Franzi now fear. Indeed, had the United States been settled from west to east rather than the other way around, the big government agencies necessitated by scarce water would have preceded the freeman tradition that took root on the well-watered eastern slopes of the Appalachians in the eighteenth century, and a mild form of what Karl Marx called "Oriental despotism"—highly centralized and authoritarian regimes like those that built the great water- and earthworks in India, China, and Mexico—might have arisen here.

But the claims of the militia movement and other libertarians notwithstanding, government intrusion has remained limited. Once land and water were parceled out, people were free to do what they wanted, to succeed beyond their wildest expectations or fail beyond their worst nightmares. And the discovery, mapping, and exploitation of aquifers (pools of water beneath the desert) in the first half of the twentieth century have further postponed the day of reckoning for humankind versus nature in the West. But that day is coming. In 1928, Arizona's population reached 400,000, the largest it had been since the apex of the Hohokam Indian culture of the thirteenth century. Now there are almost 800,000 people in greater Tucson alone and four million in Arizona, a tenfold increase in seventy years: in a desert, no less. Referring to the Central Arizona Project, Marc Reisner, an expert on natural resources in the West, writes, "Despite one of the most spellbinding and expensive waterworks of all time, Arizonans from now until eternity will be forced to do what their Hohokam ancestors did: pray for rain." Especially as Arizonans had decided—at least here in Tucson, for the moment—that CAP water was not good enough for them and therefore their only choice was to continue to deplete the aquifer.

What the voter turnout actually suggested is that the vast majority of residents were unconcerned about this and other communal issues. While a community might exist among scientists around the globe studying the chemistry of the brain—as in the case of University of Arizona scientist Stuart Hameroff—it might not exist from one street to the next in Tucson because there are no streets. And as the crime rates and the hollowing out of downtown showed, the social and communal fabric appeared to be fraying at the very moment in southwestern history when it is needed in the oncoming battle for water. The transnational, mestizo-Polynesian Tucson of the future—one of twenty-first-century North America's economic junction points for the world's most talented individuals—will require the opposite of individualism. It will need communalism merely to survive.

Gary Snyder, an ecologist and Pulitzer Prize–winning poet, warns, "This is an age of limits."[3] But Roy Drachman, the ninety-year-old Tucson native and post–World War II real estate developer who helped build the Sun Belt, thinks that people here will pay little attention to what Snyder says. Sitting in his low-ceilinged office next to a parking lot and restaurant, Drachman told me, "There are no limits. We will eat up more and more space out into the desert and there will be more and more loneliness and, consequently, more and more need for friendships. At first there won't be a water shortage, though. The price of water will just go up, and the quality will go down. Then we'll see."

Maybe Drachman is right. Maybe the Southwest can buy itself more time. Maybe, as some visionary engineers think, the Southwest's salvation will come ultimately from that shivery vastness of wet green sponge to the north: Canada. In that scenario, a network of new dams, reservoirs, and tunnels would supply water from the Yukon and British Columbia to the Mexican border, while a giant canal brings desalinized Hudson Bay water from Quebec to the American Midwest and supertankers carry glacial water from the British Columbian coast to southern California, all to support an enlarged network of posturban, multiethnic pods pulsing with economic activity.[4]

The attraction of such schemes stems from the remarkable success westerners have had thus far in peopling the desert. Yet any number of desert civilizations throughout history—Assyria, Carthage, Mesopotamia; Inca, Aztec, Hohokam—could have boasted a similar record of success before they, too, collapsed. Even the Hohokam built two hundred miles of irrigation canals, but ultimately this did not help them.

In fact, given demographer David Taylor's vision of greater growth and racial complexity, places such as Phoenix and Tucson straddle

---

[3]Snyder made these comments in *Mother Jones,* January–February 1996.
[4]For a more detailed description of these engineering plans, see Jerry Thompson, *Diverting Interests.*

the knife's edge between bold, futuristic dreams and apocalypse. The adrenaline-charged friendliness coupled with the extreme apathy and antigovernment views I encountered suggested a no less intense loneliness, emphasizing the need for community while threatening it at the same time.

There is also the threat of 92 million Mexicans, whose border is an hour's drive south of Tucson. During the Mexican Revolution and its attendant civil wars between 1910 and 1922, more than 10 percent of Mexico's population of 13 million fled to the United States. Now, as Mexico's population climbs past 100 million, imagine the level of militarization and domination by Washington required to control a comparative flood of refugees, were Mexico's central government to undergo an unruly meltdown into a weak tributary state system.

In Tucson, I wondered if America might need a new, more candid myth than the rugged individualism that had settled the West: a region that, in truth, could never have been tamed successfully without big-government intervention and the creation of bureaucracies— the very things rugged individualists such as Jeff Smith hate. In John Steinbeck's documentary-novel of the 1930s, *The Grapes of Wrath,* the myth of the West is exposed as a deceit, as the Great Plains become a dust-blown wasteland afflicted by drought and destitution. Steinbeck dreaded the West. He feared that the Okies' destiny might become the symbolic destiny of the nation itself if wanton individualism fatally weakened the government's ability to regulate growth and settlement.

What fascinates me about America's future is that the gradual, ongoing increase in both the size and complexity of the population (our population will likely grow by 50 percent, to 390 million, by 2050[5]) will require regulatory tyranny—governing everything from water use to credit card fraud—or else there can be no justice for anyone. But such a development is bound to cause an even greater backlash by unreconstructed individualists.

[5] *Statistical Abstract of the United States 1996* is the source of the population figure.

1 6

"Our Culture Is
Getting Real Thin"

AS TUCSON SUGGESTED, America's future appeared dynamic yet fragile, an impression strengthened by my talk with Cayce Boone, a Navajo Indian who works for a local cable television company. He had built a "sweat lodge" high in the Santa Rita Mountains, southeast of Tucson, in order to teach Navajo traditions passed on to him by his grandfather, an eighty-nine-year-old medicine man who can still lift heavy boulders.

I met Boone the same way I often meet people in my travels: a friend of a friend of a friend had given me his phone number. I called Boone and said I would like to talk.

South of Tucson I pulled off the interstate and found Boone waiting for me in his GMC pickup truck. His graying black hair was tied back in a long ponytail. He wore blue jeans and a cotton shirt with two pens stuck in the pocket. A large collection of keys hung from his belt. His cratered, bumpy, yellow-brown face with its wide features reminded me of Central Asians: the resemblance between Boone and so many of the people I had met on the other side of the Bering Strait was remarkable. (Nor was I alone in my observation. In 1916, the English traveler and poet Rupert Brooke had remarked upon the "taciturn and Mongolian" features of North American Indians.) The link between the Old and New Worlds I now saw standing before me was yet another reason to be wary of the notion that America is somehow outside history, forever protected from the tragedies of the Old World.

"Get in your car and follow me," Boone said.

We climbed higher and higher into the mustard-colored hills, first on paved roads, then on dirt tracks. The temperature fell. The sweat lodge was in a clearing. It was an igloo made of oak, mesquite, and aspen branches that had been plastered with mud. Glowing coals sustained the 130-degree dry heat inside the lodge. But that morning, we found that the embankment stones surrounding the fire outside where the coals are burned had been scattered, while many branches had been ripped away from the lodge's roof. The site was also littered with empty beer cans.

"Kids!" Boone exclaimed. "This vandalism was done last night."

"How can you tell?" I asked.

"See, the footprints are fresh."

We collected some of the debris. Boone pointed out the nearby vegetation: "This is sage, this is desert broom, this is mesquite," he said, fingering the weedy clumps as though their English names meant nothing to him. "Just looking for critters," he said as he scoured the ground. His speech belonged to the Southwest as much as the three-pronged saguaro cactus. Boone was one of the few people I met in the Tucson area with a real southwestern accent. The Indians, with their cowboy boots and baseball hats, the pickup trucks that had replaced their horses, and their accents—like the gentle twang of an acoustic guitar—embodied the Old West.

Boone invited me into the sweat lodge.

"Think of this lodge as a spiritual sauna bath. It takes half a day for the fire to make the stones hot enough. We Navajos place the hot stones inside and to the left of the entrance; the Sioux and the other Plains Indians place the stones in the center of the lodge. The lodge represents the mother's womb. The heat of the stones inside the womb protects you from all the negative energy. You see, in the beginning of time there was a spider woman, or a 'changing woman.' She had two sons: a 'monster slayer' and a 'child born of water.' The two sons grew up in a world of corruption that had gone out of control. It was a world in chaos. The sun god told the two sons it was time for them to restore order, and he gave them special gifts to do it. Out of the lightning in the sky the sun god fashioned arrows for the two sons, and out of the rainbows he fashioned bows. From obsidian, the two sons were given armor. The fire was their doorway to spirituality, which allowed them to cleanse the world of corruption, chaos, negative energy. That is what we celebrate in the sweat lodge. Of course, there are many variations of this myth, among the different tribes and also among the Navajos themselves. There is no one, correct story."

Boone added, "The squirrels spoke in the first world. In the time before the spider woman, the squirrels were the earth's caretakers. The time will come when all of this civilization will be gone and we will be back at the beginning, and the squirrels will speak again."

I glanced out through the small opening of the sweat lodge and noticed his spotless pickup truck, with the ladder and other equipment for installing cable television lines neatly clamped in place. Again I noticed the keys dangling from his belt. Boone was your typical serviceman who had shown up on time for our meeting.

"I was born in 1952 on the Navajo reservation in northern Arizona," Boone said. "I was part of the generation of Navajo young people torn from our traditions by the federal government. We were made to feel ashamed of everything Indian—of our language and tribal identity—in a failed attempt to make Indians like white people." Boone said he had been forcibly sent to an American boarding school at an early age, then placed in a foster family of Mormons from Malibu, California, a painful irony given that the Mormons and Navajos had fought a protracted guerrilla war in the second half of the nineteenth century. "I was baptized into the Mormon Church. I rebelled and went through four foster homes. I did not complete high school. It was often hard for me to talk as a kid. What I remember most about my youth is silences and embarrassments. Eventually, the Mormons excommunicated me. In 1980, I went back to the Navajo reservation, where I lived in a hogan.[1] I asked my grandfather, a medicine man, Dan Chee, to teach me everything he knew before he dies.

"I built the sweat lodge here in 1992. According to strict Navajo tradition, there are no co-ed sweats, but we've made concessions to modern life. About fifteen of us, men and women, some Indians, some Mexican Americans, some Anglos, sweat together. We wear light clothes, of course; it's not a commune. While the fire purifies us of negative energy, each of us talks about our past, where we come from, who our parents are, what our home lives as children were like. Many

---

[1]A one-story, hexagonal or octagonal structure, often built of logs and mud and characteristic of the Navajo Indians.

of us don't want to remember our home lives, and at a certain point we stop talking. I've heard awful stories inside this lodge. And when I do, then would come the silence.

"Too many of us are hovering off the ground with no firm foundation beneath us. Take my own family, for instance. Half of my relatives died from alcoholism. I grew up with nothing, in a desert, with no running water, with family problems followed by a series of foster homes that completely alienated me from whatever traditions I had. But I'll tell you something: compared to the white trash I encounter in the places where I go to install cable TV, I am pretty well rooted, actually.

"If you could see what I see every day in my job, you would understand where all the guns and gangs and violence come from. Our culture—Indian, Mexican, Anglo—is getting real thin. Increasingly, we're living within a narrowing range of error and security. The wave of Western culture that washed over these parts in the nineteenth century is fast draining into the ground, and the contours of the land are becoming recognizable again. This sounds beautiful the way I just put it, but the reality is scary.

"TV is the whole existence for a new class of silent people. Look all around you in the Southwest; most of the buildings you see are mobile homes. Inside most of these homes are filthy people who can't read, who don't talk to each other, who have few or no relatives or friends, who are one unpaid bill or one small tragedy away from being homeless: people who can't put food on the table or watch over their kids.[2] The little money they have is used to install cable TV. I know. I go into these places every day. It gives me more confidence and pride in myself. And you know why? Because I am continually confronted with people who have no culture, who can't cope even as well as I can.

"When I think of the future of the United States, I think of a little girl I saw inside one mobile home, a girl who—I can tell you from my own experience—is not so untypical. She's about three years old. Her parents plop her down all day by the TV, turned to the channel for soap operas and game shows. There's dirt all over the house. There are tabloid magazines and TV schedules and beer cans. There's not much furniture, no books. It smells."

[2]According to the U.S. Census Bureau, at the end of 1995, in the Tucson area, between 10 and 25 percent of whites lived in poverty.

I thought of the people in the trailer park described by Bruce and Corinna Chadwick.

"But then, time and again, I will install a cable TV line in one of those homes in the Catalina foothills, of the rich people, where they put plastic on the carpet for me to walk on, so my work boots won't dirty the carpet. In rich people's homes it doesn't smell and there are always at least a few books, sometimes a lot. That's culture, not money.

"And there's nothing much in between—between the homes with the plastic for me to walk on and those with a trail of garbage leading from the TV. I provide cable service for the Yaqui Indians near the Mexican border. One Yaqui man told me, 'We Yaquis don't have a culture anymore, for us culture is just beer, TV, and the Catholic Church.' "

Boone stopped talking. We just sat silently for a moment on the hard-packed dirt in the semidarkness of the sweat lodge. He seemed solid, dug in, and permanent compared to the world he had just described.

17

Arizona: A Balkan Map?

I LEFT TUCSON and drove north, roughly following Coronado's trail to Kansas, passing through a sparsely populated landscape of scattered Indian reservations. The 1.4 million Native Americans account for only 0.6 percent of the U.S. population; their unemployment rate is 37 percent, half live in substandard housing, and more than 20 percent of Indian homes have incomplete plumbing.[1] Just as the posturban pods I had seen were increasingly shaping their own destinies beyond the reach of Washington—and were breaking apart along class lines from within—so, too, were these socially troubled Indian reservations: in the southwest desert I saw the emergence of a neomedieval wilderness of semi-independent settlements.

I AM AN easterner with an easterner's sensory prejudices. In the eastern United States, the shorter distances between towns, the huddled-together hills, the heavy humid air, and the ranks of tall trees that partially block the view ahead and the sky above contract the landscape, so that every curve in the road brings a new surprise, a new

[1]Sources: U.S. Census Bureau, Indian Health Service, and Bureau of Indian Affairs.

chapter in a developing story. In the Southwest, though, everything is far away and the earth is naked of tree cover. The dry, thin air of these high plateaus expands the view and the sky, so that everything is seen at once; there are no developing chapters, no narrative: just an all-encompassing monotone where one strip-mall town follows another.

As I ascended, the air quickly became colder, then warmed up again a few minutes later as I descended. The lack of trees in the Southwest leads to a lack of moisture, which, coupled with the reduced oxygen of the 4,000-foot flatlands in the Sonora Desert north of Tucson makes it that much harder for the atmosphere to retain heat. Temperature changes are extreme. Throughout the day I was constantly removing and putting on my jacket. At night in the late autumn the thermometer would drop from seventy degrees to freezing.

Yet the dimensions of the sky and desert here are fantastic to behold. At 7,000 feet the air loses a quarter of its density, which explains the dreamy combination of sharp, prismlike sunlight and deadly dark shadows—the mark of high-altitude deserts—giving every image, whether a bare yellow escarpment or a lonely gas station, a one-dimensional, dioramic quality.

I like to believe that Coronado and his soldiers also noticed the magnificent change of landscape as they proceeded northward, away from present-day Mexico and into the heart of what would one day become the United States: a change that had begun with the columnar majesty of the saguaro cacti between Nogales and Tucson. But the record indicates otherwise. Even in Bernal Díaz del Castillo's account of Cortez's expedition—the most suggestive of all the writings of the Spanish "entrances" into North America[2]—there is a missing sensibility, heightened by a crassness that would shock the most assertive nouveau-riche climbers of our own time. Reading Díaz and the other Spaniards, one encounters details more useful to an accountant than to an armchair traveler—"There was water here, but no water there; there were crops here, none there; there were wealthy-looking houses or there were poor houses; there were birds; there were extractable minerals"—but no curiosity, introspection, or even wonder (as we experience it). García López de Cardenas, who, as a member of Coronado's expedition became the first European to see the Grand

---

[2]The term "entrance" or its plural, "entrances," a translation of the Spanish *entrada,* is often used by historians of this period in describing the first forays of Spaniards into Mexico and the southern half of the United States.

Canyon—coming upon it near Grand View, arguably the most spectacular lookout point along the south rim—was unimpressed. In his
manuscript, Cardenas mentions "thirst and hunger" and the lack of
Indian settlements to plunder, but not the canyon. Historian Herbert
E. Bolton writes, "They were looking for gold, not scenery."[3]

ARIZONA, WHICH I was crossing from south to north, like many
American states, is an act of faith, fiat, and illogic. It works because determined, ingenious people created facts on the ground that have
lasted more than a hundred years, since the first Americans arrived
here. The "Official State Map" prepared by the Arizona Department
of Transportation reminded me of maps I had seen of Bosnia. I will
explain.

First, there are the Indian reservations, colored in pale orange. Almost the entire northeast quadrant of Arizona is a Navajo reservation.
Navajo lands, which extend into New Mexico, are as large as Vermont,
Massachusetts, and New Hampshire combined, and twice the size of
Israel. Within this sprawling quadrant is a smaller Hopi Indian reservation, delineated by broken red lines. And within this Hopi square
are squiggly islands of more Navajo lands. To the south, in eastern
Arizona, is another pale orange blotch denoting an Apache reservation, about three times the size of Rhode Island. Even further south,
extending northward from the Mexican border, is the Papago Indian
reservation, about the same size as the Apache one. Throughout the
state runs a pale orange archipelago of more Indian lands. There are
also vast areas in the southwest of the state marked off by both thick
blue-gray lines and broken red ones. These are military bases, such as
the Barry M. Goldwater Air Force Range—about twice the size of
Rhode Island—where the U.S. Air Force regularly bombs imaginary
enemies into oblivion. Arizona Highway 85 is the only road traversing
this area, and civilian vehicles are not allowed to leave it. Then, of
course, there are the bright green shapes signifying national parks
and monuments, pale green shapes of national forests, pink shapes
for "national conservation units" such as wildlife refuges, and gray-
colored wilderness areas. In addition, there are railroad lands and

[3]Bolton, who died in 1953, taught at the University of California at Berkeley. In
his time, he was considered the premier historian of Spain's activities in North
America. I have relied on his reading and interpretation of Cardenas's manuscript in *Coronado: Knight of Pueblos and Plains.*

mysterious white squares marked by black lines that are described as "sites or settlements" with "limited or no service." Occasionally, these territories overlap each other. John Gunther wrote fifty years ago in *Inside U.S.A.*, "About 80 percent of Arizona is still public land, and the federal government owns a greater proportion of it, some 69 per cent, than of any other state." Those remarks are still relevant, if Indian reservations are included as public land.

The larger regional map showed further evidence of the power and relevance of the federal government. In the nineteenth century, the necessity to share water efficiently and fairly led Washington to divide the desert Southwest into even pieces. This accounts not only for the neat, rectangular shapes of Arizona, Utah, Colorado, and New Mexico, but also for the gridwork of counties within each state. As for the overlapping, Balkan-like blotches I had noticed, they work just fine so long as Washington rules this part of the continent and Arizona preserves a semblance of middle-class peace. Should the social disintegration I saw in Tucson's south side ever become pervasive while our governing institutions become infirm and border crossings from Mexico increase substantially, the broken lines on a map that today appear abstract could have deadly consequences, as I would soon see.

IT WAS A day of spectacular monotony: the Arizona desert can be as inspiring and changeless as the Sinai or the alkaline wastes of Yemen, Iran, Afghanistan, and Chinese Turkestan. Beyond the Gila River—a narrow wash marking the northern limit of the 1854 Gadsden Purchase, which completed the map of the lower forty-eight states—I continued northward to the town of Superior, a series of tract houses: dirty white serrations like bad teeth along pinkish hillsides, rattled by the wind. As I drove, one mountain outcropping led to another and another, until I reached an altitude where the last of the saguaro cacti had disappeared, replaced by a flat, shimmering salt bed, the view broken only by a metal and brown-painted wooden shack with a broken door off the roadside. Where the salt bed ended, I came upon spectacular green lawns, ranch houses, country clubs, shopping centers, and retirement communities. I was traversing the edge of a strip-mall belt as much as fifty miles in breadth called Phoenix: an oasis four times as big as Tucson. Though the Salt River provides Phoenix with more water than most other places in the Sonora Desert, the profusion of trees and lush lawns maintained by sprinkler systems suggests that humankind may be pressing its luck here.

When I discerned that lawns, shopping centers, and office parks were more or less all there was to this oasis, I drove on. Sixty miles north of Phoenix, the road climbed suddenly in a series of switchbacks. This was the Mogollon Rim, a rugged, craterlike escarpment whose rosy gray walls and outcrops hold majestic, dense expanses of fir, pine, and aspen. The Mogollon Rim marks the southern edge of the Colorado Plateau, a lunar tableland 5,000 to 8,000 feet high, capped with even higher buttes, mesas, and mountain ranges.[4] This was a real geographical border. The Colorado Plateau covers northeastern Arizona, southeastern Utah, southwestern Colorado, and northwestern New Mexico. It has its own Indian history and ecosystem and defines the "high-desert Southwest."

After driving several more hours on what looked like the glazed surface of a red earthen jar, I spied the shimmering outline of the Black Mesa, a 5,000-square-mile sandstone platform that rests atop the Colorado Plateau. On the mesa's three southern fingertips live the Hopi, in the middle of Navajo country. The struggle between the Hopi and the Navajo appears to outsiders age old, but it began only in the late nineteenth century as a reaction to modern development and the conversion of imperial territories to states, which necessitated the drawing of artificial borders and the adjudication of land rights for the exploitation of water and minerals. The Hopi and Navajo may seem alike to outsiders: both are Indians of the high Southwest. Yet to each other they are opposites: the Hopi, related vaguely to the Aztecs, dwell in urban clusters, or "pueblos," while the Navajo, descended from Arctic migrants, prefer far-flung, sparsely populated settlements.

There is a vague similarity here to the Serbs and Croats, who also seem alike to outsiders, though they represent the northernmost and southernmost extensions of their own respective imperial and religious domains: the rivalry between the Serbs and Croats, moreover, like that between the Hopi and Navajo, while appearing age old,

---

[4]Mesas and buttes are the different shapes of elevated landmasses that are composed of soft rock and therefore susceptible to erosion. A flat-topped rock is called a "mesa," the Spanish word for "table"—so named by the early explorers. If the rock has eroded to the point where it is no wider than it is tall, it is called a "butte." Further erosion will narrow a butte to a degree where it is called a "monument," "pinnacle," or "spire."

also dates only to the late nineteenth century and the conversion of empires to states. However arbitrary this comparison may seem, it illuminates a crucial point: the reemergence of North America's vast and increasingly sovereign Indian archipelago, with its resurgence of ethnic consciousness—along with the attendant court battles over mineral rights and gambling concessions—can lead only to increased conflict among the Indian tribes themselves as the power of the federal and state governments declines. A more politically and economically significant Indian America will likely be a divided, balkanized Indian America.

As early as 700 A.D., a people who called themselves "Hopi," a Uto-Aztecan word that means "well-behaved," migrated northward to the Colorado Plateau. These Hopi, like other Pueblo Indian groups, are descendants of the so-called Anasazi, or Basket Makers (known for their woven, clay-fired baskets), who may have arrived in the Southwest from Mexico as early as 1500 B.C. The Hopi built a series of villages that clung to the edges of the Black Mesa's three southern fingertips. Here enough subterranean water seeps through the permeable sandstone to form springs that can sustain life for several thousand people: the Hopi population of 8,000 that today inhabits the mesas is about the same as the number who lived here in the twelfth century.

As I left the red floor of the plateau and ascended to the 600-foot-high Second Hopi Mesa, I saw a honeycombed pueblo, made of cement and cinder blocks rather than the traditional mud brick. The village of Shungopavi, which means "water place where reeds grow," looked at first glance like a hideous caricature of the pueblos encountered by Coronado's horsemen. Though the faces that looked out at me from the cement blockhouses and mobile homes resting on cinder-block platforms looked ancient, like stone carvings, the poverty looked new and crass. Shungopavi's mobile homes, spread over a rocky wasteland, are upmarket housing compared to the shacks I saw nearby, with roofs of plywood and corrugated iron held down by old tires. Outside many dwellings I saw a pickup truck, often old and rusted, its hood open. There was not a garden or even a blade of grass. The old stoves and washers in the yards, even the beer cans and bottles and rusted bicycles, were sharply defined against the hard, featureless desert. Styrofoam food trays and plastic bags blew across the ground and over the corrugated iron roofs. Many of the Hopi I saw were overweight, with bad complexions.

At the edge of the mesa, like midair platforms overlooking the sweeping, black-orange moonscape of the Colorado Plateau, stood a few wooden outhouses amid the howling winds, the growling dogs, and the icy early-winter temperatures. I watched an old man enter one of these swaying, exposed closets as he must have done on many other freezing, windy days.

At the Hopi Cultural Center on the Second Mesa, I paid three dollars to enter a one-room museum of pottery and old photographs, with crude explanatory displays made of unevenly cut paper. A sign at the entrance warned, "Do not copy or take notes, we [only] share this information with you," an attempt to copyright the Hopi past. The Hopi ran a hotel, too. In my room I found a monograph entitled *A Brief History of the Hopi-Navajo Land Problem,* which says that the Hopi-Navajo dispute "is over one hundred years old" and "is further defined by the political, economic, social, and religious differences" between these two southwest Indian groups. That is to say, the monograph makes no bones about the intergroup hatred, for the Hopi had inhabited the Southwest since 700 A.D. and had occupied the Black Mesa since 1100 A.D., while the Navajo were mere newcomers, arriving in the mid–1400s after a very long presumed migration that began in Asia and took them across the Bering Strait into present-day Alaska and Canada, before they moved south into the Colorado Plateau. Whereas the Hopi coagulated into urban settlements from which they went out to farm their fields during the day, the Navajo roamed constantly over the high desert, stealing Hopi land. Even under Spanish and Mexican rule, "the Hopi were plagued by Navajo depredations" and "complained bitterly." Then the Americans made things worse.

In the early 1860s, when severe weather and hunger had forced the Navajo to raid Anglo settlements, the Americans retaliated. By 1863, "Kit" Carson and his troops drove the Navajo into reservations, leading the Hopi to think that the Navajo had finally been put in their place. But the Navajo broke loose and migrated back onto Hopi land. The U.S. Army could do little: the Civil War had not yet ended, and it would be two decades before the federal government consolidated its hold on the Southwest. A dismal series of agreements and misunderstandings among the federal government, the Navajo, and the Hopi followed. The map of the Navajo reservation grew larger and the map of the Hopi reservation smaller, until the Hopi territory—once larger than that of the Navajo newcomers—was enclosed in the Navajo territory. Now the Hopi want back the land on which the Navajo have remained long enough to acquire squatter's rights. Though the Navajo are willing to give monetary compensation to the Hopi for this land, they are not willing to leave it. The monograph ends with a plea to visitors to write the U.S. president, the U.S. Congress, and the governor of Arizona in support of the Hopi. What will happen, I wondered, if the federal government becomes as weak here as it was in the mid–nineteenth century? Was Jeff Smith's idea that the more numerous Navajos would simply kill the Hopis too far-fetched?

From the parking lot of the Hopi-run hotel I looked out over an arid, multilayered, treeless rock cake formed more then 300 million years ago. The Indian villages here have been in existence since the twelfth century: Shungopavi, along with Oraibi, a few miles to the west on the Third Mesa, are the oldest settlements in the territory of the United States. Some call Shungopavi the "Vatican" of the Hopi world because it is in the middle of the "Sacred Circle" on the edge of the Second Mesa between the First and the Third. The Spanish had encountered Indians here almost a century before the English landed at Plymouth Rock. Yet by the middle of the nineteenth century, the Southwest still constituted the last extensive tract of unmapped, empty territory in America. Arizona was admitted to the union only in February 1912, a month after New Mexico, making them the youngest states of the lower forty-eight. Yet ancient peoples are still fighting over this land. In the Desert Southwest, so old yet so recently a part of the United States, the idea of the United States as but one phase of history occurs naturally. Disputes among Indian tribes are in abeyance rather than reconciled; while sprawling post-urban settlements are—like those of the Hohokams—threatened by mounting water shortages.

1 8

Hopi Silences and
the Land of Awe

I LEFT THE Second Mesa and drove northeast for twenty minutes across the plateau. When I reached the First Mesa, I headed back uphill until I came to the Hopi village of Sichomovi, obscured by a dust storm. I entered a room with a folding table in the middle. A half-dozen short, silent, overweight Hopi women sat in a row against the wall, selling hand-carved and -painted kachina dolls.[1] One woman asked if I wanted to buy a doll. I said "No." Thereafter, none of the women said a word to me. Nor did they speak to each other. They simply sat and looked at nothing in particular, waiting, I suppose, for the next tourist to enter: whenever that might be. They seemed to me tragic, staring vacantly, wearing secondhand clothes. They were leaning against the wall without moving; I felt as though I were seeing them in a photograph rather than in life.

Seated behind the folding table in the middle of the room was another Hopi woman, shuffling and filling out forms. I asked her when the next tour of Walpi, a traditional Hopi village at the edge of the First Mesa, would begin. In a mellow southwestern accent she said,

---

[1] Kachinas are powerful spirits who visit the Hopi from the winter solstice until after the summer solstice. The rest of the year they inhabit the snow-clad San Francisco peaks to the southwest of the Hopi mesas.

"In half an hour, three-thirty." I walked outside, where I tried talking to a group of Hopi teenagers wearing tracksuits and sports shoes. But they were interested only in selling me a kachina doll, of which they had about two dozen in the back of their pickup. With the sand still blowing hard, I walked back inside and waited. At 3:30 P.M., the woman behind the desk suddenly stopped shuffling papers, got up, and said to me, "Okay, let's go for the tour."

She walked briskly for a few hundred yards to the edge of the First Mesa, where Walpi's collection of homes stood. "My name is Florence," she told me as I hurried along beside her. It was the last information she would volunteer.

Dogs growled at my ankles. The wind blew sand everywhere, rattling rusted bicycles, sheet-metal roofs, and broken plywood doors. A ruinscape of low shacks overlooking wilderness and outcroppings of rock came into view. Walpi was located on a narrow headland of rock 600 feet above the Colorado Plateau, some 6,000 feet above sea level. I caught the sharp, spicy smell of burning juniper rising from inside the hovels as I passed.

The mesa narrowed. A few feet to my right and left were drops of several hundred feet. Walpi lay immediately ahead, where the mesa widened into an island platform. The wind rose to an even higher shriek, and some multistoried adobe buildings rose above the shanties, with soft contours and light-colored walls. The dusty lanes between the houses were empty, and, except for the wind, there was silence. This was the Hopi "Center of the Universe," the "Sacred Circle," and the center of all "vibrations." The surrounding desert was vast as an ocean.

"How old is Walpi?" I asked Florence.

"Eight hundred years," she said.[2]

Though I expressed amazement, she did not reply.

"I mean," I tried to explain, "that it was built long before Coronado."

"Yes."

"How old are the adobe buildings in Walpi?"

"It depends."

I pointed to an island of dark rock rising above the desert in the distance, and asked, "That's the Second Mesa; how far away is it?"

---

[2]Guidebooks say Walpi was founded in the thirteenth century, which would make it, in fact, seven hundred years old.

"Ten miles."

"Is this the land disputed with the Navajos?"

"No, that's thirty-five miles away."

"Where do the Hopis grown corn?"

"Wherever you see clear spaces in the desert." She meant spaces not dotted with sagebrush.

"What are these?" I asked, pointing to circular holes in the ground with ladders projecting from them at forty-five-degree angles.

"Kivas."

"What are kivas?"

"For Hopi ceremony."

(Kivas are circular underground caverns where Hopi and other pueblo people of the Southwest hold secret dance ceremonies. During some of the skirmishes with Coronado's troops in what is now New Mexico, the natives retreated into kivas for protection.)

"How do most people in these villages earn a living?"

"They make dolls."

Suddenly, a leathery old woman stepped through a creaking plywood door and gave me a hearty "Hello." Had it not been for her and the smell of burning juniper, I might have thought Walpi was deserted.

"Do you want to buy kachina dolls?" the woman asked me bluntly, holding one in her hand. "I take American Express traveler's checks with one percent commission only."

"No, thank you," I replied.

"You sure you don't want to buy dolls from this woman?" Florence asked, annoyed.

"No, thank you," I repeated.

The old woman retreated behind the door. Florence led me back to her office. On the way back I noticed a sign declaring that Walpi would be closed to visitors on Veterans Day.

"Are there many Hopi war veterans?" I asked Florence.

"Many. And many never came back from the wars."

I ran out of questions. Florence and I said nothing as we returned over the bridge. The wind whistled. Hopi silences are cruel. It is as if through their silences, the Hopi were saying "You owe us."

The Hopi refuse to conform. They refuse to run lotteries and open casinos like most other Indians. Their brazen determination to scratch out a livelihood by small-scale basic farming, doll making, and the copyrighting of their past may only slow down, rather than arrest, the erosion of their culture by drugs, alcohol, gangs, and other effects of boredom that I would hear about as I traveled through Indian country. In a land ruled by technology and economic development, such communities are highly vulnerable. I thought of the sandstone buttes and spires gradually being worn away by the wind.

I HEADED EAST back into the Navajo reservation, in the vicinity of what is called the "Painted Desert": onto sprawling uplands speckled with juniper and chaparral, only to descend again into bare tableland that, in turn, narrowed into other mesas. For easterners who came west in the nineteenth century, whose world had been circumscribed by wooded hills, the limitless scale of this landscape, with its sharp, pitiless shapes and its purple, vermilion, and bright orange hues, must have been evidence of America's greatness and ultimately sunny fate. The *idea* of the West encompasses more than just the economic opportunity of the frontier and political expansion to the Pacific. Indeed, if the West had looked like another version of the East or the Midwest, its effect on the national psyche would not have been as immense as it has been. The High Desert influenced the Mormons as the Sinai wilderness had the Hebrews. The hardness and industry of both those groups grew out of their encounters with the Truth, as it had been physically revealed through landscape.[3]

Then I saw something even more spectacular than the High Desert, a sight that brought me nearly to tears: the Canyon de Chelly.

From where I first saw it, the Canyon de Chelly (pronounced "d'*shay*," a Spanish corruption of the Navajo word *tsegi*, meaning "rock canyon") is only about 350 feet deep, less than a tenth as deep as the Grand Canyon.[4] The November day was cold and windy, with dazzling sunlight and hard blue enamel skies. The few clouds were almost at eye level, and all around me was a pounding silence, except for the croak of a raven, whose wing beat I could almost feel through the air. The only other car in the parking lot belonged to a Navajo,

[3]The Joshua tree was named thus by the Mormons, as a sign that the Hebrew prophet Joshua was leading Mormons, too, to the Promised Land.
[4]*Tse* is the Navajo word for "rock"; it is used as a prefix for many other words such as *tseta'a*, meaning "rock ledge."

selling jewelry displayed on the hood.[5] Before me was a sandstone monolith of fiery red and salmon pink, topped near the canyon rim by a conglomeration of shale, siltstone, mudstone, and volcanic ash of an even richer earthen-red cast.[6] Parts of the canyon walls were dramatically streaked with lines in shades from brown to purple, a phenomenon known as "desert varnish" thought to be caused by manganese and iron oxides leached by water and deposited either on the rock's surface or on the clay particles that have settled on the rock.[7] But the color pageant would not have made the impression on me that it did had the walls of this miniature canyon not appeared so fragile, so crumbly thin, as though shaped by human fingers ready to wash away in the wink of an eon. I was struck by the dizzying cake swirl of patterns in the red and salmon-pink rock—what geologists call "cross-bedding"—an endless, numbing calligraphy written by wind and water over millennia. Hearing the wind howl before I actually felt it against my face, I could imagine it endlessly shaping the rock.

I stood for a while longer, thinking of the historical drama that had ensued in this place since the time of the Anasazi hunters a thousand years ago: here was the wilderness that would never be mastered, as revealed by the story of the Navajo.

The Navajo number 220,000, of whom 145,000 live on the reservation, the most populous reservation in the United States. According to legend, "the People" or *Dineh,* as the Navajo call themselves, emerged from "underground." Actually, the Navajo, along with the Apache, are Athapaskan-speaking Indians who once inhabited the dense forests of northeastern Asia and migrated to the woodlands of present-day Alaska and northwestern Canada about two millennia ago. Then they began drifting south and in the 1400s settled in the arid canyons of the Colorado Plateau, where these hunter-gatherers first became farmers, with help from the Hopi and other Pueblo people (beginning an uneasy relationship between the Navajo and Hopi

---

[5]The deepest hidden rocks of this canyon were formed in the Precambrian period, 3 billion years ago, near the beginning of geologic time. However, it is the youngest formations, from the Permian and Triassic periods, just before the first dinosaurs, between 200 and 165 million years ago, that account for today's visual drama. When the Canyon de Chelly was formed, the Rocky Mountains not only did not exist, they were at least 100 million years in the future.

[6]Geologists call this a "shinarump" conglomeration. According to *Webster's Third New International Dictionary,* the origin of this word is unknown.

[7]See Robert L. Casey, *Journey to the High Southwest: A Traveler's Guide,* for an excellent geological summary of the region.

that would worsen dramatically in the nineteenth and twentieth centuries).

Perhaps it was the millennia they had spent roaming through northeastern Asia and the Arctic regions of North America as hunter-gatherers, compared to the mere two centuries they had spent as settled farmers in the High Southwest, that had ignited both the Navajo's and the Apache's passion for the swift, beautiful animals the Spanish had brought to the New World. Whatever the reason, these Athapaskan speakers became the first Indians north of Mexico to become horsemen. By the late 1600s, the Navajo, in particular, were raiding Spanish settlements for horses and livestock. When the Spanish gained the upper hand around 1750, the Navajo migrated westward into the *tsegi*, or Canyon de Chelly. But the conflict did not end, since the Spanish settlements spread westward, too.

In January 1805 (around the time Lewis and Clark entered the Montana Rockies in the third year of their exploration of the Louisiana Territory), an experienced Spanish Indian fighter, Antonio Narbona, became the first European to explore the Canyon de Chelly. With clubs, swords, and coarse lead shot, Narbona's three hundred troops from Sonora massacred more than a hundred Navajos, including women and children, who had taken refuge in a cave. Narbona wrote that he "reconnoitered" the canyon "from its beginning to its mouth. . . . [It] is inhabited by many people and by nature fortified by the cliffs that form it. . . . Its center is spacious and in it they [the Navajo] have plenty of farmlands which are watered by a regular river that runs through the middle, but this does not stop the enemy from attacking from the heights."[8] Narbona's account is chillingly functional: he came, he killed, he left. A soldier of fortune like the other Spanish explorers, he saw a landscape only for what it was literally worth. (How much water does it have? Is it suitable for agriculture? Is there gold?) Because the Spanish were not inspired by this landscape, they lost it to the Anglos, who did find it inspiring.

U.S. Army Lieutenant James H. Simpson was the first Anglo to write about the Canyon de Chelly, which he explored in 1849. In his loving, detailed narrative of the geology of the canyon, Simpson calls the red sandstone walls "stupendous . . . as if they had been chiseled by

[8]The quote is from a letter that Narbona wrote to Governor Fernando Chacón on January 14, 1805, kept in the archives of the New Mexico State Records Center and translated by David Brugge. Parts of the letter are reprinted in Campbell Grant, *Canyon de Chelly: Its People and Rock Art*.

the hand of art . . . [the canyon] is indeed, a wonderful exhibition of nature." Simpson further describes his astonishment at how the Navajo inhabitants "commenced tripping down the almost vertical wall before them as nimbly and dexterously as minuet dancers!"[9] Captain John G. Walker led a second Anglo expedition into the Canyon de Chelly in 1859. He writes:

> The approach of the Chelly is over an undulating tableland . . . with absolutely nothing to indicate the vicinity of one of the greatest of natural phenomena, until you are startled by finding yourself suddenly upon the brink of this fearful chasm, which seems to open under your very feet into the bowels of the earth.[10]

The purpose of the Walker expedition deep into Navajo country was to "show the flag": to let the Indians know that the U.S. Army could now go wherever it chose. But two years later, in 1861, Confederate deserters from the Union Army defeated U.S. Army troops in the region and Navajo raiding resumed. By 1862, Union troops had routed the Confederates in New Mexico's Rio Grande Valley, and Union Colonel James H. Carleton turned his wrath on the Navajo. Carleton told his troops, "All Indian men of that tribe are to be killed whenever and wherever you can find them."[11] To harass the Navajo, Carleton put the fur trapper and mountain man Kit Carson in charge of 700 soldiers and 326 volunteers.

Carson was the ultimate American hero: a Pathfinder straight out of James Fenimore Cooper, who lives alone, braving death, yet who, by killing the enemies of western settlement, retains his purity.[12] Moreover, his fame rests not on his exploits alone but on a very American-style publicity machine. Carson was born in 1809 in Madison County, Kentucky, near Abraham Lincoln's birthplace and in the same year. When he was two years old, Carson's family moved to the Missouri frontier. After his father died, Carson worked as an apprentice to a saddle maker in Old Franklin, Missouri, an outfitting point on the Santa Fe Trail. But at the age of sixteen, he ran away, joining a wagon train to Taos, a frontier post and Pueblo Indian encampment

[9]Simpson, *Report of an Expedition into the Navajo Country in 1849.*
[10]Walker and Major O. L. Shepherd, *The Navajo Reconnaissance: A Military Exploration of the Navajo Country in 1859.*
[11]See Bil Gilbert, *Westering Man: The Life of Joseph Walker,* for more information on Carleton and his orders to his men.
[12]See D. H. Lawrence, *Studies in Classic American Literature,* for a discussion of the mythology pervading Cooper's novels.

in north-central New Mexico, seventy miles north of Santa Fe. For the next fourteen years, he ventured from Taos with exploring parties as a cook, guide, and hunter. Carson, a mere five feet, four inches in height, was a ladies' man who dueled with other hunters over Indian girls, whom he courted and occasionally married. Though Carson lived in a tipi for years, he reportedly never learned to pitch one, nor did he, compared to a few others who were lesser known, excel as a fur trapper and mountain man.[13]

In the spring of 1842, the thirty-three-year-old Carson returned to Missouri, out of money and prospects. In Independence, he met the Georgia-born surveyor and advocate of westward expansion John Charles Fremont. Carson told Fremont that he "could guide him to any point he wished to go." Fremont, a much better publicist than explorer, saw immediately that in Kit Carson he had happened upon real gold. Carson was experienced, yet still young and unknown, meaning that Fremont could "discover" him for the American public. Unlike some of the older mountain men who had been made famous in the East, Carson—handsome, with thick blond hair—looked the part, despite his small stature. In summer 1842, Carson led Fremont across the Great Plains en route to the south pass of the Rockies, in present-day Wyoming. By the following year, when Fremont's report of the expedition was published, Carson had emerged from the ranks of frontiersmen to become an overnight celebrity, the new Daniel Boone, and a hero of dime novels.[14]

By 1862, when the army called on Carson to root out the Navajo, he was fifty-three. His long hair had gone gray. Headquartered at Taos, he had been a U.S. government Indian agent on good terms with various tribes. He objected to Carleton's brutal policy toward the Navajo but put his reservations aside and, in January 1864, entered the Canyon de Chelly, intent on wiping out resistance in the last unconquered redoubt of the suffering Navajo. Snow lay deep and ice ran in the stream at the bottom of the canyon. For Carson's men, the battle was less against the Indians than against the elements. After a few skirmishes in which a dozen or more warriors were killed, the remaining Navajo quickly gave up. Many of the Navajo Carson's

---

[13]Joseph Walker, for example—a different Walker from the one who explored the Canyon de Chelly in 1859—was considered a more skillful, accomplished trapper and mountain man; see Gilbert, *Westering Man.*

[14]See Gilbert, *Westering Man,* and Charles Averille, *Kit Carson, Prince of the Gold Hunters,* as well as the materials in the Kit Carson Home and Museum in Taos.

men captured were women and children, dying of starvation and exposure.

The bitter cold made it impossible for the cavalrymen who relieved Carson in the Canyon de Chelly to destroy the hogans and five thousand peach trees that the Navajos had planted there. But in August the army returned and destroyed every tree and hogan. Then, in the winter of 1864, the army forced 8,500 starving, disease-ridden, shivering Navajo to march to a reservation near Fort Sumner on the Pecos River, in the windy badlands of New Mexico, three hundred miles east of the Canyon de Chelly. For four years the Navajo remained near Fort Sumner, where many died of starvation. Then the U.S. government, embarrassed by the scandal and tired of feeding so many Indians, allowed the Navajo to walk back to their tribal lands. The Navajo still return to the Canyon de Chelly in the spring and fall to plant and harvest corn and to live in hogans. Navajo shepherds still draw on the cave walls with charcoal.

AFTER A FEW more hours of driving northeast I reached Four Corners, the only point in the United States where four states meet. The Navajo charge $1.50 per car to enter the area. I paid and walked toward a smooth stone monument on a polished metal platform, where I was able to stand in Arizona, New Mexico, Colorado, and Utah all at once. A middle-aged couple—he was black, she was white—joyously snapped pictures of each other on the monument. She pointed out a snow-clad peak in the distance and told me, "That's Sleeping Ute Mountain over in Colorado," where the Ute Indian reservation abuts the Navajo one. Surrounding the monument was a Navajo jewelry market under sheet-metal roofs and clumsy signs. These were the borders I liked: Indians, whites, blacks, states, all meeting, mingling, overlapping. To step on the monument was thrilling because each of these four states had a richly developed identity that gave the borders here real meaning. Yet these were not onerous borders: they did not require passports or police. The dream of so many unstable regions of the world, I knew, is to have borders as peaceful yet as meaningful as these. Europeans, excepting the Swiss and to some degree the Germans with their federal structures, have no experience in such overlapping sovereignties. The American system, with power divided among Washington, fifty states, and thousands of municipalities, may actually accommodate itself well to a future of increasingly ambiguous sovereignty. In other words, the very governing genius of the United States may both ease and permit a slow passage toward a wilderness of semi-independent principalities, some fabulously successful, others disastrous. Take, for example, the Navajo reservation.

19

Veterans Day

FROM THE FOUR Corners monument I drove into Shiprock, New Mexico. To my left, rising 1,700 feet from the desert, was the red rock for which the town is named: a volcanic plug with winglike protrusions. It had reminded the conquistadors of a ship, but in one Navajo legend, the three-million-year-old winged rock is the "great bird" that carried the Navajo here from the Arctic.

The town, whose population of 12,000 is 95 percent Navajo, is a typical run-down settlement in Indian country. On an achingly flat, gray plain of blowing dirt, where the temperature drops to freezing by evening, were miles of mobile homes mounted on cinder blocks mingling with prefabricated tract houses of the poorest kind and brutally drab strip malls. Kentucky Fried Chicken and Taco Bell were the only national chains I saw among the bottom-of-the-line stores that lined the highway, and they appeared luxurious compared to everything else around.

Most of the vehicles were old, rusted pickups. Shiprock had no greenery, no primary colors, only browns and grays. I saw tipis surrounded by fences of old tires.

I had arranged to meet Duane "Chili" Yazzie the following morning for coffee at Kentucky Fried Chicken. A friend had told me that Chili was "a major power on the Navajo Tribal Council, forty-five years old, a onetime chairman of the budget committee: tough, intense, and circumspect." Chili "might talk to you only if he sees a personal advantage," my friend warned me. When I had called Chili a few days before and mentioned that I was a contributing editor to *The Atlantic Monthly*, he had suggested I spend the night at the Best Western hotel in Farmington, about twenty-five miles east of Shiprock. "I guess that's the only place around here suitable for someone of your standing," Chili said, I thought somewhat reproachfully. Farmington was an Anglo community with a population of 35,000, featuring new banks and ATM machines. The Best Western had a swimming pool and hosts local conventions. To someone from Tucson or Santa Fe, Farmington was forgettable: a place you drove through without stopping except for gas. To a Navajo, Farmington—whose Best Western charged sixty dollars for a single room—was Paris.

Chili wore a black goatee, a ponytail, and a black headband, along with a black cotton sweatshirt and torn sweatpants. The pupil of his left eye was cloudy with what looked like trachoma. Chili's red wristband read, "USAF Lt. Jeffrey Lemmon, 4/25/71, Laos, MIA." "I'm a supporter of the MIA cause," Chili said bluntly.

He had pulled up next to my rented 1995 Toyota compact in a lumbering old automobile with a professional football insignia on the rear license plate. Like Cayce Boone, the Navajo whose sweat lodge I had visited south of Tucson, Chili looked at me as though from a distance, sizing me up. We sat at a table with a view of the parking lot, a gas station, and Thatsaburger—a low-end fast-food outlet—across the highway. Kentucky Fried Chicken in Shiprock was fairly busy at nine in the morning. The notables in town conducted business here. I noticed that Chili was missing an arm.

"What happened to your arm?" I asked.

"It was in the 1970s. I was driving. I picked up this hitchhiker, a white guy. It turned out that he was bad, had a record. But with me he finally went big time. For no reason he pointed a .357 magnum at me from inside his poncho and just shot me in the arm."

I wasn't sure I believed him. I wanted to know Chili better, so I proceeded with the interview.

"What's the most important political issue on the Navajo reservation now?" I asked.

Chili said nothing for a moment. Then he spoke: "Decentralization: decentralization's not just a Washington issue—moving money and power back to the states, I mean. Even here, within the reservation, the number one issue is about moving money and power out of the reservation capital at Window Rock [in Arizona] and dispersing it to the 110 chapters, into which the Navajo reservation is divided. We get around $250 million every year from Washington and $100 million from our own resources—mining on the reservation, whatever. But seventy percent of that money is spent by Window Rock bureaucrats. The idea is to move the money down to the local chapters and let them spend it. People are afraid, though. The money from Washington will gradually dry up. We will be on our own. We'll have to manage our money better than we do now. But at the chapter level there is often no expertise or formal mechanism for that. Some chapters have talented people, but many are full of incompetent, uneducated people. Instead of dictatorship from Window Rock, we could have the reverse: chaos. . . . We're beginning to enter a difficult transition."

Chili had me thinking. According to what Indians and white experts had told me, there might not even be a Bureau of Indian Affairs (BIA) in the future, given the downsizing in Washington. American Indians will then be truly independent: the only aggrieved minorities in the United States with sovereign territorial rights, more like Kurds and Chechens than like blacks and women's groups. Schools on Indian reservations were now teaching Indian history rather than American history, challenging the American belief that one of the primary duties of education is to assimilate every child to a common past and sense of place in the national culture.[1] Tribes were assuming some of their former characteristics, having broken free of the homogenizing mold imposed by Anglo boarding schools and BIA controls. For example, the Mescalero Apache[2] in southern New Mexico had enraged other residents of the Southwest, particularly white environmentalists, by turning their reservation into a nuclear waste dump in return for big cash payments. One Apache official said, "The Hopis make pottery, the Navajos make rugs, and we Apaches make money."[3] In other words, the Hopi were still the docile village dwellers, the Navajo seminomads, and the Apache, as in the nineteenth century, the most aggressive Indians of all.

---

[1]See Fergus M. Bordewich, *Killing the White Man's Indian.*
[2]"Mescalero" means "mescal people," from this Apache tribe's custom of eating parts of the mescal cactus.
[3]*U.S. News & World Report,* Jan. 1996.

Chili and other Indians I met suggested that sovereignty for each of 551 separate Indian groups would lead to intertribal battles and to political and social breakdown within various tribes, as the loss of federal aid would mean either greater poverty or destructive ways of replacing the aid, such as nuclear waste storage and casino gambling.[4] I had heard and read accounts of Satanism and gang activity among reservation youth: in Fort Defiance, Arizona, the base for the U.S. Army's campaign against the Navajo in the mid–nineteenth century, young Navajo women now sleep in shifts at night to protect themselves against rape by Navajo gang members.[5] Instead of the "time of the grandparents," when children would hear stories from the elders, there is television, thanks to relatively cheap satellite dishes. A Navajo woman conceives an average of more than four children in her lifetime, a fertility rate comparable to Egypt's, Cambodia's, and El Salvador's and twice the Anglo rate.

"Our inability to cope in the white man's world may be due to our Indian culture," Chili told me. In other words, the Navajo are an ancient people severed from their traditions through coercive assimilation, then nakedly exposed to the worst aspects of American culture: soap operas, rap music videos, and so forth. So disorientation reigns. "Shiprock is on the cutting edge of this traumatic transition," Chili said. "That's because of Shiprock's closeness to Farmington, which represents the dominant Anglo culture, unlike Gallup [in New Mexico] and Flagstaff [in Arizona], which are dominated by Indians. You would not believe the problems here in Shiprock. Many Navajos don't even look for work. The welfare culture has destroyed us. You want Indians to have dignity, then the federal government should get rid of welfare.

"But we are creating a new hybrid culture," Chili went on optimistically, "like the Japanese, who are way up in cyberspace. Our kids will be technocrats. They will go to college."

"But Shiprock looks bad," I cut in. "It looks depressed. No landscaping, not even a garden."

---

[4]The figure of 551 tribes is from Charles Trueheart and Dennis McAuliffe Jr., "Indians Demand Power, Economic Benefits as Free Market Sweeps the Hemisphere."

[5]Albuquerque's *Sunday Journal* ran a front-page investigation about a low-income housing project for Navajo in Fort Defiance that the residents call "Little Beirut," due to gang activity involving homicides, graffiti, and the terrorizing of residents; see Leslie Linthicum, "Surge of Violence on the Reservation."

Chili was silent for a moment, then said sharply, "Shiprock used to be a quaint little town until the 1970s. Then . . . do you really want to hear it?"

"Yes," I said.

"In 1970, there was this Navajo fellow, Peter MacDonald. He had been some kind of aerospace engineer, someone who had made it in the white man's world. He seemed a kind of savior. Then, over time, he got a lock on the tribal council in Window Rock. The man was in control, I mean. There were stories of questionable deals between *Mr.* MacDonald"—Chili pronounced the word "Mister" with disdain— "and the AFL-CIO. Then, in 1976 I think it was, a number of Mac- Donald's critics were killed in a suspicious plane crash. We suspected the crash was engineered, that the victims had disappeared in an- other way. There were no discernible body parts at the crash site. We heard that the chunks of flesh found at the site were sent to a lab in Texas and turned out to be pig meat. We heard incredible, totally in- credible stories about how the victims—those who had gone up against *Mr.* MacDonald—were being held captive in exotic places. The reservation went wild.

"I was a principal player in all of this," Chili continued. "Remem- ber, this was the time when I was shot by the guy in the poncho. Peo- ple here concluded that there was a connection between my being shot and MacDonald's attempts to silence his critics. MacDonald con- trolled the police here, and I was one Indian who did not care for the way *Mr.* MacDonald ran things. MacDonald controlled the reserva- tion like a centralized monarchy. That's partly why Shiprock looks the way it does: we here in Shiprock didn't like *Mr.* MacDonald, and he made us pay. We in this town were the bad stepchild of the tribal gov- ernment. MacDonald is now in a federal penitentiary for stealing land and money." Then, rather self-consciously, Chili said, "I'm sorry for being so long-winded."

An experienced journalist in the region, Bill Donovan, who had re- ported on Peter MacDonald's rise and fall, would later tell me, "Mac- Donald was sort of a Navajo version of the late Mayor Richard Daley of Chicago. He took bribes and was corrupt. But many say the reser- vation 'worked' when MacDonald ran it, and many Navajos will actu- ally tell you that when MacDonald gets out of prison, they could do worse than return him to power. MacDonald was a strong, Third World dictator."

That opinion was seconded by a long article in *Mother Jones* on

MacDonald in 1982.[6] MacDonald's story, it turns out, is a cautionary tale for the future of Third World America. Peter MacDonald's original name was Hashkasilt Begay. His great-grandfather had owned five thousand head of sheep and more then three hundred horses. This counted for nothing, however, in the BIA boarding school in Shiprock, where white teachers beat Indian children and ridiculed their names. One day in 1938, nine-year-old Hashkasilt heard someone singing "Old MacDonald Had a Farm." The boy renamed himself MacDonald and joined the Marine Corps at fifteen. Later, he graduated with a degree in electrical engineering from the University of Oklahoma and became a project engineer for Hughes Aircraft in California, where he helped design guidance systems for the Polaris missile. In 1963, after six years at Hughes, MacDonald suddenly returned to the reservation "to help however I could." In 1965, he got the job of dispersing federal antipoverty money on the reservation, and in 1970 he successfully ran for the post of tribal chairman. That year the Navajo government's annual budget was $18 million. In 1980, after a decade of MacDonald's leadership, the budget had soared to $137 million. MacDonald had accomplished that feat by exploiting—with the help of some high-priced Phoenix attorneys— the reservation's considerable coal and uranium reserves. Much Navajo land had been turned into a huge strip mine. "MacDonald's brand of development has created a classic Third World colony . . . visible signs of wealth and status in bureaucratic Window Rock [the Navajo capital] surrounded by a sea of rural poverty . . . the reservation becomes more industrialized and more colonized," wrote journalists Jeff Gillenkirk and Mark Dowie. By the late 1970s, MacDonald had emasculated the tribal judiciary, replacing judges with cronies, and people began to speak of him as a "dictator." In the 1980s, MacDonald fell from power, when his corruption finally came to the attention of the U.S. justice system.

What will happen, I thought, if U.S. law gradually weakens in an age of increased Indian sovereignty, as tribal figures build mini-empires through mining, casino gambling, and storing nuclear and other toxic wastes? Chili Yazzie, by Shiprock standards, is "very smart." But this worried me. Chili's account of the airplane accident and his own shooting suggests the kind of näiveté that makes someone like him unlikely to govern well should he one day come to power.

[6]See Jeff Gillenkirk and Mark Dowie, "The Great Indian Power Grab."

"Do you want to go to the cemetery?" Chili asked as we finished a second cup of coffee.

"Why?"

"It's Veterans Day. We're supposed to have a ceremony, though it may be over by now."

I was ashamed to admit that I had forgotten about the national holiday.

"Follow me in your car," Chili said.

The veterans' cemetery in Shiprock sprawled across a long hillside that overlooked the High Desert. The ceremony was over by the time we had arrived. It didn't matter. I was moved in a way that I had not expected to be. There was no fence, no landscaping, just tufts of gama grass and tumbleweed amid some hundred or so graves scattered beneath a vast curvature of blue sky. The graves were not orderly, and there were no stone markers. The raised dirt mounds were decorated with red plastic pinwheels and empty beer cans arranged in rectangular or circular patterns. American flags of many sizes had been stuck into each mount: some were plastic, some wooden and painted red, white, and blue. More flapped in the stiff wind. Over a few mounds where family groups stood in silence, full-size American flags had been laid out. Chili explained that each flag had been wrapped around a coffin on the day of burial; the families unfurl them once a year on Veterans Day. "Indians serve in the military in greater proportion than other ethnic groups," Chili said, "because we're defending the land itself more than just the abstract idea of the U.S.A."

Chili's wife and children drove up in a truck to meet us, and we all walked through the cemetery together. Because of his missing arm, Chili hadn't served in the military. He told me he felt bad about that. Otherwise, none of us said much. Looking out over the sharply defined, high-altitude hillside crested with snapping American flags—planted amid beer cans and pinwheels on mounds covering dead soldiers—I thought that whatever America's destiny, it had already been incorporated into the native religion of these Navajo. Those cheap plastic and cloth flags had a permanent, mythic feel that sent a chill up my spine.

FROM SHIPROCK I drove south on U.S. 666 to Gallup, ninety-three miles away. U.S. 666, which traverses the eastern edge of the Navajo reservation—connecting the Ute reservation to the north with the

Zuni lands to the south—has a reputation for high-speed, drunken accidents, especially among Indians. It is said that the three digits, 6—6—6, are unlucky, and there have been calls for changing the numerical assignation of the road.

In Gallup I checked into El Rancho Hotel, a neon palace on old Route 66 by the railroad tracks with a two-story lobby featuring Navajo rugs and animal heads mounted on the walls. A brother of D. W. Griffith (America's first major film director, who made *Birth of a Nation*) had opened El Rancho in 1937. Many Hollywood stars had stayed here while making grade B (and occasionally grade A) westerns in the nearby sagebrush desert.[7] Five miles further along old Route 66 was the Shalimar Lounge, a cavernous space with a bar at each end backed by mirrored signs framed by colored neon advertising beer, gin, and so forth.

Dozens of couples clutched each other in the dark and danced to the loud, syrupy rhythms of an electrically amplified western band. This was the real West: I saw every manner of cowboy hat but not a single baseball hat. I noticed two short, thin men on the dance floor, with thick glasses, crew cuts, electronic beepers attached to their belts, and big felt Stetsons tilted atop their heads. Whites, Indians, and Hispanics mixed easily, and I saw several mixed couples and table groups of various ethnic combinations. One table of half a dozen blacks kept apart; a man at that table was shouting profanities that made the other blacks at his table uncomfortable and that the whites, Indians, and Hispanics studiously ignored until a policeman told him to shut up. A number of cops circulated in the crowd, and more at the entrance, with guns and clubs, checking IDs. At midnight, as I headed back to El Rancho Hotel, Route 66 was an eerie succession of pulsing neon broken by patches of black and the sound of train whistles and police sirens. The nightclubs and gas stations appeared as transitory as the train whistles.

The next morning I saw Ben Shelley, a full-blooded Navajo and the commissioner for McKinley County, of which Gallup is the seat. He is also a member of the Navajo National Delegation and chairman of the Navajo Gaming Committee. Shelley wore a plaid shirt and jeans, and his boots were muddy. "The Navajos in New Mexico are more ad-

[7]These films include *The Bad Man,* with Wallace Beery and Ronald Reagan; *Colorado Territory,* with Joel McCrea; *Streets of Laredo,* with William Holden and William Bendix; and *Quantrille's Raiders.*

vanced than those in Arizona," he told me. "We in New Mexico are not as isolated from the big Anglo towns as our relatives in Arizona, so we know what needs to be done. It was the Arizona Navajos who voted down gambling casinos in the last referendum in 1994; the 'yes' votes came mostly from this side of the state line. Then there were the church people—both in and outside the reservation—who opposed gaming. But everyone knows it's coming. We all know we're short on revenue. We lack the money for environmental enforcement of our coal mining, and we don't have a landfill for people to burn their wood and garbage. Let's face it, we're going back to the Old West. In the future, there will be no more money or rules from the white man's government in Washington. Washington doesn't have the money or the will anymore. The Navajos will be on their own. We have to be. Everybody wants guns, fences. Society is breaking down, but gaming will help raise the revenue to patch it all together: sixty million dollars a year. We have a five-to-ten-year pilot project ready to go the moment we win the next referendum. Everything is in place. We will run buses from all over the reservation and from the major Anglo towns outside the reservation to the casinos. The casinos will need day care and video arcades; you can't let the kids hang around in parking lots with nothing to do. The Navajos and the Hopis are among the only holdouts against gaming in Indian America. But that situation is about to change. The Navajo gods have always gambled."

Driving east to Santa Fe, I stopped at the Sky City Casino, located on the Acoma Indian reservation.[8] The highway sign was typical: WELCOME TO THE ACOMA INDIAN RESERVATION, TURN RIGHT FOR CASINO. The casino's air of hushed wholesomeness and sterility was devastating, like that of sex houses in Bangkok where credit cards are accepted and copulation with teenage beauties is safe, easy, and mechanical. Sky City was a brightly lit indoor stadium with nothing but long, yawning rows of beeping slot machines, operated by transfixed truck drivers, retirees whose chartered buses had brought them this weekday morning, and pregnant mothers with toddlers at their feet. Except for a few noisy children, the carpeted aisles had the whispering, cubicled hush of a roomful of computer terminals. There were

[8]Acoma are Pueblo Indians, like the Hopi, Zuni, and Taos: members of the Uto-Aztecan language group. Don Juan de Oñate, a native of New Spain—as Spanish-colonized Mexico was then called—led a group of settlers into the territory of these Indians around 1600, in the course of which he massacred six hundred to eight hundred Acoma.

cashiers, ATM machines, and uniformed Acoma Indian attendants patrolling the restrooms with mops and extra toilet paper. There was no socializing and certainly no drama, no hint of the romance of the roulette table, over which elegant men and women once flirted. There was no roulette at all here or even blackjack, only slots and long rows of solitary, mostly overweight people compulsively pumping coins into them—masturbating. Playing "the slots is an autistic activity—mindless, solitary, and addictive," writes the English critic A. Alvarez. These people were fat for the same desperate reason they gambled: the hopeless quest to satisfy gross material desires. In the early 1990s, slot machine revenues were climbing by almost 40 percent annually while table game revenues were declining. By 1995, legal gambling was generating $37 billion yearly in the United States, nearly half the cost of the former federal welfare and food stamp programs and cash assistance to the elderly poor combined.[9] Americans place more than $400 billion annually in legal wagers, that is, more than three times the amount spent at the cinema box office or to see professional sports.[10] With real wages tapering off and gambling—as Ben Shelley's soliloquy suggested—still a growth industry, there seems to be no end in sight, though of course there will be.

[9]See Robert Goodman, *The Luck Business.*
[10]See John Kifner, "An Oasis of Casinos Lifts a Poor Mississippi County."

20

Onstage in Santa Fe and Taos

AN ESPRESSO BAR, a woman in L. L. Bean gear pushing a baby in a Mothercare pram, a sign advertising African drumming lessons, and several bookstores—one offering rare editions—startled me. From the Acoma reservation I had driven 90 minutes eastward and entered the tangy, pine-scented air of Sante Fe, 7,000 feet high. The wooden shop shingles, hand-painted in earthen shades; the tasteful, pale orange adobe facades; the Nissan Pathfinders; along with the road signs pointing to "condominium developments" told me that the price of real estate had risen sharply at a certain invisible line a mile or so back. While a luxury villa with a swimming pool and a Jacuzzi costs $125,000 in Gallup, in Santa Fe a town house apartment costs $350,000.

Santa Fe is the Hamptons-plus-Malibu in the heart of the blue-collar Southwest, where the immensity of a deep blue, high-altitude sky substitutes for an ocean. The aesthetic perfection of the lean, sculpted men and women on the streets and in the shops was shocking after the lumpy people I had seen on the Indian reservations and elsewhere.

I found myself staring at a man in a magnificent Navajo vest—the kind Navajo never wear—reading *The Wall Street Journal.* As I scribbled in my notebook, my last Bic pen ran out of ink. I went into a shop selling Navajo rugs for several thousand dollars apiece to ask where I could buy a pen, since all I saw around me in the main square and streets of downtown Santa Fe were boutiques. There were no other customers in the shop. A woman wearing a designer T-shirt and expensive jewelry was talking on the phone in a New York accent discussing Federal Express. She was using a laptop computer. Federal Express, *The Wall Street Journal, The New York Times* were commonplace in Santa Fe but all but unknown almost everywhere else I had traveled in the Southwest: Santa Fe was another cultural and economic oasis, another specialized community like the Indian reservations I had passed through, though prosperous, of course, and not dysfunctional like the reservations. Yet it, too, was a distinct island in a desert sea, full of designer magazine homes with luxurious English gardens (supported by expensive sprinkler systems) and gated luxury communities.

I struggled to get the woman's attention. She ignored me. Symphony music filtered through small speakers. I left the shop and entered a similar one, this one selling Asian art and with chamber music in the background, and the same sort of slightly underfed, vaguely bohemian woman at the center. It turned out that Woolworth's was the only place in downtown Santa Fe where I could buy cheap pens, but when I went to Woolworth's I found that its lease had run out and it was clearing out the remaining items it had left. Luckily, I was able to buy some pens.

I found a restaurant offering a mixture of fancy Mexican and Lebanese food. Three men sat at the adjoining table, one with a ponytail, another wearing a poncho and beret, the third a cowboy hat with a feather stuck in it. They were talking in East Coast accents about Georgia O'Keeffe and then about "Native Americans." This was the first time I had heard the term "Native American" since entering what Navajos and Pueblo Indians themselves—along with the signs—call "Indian country." Then they talked about diets, and I overheard the usual chatter about cholesterol levels . . . triglycerides . . . antioxidants . . . saturated fats, and San Pellegrino versus the hardness of the local water.

The restaurant was across the street from the oldest public building in the United States, the Palacio Real, built of white adobe and dark wood between 1610 and 1612. Here General Lewis Wallace of the Union Army, the governor of the New Mexico Territory, wrote *Ben Hur* in the late 1870s. The building is now a museum: in the gift shop

were two saleswomen with East Coast accents who talked with satis-
faction about the seventy-degree sunshine here and the snow and
freezing rain in New York. A few blocks away from the Palacio Real is
the dead drop where associates of Julius and Ethel Rosenberg passed
nuclear secrets from the nearby Los Alamos laboratory to the Russians. A few blocks in another direction is the jail where Billy the Kid
was imprisoned between December 1880 and April 1881, before he
escaped and was shot to death later that year by Sheriff Pat Garrett.
Billy the Kid was born in New York City, and his real name was probably Henry Bonney or Henry McCarty. Personal reinventions are not
new to Santa Fe. What is new is the scale at which they now occur.

THE SPANISH MAY have established Santa Fe as early as 1607, mak-
ing it older than Jamestown, the first permanent English colony in
North America. In 1825, President James Monroe, the last of the
Founding Fathers, in one of his last presidential acts, appropriated
$30,000 to survey and mark the Santa Fe Trail, linking the westering
Anglo-American empire with newly independent Mexico, which, with
the departure of the Spanish, could now trade freely with the United
States. The Santa Fe Trail, which started near Fort Leavenworth and
continued in a southwesterly direction to Santa Fe and Taos, was one
of the continent's main trade routes and a vector for Manifest Destiny
until the arrival of the railroad in 1880, which brought among other
cargo, artists and writers.[1]

It is impossible not to be struck here by the sensuous Spanish dress
and architecture; the aroma of piñon, sage, and juniper; the cut-glass
clarity of the light; and the high-altitude vistas of the pink desert and
the Sangre de Cristo (Blood of Christ) Mountains. "No man who has
seen the women, heard the [mission] bells or smelled the pinon
smoke of Taos will ever be able to leave," Kit Carson said. Mabel
Dodge Luhan, who from the tail end of the Gilded Age through
World War II presided over a movable salon—first in Florence, then
in Greenwich Village, and finally in Santa Fe–Taos, which she "discovered" after the First World War—found here a landscape that "was
like a simple phrase in music or a single line of poetry . . . and re-

---

[1]Between 1822 and 1866, thirteen thousand Conestoga wagons transported $45
million in merchandise along the trail. It was along the Santa Fe Trail that
American troops marched off to the Mexican War in 1846.

duced to the barest meaning."[2] Georgia O'Keeffe, D. H. Lawrence, Willa Cather, Sinclair Lewis, Edna Ferber, Thornton Wilder, Jean Toomer, Thomas Wolfe, Robinson Jeffers, and Carl Jung were all beguiled by the Santa Fe region, as were the members of another specialized community: at the Los Alamos laboratory, less than an hour's drive from Santa Fe, the first atomic bomb was developed. J. Robert Oppenheimer, a leader of the Manhattan Project, which built the bomb, had owned a cabin in the mountains near Santa Fe in the 1930s and responded to the landscape with the same passion as the artists and writers who were his neighbors. It was he who convinced the U.S. Army to choose Los Alamos as the secret research site.[3] The mixture of artists and physicists still makes for an eclectic environment. At one cocktail party given by Site Santa Fe, a gallery specializing in modern art from all over the world, I talked with a man in a fashionable Navajo tie about the medieval entry of the Magyars into Europe; he was Murray Gell-Mann, the 1969 Nobel laureate in physics, who had discovered the smallest particle of matter yet found and named it the "quark," after the word he had come across in James Joyce's *Finnegans Wake*.

Any doubts that Santa Fe was "in" were put to rest in 1986, when *Santa Fe Style*, a coffee-table book on the art and architecture of Santa Fe, became a best-seller.[4]

From the time of the first Spaniards to the 1970s, Santa Fe developed in a straight line: from a frontier outpost of New Spain to a simple Mexican territorial capital to a modern American city with heavy Spanish influence. But as I soon saw, there were now two Santa Fes: the designer fantasy that occupies the old downtown and a new, unregulated settlement to the south, known as Agua Fria (Cold Water), with mobile homes, strip malls, a waste dump, a detention center, and "affordable housing" for middle-income families, many of them state employees.

In 1970, Agua Fria, or south Santa Fe, was still open country, but by the late 1970s it developed rapidly as wealthy out-of-towners began taking over Santa Fe proper. In Agua Fria, J. C. Penney, Sears, and similar stores have relocated from the downtown area to serve the poor Mexican immigrants who have settled there. Agua Fria looked

[2]Mabel Dodge Luhan, *Edge of the Taos Desert: An Escape to Reality*.
[3]See Lois Palken Rudnick, *Mabel Dodge Luhan: New Woman; New Worlds*.
[4]See Christine Mather and Sharon Woods, *Santa Fe Style*.

like so many other places I had visited in the Southwest, a desert littered with mobile homes. Adobe, the region's traditional architecture, a product of Arab genius brought to the New World by the Spanish, is now almost exclusively for the rich. (Navajo rugs are another example of how the Arabs, by way of the Spanish and the Indians, influenced the artifacts of the Southwest.)

"It was the railroads, or, I should say, technology, that changed history," explained Carmella Padilla, a reporter for a local Hispanic newspaper.[5] "Not only did the railroads close the Santa Fe Trail, they also brought in luxury goods and allowed easterners to visit and settle in significant numbers. Since 1980, this migration of coastal people has gone out of control because technology—now in the form of home computers and airplanes—changed history again.

"People have come here from New York and California, renovated adobe houses, built high walls around them—real gated communities—and continue to do business in places like New York City and L.A. Some are real rattlesnakes: women from the East who dress in leotards and the most expensive cowboy boots, whose husbands have bought them real estate licenses in Santa Fe to keep them busy.

"When I grew up in Santa Fe twenty years ago, there was much less mention made of 'Hispanics' and 'Anglos.' Now we all have labels to go with our economic status. Because I cover the art scene, I mix with these people. I'm Hispanic, but I don't look Hispanic—I'm not dark and short—so people occasionally say things in my presence which are hurtful." Carmella, who is tall and slim with blue eyes and long brown hair, and fashionably dressed, explained, "In Santa Fe, if you don't look the part—if you don't wear, say, expensive-looking jeans and a sharp blazer—you're totally snubbed": it's like being in Washington, D.C., without a suit and tie. The public schools here mirror the class divide: whereas nationally 12 percent of enrollment is in private schools, in Santa Fe it is 20 percent and rising as more private schools are built. Santa Fe is further proof that there are two Americas: the people who own stocks and mutual funds and have seen their assets rise dramatically in the 1990s and those who are completely dependent on wages, which have risen far less if at all.[6]

---

[5]Spanish speakers in New Mexico are called "Hispanics" because, in most cases, they are descendants of the original Spanish settlers. Rarely are they Mexican immigrants or descendants of Mexican immigrants.
[6]See Jeffrey Madrick, *The End of Affluence* and *Statistical Abstract of the United States 1996.*

"People give you all these reasons why they come here," she went on. "They say they come because they love the Indian culture, because they love the Hispanic culture. But when they get here, they have nothing to do with the Indians or the Hispanics. To them we're slow, stupid, inefficient. After the scenery and the sophisticated environment, one lurking reason why they come here may be that there are no blacks."

I recalled a conversation I had overheard the day before in an espresso bar. A middle-aged man in olive-green shoes and an olive cable-knit sweater whose color matched that of his shiny Ford Explorer had ordered "espresso romano," the kind served with a lemon rind. "In Washington, just three blocks away from the White House in the wrong direction," he told a friend, "and, well, you're in trouble. Like in *The Bonfire of the Vanities*."

By implication he was, of course, admitting what had brought him to Santa Fe. But white flight explained only part of what was happening here.

I DROVE THE seventy miles north to Taos, passing the Rio Grande off to the left, a streak of silvery blue flowing down from the mountains of southern Colorado toward the Texas-Mexico border, lined with golden aspens in the intimate autumn light. Eventually the landscape reverted to red sandstone hills spotted with piñon trees heaving upward toward a vast desert tableland 7,000 feet above sea level, split by the Rio Grande, which now ran through the bottom of a deep chasm. In the distance, at the encircling northern and eastern edges of this tableland, were the 13,000-foot-high, glacier-carved pinnacles of the Sangre de Cristo Mountains: the southern rampart of the Rockies where, twenty-five miles away, in the Kit Carson National Forest, the ashes of D. H. Lawrence lie in a small white chapel. In the middle distance, speckled on the flat wasteland near the foot of the mountains, is Taos.

Taos, originally a pueblo, is a double-espresso version of Santa Fe, with 5,000 full-time residents rather than Santa Fe's 60,000, and even more stylish in places; its surrounding area is even more primitive and barren than the outskirts of Santa Fe.

The desert ended where the town began. But rather than the corrugated iron of a Hispanic village, I saw wooden shingles, art galleries, adobe facades, expensive jewelry stores, rare-book shops, and some stylish men and women in subtle tweeds walking their dogs in a circle in a park: a woman with a whistle stood in the middle, ordering the dogs and their masters to reverse direction, then reverse again. In a bookshop, I bought a 1927 second edition of Lawrence's *Mornings in Mexico* for $50.

PETER RABBIT TOLD me he was a "communist," that is, a "com-mune-ist." Peter Rabbit's real name used to be Peter Douthit. He was born in 1936 in Bradford, Pennsylvania, came to Taos via New York City in 1954, and legally changed his name to "Peter Rabbit" some-time in the 1960s or 1970s. "In 1954, you had an artists' and writers' colony in Taos," he explained. "But it was of reasonable size. There were still no ski resorts, and everyone had to learn Spanish. You couldn't get your gas tank filled back then without knowing some Spanish."

"Why did you come here?" I asked.

"Creeley was here.[7] And where else would a poet be able to get a mortgage?"

Peter was nearly sixty, an ancient, as close as you come now to an original citizen of Taos, Indians and Hispanics excepted. Peter, as he himself puts it, is a "pre-Beat bohemian" who hit the "open road" around the same time Kerouac did. I arrived at Peter's house on the outskirts of Taos almost an hour late. Nobody cared. It was midday, and Peter and Anne, his common-law, scraggly-haired wife in work clothes, and a friend were sitting at the kitchen table smoking ciga-rettes and drinking sour mash bourbon that Peter had brought back from Kentucky, where one of his children lives. Except for the shelves of books and the soft jazz filtering through the speakers, I could have been in a mobile home. Dust was everywhere. Peter, his grizzled beard, jug ears, and long reddish-gray hair protruding from his gas station–style baseball hat, spoke in a low, raspy voice; his expression alternated between blunt and impish.

"Yeah," Peter said, "now everybody wears these baseball hats. In the beginning they were 'gimme' hats: they'd have 'em stacked by the feed store with the store's name on them, and customers would say, 'Gimme one of those hats.' They were a cheap form of advertising. It may have started with the 'good old boys' in the South, with John Deere Company. Now they're everywhere."[8]

---

[7]Robert Creeley, a contemporary American poet.
[8]I had first thought that the popularity of baseball caps off the field indicated a

Peter helped start the commune movement. In 1970, he published a book, *Drop City*, which became an underground classic.[9] "It was a study, written in the heat of battle, of what it was like living on a four-hundred-acre commune in Trinidad, Colorado [twenty miles north of the New Mexico line]. *Drop City* stood for droppings-in: that is, happenings, events, never-ending street theater. The commune was ecological, spiritual, sexual. It was about lost causes, 'save the wolf,' and all that stupid shit." In 1979, the Colorado State Organized Crime Strike Force broke up the commune and arrested Peter.

"They came in at five A.M., fifty-seven guys with M-16s. I was arrested and convicted of 'attempt to possess with intent to distribute a controlled substance.' In other words, I was convicted of being a metaphysical clown."

"Were you guilty?"

"Sure, we were doing all kinds of crazy shit. The commune was a radical social experiment, a serious educational institution. We had been harboring fugitives. Years before, the police thought Patty Hearst was at our place."

Peter served a year in prison in Canon City, Colorado. "It was a monastic experience. I was in with murderers, rapists . . . they were hard on me. I taught basic literacy to other inmates. I also wrote pornography for their enjoyment.

"We thought we were going to change the world. But this world is a spaceship, and the engine room has to get along with the kitchen. In the 1980s, we've learned to get along. Big government is bad, yeah, maybe the Republicans are right. We're entering a period of specialized communities: Santa Fe, Taos, Atlantic City, Las Vegas. Anything is possible; all you need is imagination and consenting adults," Peter explained. "Seriously, consensus building is slow, and even then it only works with a small group of people. As individuals become less fatalistic and more empowered, the U.S. may be too big to survive in the future. We'll have to split up into parts."

Peter is currently known for hosting the annual World's Heavyweight Championship of Poetry in Taos. "It's just a fucking poetry

---

slide in dress codes and self-esteem. Then I ran across a passage by William Dean Howells in *The Rise of Silas Lapham* about straw hats in late-nineteenth-century America: "To a straw-hatted population, such as ours . . . no sort of personal dignity is possible. . . . In our straw hats . . . we are no more imposing than a crowd of boys."

[9]Published by Olympia Press, New York.

reading. We call it the 'World's Heavyweight Championship' because hype is everything in an era of pop culture."

I noted the Knob Creek sour mash bourbon on the kitchen table. "Yeah, rural Kentucky's something. There's this fellow, Bo. Bo was shot through the head at two and has never been right since. He's got a cannon facing down the dirt road from his shack. Bo's been chewing tobacco since his diaper days, and the tobacco stains have eroded his skin between his mouth and jaw: they're permanent, darkened streaks. Bo's poor white trash. You know what the poor white trash in Kentucky still call black people?" Peter asked with a grimace. "They call 'em 'yard apes.' 'Yard apes,' imagine that." Both Peter and Anne took swigs of bourbon.

I liked Peter and Anne. Unlike some of the famous sixties radicals who went on to write cookbooks and work in investment houses, Peter and Anne are authentic hippies who barely scrape by.[10] I went with them to a cheap Mexican luncheonette where Peter talked a bit enviously of his friend the poet Gary Snyder, who had "lucked out" with a tenured teaching job at the University of California at Davis. Regarding 1990s Taos and Santa Fe, Peter remarked, "Yup, there's a designer theme park culture here which has walked over the corpse of the hippies. Beatles songs have been turned into elevator music. The art galleries sell mostly dreck—kitschy paintings of adobe houses that tourists consider serious art only because of the high prices. Taos isn't as bad as Santa Fe, though. [Greater] Santa Fe is already fifty percent Anglo, while Taos is sixty-five percent Hispanic, eight percent Indian, and only twenty-seven percent Anglo. Taos is more remote and therefore less spoiled. Here's the real problem: Georgia O'Keeffe lived here. And she was married to Stieglitz. Willa Cather lived here, too, over at Mabel Dodge's place down the road, along with D. H. Lawrence," Peter went on in a bored, fatigued tone. "You see the problem, don't you? This whole area is just too fucking hip!"

I DROVE NEXT to the local cemetery in the center of Taos, where Kit Carson and Mabel Dodge Luhan lie buried in the shade of big

---

[10]National Public Radio commentator Andrei Codrescu had a similar reaction to Peter Rabbit in his book *Road Scholar: Coast to Coast Late in the Century.* I read Codrescu's book only after Peter and Anne had told me they were in it. I experienced a bit of envy when I learned that I had not discovered Peter and Anne myself. Yet I was heartened that Codrescu had liked them as much as I did.

cottonwood trees by the clearing where I had seen people walking their dogs in a circle earlier in the day.

Carson's tombstone comes first, heralded by a wooden sign at the entrance of the cemetery that announces:

KIT CARSON
1809–1868
SCOUT-CITIZEN-SOLDIER
"HE LED THE WAY."

In the cemetery's far corner another stone marker reads:

MABEL DODGE LUHAN
2/26/79–8/13/62

Kit Carson, who had run away from Missouri, then remade himself through sheer force of will as a mountain man before shrewdly befriending publicist John Charles Fremont, had made himself a celebrity against a backdrop of pine-scented mountains and the Indian and Spanish cultures of Taos. Carson was part real, part his own artifice, but less an artifice than Mabel Dodge, who fabricated a life out of a harmless confidence trick. Born wealthy in dreary Buffalo, New York, she married dull, wealthy men who paid for her exquisite salons and then left her alone. Though her villa in Florence gave her prestige among an advantaged cultural elite, she sensed that Italy was only a sideshow for the artistic and literary ferment of the early twentieth century. Greenwich Village was the center, but others had been there first. She needed a world of her own creation, which she found in Taos. She divorced her second husband and married a local Pueblo Indian, Antonio Luhan, who both enhanced her status and became her exotic pet. Without having written anything memorable, she became an institution by establishing a commune of the kind to which the New York cultural world could relate.

But isn't the "masquerade" the appropriate symbol for American life? For the Founding Fathers and for generations of immigrants, becoming an American has often meant inventing oneself. American literature is full of such self-willed identity changes, whether the poor boy Jimmy Gatz becoming Jay Gatsby, Fitzgerald's socialite, or Sal Paradise replacing his dismal life with his aunt in Paterson, New Jersey, for that of the western traveler in Kerouac's *On the Road*. Isn't the deeper significance of Santa Fe and Taos more than a case of white flight? Isn't it, as the New Yorkers and Californians in designer western wear attest, that these two towns are yet another theme park where Americans can dress up and play new roles?

21

The Greyhound Underclass

FROM TAOS I drove south through Santa Fe to Albuquerque, on the Rio Grande, which the Spanish settled more than three hundred years ago. But Albuquerque looked as if it had no history. As I approached the city I saw only a grid of one-story clapboard houses followed by a downtown of empty streets and stone buildings, whose windows were blank stares. At the western edge of the city near the river is Albuquerque's restored "Old Town," where I parked. Old Town is a stage set of adobe facades, espresso cafés, and boutiques offering expensive jewelry and "fine leather apparel," as in Santa Fe and Taos. Like the Gateway Arch Plaza in St. Louis, Old Town is a tourist bubble, offering the same globally manufactured mugs and other trinkets, in addition to a stylized, nostalgic version of the past that suggests what Albuquerque ought to be, rather than what it is or even was. Black metal grilles secure the shops at night. A shop owner warned me not to walk here after closing time. I did anyway and had no problem, but I was alone on the streets.

Albuquerque is typically American in that the future here appears more palpable than the past or present. The proximity of Intel, Sandia, and other high-technology firms nearby will lead to an influx of 86,000 highly skilled workers and their families, according to city officials. Not everybody is happy about that. Riding back from the local airport, where I had returned my rental car, I encountered a talkative cabdriver, a burly man with a red plaid shirt. "I'm from northern Wisconsin. I came to Albuquerque twenty years ago. I was in the service in Germany, then the army shipped me to the White Sands missile base [where the first atomic bomb was tested]. I fell in love with New Mexico. But it's being ruined by California people. They bring their political values, their animal rights, their environmental causes, their high prices. Wood here has gotten expensive because of restrictions on logging. The loggers can't work because these California people want to save the spotted owl, which isn't even native here. Rents have nearly doubled because of them." Yelling at a driver of a passing luxury sedan, he interrupted himself: "All right, jerk face, you can turn first!"

IN THE VISITOR'S guide to Albuquerque that I had found in my hotel room, there was no mention of buses under "transportation," even though airlines, Amtrak trains, and various charter bus services were listed. I soon learned why.

The next day before dawn, I took a cab to the Greyhound station, a sprawling, drafty hall with rows of machine-molded plastic chairs, darkened with food stains and anchored to the floor, where people in mismatched hand-me-downs wandered about with hard, contorted faces. The bus I planned to take had originated in Los Angeles, stopped at Phoenix and now Albuquerque, and was bound for Amarillo, Oklahoma City, Tulsa, and St. Louis. For forty-nine dollars, I bought a one-way ticket for the five-hour journey to Amarillo, three hundred miles to the east. An announcement directed the passengers to form two lines: one for those reboarding the bus, the other for those like myself, who were beginning their eastbound journey here. The line for those reboarding was much longer. It included a woman in a green flower-print plastic jacket, torn pink cotton sweatpants that exposed her thighs, and beach thongs without socks, though it was freezing; a man with a baseball cap with a picture of the Virgin Mary on it and a sneaker on one foot and a laceless hiking boot on the other; another man who was wearing headphones that were not connected to any audio device; a third man who had been begging with an empty can that had once contained spaghetti sauce; and a teenage mother with two little boys with punk hairdos. There were many ragged haircuts, bad complexions, grimy baseball hats turned backward, people coughing and smoking cigarettes, and bulky old bedrolls from the era before nylon and goose-down sleeping bags. I noticed very few wristwatches, fewer shoelaces, and only four white faces (including mine and the bus driver's) among some forty passengers. Of the two other white passengers, one was a grossly overweight woman with a skin rash, the other a scrawny man with long blond hair, a denim jacket, and an exhausted, vacant expression. The rest were blacks and Mexicans, along with several Indians. At 6 A.M., the passengers were eating candy for breakfast. One ate a chili dog.

Inside the bus—a Greyhound Americruiser with an American flag emblazoned on the outside—the driver, a thin, poker-faced man with straight white hair, was barking at a woman who was trying to stuff her bedroll overhead: "Put it below!"

At that moment a middle-aged black woman with a sad, wasted face asked meekly if it took longer to continue on to St. Louis than to go back to Phoenix. The driver said the ride back to Phoenix was shorter. "Okay, I think I'll go back to Phoenix if I can get a refund." She offered no explanation, then stepped down from the bus with her bedroll and box of candy: all she had. I asked her why she wanted to go back to Phoenix and if I could help her in any way. She looked at me in astonishment and shook her head, as if I had a problem of my own.

The bus left at 6:35, twenty-five minutes late. The driver announced to the passengers, "Welcome to Greyhound's service from Los Angeles to St. Louis, with connections there to all points further east. No smoking, no alcoholic beverages, no drugs, and no abusive language will be tolerated. If anyone has a radio, he must play it with headphones, so as not to disturb other passengers."

Dawn broke as the driver eased the bus into the eastbound lanes of Interstate 40, the old Route 66. The black sky gave way to purple mountain silhouettes topped with snow. As the sun rose in the east directly ahead, I realized that I was the only passenger with sunglasses. At the end of the twentieth century, to cross America by land by public transport often means to travel among the poor. Long-distance trains offer relatively few routes, particularly in the West, while the decline in domestic plane fares has made air travel possible for the middle class and up; booking a discount plane fare often requires more ingenuity than poor people can muster. Left to the bus stations, therefore, are people who are either homeless or a small misfortune or two away from it; people whose entire belongings can fit into the bus, taking up less space than my duffel bag and rucksack. *U.S.A.: The Rough Guide,* a veritable bible for low-budget foreign travelers to America, warns that "many bus stations are in fairly dodgy areas." It advises women, in particular, "to sit as near the driver as possible" to avoid "hassle."

"Stop it, I don't like people touching me!" the woman sitting behind me exclaimed.

The driver pulled over, got up from his seat, and walked over to her.

"Ma'am, do you have a problem?" he asked politely.

I turned to look for a moment. She was black, in her late twenties I would guess, with slept-in clothing, a sad, anxious expression, and uncombed, unshaped hair. Twitching slightly, she looked as though she hadn't slept properly in days. Words such as homeless . . . disembodied . . . disoriented crossed my mind.

"I don't have a problem," she said, on the verge of tears.

"But it seems you do, ma'am." The driver's voice was now like that of an understanding parent.

"I don't have no problem," she repeated, louder. "I just don't like people touching me. Men always been *touchin'* me."

"I ain't been touchin' her," said the man next to her, who appeared to be in equally difficult straits. "She's crazy!"

"I ain't got a problem, I don't want anybody to ever touch me again—you got the problem!" the woman shrieked at the driver.

"But it seems you do have a problem, ma'am," repeated the driver, calmly. "Do you want me to change your seat?"

"Don't scream at me!" she shouted.

"I'm not screaming at you, ma'am. I just want to help. But if you don't settle down, I'll have to ask you to leave the bus."

"All right, I'll go sit on the floor. I ain't *gonna* sit next to nobody."

"You can't sit on the floor, ma'am, that's against regulations."

Finally, she consented to having another woman sit next to her. The driver returned to his seat, and the bus moved on.

Soon children were screaming and running up and down the aisles. The driver asked the teenage mother to "please control them." Stone-faced, she ignored the driver, while her children continued their noise. The driver announced, "If those children are not controlled, I will have to discharge them and their parent at the next stop." The mother shouted profanities at the kids and grabbed them, and they became quiet. The driver was like a benevolent despot in a Third World state. Can democracy flourish among people like this?

At Tucumcari, in eastern New Mexico, the bus pulled into a fast-food dive for our promised "rest stop." The passengers fell out of the bus, lit cigarettes, and took deep drags as quickly as they could. Then they bought Cokes. Almost nobody ordered orange juice or coffee. Throughout the Third World and eastern Europe, I had been among even poorer people on buses that were not nearly as well maintained as this one. But, with the exception of some drunken bus passengers in the former Yugoslavia, I had never traveled among a more rootless or unstable crowd whose members took such poor care of themselves as these homeless: never in Africa, certainly not in Mexico. (Though the constant coughing of some of the passengers evoked the tubercular atmosphere of buses in the Indian subcontinent.)

I tried talking to one man. He was white, with freckles, long blond hair, and a feedlot cap. "Where are you going?" I asked.

"O.C., *Momma!*" He tapped his palm on his knee as though playing the drums, then showed me his gums with many missing teeth. He meant Oklahoma City.

"Why?"

"*Hey,* why not, *Momma! Yo!* Money, money, money, yeah, that's all those crazy fuckheads in Phoenix know. Some heavy shit goin' down in Phoenix—rumble in the park with naked women, yeah, that's all I want!" He smiled and nodded to himself, staring straight ahead. Another fellow told him, "Shut up!" They shouted at each other obscenely. I tried talking in turn to each of them, but their conversation became more incoherent. Remembering how, in *To Jerusalem and Back,* Saul Bellow had gotten a negative reply after he had asked a Hasidic Jew sitting beside him on the plane if he had ever heard of Einstein, I asked these two if they had heard of the mass-market thriller writer Stephen King. They hadn't.

No one had a book or even a tabloid newspaper. This bus was like a prison van, transporting people from one urban poverty zone to another. I asked another group of young men on the bus where they were going. They told me—again, in nearly incomprehensible speech—that they were looking for work in Oklahoma and Kansas, where slaughterhouses were hiring low-wage, unskilled labor.

The driver smiled at me as he entered the fast-food joint, where he ordered eggs and coffee. He must go through this every day, I thought.

The bus continued eastward. The Rocky Mountains had retreated to the distant horizon, and the rolling, snowy desert of sage and thornbushes gave way to patches of bunchgrass. The wilderness floor was imperceptibly sloping downward, and the ground, consequently, was less arid; enough water for grass tufts but not for a continuous carpet. We came near the Pecos River, little more than a dry wash during most of the year. When Coronado had approached the Pecos in the days before dams, reservoirs, and cities, it had been a wide river, and his troops had required four days to construct a bridge across it, a few miles away from here.

After wintering near Albuquerque, in April 1541 Coronado's army had set out for the land of "the Turk" to the northeast. "The Turk" was the nickname the Spaniards had given to a Plains Indian who had been captured by the Pueblos and throughout the winter had entertained the Spanish soldiers with stories about cities of gold in Quivera, an Indian territory in present-day Kansas, near his home. Disappointed not to find the fabled "Seven Cities of Gold" on the Colorado Plateau and having suffered days at a stretch without water, subsisting at times on half-roasted horsemeat and marching at night through blizzards to keep from freezing to death in their sleep, this desperate army had now talked itself into a renewed frenzy of hope and dreams based on one Indian's lively imagination.

The sharp, snowy peaks fell completely from view as we approached New Mexico's eastern border with Texas. As we descended from more than 5,000 feet to around 3,500, the atmosphere became less rarified, and in the thickened air objects seemed less focused. The gaudy primary colors I had been used to in the Southwest had washed away. Spiny mesquite branches no longer clashed with bright orange or yellow sand; instead we entered a wilderness of silt, gravel, and short grasses: mesquite[1] and blue stem, with a bit of tumbleweed and gama grass mixed in. Mainly I saw an unending cover of buffalo grass—dry and stiff, burnt brown in winter, as short as beard stubble, with a scorched-earth look. We had left the ancestral land of the desert Indian tribes—Navajo, Hopi, and so on—and entered that of the more warlike, nomadic Indians of the southern plains: Comanche, Cheyenne, and Kiowa Apache (distinct from the desert Apache).

Coronado's army called this region the "Llano Estacado," the Palisaded or Stockaded Plains. English-speaking Americans later mistranslated the term as "Staked Plains," believing that the flatness and

---

[1]Mesquite trees, to which I refer here, are distinct from mesquite grass.

uniformity of this territory had caused Coronado's solders to drive stakes into the ground to keep from getting lost.[2] Coronado writes, "I came across some plains so vast that in my travels I did not reach their end. . . . [They were] as bare of landmarks as if we were surrounded by the sea." Here the conquistadors encountered large herds of buffalo for the first time. There was "nothing but cattle and sky. . . . The country where these animals roamed was so level and bare that whenever one looked at them one could see the sky between their legs." Perhaps some of the conquistadors thought they had indeed reached Asia.

A little later, the driver announced, "We are now entering Texas, the Lone Star State. We have left the Mountain Time Zone and have entered the Central Time Zone. Set your watches back one hour."

Only a few of the passengers had watches.

A big sign in the shape of Texas welcomed us. There was no longer even wilted grass, only a flat, dirt expanse waiting for sorghum and cotton to begin growing, like an endless, empty parking lot. Amid this lunar austerity, the road signs seemed even bigger than they actually were: GREAT STEAKS, NO BULL! . . . HO-MADE PIE! . . . BOOTS 'N JEANS . . . CAMELOT INN, ROOMS $29. . . . As these signs became more numerous, a smaller one announced that we had entered Amarillo. Soon I saw more auto dealerships than I had ever seen before in one place, displaying enormous American flags: though the American flag as some sort of an insignia may punctuate the continent into the future, the question, of course, is what it will stand for: a healthy democracy, a corporate oligarchy that wears democracy's trappings, an extremist caricature of what the Founding Fathers intended for militias and other isolated individualists?

The driver told us to look to our right. For the first time, his voice became animated, even enthusiastic: "Look over there in that field. See the world-famous Amarillo Cadillacs. People come from every continent to see them. They come out in the rain, in the sleet, sun, and snow. These Cadillacs have been written about in every newspaper and magazine. . . ." In a muddy pasture strewn with cows, I noticed ten Cadillacs buried partway in the ground in a straight line, as though they had nose-dived in formation from outer space, their exposed tail fins indicating the different models from 1949 to 1963. They had been planted there by Stanley Marsh III, an eccentric who

[2]See Herbert E. Bolton, *Coronado: Knight of Pueblos and Plains.*

had made a fortune exploiting local helium reserves. The vehicles were streaked with rust and defaced with graffiti. It is the only art exhibition I knew of where vandalism is actively encouraged. People come at all hours with spray paint to improve upon this apocalyptic vision of a junked, rusted desert civilization.

A young man behind me said, "I think I learned something about that in school."

At Amarillo the bus turned off the interstate and into a homely patchwork of stucco and brick buildings; wide, empty sidewalks; asphalt-roofed churches; bail-bonding offices; and other structures with an erased, written-over look. Only the art deco Santa Fe Railroad building, erected in 1930 and now empty, stood out.[3] The driver told the passengers that the bus would stop at Amarillo for half an hour and directed them to a room inside the station where they could smoke. As I left the bus and retrieved my bags, about thirty ill-dressed people squeezed into a chamber, taking long drags.

It took me forty minutes to find a taxi. Amarillo had few cabs, and, given the poverty of the long-distance bus clientele, the station provided little business for the handful of local drivers. The airport, where I went for a rental car, was as shocking as Santa Fe had been: so clean, so prosperous with its high-quality deli food after the squalor of the bus journey. I recalled a trip some years ago, when I had crossed into Austria after a month in Yugoslavia on the eve of war in that former country: the heating in the train came on, well-dressed people filled the cars at the first stop, and hot food became available for the first time. Amarillo's was just another medium-sized airport with gray, tubular decor. But I had crossed a real border, back into middle-class America. The passengers I had left behind on the bus inhabited another country. I wondered what would become of them and of all those left behind in this ruthless, albeit efficient, global economy.

[3]Actually, downtown Amarillo had looked even worse in the 1980s. When I visited again, it was beginning a limited revival. There were hopes of renting office space in the Santa Fe Railroad building as part of a revitalization campaign.

22

A Desert Culture

AMARILLO, WITH A population of 150,000, is the heart of the Texas Panhandle, true wilderness country, prone to drought and cyclones, where fortunes have been built on oil, helium, and natural gas, as well as on cattle ranching and wheat farming: water-intensive operations that are slowly depleting the great underground pool known as the Ogallala Aquifer. More cattle have been slaughtered in Amarillo than anywhere else in the world, and more nuclear weapons have been produced here than anywhere else.

Amarillo is the final assembly hub for every plutonium and hydrogen bomb in the U.S. arsenal. During the Cold War, it was an "A-1" first-strike target of Soviet nuclear planners. The local area has three hundred Evangelical churches. Friday-night high school football is a religion. The Panhandle is conservative, and in 1964 it voted against Lyndon Johnson, a fellow Texan, and for right-wing Republican Barry Goldwater. Amarillo lacks the cosmopolitan culture of Dallas, Houston, and other posturban pods; nor does it have an intellectual community like the university towns of Austin and College Station, with their computer software firms. This is still unadulterated, barren Texas, with state flags everywhere and a corrugated look to everything, especially when the wind blows the gritty dust against the road signs.

Towering over a highway south of Amarillo is the "world's Biggest Texan," a forty-seven-foot-tall, seven-ton, gray concrete statue of a cowboy with painted black hair, boots, and spurs, constructed in 1959. Part of his red concrete bandanna has fallen to the ground, chunks of his concrete, lead-painted bellbottom trousers have flaked off, and birds have built a nest in the crook of his neck. Next to the statue is a vacant restaurant with old Christmas decorations in the window.

From downtown Amarillo I took side roads rather than the interstate. The roads were not well lit, and I felt vulnerable driving through this dark, strange emptiness. Then came the Texas Panhandle equivalent of a skyline: Shoney's . . . Black Eyed Pea . . . Chili's . . . Arby's . . . Steak: $4.85. . . . It occurred to me that just as the flat brown wastes had made the restaurant and gas station signs appear bigger than they actually were during the day, the unlit darkness and yawning distances between the points of human habitation in Texas made the neon lights of these establishments appear brighter, friendlier, and more significant at night. The advertisements seemed to scream at you. I saw a park bench beside a public library bearing the logo "Imperial Body Shop."

"You're the guy who ordered a Michelob and sat at this same table last night: you're a real creature of habit, aren't you?" said a waitress in a high, drawn-out, lingering key that pulled together wonderfully the gentle acoustic twang of the Southwest, the flat oatmeal accent of the prairie, and the drawl of the Deep South the second night I came to her restaurant. Even the fast-food places here evince the lively togetherness of a late-night bar in the middle of nowhere, where people drive from miles around just to talk and sip drinks. A nineteenth-century cavalry officer called the Texas Panhandle "the Great Sahara of North America."[1] Indeed, Texas constitutes just another friendly desert culture, similar in its fundamentals to what I encountered in Arabia and other places, where great distances and an unforgiving, water-scarce environment weld people closely to one another at oases, while demanding a certain swaggering individualism out in the open—as well as religious conservatism. "Amarillo is full of Methodists, Church of Christ people, lots of Baptists, other Protes-

---

[1]Captain Randolph Marcy made the remark in 1849; see Frederick W. Rathjen, *The Texas Panhandle Frontier.* Also see A.G. Mojtabai, *Blessed Assurance: At Home with the Bomb in Amarillo, Texas.*

tants, of course, and some of the strangest Evangelicals you ever saw," a shop owner told me.

William Elton Green, curator of history at the Panhandle-Plains Historical Museum in Canyon, Texas, fifteen miles south of Amarillo, explained, "Political, social, and religious conservatism emerges partly from the uniformity of the landscape. The sameness of the view engenders conformity of thought. Because the plains just go on and on for hundreds of miles, without alteration, there is, I suppose, a subconscious conviction that the whole world must be like this, and that, therefore, everyone else will have to become like us—to think like us."

Bill Green's office was lined from floor to ceiling with old books about Texas and the Great Plains; his several desks were covered with papers and exotic bric-a-brac. Teddy Roosevelt and Rudyard Kipling would have felt at home here. Bill's particular specialty was the Alamo, the San Antonio mission besieged in 1836 by a Mexican army led by Santa Anna. The siege began February 24 and ended March 6 with hand-to-hand fighting, as the Mexicans scaled the walls and killed the 180 Texan defenders, who included Jim Bowie and Davy Crockett. The cry for revenge—"Remember the Alamo!"—helped lead Texas to independence from Mexico, followed by the Lone Star Republic's incorporation into the Union. "Oh, I know 160 things at least about the Alamo," Bill said. "I've got books and books on it. For instance, do you remember when LBJ said he would 'draw a line in the sand' in Vietnam; and when [President George] Bush said he would 'draw a line in the sand' against Iraq? Well, that phrase, 'draw a line in the sand,' was first used at the Alamo. Johnson and Bush, being Texans, knew that; their statements were not accidental."

He added, "I read recently that only one out of four Americans knows that the first atomic bomb was used against Japan. The less we know about our history, the easier it will be to invent it. Like the fact that welfare is un-American. What do you think 'free land' out West was about in the nineteenth century, when the government gave 160 acres to anyone willing to farm it? Wasn't that a form of welfare? And when the drought in the 1930s turned that same land into a dust bowl because it was overfarmed, Roosevelt instituted 'relief'—modern welfare, that is."

I kept listening to Bill, a middle-aged man with gray hair and a beard who has never been overseas and rarely away from the Great Plains: "Texas is the only state that was once an independent country."

"Wrong," I interjected. "Vermont was, too, from 1781 to 1790."

"Fine," Bill said with a smile, "but people in Texas never heard of that! The perception here is that we are fundamentally different. Real Texas is west Texas, and the most real part of west Texas is the Panhandle. Though I'd make an exception for College Station in east Texas, the friendliest town I know of. Here in the Panhandle, everybody owns a gun and there is almost no crime—no blacks or Hispanics, that's why. I know that's racism, and racism runs deep in Texas. I have a terrible memory from grade school. Our teacher had delivered an emotional description of what happened at the Alamo. There was one Mexican boy in our class. He was skinny and short, and the big kids pulverized him in the playground afterwards.

"People accustomed to mountains and tree cover go crazy out here. But I just hate trees and mountains. I went to Virginia once. I felt so fenced in by the landscape that I could scream. When I was in Chicago, the skyscrapers made me feel the same way. I can't imagine spending your life in a place where you can't see for miles in all directions. . . .

"Of course, the ranching culture is coming to an end. There are all kinds of schemes and experiments going on with new crops and more efficient irrigation: soybeans, sugar beets, sunflower. . . . Wineries are getting popular, since grapes require much less water than cotton or ranching. We hunger after the old lifestyle, but we can't have it, so we fake it for a while—a few decades or a half century, perhaps. By then the fake reality has worn off, and one day we realize that the whole world has changed. What do you think country-western music is all about? You hear it everywhere, on every channel in the Panhandle, because we need it now more than ever—to convince ourselves that we're still cowboys. You see that gold-framed picture of the Alamo on the wall? It's not gold, it's fake gold paint. See this table"—banging his hand on it—"it's not wood, only plastic that looks like wood. Instead of beef with fat, we now have it without. Sometime in the future, there will be no cowboys, no gold, no wood furniture, and no beef in Texas. By then what will Texas, or America, have become? Could Texas and America—as concepts, I mean—seep gradually into the ground beneath us?"

Bill and I drove twenty miles eastward to the Palo Duro Canyon, where, in the spring of 1541, Coronado had made final plans for sending most of his thousand-man army back to the Albuquerque area, while striking out to the north with a handpicked force of thirty

to Quivera, in what is now Kansas, looking for gold. The Texas landscape here looked like an upscale version of Kazakhstan: a bony,
fleshless surface in which the A-frame houses looked like beached
boats and every wire fence, windmill, and rusted, tomato-colored
pickup truck stood out grotesquely. Bill talked easily about the beauty
of the yucca cactuses and mesquite trees, and about the miracle of the
playas: natural, saucerlike depressions on the plains where water col-
lects. He pointed to a lonely frame house on a tan dirt hillock, with a
pickup truck parked next to it. "What a beautiful location for a
house," he said. "You can see for miles from there. I always thought
that some lucky person would build on that property, and now someone has."

We descended into the Palo Duro Canyon, a geologic timetable,
with 250-million-year-old gray Permian period stone at the bottom
and 2-million-year-old yellow Pliocene sand near the top. A campsite
off the road reminded Bill of the "RV World War II guys" who crowd
the canyon from spring till fall: "These are retired World War II veterans who drive all around the country with their wives in RVs [recre-
ational vehicles]. They're patriotic as hell, you know the type. They're
incredibly interested in the local history and landscape of every place
in America they visit, and they carry lots of guidebooks. I guess it
grows out of their obsession with the meaning of World War II.
They'll all be dead within a few years. I wonder how that last great
struggle will be reinterpreted seventy-five years from now, long after
even the baby boomers are gone?" I looked at the Permian period
stone, thought about only one in four Americans knowing that the
first atomic bomb had been dropped on Japan, and had no idea.

Later we stopped at a trading post that sold refrigerator magnets
with the Texas state seal, along with "official Texas mosquito traps,"
whiskey glasses with pictures of the Alamo on them, American flags,
and other "Texacana" and "Americana" for tourists. The items, like
those sold in Albuquerque's Old Town and St. Louis's Gateway Arch
museum, were made in China or Taiwan.

"PEOPLE HERE DON'T like to talk about Pantex," Bill said. "We put
it in the back of our minds. After all, it's secret, and people figure that
what they don't know won't hurt them. It's sort of like the way people
who lived near Buchenwald must have felt. After all, Pantex is something we don't want to brag about."

To see what Bill meant, I drove east out of Amarillo on Interstate 40. After about twelve miles, I turned north onto Farm Route 2373 and passed through flat, yellow-brown fields for seven miles: the picture-book Great Plains. Then, on my left, I saw a sprawling complex of wire fences, cement guard towers, one-story sheds, and forests of antennae. It did not look particularly high tech; from some angles it reminded me of a prison. As I turned into the entrance, I saw a blue sign emblazoned with an American eagle that read:

U.S. DEPARTMENT OF ENERGY: PANTEX PLANT

PURSUIT OF EXCELLENCE: IMPROVEMENT THROUGH INVOLVEMENT

The Service Facility Building where I parked looked like a modern public library branch. Children were leaving the building, brochures in hand, stepping onto a schoolbus. I walked up to the front desk and signed the visitors' book. Behind the receptionist I noticed a wedding photo of a fellow employee, a stuffed teddy bear, a calendar promoting a local athletic team, and a sign that read, "Our Policy Is to Blame the Computer." The front door opened automatically as a handicapped man wheeled himself inside.

"Are you a U.S. citizen?" the receptionist asked me.

"Yes."

"Fine, just sit down and wait."

There was piped-in country music. Three security guards ambled through the door: two males, white and black, and a blond woman with a smiling cheerleader's face. All three wore khaki battle fatigues and black boots and carried assault weapons, flashlights, and communications gear. Each wore three different laminated photo IDs around his or her neck. Other men and women went into and out of offices in the nearby hallway, dressed straight out of Washington, D.C., in suits, ties, and suspenders for the men and attractive, neutral-toned skirts and blazers with high-heeled shoes for the women. After the denim-and-plaid world of the Southwest, the dress code here seemed odd: except for the heavily armed security officers and the stack of IDs around everyone's neck, I might have been in the State Department. (At State, people wear only one ID.) I was in an oasis of the federal government.

A public relations officer, a handsome black woman who chatted with me about skiing in New Mexico, escorted me into a room with several chairs and a framed portrait of Coronado looking out over the

Palo Duro Canyon. I had asked to meet several plant workers, though none in particular. Four people in civilian clothes and triplicate IDs followed us into the room. They worked in final assembly, and therefore did not dress formally like the front-office people.

F. W. George, a former Santa Fe Railroad worker, born and raised in Amarillo, who dressed like a cowboy, spoke first: "The Cold War secrecy is over. Who knows, we may even have joint ventures with the Russians," he said unhappily. "There is a definite openness to disclose our security systems and to inform the media of what we do here. It's a breach of national security, and I am personally against it."

R. W. Zerm, a Vietnam veteran from Ohio with a "defense R-and-D" background, whose cool, government-issue appearance could have qualified him as an extra for a Hollywood movie about the CIA, tried to minimize the danger of what Pantex does. "I've worked for Rockwell, on the B-1 bomber, and in the civilian airline industry, and I can tell you that it's safer here. Here there are more personnel backup, more redundant systems if anything goes wrong. For instance, in the civilian airline industry you sign a form after doing some maintenance work, and if the plane crashes you might go to jail! Now, that's stress! But here at Pantex we all work together, we train and train and retrain."

J. C. Clark, a black military veteran from North Carolina, added, "We conform to all OSHA [Occupational Safety and Health Administration] standards." As at Fort Leavenworth, everybody here, despite race and geographical origin, looked and talked alike.

"There is lots of camaraderie," said Sofia Delosantos, who has worked here since graduating from high school in Amarillo eighteen years before. She is married to another Pantex employee. "Many of us belong to the same bowling leagues, the same golf leagues and volleyball teams. We go to the same dances. We look after one another. If one of us dies, it's like we've all lost a member of our family." The others nodded. I learned that Pantex (which stands for "Panhandle Texas") is the largest contributor to the United Way in the Amarillo region.

"Let me tell you something else," George said. "We take great pride in what we do. We take pride in furthering technology. We take pride in the fact that everything we manufacture here, from top to bottom, down to every last screw, is made in the U.S.A., to protect U.S. national security. We are the public's first line of defense. And we can guarantee that our products will perform exactly as they are designed to."

Clark interjected, "I feel that if we didn't have these weapons, a lot more people would have been killed over the past fifty years." Delosantos added, "We take pride in being able to protect our country and our families."

"What is it like making nuclear bombs all day?" I asked. "Is it like an automobile assembly line?"

Delosantos protested, "Even with this new policy of openness toward the media since the end of the Cold War, I don't feel comfortable talking about it to strangers like you."

George helped her out. With an affirmative nod from the public relations officer, he explained, "Let's say we're assembling a B-61 . . ."

"What's a B-61?" I asked.

"Oh, it's just one type of nuclear bomb. We make several different warheads and bombs. Warheads are missile-launched, bombs are dropped by planes. Now, there is no assembly line here like at a car plant. It's more like an operating room at a hospital. Six of us will surround the patient, the B-61, for example. Around us are lighting, alarm, and air filtration systems and other safety backups. One of us will read from the instruction book. Two others do the assembling, and each of them has a backup: a person who verifies that the other has actually put this screw, for instance, where it is supposed to go and, if necessary, restrains the other from doing something wrong or dangerous. We work on the buddy system."

Clark added, "Any of us can stop any process if we feel something is wrong. Whistle-blowers are encouraged here, not intimidated. All of us are trained in every facet of bomb assembly. So the person reading the instructions can take over from the ones putting the weapon together."

"With the Cold War over, are you people worried about losing your jobs?" I asked.

Everyone nodded "Yes" and explained that, in fact, since 1989, they have been "disassembling" bombs rather than assembling them. "Disassembly" is just as delicate and complex a process as assembly. A B-61 nuclear bomb, for instance, has six thousand parts and can take between one and three weeks to assemble or disassemble. But there are just not enough bombs to disassemble beyond a few more years. "This plant could close in five years," George said. "On the other hand, something could happen in the world which could make mass production of nuclear weapons still a possibility. I think we're fine through fiscal '97 or '98. After that, nobody is sure."

Delosantos said, a bit upset, "I'm just not comfortable. What am I going to tell prospective employers if I have to look for a new job? That I built nuclear bombs for ten years, then took them apart for another ten years?"

PANTEX, A CONVENTIONAL bomb plant in World War II, became a nuclear weapons facility in 1951, when the U.S. Atomic Energy Commission awarded the first five-year management and operating contract to Procter & Gamble. (The joke was that Pantex manufactured soap.) Since 1956, Mason & Hanger, a Kentucky-based engineering firm that helped build the Grand Coulee Dam, has operated Pantex for the U.S. government. After other nuclear weapons facilities in Texas and Iowa closed in the 1960s and 1970s, Pantex became the sole producer of nuclear weapons in America. In addition to the tens of thousands of nuclear weapons being assembled and disassembled here, Pantex also manufactures the high explosives that surround the plutonium and uranium cores inside the bombs: explosives that can be compressed to thirty thousand pounds per square inch. Finally, Pantex is where thousands of "plutonium pits"— hermetically sealed plutonium spheres, the radioactive hearts of disassembled bombs—are stored. Nuclear weapons enter and leave Pantex in radar-tracked, heavily armored train and truck convoys, whose guards are authorized to use "deadly force" to protect their shipments.

As I passed through the entrance gate of the bomb complex, I saw a sign that read:

GIVE TO THE CHRISTMAS PROJECT

My guide told me that the government spends $20,000 per employee to run a security check on each of the 3,600 people here. He also said that Pantex is a self-sufficient city, with its own machine shops, explosive-testing facilities, and electricity, water, and self-defense systems. A nuclear bomb, after all, requires its very own motorized trailer, drumlike container, custom-designed tool kit, anchoring chains, and so on, all of which must pass federal safety standards, and the paperwork for all this is monumental. (This is in addition to the armored trucks and trains for long-distance travel.) There is even a specially patented, remote-controlled racking and shelving system for packing and moving large numbers of bins that, in turn, contain bombs and plutonium pits, so as not to expose workers to radioactivity. I was not allowed to witness the actual disassembly of nuclear bombs, but I was permitted to see the storage and assembly-disassembly buildings from the outside (buildings that had no names, only numbers). Nevertheless, I was awed by what I saw.

The assembly-disassembly process is more complex and potentially dangerous than the four workers had let on. Indeed, they were a bit modest about their responsibilities. Disassembly is divided into three stages: First, the nose of the bomb, where the radar equipment is located, is taken apart. Second, the "nuclear physics package" is removed. This all occurs in a bomb bay, the operating room that George described. But the third stage of disassembly—in which the nuclear physics package itself is disassembled and the plutonium pit is disentangled from the heavy explosive and insulating material—takes place in a "gravel gertie": a reinforced concrete cell covered by graded gravel and heavy earth, designed to cave in on itself, burying the workers and minimizing the blast and release of radioactivity in the event of an "accident."

These silver-lined gerties, each about forty-feet high, are sloped like pyramids and suggest the chilling monumentality of a Near Eastern imperial city. There is also the vast panorama of the hundreds of other buildings, the sixty-seven miles of razor-wire fences, the towering radio antennae, the closed-circuit visual scanners, the armored security patrols, and the seismic motion pods that stick up from the ground and can detect a single field mouse or prairie dog scurrying across the dirt. (The nuclear storage area of Zone 4 attracts prairie dogs because the high-powered orange night lighting protects them from coyotes.) In the midst of this complex are several rows of "staging bunkers," each about a quarter mile long. Thirty-eight of the bunkers are for storing nuclear weapons, twenty-two for storing plutonium pits. Each bunker is built of 100,000 pounds of reinforced concrete and is covered by grass and topsoil. From a distance, these earthen mounds look like giant tombs or dolmens, a city of the dead unearthed by archaeologists. Inside them are the plutonium pits—if not the entire explosive apparatus—for 12,000 hydrogen bombs: 12,000 man-made stars, for the energy of hydrogen as it is fused into helium at millions of degrees Fahrenheit creates the explosion that allows a star to burn for eons.

Here were thousands of such deities, assembled in one place and rendered more or less harmless by a regimen of security and environmental controls that only the most massive, overbearing, and modern bureaucracy has been able to muster: to wit, each plutonium pit and weapon, though hermetically sealed in stainless steel, is nevertheless tested repeatedly for alpha-ray emissions as part of a regular examination: as if it were a human being with the finest medical insurance begetting its own prodigious paper trail.

Say what you will about the logic, or illogic, of being able to destroy human civilization many times over; or about the cancer-causing radioactivity that the U.S. nuclear weapons program inflicted on its own citizens in the 1950s and after; or about other abuses that may have occurred over the decades. Still, never before in history, certainly not under any of the great bureaucratic despotisms of ancient Egypt or China, not in Aztec Mexico, not even in the vast death apparatuses of Stalin's Russia or Hitler's Germany, has so much destructive power been overseen so seamlessly and politely, with press tours given to any journalist who bothers to phone in advance and can prove American citizenship.

Will the United States be around as long as these weapons exist and the plutonium cores remain lethal? Even after hundreds of years, some sort of government bureaucracy will be necessary to furnish maps of their underground locations. Even if science discovers a way to remove all the radioactivity instantly, that process, too, would require rigid government oversight. Moreover, the possibility that the coming century will see the elimination of nuclear weapons is unlikely: "Nations prefer familiar uncertainties to thoroughly unfamiliar leaps in the dark," said Harvard professor Stanley Hoffmann.[2] Can the city council of Amarillo or even the state of Texas be trusted to oversee Pantex? I think not. That is the conundrum. The collapse of distances and the increasing interconnectedness of the world economy argue against the permanence of Washington. The visit to Pantex made it clear to me that the future (if there is to be one) will depend on the transformation of the federal government into an as-yet-undiscovered alloy—a far more flexible, lightweight version of itself—so as to appear almost invisible, even as it retains the power to oversee not only nuclear weapons but, for example, ever-scarce water resources. Whether this is likely, who can say?

*   *   *

[2]Hoffmann's remark is from his "Report of the Conference on Conditions of World Order—June 12–19, 1965, Villa Serbelloni, Bellagio, Italy," first published in *Daedalus,* Spring, 1996.

A WEEK LATER, I met someone in a small Oklahoma town who told me what it is like when a truck carrying nuclear weapons passes through on its way to or from Pantex.

"It's not like what you think," he said. "There is nothing obtrusive about it. The vehicles don't have their high-beam headlights on during the day, for instance. And the truck looks like any old eighteen-wheeler. The fact that it's armored is not immediately noticeable. Still, the truck is escorted by Suburbans with two-way mirrors so that you can't see the people inside, who are armed and who can see you. And there is a garden of antennas on all the vehicles. Sometimes they stop, and the guards get out, if they have to use the toilet or buy something to eat. And they answer questions good-naturedly. 'What happens if someone tries to break into the truck?' I once asked one of these guys. He told me that 'the truck has mechanisms so that it can defend itself.' "

"A truck that can defend itself!" I said.

"Yeah, it's got explosive devices if you try to break the door lock. It's incredible what it takes to protect a nuclear bomb." How future generations will deal with the legacy of Pantex remains an awesome question.

2 3

The Dry-Land Sea

THE OKLAHOMA PANHANDLE, where I headed next, furthered my understanding of how the international economy is shaking the foundations of even the most isolated of regions. First, though, a word about topography.

THE CENTRAL UNITED States is divided into two geographical zones: the Great Plains in the west and the prairie in the east. Though both are more or less flat, the Great Plains—extending south from eastern Montana and western North Dakota to eastern New Mexico and western Texas—are the drier of the two regions and are distinguished by short grasses, while the more populous prairie to the east (surrounding Omaha, St. Louis, and Fort Leavenworth) is tall-grass country. The Great Plains are the "West"; the prairie, the "Midwest."

Like the sea, the Great Plains are exposed to the strongest, steadiest winds in America.[1] Also like the sea, the Great Plains are subject

---

[1] The average wind velocity in the Texas and Oklahoma panhandles is twelve to fourteen miles per hour. The only higher average velocities in the lower forty-eight states are off the coast of Washington State.

to moods, depending on the time of year and the degree of cloud cover. "The plain has moods like the sea," wrote the early twentieth-century poet Hamlin Garland in *Prairie Songs.* In winter, under a leaden sky, this sea of wilted buffalo grass evokes the desolation of a lifeless planet; yet in the summer sunshine the brilliant yellow-green iridescence of the cereal fields seems almost manically happy. If you study the Great Plains long enough, you will see great distinctions in color and terrain. The expanse of buffalo grass, for instance, achieves a luxurious autumn texture if dotted with yucca cactus and Kentucky bluestem, as in western Oklahoma. The Great Plains are not truly flat. Flatness, here, soon becomes relative. After driving for several days in western Oklahoma, for example, I began to notice choppy seas composed of the tiniest of hills, as well as slight rises and declivities in the landscape, like the movements of the wind on a lake. The very extent of these plains made the world beyond seem remote. For two decades I have been a foreign correspondent, yet in the Great Plains I lost interest in the foreign news I could hear on the BBC shortwave service. Such was the effect of this landscape: a veritable dry-land ocean in midcontinent where even the East and West Coasts of the United States, to say nothing of Europe or Asia, seem far away even as they grow closer. Isolationism is not an American character failing; it is an adaptation to terrain.

The Great Plains, even more so than the tall-grass prairie to the east, are America's isolated center, where social and cultural tremors emanating inland from the two coasts—upheavals both good and bad—either peter out or arrive years later in diluted form. Whereas the East Coast attracted blacks from the Deep South, as well as Italians, Jews, and others from southern and eastern Europe; and whereas the West Coast drew Asians; the Southwest, Mexicans; and the prairie of Illinois, Iowa, and the eastern halves of the Dakotas, German and Scandinavian immigrants, the Great Plains, until recently, have been home to mostly Anglo-Saxon stock. It is the Great Plains, again, even more than the prairie, that provide the nation with its perception of immense, inviolable space. Much of the Midwest prairie has now become urban and suburban, but in the Great Plains rural life has held out longer.

Most of all, the Great Plains—the heart of the "Great American Desert" until underground aquifers were discovered and exploited in the twentieth century—constitute the nation's unalterable geographical fact. Walter Prescott Webb, in his classic 1931 study, *The*

Great Plains, argues impressively that the geography of the plains, more than Lincoln or even the Civil War itself, defeated slavery.

The small farms, free labor, and industry of the North and the slave plantations of the South were in place following the War of 1812. The question then became which system could expand faster into the West, for it was western settlements that ignited the Civil War: the North and the South might have existed side by side, however uneasily, had there been no new territory to settle one way or the other. Though much of the West was opened to slavery, the South, Webb explains, could not occupy the Great Plains because its economic system of water-intensive cotton agriculture based on slavery was circumscribed by climate and water resources. In the West, aridity stopped the slave economy in its tracks just as cold weather did in the North. Vast, waterless desert spaces required individual initiative, rather than forced, uncreative labor, for development.[2] When the Great Plains prevented the South from dominating the Union, the South seceded rather than acquiesce. And since a weak, divided American continent would have been easily dominated by the European powers, Lincoln knew that war was necessary: that an expanding, industrialized economy of scale required a landscape of scale.

Geography, as I would continue to learn—particularly when I got to the Pacific Northwest—will be as crucial to our future as it has been to our past.

A FEW MILES north of Amarillo en route to Oklahoma, I spotted the arched wrought-iron entrances to the Bud Crawford and Coon ranches, bordered by long stretches of barbed wire. There were absolutely no landmarks to define these ranches: no line of hills, trees, or creeks. Rising from an utterly flat surface of inch-high, monochrome short grass, the iron gateways and wire fences appeared arbitrary. No wonder property rights are sacrosanct in the treeless West

---

[2]Ironically, the future president of the Confederacy, Jefferson Davis, had a similar view of how the Great Plains would fundamentally change America. Davis, the U.S. secretary of war under President Franklin Pierce in the 1850s, saw how great and arid distances must affect the army. Rather than occupy the Great Plains the way it did the transappalachian region, Davis thought the army should deal with the nomadic Plains Indians the way the French were then dealing with Arab tribes in Algeria: by putting garrisons near the edge of white civilization and making forays into Indian territory as required, to inflict retribution or to escort settlers.

and trespassing a major crime. Either a fence in the middle of the Great Plains is holy writ or it is nothing, anarchy.

As I crossed into Oklahoma, I was pulled over by the Oklahoma District I: Narcotics Police. They had sniffer dogs and were clad completely in black from baseball hat to shin-high leather boots. "You have a nice day, now," the policewoman said to me after she was satisfied with my papers. Her blond hair stuck out through the back of her hat. Oklahoma was poorer and grittier than Texas. Just beyond the roadblock came a billboard map of the Oklahoma Panhandle: rather than a standardized metallic billboard that glowed in the dark like those I had seen in Texas, this was made of plywood, held aloft by bare two-by-fours.

"No Man's Land," "the Neutral Strip," and "Unofficial Lands" are the names Oklahomans have used for their Panhandle, nearly 170 miles long and only 36 miles wide. The Panhandle began as the stepchild of Civil War politics. It was the neutral strip between the 100th and 103rd meridians and between 36.30 degrees and 37 degrees north latitude that separated Texas, admitted to the Union as a slave state in 1845, from the territory to the north (eventually to become eastern Colorado and western Kansas), where, under the terms of the 1850 Missouri Compromise, slavery was restricted. This flat, puzzle-shaped piece of territory—a windswept panel of short grass the sight of which made me dizzy—truly belonged to no one. Except for the Cherokees, who made a halfhearted attempt to occupy it in the 1880s as an extension of their northern Oklahoma lands, not even the Indians claimed it. An act of Congress attached No Man's Land to the Oklahoma Territory in 1890, only seventeen years before Oklahoma became one of the last states to enter the Union. I found the Oklahoma Panhandle among the bleakest landscapes of the Great Plains. Barely 9,000 people inhabited the largest town, Guymon. It was the refugees from the Oklahoma Panhandle, migrating west after their overplowed fields had turned, literally, into a dust bowl, who gave the name "Okies" to all the migrants from the Great Plains in the 1930s. The survivors of this and other deprivations earlier in the century in the panhandle were truly "the last pioneers of the Old West."[3]

The next ten miles northward on U.S. Route 54 offered a panorama of gigantic center-pivot sprinklers, circular irrigation devices

[3]Nancy Laughlin Leonard, *Images of a Past: No Man's Land.*

several hundred yards in diameter. From the air, large sections of the Great Plains look like a network of circles because of the patterns created by these massive rotating sprinklers.

I pulled into the town of Goodwell, site of Oklahoma Panhandle State University. "It's an itty-bitty school, and I teach European history and sociology, though I'm not trained in those subjects in a formal sense," explained Sam Nelson, an associate professor, behind a haze of cigarillo smoke and a wall of books that included all six volumes of Edward Gibbon's *The Decline and Fall of the Roman Empire*. "In the Panhandle we don't even have e-mail yet, though we probably will in a few months, once the phone company installs the equipment. I have a sister in Ankara, Turkey, who communicates with friends all over the world on e-mail, but not with me."

I had called Nelson ahead of time to set up a meeting. He was a friend of a friend of a friend whom I had never met before. Born in Amarillo fifty-three years ago, he seemed a bit shy and withdrawn at first. I just let him talk. I don't think he knew how interesting he really was.

"Almost everybody was poor here until the 1940s, when oil arrived. Hooker [twenty miles northeast in the Panhandle] was the center of the Dust Bowl, a subsistence economy. Depression-ridden people who couldn't cut it picked up and left. To those who stayed, the deserters were weaklings. Because of the harsh climate and wilderness landscape, there is no empathy in this part of the world for those who can't survive on their own. As regards those unwed mothers on welfare and the teenagers on drugs that we read about, there is a local attitude that says, 'Tough shit, we made it without help, why can't you?' The Panhandle is an exaggerated allegory of America. In the 1970s—I think it was—a woman went into a local diner and killed her husband with a twelve-gauge shotgun. She wasn't even indicted. Everyone knew he needed killing."

(Throughout my travels, I did not find much sympathy for blacks who require special help. Affirmative action evidently runs counter to the American notion that the scramble for wealth, jobs, and positions be unaffected by government. Of course, for so long blacks were denied such equality that affirmative action is simply an imperfect way of redressing grievances and fostering social stability by quickening their entry into the middle class. Though government may not be able to alter vast social and economic forces such as the disintegration of inner cities, that does not mean that it cannot soften such painful blows. Throughout history, social stability has been achieved by pacing out change so that it is never too burdensome and therefore destabilizing. Affirmative action fits well within this historical tradition of easing the burden of change—the death of inner cities and the creation of a sizable black middle class. But it has to be applied extremely judiciously, or it may split society rather than unify it.)

"Big changes are on the way," Nelson continued, "and I'll bet that seventy percent of the people here are not super looking forward to it. Guymon is either going to die like so many towns on the Great Plains or change drastically."

What Nelson meant was the effect of the corporate pig farm that was beginning operations in Guymon, ten miles to the north, that would soon draw many blacks and Hispanics to the unskilled, low-wage jobs it offered. "Already we have more migrants from Mexico here than ever before." Indeed, the cattle industry was on the ropes because of lower beef consumption in the United States, while a new middle class in the Far East and South America offered a growing export market for pork. "Low-wage pig farms in Garden City, Kansas, have already resulted in more minorities, more crime, AIDS, and social change. On the other hand, the economy in the Guymon area is in trouble, and nobody's kids are staying here because the retail business was bad and there weren't any jobs left until the pig farm came. Change or die, that's the future. Even in the Panhandle, a world market is replacing the United States market. Why, near Boise City, a town of under two thousand people, they're raising beans for export to India and Japan. People are even raising ostriches for export. They're trying anything. . . .

"Of course, water is a big problem that will get worse. But it's so gradual that people don't admit it. Water does not just disappear; what happens is, it first gets expensive, little by little. Even that occurs indirectly. Center-pivot sprinklers have replaced ditch irrigation, which was too wasteful. But these sprinklers cost so much money, while ditch irrigation required no equipment: that's how water rises in cost. The sprinklers run all summer long, twenty-four hours a day, on natural gas. In winter, we sell the natural gas to the East. Ultimately, we'll run out of natural gas, too. Of course, we'll find a solution, but it will cause big changes.

"We are in the beginning stages of a formidable social revolution, and people are scared. When they get scared, they try to refuel old value systems. That's what all these Evangelical churches are all

about—go back to the 'good old days' when the worst problem in
school was kids chewing gum. When society is in a state of upheaval,
everything changes, including religion. We're edging toward a new,
postindustrial brand of religion that may ultimately bear no relationship to how we worship now."

I thought of the Christian television channels I had been watching
at night here. One preacher after another would sermonize, then ask
for donations to be phoned in to a toll-free number posted at the
edge of the screen. "God speaks to me. . . . I argue and commiserate
with God. . . . He has sown a seed of five thousand dollars; now it's up
to you. I promise that something good will soon happen in your life."
To the most telegenic preachers with the most appealing message go
the contributions and a new community of believers. We are at the beginning of long-term changes, and new communication technologies
will subtly transform and, perhaps, trivialize religious worship as they
have politics: the Crystal Cathedral in Anaheim is a case in point.
And, as I would learn later in Nebraska on my way to the Pacific
Northwest, the line between cults and reexperiencing Christianity in
its first-century form is a fine one: both are driven by loneliness, fear
of the future, and the belief in miracles. Economic uncertainty for
many and increasing reliance on television and computers have enormous implications for religion, particularly in the underpopulated
Great Plains.

AT FIRST GLANCE, Guymon looked as bleak as an Indian reservation: treeless and windy, with biscuit-brown yards of short grass and
houses of liver-colored brick. With their narrow window slits, they
recalled the windowless sod shacks of the nineteenth-century pioneers. The houses of the poor needed paint. The yards were littered
with old appliances. The facades on Main Street were dominated by
cheap aluminum siding. The desolation was overpowering. In this
grainy, black-and-white artifact of a town with the industrial detritus
of a desert culture, I recalled Henry James's remark in *The American
Scene* about how, in America, "there is too little history for dignity
of ruin" so that poverty (and wealth, too) occurs "in a void." Thus,
James writes, America has "no constituted mystery . . . no saving
complexity."

That, of course, is a European way of seeing this landscape. There
is another perspective.

*   *   *

"ISN'T IT JUST so stark and pristine? I love it. You should see it in the spring, when the grass is lime-colored and the winter wheat is pure gold. The autumn is truly spectacular: golden grass, green wheat, bright orange soil, and a mass of yellow corn," said Carol Grider, an artist and real estate agent. Just then about a dozen Hereford and Black Angus cattle broke into a run across her field outside Guymon, a stunning sight amid this flat, endless landscape of black soil, empty except for the windmills, the sprinkler cranes, and the lone family farm, with 2,400 acres of land, belonging to Carol and her husband.

Carol told me, "We're still innocent out here. People still don't lock their doors, everybody knows everybody. There is no greater thrill than going out of the house here to watch the sunset, or to wake the kids up late at night to see a thunderstorm in progress several miles away. The landscape is consistent, comforting. Where the malls are, it used to be just dirt until the 1970s. So we're grateful for the malls. Of course, a lot is going to change, on account of the million pigs from Seaboard Farms over the next two years."

Carol, in her thirties, was clad in a stylish black skirt and Indian print vest. Over a pot of tea in her living room in the middle of the afternoon, I let her talk. The only sounds were those of the sparrows and meadowlarks at the window and in the nearby Chinese elm. A feeling of silent peace had descended on me, as when one stares at a spider's web in a field.

"Yeah, it's become a hobby to bitch about the decline of the cattle industry. All these guys with big belt buckles, high boots, and cowboy hats eating mom-and-pop food and saying 'Poor old me.' There used to be cattle in the streets of Guymon. But the educated sons of ranchers are not coming back. We're headed toward corporate farming: you get paid six dollars an hour for slaughtering pigs. Already we've got mobile homes for low-wage earners from Mexico, some blacks. . . . I've even seen a few homeless in Guymon; not all the migrants can get jobs in the plant. The problems, and some of the possibilities, of the East and West Coasts are finally coming to the Great Plains. A three-bedroom house in Guymon in 1990 cost $80,000. In 1996, it costs $150,000. But you should see these pigs, it's a terrifying sight: hundreds of them in a shed with no room even to walk or move their legs; butting their noses up against a panel for food or water until they're fat enough to be slaughtered. I'm no animal welfare nut, but I challenge anyone to look inside these corporate pig farms and not be unnerved. . . .

"Why do people have narrow slits for windows, you ask? Not against the dust, but because they simply have no imagination. No woman here keeps her own name after marriage. People in the Panhandle are more afraid of change than of death. But you can sense this undertow of change about to grab you—more and more blacks in the schools. Did you know that the Guymon public school system is already seventy-five percent Hispanic? Just wait till the pig farm starts twenty-four-hour operations, then that percentage will rise. We have no private schools here, there's nowhere to escape. We're all in this together. Both of my brothers are New Age Christians—Evangelicals. Maybe they fear the loss of patriarchy, I don't know. Have you noticed how kids don't play outside as much as they used to, how they're more overweight? Even when they're inside, they don't read, they play video games."

I glanced around Carol's living room. The chairs were pink, and the large paintings on the walls were full of bright yellows and greens. Through the window were dirt fields as far as the eye could see. I thought of a Persian carpet in the middle of a brown desert. There is a nomadic, unstable quality about any culture that attempts to occupy an arid wilderness, no matter how ingeniously and efficiently it exploits the ground resources. On the Great Plains the present day seems like a vague dream before waking, soon to fade.

"THANKS A BUNCH for coming over. You need fixin's in your coffee—milk or sugar?" Paul Hitch asked me. I said, "No." He led me into his sprawling office in the back of a small shopping mall in Guymon. I noticed a glass tabletop supported by a wagon wheel that displayed gold-plated belt buckles and turn-of-the-century pocket knives; a late-nineteenth-century Winchester rifle, a large coyote skin, and massive longhorns held in place by leather straps on the wall; and a saddle, rope, scabbard, and cowboy hat in the corner. "These are all mementos of my grandfather."

Hitch, with short, grayish hair and aviator glasses, wore cowboy boots, blue jeans, and a blue plaid shirt. Behind his computer terminal was a rack of guns. Hitch is the scion of the richest ranching family in Texas County, Oklahoma, which constitutes the middle third of the

Oklahoma Panhandle. The day before, Carol Grider had driven me through a part of Paul's 17,000-acre ranch. The foreman's house was larger than most homes in Guymon.

Paul kneaded a wad of chewing tobacco and put it into his mouth, then told me the history of his family.[4] The Hitches immigrated from England before the American Revolution, settling in Maryland and Virginia. Around 1800, some family members meandered down the Shenandoah Valley into eastern Tennessee. There, James Kerrick Hitch, a lad of twenty in 1875, took the family savings of ten dollars and left home at dawn after writing a contrite note. He traveled west through Tennessee and across the Mississippi River. Young Hitch settled in Springfield, Missouri, where he found work with a well-off farmer. When the farmer migrated to southwestern Kansas to go into the ranching business around 1880, Hitch went too. He later married the man's daughter.

In 1886, Hitch and his wife moved into the Panhandle. But in January of that year, a blizzard killed much of the region's cattle. Carcasses lined the roads, and that spring the odor of death lasted for weeks. Hitch skinned five hundred carcasses and sold the hides to cover his losses. Another blizzard hit the following year, with more cattle losses. Then came a drought, which persisted on and off until the mid-1890s. Amid these hardships there was the national depression that began in 1893 and lasted three years. Then there were the extreme loneliness and isolation of living in No Man's Land a hundred years ago. There was not even a post office, nor a school until 1889. Supplies came from Dodge City, Kansas, 125 miles away. Though located in the geographic heart of the country, Oklahoma was the last frontier of the West, opened officially to large numbers of white settlers only in the late 1880s and early 1890s. No Man's Land was the frontier of this frontier. "There were no runs out here," Paul Hitch told me, referring to the mass settlers' rushes across the Oklahoma state line to stake out land claims.[5] "There wasn't even farming in this area until the 1920s. Before 1920, it was just grass and cattle."

There was personal tragedy, too. In 1891, Jim Hitch's wife, Mary Frances, died, leaving him with three children to raise. But Hitch had

---

[4]For a complete history of the Hitch family and the Panhandle, see Donald E. Green, *Panhandle Pioneer: Henry C. Hitch, His Ranch, and His Family.*
[5]For a poignant description of one of these rushes, see H.W. Brands, *The Reckless Decade: America in the 1890s.*

help. Besides his wife's family, his brother Charlie had relocated from eastern Tennessee to join him and married here. The question a hundred years later is how such a family-based community can be re-created, in the same or different form. Paul answered with a story.

"One of my friends made a trip to Louisiana to check out the cattle there. He came back and told me, 'Paul, I saw the damnedest thing.' My friend described an alligator swamp filled with tall grass where cows were feeding. Up on the berm, or ridge, safe from the alligators, were all the little calves. Because so many of the cows were down in the tall grass feeding, every cow that remained on the ridge had three calves sucking milk from it. Only if you know cattle can you know how incredible this was. A cow usually allows just one calf to suck on it at a time, never three. But the cows had to feed, or else they wouldn't have milk for their young. Though the cows were too big for the alligators to mess with, their calves would have been attacked in the tall grass if they came along. So the mothers took turns feeding, and those up on the berm milked everyone else's calf. A communal order had emerged because of the danger posed by the alligators—a new society was created because of new conditions."

Paul put his boots up on the table and more tobacco into his mouth. "In the 1920s, there was a great upheaval here. As I said, farming began back then. The Hugoton gas field was discovered, and so was the Ogallala Aquifer. The aquifer allowed for big-time irrigation, and the natural gas provided the fuel for electricity to run the irrigation systems. Irrigation caused the center of gravity of the cattle-feeding industry to move from the northern corn belt to the southern Great Plains by the 1940s. Because we had nonunionized labor, we also became a center of the meatpacking industry.

"Well, in the 1990s beef consumption has gone downhill. In a world market there's competition from abroad, dietary habits are changing, the gestation time for cows is much longer than for chickens, which are eaten a lot more now, and cows are much more expensive. Water and natural gas—which you need to irrigate grasslands—are being slowly depleted. Beef's become the whipping boy for the thugs in the media—all these stories about high cholesterol and so forth. The meat market is ninety percent domestic: it's not the future. Cattle ranching has lost its stature. Pork's become the big thing, it's the most consumed meat in the world, and the export potential is certainly there. Across the Pacific, millions and millions of rice eaters are becoming pork eaters. Already, the corners of those circular sprinkler fields are being filled with pig barns. With pig farming, Guymon could double in size.

"We were looking pretty tattered, with empty storefronts on Main Street, until Seaboard Farms opened their plant here in 1993. They're still not working at full capacity. Fourteen hundred mostly low-wage workers are going to settle here, with their families. It's going to be a big bite of change to swallow. There will be growing pains: vandalism, gangs. . . . We got our first trailer park last year. There is a new school under construction. Guymon has a reputation for friendliness, but now for the first time we're going to have lots of nonwhite folks. We're going to find out just what kind of people we really are. There's going to be no savior except ourselves. People may think, 'God, please send us another oil boom [like in the 1980s], we promise not to fuck it up this time.' Hell, we don't have the possibility of IBM relocating here with $85,000-per-year jobs for everyone. Seaboard pig farms is all we got."

"What about ostriches? I've seen a few of them off the road. Are they a new thing?" I asked.

"Oh, everybody's experimenting with new ways to make money these days. Ostriches, that's got to be a Ponzi scheme—you raise 'em to sell to someone else, who sells 'em at a higher price to someone else. . . .

"The land is in a ferment. Everything that happened in the U.S. has happened in a more compressed period of time in Oklahoma. Remember, this land was not even settled by cowboys and farmers until the 1890s. Now the world economic upheaval is arriving all at once: blacks, Asians, Hispanics, big-city problems. We'll all have to learn to live with each other. My wife has already started a homeless shelter, because we *will* have homeless people. Why wait till it happens?"

A FEW BLOCKS away, I stopped in on Brian Test, a nature artist and baseball coach, among other things, at Panhandle State University. "People are tired of illegal Mexican aliens coming here. But white people won't do much of the work that Mexicans are willing to do, and when the Mexicans buy things here, their money is as good as anyone else's. I'm curious about how Guymon is going to treat the Vietnamese and Laotians who will come to work in the pig-processing plant. I remember the Vietnamese from college at Southwestern Oklahoma State. In daytime, they're the smartest kids in the class, and at night they're your waiters, serving you your dinner. Folks here have never yet had to compete with people who aren't white and whose work ethic is even more dynamic than their own. It'll be interesting . . ."

I thought of the revolution on the plains in the mid–sixteenth century, when Coronado's army had introduced horses to the Indians, unleashing survival talents that the Comanche, Cheyenne, and others never knew they possessed. Will the compression of distance caused by world trade and the large-scale movement of peoples have a similar effect on the current inhabitants of the Great Plains? In Guymon I realized that isolationism is becoming an obsolete term. Isolationism connotes the withdrawal of the United States from international affairs after World War I, which allowed for the spread of German and Japanese fascism. But the revolution in world trade and communications has made economic and political withdrawal impossible. What is at issue here in the Panhandle, as in such places as Tucson, Los Angeles, Omaha, and St. Louis, is America's identity as it melds with the rest of the world.

Before leaving Guymon I stopped at a Wal-Mart. I passed through the electronics section, featuring the latest laptop computers and audio systems, through the sporting goods, the toys, the gardening supplies, and so on. It all looked familiar. I had seen the same merchandise on sale in shopping malls in western Omaha and western St. Louis, at similar prices. Guymon's traditional stores on Main Street could never offer such bargains. One benefit of the chains has been their unifying effect: Guymon, Oklahoma, is experiencing the same product revolution as elite Johnson County, Kansas, for example. But does this make us more of a nation, considering that chains in Asia and Europe offer the same products?

THE FLATNESS OF the road west from Guymon to Boise City, Oklahoma, was misleading: my car had climbed a thousand feet. The shadows were deeper here, and the buildings looked like lonely cutouts against a few treeless, dust-blown streets. A recent frost had turned the bluestem grass red.

I had called Jim Roseberry, the owner and editor of *The Boise City News*, in advance. Jim was the Oklahoma Panhandle equivalent of an Arabist or other foreign-area specialist. Like them, Jim and many other small-town newspaper editors in America tend to go a bit native in the region they cover. Jim's desk was in an office supply shop. The newspaper presses stood behind him in a gloomy, dust-ridden room. "A few years back, this newspaper came up for sale. My wife and I were truly tempted. I'm from Texas, and we were living in Guymon at the time. People in Guymon said awful things about Boise City, about how there were weird churches here, John Birch strongholds, and armed guerrilla groups. But after a year we bought the paper anyway. We figured, if we don't do it now we'll never own anything, and we'll always be working for someone else. Well, dog-gawn, you know what—about all those rumors, I mean—to a certain extent they're true. There are people with real extreme philosophies out here, people with unreasonable and highly complex theories of who's really running the government in Washington. But even the looniest ones will always help you in an emergency, no matter how much they hate the editorials you write in the newspaper."

"What's the circulation of the *News*?"

"Eighteen hundred."

"That's a bit more than the population of Boise City?"

"I know. We have a lot of Dust Bowl subscribers: people who left the area in the 1930s and migrated to California but who want to keep up with the place where they were born and raised. They're old and dying off. And you know something, they did extremely well in California. People who stuck it out here don't like to admit that; it goes against the myth."

"What are you going to do when they all die?"

"I really don't know. The population here is dwindling. All we do is agriculture, and agriculture is changing. The days of farm subsidies will end soon. Family farms are dying, the kids are growing up and moving away. The future could be a combination of corporate farming and a Great Plains theme park, with barracks for immigrant workers instead of the traditional white frame house with its nuclear family surrounded by a clump of elms, which took decades to grow. Towns will die, buffalo herds will be reintroduced for tourists and environmentalists, and theme park companies will pay corporate farms to reintroduce more native grasses for the buffalos. The Santa Fe Trail passes right near here, and nostalgia for that type of thing is coming on stronger than ever."

I asked him how he liked living here.

"I'm from a part of Texas where there are some trees. That's what I miss the most. It's despairing to step outside into the blank wilderness and realize, 'Oh, shit, I'm alone!' . . . This is still No Man's Land. Oklahoma's not here, it's back over there, in Guymon. Oklahoma state inspectors [for taxes, the environment, and so on] rarely get this far west. They hate coming here, and we hate it when they do."

Jim and his wife invited me for a meal at a Mexican restaurant, where Jim gave me a locally published book, *Not a Stoplight in the County*. In it I read that:

- As the title of the book suggests, there is not a single stoplight in Cimarron County.

- Boise City has no clue where it got its name.

- Boise City's claim to fame is that it was bombed by mistake in World War II. On the night of July 5, 1943, a wayward B-17 from nearby Dalhart Army Air Base dropped six practice bombs on the sleeping town. The "bombs," which consisted mainly of sand, tore through the roofs of several buildings but caused no injuries. After the attack, it was said that the city could use some searchlights and anti-aircraft guns.

Jim warned me that Kenton, a town forty miles west of Boise City near the New Mexico state line, was even more remote.

IN MY REARVIEW mirror, Boise City disappeared in an instant. A few indentations in the hard-packed sand—wagon wheel markers that had survived for more than a century—indicated the Santa Fe Trail's "Cimarron Cutoff," which had saved many days of travel from Kansas and Missouri by cutting directly through No Man's Land into New Mexico toward Santa Fe. After driving for another quarter hour, I felt as if I had reached a shoreline of the great dry-land sea. Bluffs appeared on either side of the road: crumbly, bright orange sandstone speckled with juniper bushes. Turquoise lakes filled the depressions. Then I saw piñon trees. I had left the Great Plains and come back to the edge of Rocky Mountain country, where many bird species, including golden eagles, live at the eastern- or westernmost point of their range.

I pulled into the town of Kenton, where I saw a number of signs proclaiming "Jesus Is the Lord." Yet again, the need to proclaim the obvious suggested the insecurity of the believers. A man with a beard and suspenders greeted me in the general store. He introduced himself as Allen Griggs. A dark-complexioned young man was watching a soccer match on television. "This here's my son," Allen said. "He was raised in Saudi Arabia and is hooked on soccer." Allen explained that he had been an engineer for the Arabian American Oil Company (ARAMCO) before buying the store some years back. I told Allen that I had been a journalist in the Middle East, and we launched into a discussion of Middle Eastern politics. Then I asked him about Kenton.

"We're the bird and dino capital of America," he said. "It seems that this was the only part of the continent on dry land during some phase of prehistory, that's what accounts for the dinosaurs. Oh yeah, we get all kinds of bird-watchers, dinosaur people, and European tourists here in the summer—French mostly, they're very adventurous. Now, here in Kenton we've got a population of forty-five. This includes writers, artists, a photographer, and four Evangelical churches. The church people come from all over the area on Sunday. We're on Mountain Time, not Central Time like the rest of Oklahoma."

"But according to the map, Mountain Time doesn't start until you cross into New Mexico," I said.

"Forget the map. Kenton's on Mountain Time."

I noticed the rack of brochures by the counter, advertising tourist sites in the mountain regions of New Mexico and Colorado. "Nothing much about Oklahoma," I remarked. "Hell," he responded, "Oklahoma and the Great Plains are back there, in Boise City. The Panhandle is the stepchild of Oklahoma, and we're the stepchild of the Panhandle." I asked Allen about some burnt-out house foundations I had seen. "Used to be hundreds of people here in the 1890s, with saloons, topless bars—well, maybe not topless. You saw some of the ruins. But give us time, if a few more writers or artists settle here, we could develop into a small Santa Fe or Taos. We need interesting foreigners. Land's cheap, it's beautiful, and you can communicate anywhere with computers. What else do you need?"

Allen pushed open the screen door to let me leave. "Hello, wind!" he yelled. I waved good-bye.

I DROVE NORTH into Kansas, then northeast across the entire state and back to Fort Leavenworth. On the dust-blown desert of western Kansas, outside the town of Ulysses, I reached an oasis: a restaurant surrounded on three sides by gas stations.[6] Beneath the restaurant's bright lights, Mexican laborers filled the booths. From Ulysses, I continued northeast and reached another Santa Fe Trail marker on the tree-lined banks of the Arkansas River. The river here had been the international boundary between the United States and Mexico in the early trail years, until the Texas Territory (which had extended into southwestern Kansas) seceded from Mexico and became the Lone Star Republic. The signs proclaiming "Mexican Baptist Church" suggested that this far north Mexican culture was being altered by its exposure to Anglo religions.

Dusk fell as I arrived in Garden City and checked into the Wheatlands Best Western. In the lobby, I noticed a black-and-white photo of Truman Capote standing in front of the hotel, his head tilted sideways, his classic impish smile on his face. Capote had said that while researching *In Cold Blood,* his 1965 documentary-novel of a celebrated murder in nearby Holcomb, he had lived "in ghastly motels in the wind-swept plains of western Kansas."[7] Well, I had a comfortable room, an excellent steak at a restaurant across the street, and a friendly hotel receptionist who worked part-time for the local NPR affiliate and whose dream was to be a reporter for *All Things Considered.* I suspected that what Capote meant by "ghastly" was just the sharp-contoured loneliness of one-story buildings without an architectural past, set against the moaning wind.

GARDEN CITY, KANSAS, represented the future for Guymon, Oklahoma. A pig-raising plant opened in Garden City in the late 1970s, attracting Vietnamese "boat people" and Mexican immigrants. Garden City, with 18,000 inhabitants, was now twice the size of Guymon, multiethnic and crime-plagued: signs of dynamic change. The rich soil and relatively homogeneous landscape of Kansas had ultimately ground down the differences among New England abolitionists, southern slavers, and various white immigrant groups. Now the boun-

[6]The town of Ulysses is the seat of Grant County. The Civil War and its heroes are ever present in Kansas, where violence between groups of abolitionists led by John Brown and southern slavers in the late 1850s constituted a mini–Civil War of its own, earning the western territory the epithet "Bleeding Kansas." After 1865, many Union Army veterans settled here, entitled, as they were, to 160 acres of free land.
[7]See Robert Smith Bader, *Hayseeds, Moralizers, and Methodists: The Twentieth-Century Image of Kansas,* for more about Capote's sojourn.

daries were being stretched again to include nonwhites. There are 2,500 Vietnamese in Garden City. The Mexican community is larger still. Here is one story.

Quang Nguyen owns the Garden City Specialty Cleaners. At night, he prepares federal tax returns for Vietnamese and Mexicans who do not know English well. He files the returns electronically on his laptop computer. I met him for breakfast at a franchise restaurant. In a part of America where people dress informally, he wore a pin-striped shirt and tie and had a collection of newspapers under his arm.

Nguyen was born in 1959 in South Vietnam, the son of a businessman. After the fall of Saigon in 1975, he escaped with hundreds of others on a rickety fishing boat. They drifted with little food or water for three days in the open sea before an American vessel rescued them. Nguyen and the others were sent to a refugee camp in Thailand. In 1981, after years of delay, he arrived in Oakland, California, then flew to Wichita, Kansas, where he knew a Vietnamese family. He soon learned that the new pig-raising plant in Garden City had jobs to offer. "So I came here and never left.

"I came with a friend, another Vietnamese I had met in Wichita. I was young, thin, and short. I was one of the first Vietnamese to come here. The people at the plant wouldn't hire me. They said I was too small to hack pig meat all day with a knife. My friend and I slept in an old car we had—we had no money to rent a room. We slept all winter of 1981–1982 in the car, by the highway and in the park. We came back to the plant every few days, begging for work. Finally, one of the foremen felt sorry for us. I started working nights at the pig plant and immediately registered for school during the day. I had studied electrical engineering in Vietnam, but I knew that I was not in a position to continue that here: I had to learn proper English.

"I saved money to sponsor my sister to come, and I always studied, I tried never to sleep. I got together with some other Vietnamese to start a restaurant, and I worked there for two years after quitting the job at the feeding plant. But the restaurant was not really a success. So I read manuals about fixing cars and in 1985 opened a body shop. In 1987, I sold my share in the body shop and bought the Rainbow Laundry, then the Specialty Cleaners. After I became a citizen, I studied the U.S. tax system and started preparing tax returns for the other Vietnamese. In 1991, I married a Vietnamese. My wife and I met at a bowling alley.

"My youth was all work and struggle and cold and heat and lonely with a strange language. In this country, if you don't work hard you either sink or stand in place, which is just as bad. You always have to calculate to get ahead. You know, I have to pay $250 each month for health insurance, and then there are the mortgage payments. I have four children; two are in Head Start programs. If I didn't have to sleep, I could make more money, though." He smiled.

"I'm thinking of buying a liquor store. You have to go forward here. I sold the Rainbow Laundry to my brother-in-law and now have just the Specialty Cleaners. But that's not enough. Now I study Spanish so I can deal better with my Mexican customers. I think that we Vietnamese have fairly good relations with the Mexicans. There are very few blacks here—it's hard to get on welfare in Garden City." (I let Nguyen continue rather than challenge him, though perhaps I should have. He would have been surprised to know that many West African immigrants in the Washington, D.C., area drive cabs at night and go to school during the day: their stories are little different from his. Yet this statement shows how immigrants pick up not only native attributes but prejudices, too.)

"You can do anything in this country! I woke up in the morning and decided I wanted to start an automobile body shop, and I did it. In America, there are no limits. Here you work on your own initiative or you drown—and that's good." Nguyen smiled again.

FROM GARDEN CITY I drove fifty miles east to Dodge City. In 1872, Dodge City became the western terminus of the Santa Fe Railroad and then a center for shipping buffalo hides and cattle east. By 1875, most cattle trails led to the railroad terminus here, making Dodge City a rendezvous point for a transient population of buffalo hunters, cowboys, soldiers, railroad gangs, fur trappers, prostitutes, thugs, and gamblers. Between 1876 and 1884, 10 million head of cattle passed through town. Directly opposite the reconstructed historical area, with its hokey Boot Hill Cemetery and Wax Museum, stood a complex of railroad tracks, cattle feedlots, and meatpacking plants operated by immigrants from Mexico and Southeast Asia. It was ugly, but it was real: the way the Dodge City of the 1870s and 1880s might have appeared to a traveler of that period.

I heard as much Spanish as English in the Burger King, where I bought a copy of the Sunday *Wichita Eagle*, whose front page was dominated by an investigative report about Laotian-immigrant gang violence in Kansas. My motel room in Dodge City had three inside locks and a sign warning me against break-ins. In the restaurant that Sunday night no alcohol was served because of Sunday blue laws, a relic of a rootless desert culture where errant behavior was countered by strict religiosity, the only available belief system in a capitalist culture that eschewed ideology. Two miles away from my truck-stop motel I saw winding suburban streets near a country club, with big lawns, no sidewalks, and late-model foreign sedans instead of pickup trucks. These streets were empty except for a few joggers in expensive sportswear. Here Dodge City looked like a minipod version of western Omaha or western St. Louis. Nguyen and others like him were probably headed here.

Further east I passed an increasing number of tree-lined streams. By the time I got to Great Bend, the short brown buffalo grass gave way to tall grasses waving in the wind. Here the air was thicker and the horizon closer. Kansas is a giant slab that slopes gradually downward from west to east, but it was between Dodge City and Great Bend, near the center of the state, that the lower altitude achieved critical mass and the horizonless clarity of the air that helps define the West began to dissipate. Great Bend is located on the "great bend" of the Arkansas River, a formerly treacherous torrent that is arguably the greatest east–west river of the continental interior after the Missouri: 1,450 miles long, rising in the Colorado Rockies and flowing into the Mississippi. Coronado and his chosen thirty—having ridden all the way from Mexico in search of gold—forded it not far from here. Now it is reduced to a creek because of irrigation, dams, and other diversions over the decades. "Here, I'll show ya," Ray "Jiggs" Schulz, a semi-retired attorney, told me as he began flipping the pages of a book to find a picture.

"You call it the Ar-*kan*-sas," I noted.

"Maybe I'm just a patriotic Kansan. Maybe because words change. When I was growing up, it was quite all right to call someone a Negro; then you had to call him a black; now I hear it's African American. No one knows what they'll call him in fifty years. Say, you know that buffalo grass can stay inundated in floodwater for twenty-one days without dying? Gee, I'm still searching for this picture I wanted to show ya."

"Are you from Great Bend, Mr. Schulz?"

"No, I'm from fifteen miles south. But I shopped here as a boy. I'm eighty-five now. My grandfather fought at the Battle of Gettysburg.

His stories never began with 'Once upon a time . . .' but rather 'We were on retreat . . .' Now, Phil Sheridan was a great Union general, but after the war he became a terrible Indian fighter. He had no understanding of the Indians. Americans can't deal with native, non-Christian cultures the way the British could. Outside of a few mountain men who took Indian girls as wives and learned the tribal languages, we had no pragmatic experts like the British had for their dealings with Arab and Africans. Ah, here it is, the picture I wanted to show ya."

Schulz showed me a painting of a covered wagon fording a wide river in 1872. "This was the Ar-*kan*-sas at Great Bend. Yes sir, the Santa Fe Railroad arrived here on July 15, 1872. Five days later, forty-six carloads of cattle were shipped east from here. We became a homesteader's town. Anyone willing to work hard could have 160 acres of free land. The town was established with 640 acres of land: this was big government, and it worked! We had a burst of prosperity in the mid-1880s because of flour milling. A hospital, a college, a street rail system, and new buildings on Main Street went up. From 1932 to 1980, we were essentially an oil-producing town; the town's population went from 5,000 to 20,000. Oil got us through the Dust Bowl and the Great Depression. Yes, the Dust Bowl: globs of black dust from the oil fields, so black that a flashlight wouldn't do you any good. . . . In 1980, the end of OPEC caused a mini–oil boom here, then it all went bust. Now it has stabilized. Great Bend makes hydraulic cylinders for export to oil-producing countries abroad. There's a packing plant across the river which provides work for Mexicans and Asians. Since the nineties"—Schulz meant the 1890s—"there were Mexican section hands on the Santa Fe Railroad. There is nothing new about nonwhite immigrants. It's the proportions that have expanded, and that is changing everything."

I DROVE EAST into east-central Kansas. The horizon kept shortening, and soon there were low, caressing hills all around, spotted with trees. This was Quivera, near the geographic center of what was to become the United States of America, which Coronado and his men reached in the summer of 1541, forty-nine years after Columbus had landed on San Salvador. A stone marker depicting a cross and a sword at the top of a hill commemorates the end of Coronado's journey. The Spaniards spent twenty-five days here, then commenced the long march back to Mexico City. Coronado had found nothing of value:

What I am sure of is that there is not any gold nor any other metal in all that country, and the other things of which they [the Indians] had told me are nothing but little villages, and in many of these they do not plant anything and do not have any houses except of skins and sticks.[8]

Though the soil was rich, without a large and settled population as in Aztec Mexico there were simply not enough native inhabitants for the Spanish to enslave and exploit. The local Quivera Indians had no houses to plunder, nor did they raise crops from which the Spanish could exact tribute. Spain's policy, which reflected ancient Rome's, was, in the words of Walter Prescott Webb, "to conquer, convert, exploit, and incorporate the native." But that approach did not apply to a nomadic, propertyless people. So there was nothing here for the Spaniards except possibilities, which could be realized only with initiative and years of work. So they left, just as they had reached the edge of the tall-grass prairie: a flat panel of rich farmland where, three centuries hence, human differences would be ground down into a distinctive American nation.

Almost exactly where Coronado turned back toward Mexico is the town of Lindsborg, settled by Swedes in 1869, with a college, an art museum, and a network of perfect, spotless streets and storefronts—a rebuke, I thought, to Spanish underdevelopment. The cold emptiness of much of this continent was suitable only for those with a strong work ethic.

Coronado had found scattered, unstable communities of various Indian cultures throughout the Southwest. I found an archipelago of separate nations, including Third World Indian settlements, a bus-riding underclass, a global elite in Santa Fe that was closer to New York and Paris than to Agua Fria (south Santa Fe), an Oklahoma town more affected by markets in South America and the Far East than by the East Coast, and a government fortress with more destructive power than history has ever before seen, even though the government might no longer control the future of anything except those weapons, and perhaps in the long run not that future either.

Another hour of driving, and I was in Abilene. In a frugal white frame house of tiny rooms that shook with every passing freight train, five boys of German immigrant background had grown up at the turn of the twentieth century. The bedside footstools had been made by

---

[8]George Parker Winship, *The Coronado Expedition, 1540–1542.*

the boys in high school shop classes. Their father had worked in the local creamery while the boys had put themselves through college. On the living room shelves I saw several books on "success." One of the boys, Dwight, who liked reading classical history, grew up to become the president of the United States during the height of this country's imperial reach and cohesiveness. A few steps from the house is Dwight D. Eisenhower's tomb, inside a stark, cold, angular Protestant chapel. On the wall is an excerpt from the speech he made at Abilene in 1952, during his first campaign for the presidency:

> The real fire within the builders of America was faith—faith in a Provident God . . . faith in their country and its principles that proclaimed man's right to freedom and justice.

The God of the northern Europeans who settled North America from east to west was—unlike the God of the conquistadors—"Provident." He would provide, but only for those who provided for themselves. He was a God of work whose message went hand in hand with "freedom and justice." The dripping water in the fountain beside Eisenhower's tomb seemed to mark the passing of the years, decades, even centuries. I looked up at the stained glass and knew that the economic opportunity this new, secular deity of the Enlightenment had provided his followers would, ultimately, test the limits of nationhood itself as the prospect of material gain drew people beyond the national community into the global one.

THE ACCOUNT OF my travels to the cities of the Midwest, to southern California, from Mexico to Kansas, and so on is chronologically out of sequence. In fact, from Omaha I traveled to the Pacific Northwest. But the logic of this narrative suggested that I tell the story as I have done. So now I will pick up my journey from Omaha.

THE

NEW

EMPIRE

24

———

Imperial Outpost
and the Small Town

FROM OMAHA, LINCOLN was forty-five minutes away to the south-west on Interstate 80. The approach was impressive. Next to a series of massive, dark gray highway overpasses was Memorial Stadium, a gray edifice with a capacity of 80,000, home of the University of Nebraska Cornhuskers, one of the best college football teams of the past several decades. On the Friday after Thanksgiving, the stadium becomes the third largest city in Nebraska after Omaha and Lincoln, when it fills to capacity for the game against the University of Colorado Buffalos. Because Nebraska has no professional football or baseball team, it is the Cornhuskers, more than the arbitrary borders of this 450-mile-wide state divided between western ranchers and eastern farmers and suburbanites, who unite it.

Behind the stadium rises another edifice in sullen dark and stately iron-gray shades: the four-hundred-foot-tall Nebraska Capitol building, completed in 1932, one of the great "transition" buildings of the era, blending the "romance and sentimentality" of "belle epoque classicism" with the modern Bauhaus tradition, according to a plaque. As I parked my car in the freezing rain and walked into the Capitol building and through its dimly lit corridors of massive stone past Byzantine murals, Lincoln, Nebraska, suggested to me nothing so much as one of the great provincial cities of the Roman empire come alive.[1] Of course, unlike Rome, this imperial building signified something unique in history: the authority of just one of fifty states within a larger federal system, a decentralized, divided sovereignty that has conferred a vibrancy and flexibility that Rome and all other vast empires lacked.

Two miles away from the Capitol is Fairview, the Classical Revival home of the newspaper editor, Washington-hating politician, and long-winded crier of Middle American populism William Jennings Bryan, who accepted the Democratic Party's 1908 nomination for president from his front porch. Bryan's politics were a howl from the provinces against East Coast economic interests, which, according to him, were exploiting midwestern farmers and new industrial workers: "The great cities," Bryan reminded his followers, "rest upon our broad and fertile prairies."[2] Bryan's movement, like those of other populists, rose, rippled across large sections of the country, and then died, even as its more benign elements were incorporated into the progressive politics of Woodrow Wilson. (Bryan served as secretary of state during Wilson's first term.) Among history's immense and contiguous land empires, such peacefully concluded and ultimately productive rebellions are unique to the United States. Meanwhile, Bryan's rebellion against the national capital continues, for the most part peacefully, to this day.

I visited Jerome Warner, a member of the Nebraska Legislature for thirty-four of his sixty-eight years. Though a Republican, Warner, like the other forty-eight members of the unicameral body, was elected on a nonpartisan basis. His office was at the rear of a warren of dimly lit rooms. His tone was gruff. "The idea of political power reverting to the states is nonsense," he told me. "The Feds have so narrowed our options that local control is a myth; this is particularly true of urban areas, which require more regulations. The national Republican leaders talk about states' rights, yet they have tightened their control over state parties like ours. We've become pawns in a machine run out of the Republican National Committee's headquarters in Washington. But this is a natural development: technology and

---

[1] I refer, in particular, to El Djem in Tunisia. Its Roman colosseum—though situated in a rural province—is as large as the Colosseum in Rome, an ancient equivalent of Lincoln's Memorial Stadium.

[2] The words are from Bryan's famous "Cross of Gold" speech at the 1896 Democratic Convention, in which he said, "You shall not crucify mankind upon a cross of gold!"; see H. W. Brands, *The Reckless Decade: America in the 1890s.*

communications have simply made it easier for Washington to influence us."

There are other, more subtle forms of centralizing tyranny, according to Warner. Local political races are now influenced by out-of-state money to an unprecedented degree, so that many a local race is increasingly a national race. "Because of the growth of television," Warner said, "more money is needed for campaign advertising, so candidates have to look beyond the community for help. When I entered the legislature, a typical campaign for a member cost a few thousand dollars. Now it can cost a hundred thousand."

Despite Washington's presence in local politics, the world economy has given Nebraska new freedom in other ways. "The idea that the governor would be leading trade missions abroad was unthinkable even a decade ago," Warner said. "What else do you want to know?"

I asked how state politics has changed since he entered the legislature.

"When I first started here in the early 1960s, most of the mail was positive. Now it's overwhelmingly negative. People are upset with government in principle. By that I mean that they want more and more from government but expect to pay less. Property taxes have always been the issue. 'They're too high!' people say. Because distances are great in Nebraska, the only thing people are willing to pay for is roads. But when we give them roads, they complain about the cost and then want their taxes reduced.

"It's funny, but the communications revolution has actually hindered the crucial sorts of communications that a healthy democracy requires. People read newspapers less, so there is less in-depth discussion between politicians and the public on the state and local level." As he spoke, I thought of the TV weathermen who are not meteorologists and cabinet secretaries who do no more than perform well at press conferences and become television heroes, while competent officials, to say nothing of real heroes like Joe Edmonson and the Bluvases, go unknown.

Warner suggested that relentless technological change may undermine our system of government. The Founding Fathers might have agreed. Indeed, they had rejected as a model such ancient republics of patriotic "virtue" as Athens and Sparta, partly because social and technological development had already created a more complex society in which individuals had less time for communal concerns. Thus, the Founders (Madison in particular) saw government less as a force for ideal good than as a referee among competing selfishnesses. So far, Western democracy has existed within a rather thin band of social and economic conditions: high literacy, an established bourgeoisie, and a flexible hierarchy in which people move up and down an economic ladder, most of them bunched in the middle, instead of vast and rigidly separated classes. But what if such wide, rigid class distinctions re-emerge—with a deepening chasm between an enlarged underclass and a globally oriented upper class—while the dialogue between ruler and ruled becomes increasingly ritualistic and superficial? Will the forms of democracy remain while its substance decays?

As I drove westward out of Lincoln, the Capitol and Memorial Stadium receding on the biscuit-brown plain, I continued to speculate.

For instance: As the size of our population and the complexity of our lives challenge the traditional national community—creating a wilderness of region-states and suburban oases linked to a global marketplace—will the gulf widen still further between the citizens of these new entities and the bureaucratic overseers in Washington, who must manage an elite, volunteer military (like what I had seen at Fort Leavenworth) and Information Age weapons in an unstable world?

The reddish brown of corn husks painted the fields for mile upon mile. Giant, mantislike sprinkler cranes appeared once more as I left the tall-grass prairie and re-entered the water-poor Great Plains, with its short grasses. Snow blew in patterns across the road. Then came the windy, frigid Platte River, laden with ice floes, from which Nebraska gets it name: the Otoe Indians had called this east–west artery "Flat Water," or *Nebraska* in their language. I imagined rickety wagon trains, low on supplies, packed with children and pregnant women, traversing this vastness, empty except for hostile Indians. I grafted my trekking experience in war-torn Afghanistan onto this even more brutal climate and terrain and grasped, if only marginally, the horror of nineteenth-century pioneering. This dreary emptiness, ransacked by winds, makes any civilization that exists upon it seem forever fragile; thus my bleak meditations—for the moment.

A WINTER WEATHER advisory was in effect. The temperature was minus seven, and snow blew more fiercely across the cornfields. I was headed southwest on U.S. Route 30, the Platte River over the horizon to my left and a hundred-car freight train of the Union Pacific less than fifty yards away to my right. Towering elevators stood directly over the tracks, ready to fill cars. Every twenty miles there was a Pump

& Pantry, a general store and gas station where drivers in old pickups gathered for hot soup, sandwiches, and coffee. The odor of diesel from the locomotives and heavy trucks was everywhere. There was an Industrial Age glamour to these rest stops along a main artery of an agricultural empire, where men who spent hours on end alone in vehicles on near-empty roads without cell phones came to Pump & Pantry to talk and call friends. Vanilla-colored cappuccino machines were the only sign, thus far, of a larger world.

Back in the car, I listened to a confession on the radio from a local basketball player. Jesus had helped her team win the championship, Jesus had saved her from illness, Jesus had helped pay the family mortgage, and so forth. "To stand up and say you are a Christian is to make yourself a target," she said, "because there are too many people in America who won't accept the truth—that Jesus is the only Lord."

Reliance on God, along with the demand that everyone share the same belief, seemed appropriate to this landscape, where nearly everyone's economic fate is literally in the hands of nature, and where, as Bill Green had told me in Texas, the monotonous scenery encourages the belief that what is over the horizon is no different from what is here. Such faith has been part of the social pattern here since the nineteenth century, when homesteaders faced the most arbitrary of demons (hail and locusts, for instance), from which their only protection was faith. Like the smell of diesel and the old pay phones, the confession, which I heard in a driving snowstorm alone on the road, sounded less exotic than it might have had I been hearing it in, say, New York or Washington.

Interstate 80, which crosses Nebraska from Iowa in the east to Wyoming in the west, gives the state a bad name. Located in the floodplain of the Platte River Valley for much of its 450 miles, I-80 shows cross-country travelers little of Nebraska except for achingly flat vistas, causing many drivers—anticipating the Rocky Mountains—to slam the foot on the accelerator and get Nebraska behind them. Actually, the moment one leaves the I-80 floodplain, both central and western Nebraska become a sublime tapestry of domed, wind-scraped hills of yellow loam and sand, which in the snow look glazed and crystalline under the hard blue enamel skies of below-zero weather.

Thus, I followed U.S. Route 30 parallel to the Union Pacific rail line until Kearney, then headed northwest into Nebraska's dead center. Soon the clouds lowered as the ground heaved upward. Cattle and sky filled the view: I don't mean a few hundred cattle but thousands, for miles on end. I had again crossed that mythic boundary into the Real West. A sign said that I had entered Custer County, where I planned to spend a few days. In Omaha I had heard that Callaway and Broken Bow were "nice" and "interesting" towns. I wanted to find out what those words meant and to learn more about small-town life in this age of posturban sprawl.

Callaway, with 539 inhabitants, was founded in 1885 on a spur line of the Union Pacific and named after an early president of the railroad. The population density of Custer County is four inhabitants per square mile, low even for Nebraska, where the average density is twenty persons. Further north, near the border with South Dakota, the density falls to two persons per square mile, the lowest in Nebraska. (Indeed, the population patterns not only of Nebraska but of all the plains states are yet another argument for how climate helps determine human destiny and even character. While Kansas, Nebraska, South Dakota, and North Dakota are all similar in size, the population dwindles as one goes north: Kansas has 2.5 million inhabitants, Nebraska 1.6 million, South Dakota 715,000, and North Dakota 635,000. And as one goes north, per capita personal income also declines. So does crime.[3] According to all reports, loneliness, depression, fatalism, and spirituality all intensify as one goes northward into the Dakotas and eastern Montana.[4])

As I eyed Callaway's frame houses with their intricate roof arrangements rearing up above the snowdrifts, I was struck by an intimacy born of toil and endurance. Sinclair Lewis's phrase about the Midwest, "Plymouth Rock in sleet-storm," came to mind. Callaway was a neat cluster of brick buildings emerging from an intersection. It had a huddled-together verticality manifesting community that I associated with Europe, the same quality that makes many New England towns appear inviting. Beyond the brick buildings of the business district were the old frame houses with porches and big trees.

---

[3]Though income drops only from about $20,000 in Kansas to $17,000 in North Dakota, the differences in crime are dramatic. According to the FBI, Kansas has 5,300 incidents of crime per 100,000 inhabitants, Nebraska 4,300, South Dakota 3,000, and North Dakota 2,900. While there are six murders per 100,000 people in Kansas, the rate in the Dakotas is less than one. The incidence of rape drops in half as one travels from Kansas to North Dakota; house break-ins drop to a third.

[4]Compare, for instance, Willa Cather's writing on Nebraska with Kathleen Norris, *Dakota: A Spiritual Geography,* and Jonathan Raban, *Bad Land: An American Romance* (about the section of eastern Montana near the border with North Dakota).

Callaway certainly looked less lonely close up than it did on the map. So many American hamlets I had seen, in the desert Southwest especially, had been just a scattering of trailer homes with a restaurant, a post office a few hundred yards away, a gas station–general store another quarter mile distant, and, perhaps, also, the detritus of an earlier era of expansion—for example, a derelict miniature golf course.

My car skidded onto the snowy lawn of a Victorian house on Main Street that I had been told was a bed-and-breakfast. Inside, surrounded by boxy furniture, dark wainscoting and wallpaper, I met Mike and Suzanne Wendorff. Mike, a former platoon sergeant at the Aberdeen Proving Grounds in Maryland, was stockily built and dressed in sweats, with clipped black hair and a mustache. Besides helping Suzanne run the bed-and-breakfast, he edits the weekly *Callaway Courier.* "We want to give a visiting journalist a good impression. This is a real airy little town," Mike said. Nobody I was to meet over the next few days would be shy about such boosterism. Like that of many such communities, Callaway's survival was on the line, and survival required good publicity that would make people want to live there.

Before I went up to my room, I learned that Callaway has its own museum and hospital, an "excellent school," a "youth-oriented business community," a hundred-member chamber of commerce, and weekly get-togethers for newcomers. "It's a regular New England town-meeting atmosphere," Suzanne said, with pheasant, quail, and deer hunting. "We all," Mike said, "have gun racks for our pickups. We all carry pocket knives around here, but there is no crime."

Mike took me to the local museum, a multistory building on Main Street with dusty corridors, crammed with display cases holding old pencils from the 1940s, barbed wire, typewriters, cash registers, Bibles, family photos, guns, flints, furs, Sioux and Cheyenne arrowheads, buffalo jackets, and so forth, each object identified by a handmade label. In the basement I saw a telephone operator's switchboard from the 1950s. (The phone book for the entire county is still less than fifty pages.) In one room filled with American flags I noticed dog tags donated by Wayne Thurmon, a Callaway World War II veteran. On an ancient Underwood he had typed, "I'm an old-timer: 50 missions, 330 hours in the air over Europe from Africa in P-38 and B-17 combat aircraft . . ." The amateurish nature of the exhibition made it all the more poignant, as each object evoked midcentury memories.

Mike and I walked back to the house in the radiant twilight. The temperature was below zero. The wind worked its way around my bones. The empty streets, encased in snow and ice and reflecting the silhouettes of Victorian houses, seemed frozen in time, too, as if all the certainties of an imagined golden past were still valid.

Mike and Suzanne took me to Callaway's only restaurant. I tried to pay, but Mike wouldn't let me. "We've got money from the chamber of commerce to entertain important guests," he said. "We've got to make a good impression." The restaurant was like an unfinished basement with Formica tables and plastic salad bowls. The customers were in overalls or checkered shirts, and they all knew one another. Conversation flew back and forth among the tables as at a family gathering. We drank our beer from the bottles. There was no wine. "You can get only Miller and Bud here," Mike said. "Now, when Suzanne and I lived in Kearney, we had everything—hamburgers at Wendy's, fries from McDonald's." Then, as if suddenly reading my thoughts, Mike laughed and said, "Yeah, I know, we're just peasants. Junk food is our equivalent of fine dining." But they weren't anything like peasants. If America has peasants as they have been defined in Europe and the developing world, they are probably racially and economically oppressed inner-city blacks and the growing pool of underpaid Mexican laborers.

The next day Mike introduced me to Brian Gardner, Callaway's mayor. While Mike both played and looked the part of a politically conservative, small-town military type, Callaway's mayor—a high school teacher and local representative of the national teachers' union—looked like the people I had seen in the Garden Café in prosperous western Omaha. "I voted for Clinton, that makes me far left here," Brian joked. He dismissed the notion that small towns on the plains were dying. "That was only a temporary trend," he said. "The whole thing has really turned around in the last few years. There is a resurgence of small communities everywhere as the nation's population gets a bit too large and too impersonal for itself. The *Omaha World-Herald* reported that most of the rural counties which showed a loss of population in the 1990 Nebraska census have gained in population—and some strongly—over the past six years. The trick is to combine the appeal of rural life with the economic possibilities of urban areas."

Brian and Mike told me that the Internet could save Callaway, which was about to get its own Web site to attract "city people with progressive views" to move here and telecommute. "We're not the only small town doing that," Brian said. "Communities will fight for desirable immigrants via the Internet. The information superhighway is not a cliché; for towns like ours across America, it's salvation." The local high school, for example, has long-distance learning rooms, where students take courses via satellite from Chadron State College, two hundred miles away. Brian admitted, "There are not a lot of employment opportunities here. Many people make ends meet by holding two and three part-time jobs. We're offering only a nice living environment for people who can make their money somewhere else. Our high school has a zero dropout rate. The overwhelming majority of students go to college. . . . At our weekly seven A.M. council meeting, the first few minutes are called 'wild and crazy,' when we just throw out ideas for improving the sense of community. One idea was the Labor Day Kite Fly, which is now a tradition in Callaway."

The attempt to woo people to small towns is as old as America itself. In the nineteenth century, the northwestern railroads held out the promise of wealth to attract people to what would turn out to be drought-riven wastelands, plagued by locusts in summer and arctic temperatures in winter. Towns bravely sprang up along the track, struggled for a few years or decades, then died when rain did not— as it turned out—follow the plow.[5] But Callaway's mayor was not promising wealth, only a more intimate quality of life in a setting that, because of modern communications, is far less isolated than the northern plains were a hundred years ago. What could be more wholesome, I wondered, than a Darwinian competition for survival among small towns, based purely on the quality of life they offer? If continuing advances in communications technology neutralize geography further, the only remaining difference among places—other than climate and scenery—will, in fact, be the caliber of community life.

In Johnson County, St. Louis, Omaha, Orange County, and Tucson I had caught glimpses of how the communications revolution is weakening America's national cohesion as posturbanites develop overseas relationships while loosening their bonds to poorer people close by. In Callaway I glimpsed an opposite possibility: the potential rescue of many an isolated town from the boredom and closed-mindedness that are consequences of loneliness and lack of opportunity.

[5]See Raban, *Bad Land.*

*   *   *

MARY RIDDER, WHO with her husband, John, owns a ranch outside Callaway, crystallized some of this for me. Their home was contemporary, with light colors and modern furniture and appliances. Two of Mary's six children sat on a couch, quietly reading amid maps, encyclopedias, and a home computer. "The new generation of ranchers," Mary explained as we sipped coffee and enjoyed the sunny view beyond her window, "do not want their children to suffer like the ranchers of a century ago. We want the same living standard and some of the same cultural and aesthetic influences as our friends and relatives in the suburbs. We're not isolated anymore."

"How much land do you have?" I asked, awestruck by the bumpy yellow tableland of hay, corn, and soapweed where Hereford and red Angus cattle grazed. The fields stretched for miles downhill from the window, toward horizons more distant than any I can ever recall. The branches of the cottonwood trees near the house cracked in the breeze. Otherwise all was silence but for our voices and the movement of tawny grasses. Mary smiled. "Never ask a rancher how much land he has. It's the equivalent of asking how much money he makes, since anybody around here familiar with ranching will be able to figure out our income based on the number of acres we own.

"I love ranching," Mary went on. "It would be more fun if we knew that we could make a living from it in the future. John and I discuss world economic issues all the time. With the future of beef less bright than in the past, and with ranchers demanding a higher living standard, I suppose that my kids will be doing something different and that ranching, like farming, will become corporate, with Asian and Hispanic laborers. Only two percent of the population produces the food and fiber for everybody else. So in a way we're the last individualists, the last pioneers—a family able to grow food for profit. But I believe that we have to preserve rural America. I wouldn't send my kids to school anywhere but Callaway. The average class here has only fourteen pupils, and people still don't lock their doors. What would happen if there is nothing on this continent but suburbs and wilderness, without any real communities?"

I sympathized with this vision, but I also knew that as a crucible of unrestrained capitalism on an unfettered landscape, America can never be anything but a land of chronic social and economic impermanence. So, as in the century-old Nebraska of Willa Cather's stories, the future here looked grim, despite the endless emptiness and the illusion of infinite possibility, of which dreams like Mary's are forged.

I DROVE TO Broken Bow the next morning in blinding sunlight. Frozen tree branches and yucca stood out sharply on a fire-and-ice sandstone tableland, sculpted by snowdrifts. Broken Bow, with a population of 3,800, has twenty churches, of which some are Evangelical. "Because of the clean air, the clean water, and no crime, the migration pattern has been reversed," Todd Larimer, a former mayor, told me over breakfast one Sunday morning. "During the Dust Bowl of the 1930s, people fled Custer County for California, but now Californians are slowly filtering back. Broken Bow already has a home page on the Internet. We've got a video learning center for Spanish. We need younger people to move here; sixty-five percent of our population is fifty or older. In America, if you want things to stay as they are, then your community will die."

The Evangelical Free Church was located on the outskirts of Broken Bow, a bare aluminum frame shed that looked as if it had been put up overnight. The marquee announced, "The Poorest Man Is He Whose Only Wealth is Money." I counted thirty-five cars, mostly old, in the crowded parking lot. The service was over, and adult Sunday school had just begun, when I took a seat in the rear. On the wall I noticed a map of the world marked with lights signifying Evangelical churches around the globe. Then the lights went dim and a film began with a close-up of Israeli soldiers in the Judean desert.

I saw the Herodion, a fortress built two thousand years ago by King Herod of Judea. At first the narration seemed to have been scripted by the World Zionist Organization or the Israeli Tourism Ministry. The geology, flora, and fauna of the Judean desert was described in rich detail. The Jews were extolled as hard, God-fearing farmers who loved the land and wrested life from the all-encompassing death of the desert. The narrator provided a detailed summary of ancient history in the eastern Mediterranean: Judea, Edom, Syria, Petra, and so on. After the magnificent circular ruin of the Herodion and King Herod's glittering funeral procession were described, the narrator said, "See the greatness of Herod! Look around and see his magnificence—the Herodion, the monuments of Jerusalem. . . . Yet all that is remembered of him today is that he was the king at the time of Jesus's birth. Despite all of his wealth, Herod was an Edomite, a descendant of pagans, while Jesus was a descendant of Jacob, whose other name is 'Israel,' meaning 'he who sows,' he who is industrious.

"Imagine," continued the film's narrator, "the courage of those early Jews who believed in Jesus—who had nothing, while Herod had everything! See how insignificant material wealth is! The only thing the world remembers now about Herod, the owner of that great fortress in the desert, is that he killed a lot of babies at Christmastime!"

The lights came on, and a man in an old sweater got up from a middle row and said, "Now, you guys, wasn't that neat?" The unadorned setting, with neither neon nor slick architecture, the utter absence of ritual and hierarchy or stylish clothes, and the evocation of modern Israel reminded me of a kibbutz meeting. "Now, you guys," repeated the lay pastor, "we Christians often complain about being beat up upon. But imagine the faith of the Jewish people through their travails! And imagine the persecution of Christians elsewhere in the world today! We are wealthy and privileged compared to Christians elsewhere. If that story about Herod teaches us anything, it is that the materialism all around us will ultimately be as insignificant as the wealth of Herod. And that there is nothing—not AIDS, not world hunger, not racism—that cannot be conquered purely through faith in Jesus Christ. Next week in Sunday school we will focus on the Hebrew prophet Amos and how his message against social injustice and hypocrisy at a time of great wealth and political power in ancient Israel relates to our own society."

The meeting affected me. Out in the parking lot, slipping on the ice, I felt relieved of some of my own material worries even though I was neither a Christian nor badly off financially.

The same day, I returned to Callaway to visit the Callaway Community Church, run by pastor Albert Seadore, with whom I talked for an hour. His church, like the one in Broken Bow, was Evangelical and poorly constructed. It had been a honey jar plant, then a bar and grill, before it became a church. Seadore lived in the mobile home next door with his wife and their younger children. In his church, too, I saw a world map.

"All of these Evangelical churches look so humble," I said. "I don't see an expensive old brick building with a white steeple on it at the center of town."

"You understand well," Seadore said. "For too many in our troubled times, religion means you have a building where you put God so that you can visit him on Sunday, without taking him home the rest of the week. Many people go to church in magnificent buildings, but they don't literally believe in God. But for us God is present all the time. We talk to God and worship him continually, because we accept that Jesus Christ died for our sins." His tone was quiet but firm. "Our church is, therefore, just another humble building. Jesus would recognize it in a minute. He knew humble places like ours."

"What is an Evangelical?" I asked.

"You mean, what is a Christian? Well, a Christian is someone with a firsthand spiritual experience, someone who takes spiritual direction directly from the word of God: a person for whom the Bible—the Old and New Testaments—is the foundation stone of his life, without any intermediary texts or hierarchies or priests. I am not a priest, only a pastor, a servant of Jesus." I noticed that Seadore, like the pastor in Broken Bow, was dressed informally, without a jacket or tie, though it was Sunday.

Seadore was born in Long Pine, Nebraska, a town even smaller than Callaway, near the South Dakota border. "I was one of ten kids," he told me. "I quit high school as a sophomore, worked carnivals, state fairs, and circuses. I thought I was pretty tough until I went to work in a mine and realized that I wasn't as tough as I thought. Nearby, a poor missionary and his family were rebuilding an old shack. They had a lot of kids and no money, and I was just waiting for the drunken fights to start between the missionary and his wife over car payments, or whatever. But the fights never came. Given my experience until then, that perplexed me. Finally—I was twenty-one at the time—I walked up to the guy and said, 'Fella, I don't know what you got, but whatever it is, I want it.' Since then I have shared the word."

Seadore continued, "Christians face only petty discrimination in America compared to what they put up with in other parts of the world, like in the Orthodox countries of eastern Europe. But it's good that Christians are going into politics in America. Historically, it's a misinterpretation that there should be separation of church and state."

By "Christians," Seadore obviously did not mean members of established churches, whether Orthodox, Protestant, or Catholic. He meant only those who had discovered Jesus on their own and who worshiped together in informal, humble surroundings like his. In the minds of Seadore and other Evangelicals, the two thousand years of accumulated Christian tradition and the pursuit of wealth had to be abandoned so that people could re-experience Jesus as his Jewish followers in first-century Palestine had. For preachers such as Seadore, economic and technological upheaval was forcing a return to a more elemental belief system, despite those Evangelical churches elsewhere in America that featured expensive multimedia pageants that filled large auditoriums.[6] Because economic optimism is the closest thing America has ever had to a real ideology, economic uncertainty among low-wage Americans encourages religious awakening as an alternative.

While the beliefs of some religious groups infringe on those of others, James Madison observed in *The Federalist* that the sheer variety of religious movements in America would ensure stability as each sect canceled out the other, making it hard for any to gain pivotal political influence. What Madison could not foresee was a single, highly politicized religious movement amplified by television, like Pat Robertson's. Though Seadore represented a stabilizing moral force with which I felt comfortable, give his or any other religious group too much power and, as the Founding Fathers warned, the fragile consensus holding together a democratic society passing through one technological transformation after another could shred. The Evangelical Christianity I saw in this Nebraska county was raw and literal, as if Jesus had just died on the cross last week and the story was spreading by word of mouth, with an intensity that overwhelmed other faiths and opinions. Whoever can unite such Evangelicals into a political force, as Robertson hopes to do, will threaten the increasingly fragile bonds of union.

[6]See Charles Trueheart, "The Next Church."

25

The New Localism

IN JULY 1893, Katharine Lee Bates, a New England schoolteacher, journeyed by rail from Boston to Colorado Springs to teach a summer course at Colorado College. The high point of her journey came after she had spent days crossing the flat, piecrust monotony of the summer prairie and Great Plains: suddenly, there was the dizzying wall of the Rocky Mountains. After ascending Pikes Peak, she composed the words to "America the Beautiful."

I know of nothing that better sums up the geographical bounty of the United States than crossing the flat middle of America by car or train, from, say, central Ohio to central Colorado, Wyoming, or Montana, and being rewarded by the sight of the Rockies. "I took a deep breath," wrote Jack Kerouac about encountering the Rockies for the first time in southeastern Wyoming.

With the arrival of budget air travel, this landscape experience has been rare: seeing the Rockies from the air before landing at Denver airport is not the same as craning your neck at them from the ground after days on the plains. In the late 1990s, I traveled the same route as Kerouac, from Nebraska into Wyoming. I have visited forty-six of the fifty states, and the Front Range of the Rockies is the only natural sight I know that is so likely to inspire feelings of patriotism and faith in the future begotten by the unfolding wonders of a continental landscape. But the patriotism I felt was valedictory: not just because fewer Americans drive west into the Rockies, but because for many inhabitants of the West, the intense, lump-in-the-throat beauty of these mountains—and of the Cascades farther west—now inspires other feelings than the traditional love of country.

I'll begin with a discussion with Dorothy Bradley, a Democrat, who in 1992 came within a few votes of being elected the first female governor of Montana.

WE MET IN the lobby of an old hotel in Bozeman, Montana, on the northern edge of the greater Yellowstone region. Bradley, a tall woman with light brown hair and a lively manner who lives in an apartment in the hotel, repeated what Jerome Warner, the Nebraska legislator with whom I had spoken in Lincoln, told me. The theme was the decline of traditional state politics.

"In the 1970s, perhaps as an outgrowth of the antiwar movement, citizen politics were at a high point, with all kinds of activists clamoring to attend committee meetings of the Montana Legislature. Environmentalism then, for instance, was a popular movement, full of rough-hewn blue-collar types. Now environmentalists are extremely sophisticated and well funded and seen as elitists: just another lobby, in other words. . . .

"Technology is at a point where it undermines traditional democracy. We have pressure groups like the AARP [American Association of Retired Persons] armed with all the Information Age tools of electronic domination—e-mail, faxes, mass mailing lists, and so forth—and they use it to create instant anger over a specific issue in the course of one eight-hour business day. Anger plus media power equals waves of public irrationality just at the moment when a specific issue is up for legislative decision. Everyone is angry about something, yet nobody knows anymore who his legislator is or, perhaps, whom he voted for at the last statewide election. Meanwhile, in addition to corporations, we have public pressure groups and citizens' lobbies, which have taken on the attributes of corporate beasts, even as the average citizen is both more dissatisfied and more passive."

"What about Montana?" I asked.

"This is a big state, there's a lot of dirt between the lightbulbs. And it's not really a state. The Great Plains of eastern Montana are an extension of North Dakota, while we're part of the northern Rocky

Mountain West, together with northwestern Wyoming and Idaho. Eastern Montana never heard of tourism, while we live on it. We really have little in common with the other half of the state: Montana as a governing entity is losing relevance. We have the lowest-paid university faculty in the nation. While local tax revenues are rising, state revenues are falling. Not just in the plains, but in the mountains, too, the future is city-states. Little towns are gone, and places like Bozeman and Missoula are enlarging as regional hubs, which, in turn, are defined by ecozones like river valleys."

All the experts I met said the same thing about America's transformation into posturban pods, even though I had found these people entirely at random. Indeed, each was an acquaintance of an acquaintance, usually several times removed: there were few I had specifically sought out. Yet this agreement on the city-state character of the continental future was something I rarely heard on the East Coast, where I live and grew up.

Bozeman was booming, with crowded sidewalks, pricey stores and restaurants offering international food and products, new hotels strategically located by Interstate 90, and spreading suburbs. "The rugged rural individualist of western myth never did exist," Bradley told me. "The arid West has always been more urban than many other parts of the country. Out here the only real individualists wound up at the wrong end of a rope. The Freemen"—she meant the extremist right-wing militia group that had a standoff with the FBI in 1996— "are part of the intensely isolated Great Plains culture of eastern Montana; even there they are an irrelevant mutation."

The real battle here is not ideological but economic and cultural. It has nothing to do with different interpretations of nationalism and everything to do with something more meaningful now that traditional nationalism is receding: the fate of the land itself.

"THERE IS A war going on here between developers and environmentalists like me," said Mike Miles, a former Jesuit priest, now married and an ex-gubernatorial aide. He wore a feedlot hat over his white hair and had a soft, calming voice. He took me for a hike to a mountain meadow ringed by the snow-shrouded peaks overlooking Bozeman. "Over there is Bridger Mountain, named for the fur trapper and mountain man Jim Bridger. There is Sacagawea Mountain, named for the Shoshone Indian woman who helped Lewis and Clark.

There on Mount Ellis was a calvary post from which the telegram announcing that Custer and the Seventh Cavalry had been wiped out
was sent to Washington. It's all threatened by the development of condominiums and trophy ranches for wealthy people from the two
coasts. The land rush is on. The yellow pages are full of real estate
agents. When they say, 'We sell Montana,' they're not kidding. Look,
there are two swallows, the first I've seen this spring—they're threatened, too."[1]

I noticed several more beautiful birds—blue, white, and black—in
an aspen tree. "What are those?" I asked.

"Bigtail magpies. They're tough scavengers, here twelve months a
year. Lewis and Clark made a note of them."

Miles went on with his main subject, still in a calm, numbing tone:
"Locals are being priced out by seasonal Californians. Twenty-five
years ago, an acre was $500; now it's $10,000 and up. The population
of Bozeman was 14,000 when I was growing up; now it's 50,000."

"But the downtown is thriving and the suburbs don't look too bad,
or too big," I remarked.

"Downtown density is not succeeding as it should. Nobody comes
to Montana to live in an apartment. Outsiders with money want land
and ranches, which swallow up water resources. They all want to be
'western individualists.' They don't know that the myth is a lie and will
destroy us. Because of the seasonal rich with their Disney ranches and
homes, we've got class divisions that we never used to have: our own
local ranchers live next door to the poor and don't show off their
wealth."

Miles, like other environmentalists I met in the area, was careful to
make an exception for Ted Turner and Jane Fonda, who own a ranch
in the Gallatin River Valley, south of Bozeman, toward Yellowstone
National Park: a river valley that William Clark, Ronald Reagan's interior secretary, once called the most beautiful in America. "Turner's
put all of his land under conservation rules so that developers can't
get at it. He's set a good example." (Turner and Fonda are generous
supporters of the western environmental movement.)

"The realtors," Miles said, "are ready to pounce on ranchers with
property to sell along the Bozeman River. They'll subdivide the whole
riverfront, use up more water, and threaten it with the possibility of

---

[1] I was in Callaway, Nebraska, in fall 1996 and in Bozeman in spring 1997. I broke
up the journey to return home to write.

leaks from oil and gas tanks that will have to be installed to heat the new condos. We'll need more reservoirs and dams to support the rising population. More concrete canalization of water will aggravate the already bad problem we have with spring flooding. The bobcat, the mountain lion, the black bear, the elk are threatened. So is the cutthroat trout, which requires pure stream water. It's a magnificent fish, only five percent of them are left, and their loss would affect the grizzly bear, which hunts it." Miles was happy about one thing, though: the return of the wolf to Yellowstone after seventy years.

"I'm doing the little I can to save 'the last best place,' " Miles told me softly, not in the least self-conscious about his use of the cliché. "I think it's worth devoting a life to. If you don't have a sense of place that's bigger than one's bank account, if you don't have that, then the center does not hold. Tocqueville knew that the basis of American democracy, the common good, was sense of locale."

We walked down from the mountain meadow, past foundations for expensive new homes "stacked," as Miles said, "like cordwood along the hillside."

I THOUGHT THAT if I could really understand the spirit of environmentalism from the inside, maybe I could experience the kind of communal emotion that will succeed patriotism, because despite the references to Lewis and Clark and Jim Bridger, Miles's concern for purity of place was different from Tocqueville's. But before I consider the differences between these two localisms, I should describe the physical setting of Miles's world, the home of the bobcat, the elk, and the cutthroat trout.

Even the East at its most forested (like the belt of forest stretching from Vermont's "northeast kingdom" to the Maine woods) cannot compare in dimension and sheer beauty to the part of the continent beyond the Front Range of the Rockies. New England landscape may, *may* be more intimate and suggestive, as well as more colorful, for a few weeks in the autumn. The isolation of the Great Plains encourages meditation, and other parts of the continent have their unique qualities as well. But the West has no equal. The nineteenth-century Hudson River School of American landscape painters—Thomas Cole, Albert Bierstadt, Frederic Church, Jasper Cropsey, and so on— may have concentrated on northeastern forests, but the sanctum of holiness and undefiled freedom that their work emphasized found fullest expression in Bierstadt's paintings of the Rocky Mountains and the Sierra Nevada.

Take the trees. I own a property in western Massachusetts bordered by tall pines, but whenever I return home from the West I realize that they are just trees, thin and maybe ninety feet high, what in western forests they call the "understories" beneath the real trees, which are hemlock, red and Port Orford cedar, balsam and Douglas fir, Sitka spruce, and sugar pines as wide as spruces and 270 feet high. This is to say nothing of the California redwoods, which are taller still and known to be as much as fifteen hundred years old. "Here are the greatest and most valuable forests on the continent, if not in the world," wrote Ray Stannard Baker in the March 1903 edition of *Century Magazine*. The big trees in the West are not trees: they talk to the heavens like the spires of medieval cathedrals, emblems of the savagely beautiful landscapes that overpower one here, inspiring a loyalty that at times transcends even one's human loyalty.

One day I drove south from Bozeman to Yellowstone National Park along the Gallatin River, a thundering opalescent slick between canyon walls clothed in aspen, fir, and red cedar, with creases of deathly white snow pouring down from granite pinnacles above. Off to the west a few miles is Spanish Creek, where on the volcanic grasslands of Ted Turner's ranch—I had previously gotten permission from the foreman to enter—I saw more than a hundred bison; on the Madison Plateau in Yellowstone National Park that same cold and rainy spring evening, I saw several hundred more of them, as big and numerous as boulders on the plain, their calves playfully charging. Before the park entrance, the Gallatin splits into various channels over a monumental, bone-brown tableland where the wind shrieks continually, like the crack of ice on glaciers.

It is like that throughout the mountain West: a searing beauty that obliterates words. On one trip to Oregon I hiked along the Rogue River in the southern part of the state and found myself amid the cut-glass purity of the Three Sisters (blue-white snow cones each more than 10,000 feet high). I stood ankle deep in magnesium mulch, surrounded by redwoods and aromatic red cedars mantled in oil-green moss, and watched two other backpackers, their eyes closed, sitting on a dead, lichen-covered "nurse log" from which a Douglas fir was growing. They were taking deep breaths to the beat of the swishing-of-the-womb sound of the dark, crystalline river. In an age when religion is increasingly electronic and posturban pods, with their unrelenting pace, are like ant colonies governed by the stopwatch, an environmentalism that harks back to a landscape before human habitation is powerfully attractive.[2] Some of this I experienced in the underpopulated Southwest: outside Santa Fe and Taos, in the Sonora Desert, and especially in the Canyon de Chelly. But in the water-starved wastes of New Mexico and Arizona, conservation is a much simpler issue: there is only the bare rock to protect from strip mining and nuclear waste dumping. Further north in the American Northwest—from the Rocky Mountain region of Montana, Wyoming, and Colorado westward to the Pacific—where there are more water sources and whole forest ecosystems to guard, environmentalism is more highly developed, both philosophically and politically.

Miles's obsession was understandable: those spreading human anthills, dedicated to nothing but ruthless, economic efficiency, now indisputably imperil this landscape. Driving south along the Gallatin River, beyond the Turner ranch, I saw a tacky ski resort owned by a logging conglomerate. Then came the town of West Yellowstone, a hideous sprawl of metallic signs, outlet stores, T-shirt shops, mini-malls, an IMAX theater, and a zoo (of all things) at the entrance to Yellowstone National Park.

CAL DUNBAR, SEVENTY-TWO, a World War II Japanese language expert and descendant of Mayflower Pilgrims, born in Kittery, Maine, owns a supermarket in West Yellowstone, where he has lived for decades. Over flapjacks and syrup for breakfast he told me the short history of the town: "The Union Pacific railroad established the place in 1908. But West Yellowstone wasn't incorporated until 1966, when the population was about five hundred. Because of the invention of snow machines about then, we suddenly had a winter economy with reliable skiing to go with a summer economy of park visitors. Then came a three percent retail tax on tourist items. In 1986, we took in $485,000 annually in local tax revenues; now we take in $1.6 million. In 1988, we paved the streets; before then we looked like Tijuana on a bad day. Now it's boomtown: twelve hundred full-time residents, with young families, including Chinese, moving in. Property prices are up. We're benefiting. . . .

---

[2]I have borrowed the image of the future American city as a clock-driven ant colony from the first volume of Robert Musil, *The Man Without Qualities*.

"IMAX [a theater based on high-resolution, wide-angle film technology] came in 1988. You see, Americans are impatient as hell, and they have all their kids with them. 'Are we there yet?'—that's the motto of the American auto vacation. Most of the tourists come from sidewalk city, and they see IMAX as normal. They don't want to wait to see the majesty of Yellowstone steal up on them. They want it all instantly, in the comfort of a theater where technology makes it practically real. They know there are grizzly bears in the park, and they've read about the introduction of the gray wolf in the region. But grizzlies and gray wolves are often extremely hard to locate. Nevertheless, they've paid their money to drive all the way here. So we've got this little zoo, that way they can go home and tell their friends that they saw grizzlies and wolves. Oh, sure, the park itself is overcrowded from Memorial Day to Labor Day. Soon you'll be buying tickets to the park through Ticketron, the way you buy tickets to a Broadway show."

Yellowstone National Park, the world's first preserved wilderness, established by President Ulysses S. Grant in 1872, is becoming— Dunbar was telling me—a big, crowded theater.

ENVIRONMENTALISTS HATE THIS development. They want fewer people, not more, to visit this 2,219,791-acre park in northwestern Wyoming, overlapping Montana and Idaho, even as they seek, in effect, to enlarge it. They worry particularly about the several thousand bison and more than eight thousand elk that migrate north, out of the park, to warmer, lower elevations in the fall and back into the park in spring. "The migrating herds of elk and bison on Yellowstone's northern range are unparalleled anywhere else in the lower 48 states," writes Bob Ekey, an editor of the *Greater Yellowstone Report,* the journal of the Greater Yellowstone Coalition, the region's leading environmental group. "To witness a similar migration of large ungulates on this scale, one would have to travel to the tundra of Alaska or as far away as Africa." Yet thousands of these magnificent beasts are being slaughtered by National Park Service and Montana Department of Livestock officials in an effort to control the herd size. "Not since the days of the great slaughter on the high plains [in the nineteenth century] have we seen so many bison killed," noted Mike Clark, executive director of the Greater Yellowstone Coalition. In his Bozeman office, Clark explained to me how Yellowstone and the adjoining Grand Teton National Park to the south constitute only about a sixth of the

"Yellowstone ecosystem, the biggest intact ecosystem in the lower forty-eight states. The elk and bison don't recognize the boundaries of these parks, only that of the ecosystem, so the whole ecosystem deep into Wyoming, Montana, and Idaho has to be protected." The fact that 82 percent of the Yellowstone region is already federal land means little to Clark and other environmentalists, since they know that while national parks preserve wildernesses, national forests merely manage trees as a crop—the Forest Service often encourages logging.

Clark, a tall, bearded man with a deep, theatrical voice, pulled his chair close to me and pleaded, "This is the only place left with big buffalo and elk; it's the last of the old West, the last place where the great herds can roam free. If this incredibly rich volcanic soil along the rivers here is subdivided, the herds will go! There is no other ecosystem in the lower forty-eight that can support them, along with all the moose and antelope. If everyone gets twenty acres, then we all might as well be dead. Those trophy ranches for the rich really are the pinnacles of death. I live in town, in an apartment. I think that's the way to go."

Clark grew up in poor white Appalachia. He worked with the Reverend Dr. Martin Luther King—a picture of King hangs in his office—and lived in Resurrection City on the D.C. Capitol Mall in the summer of 1968 with Ralph Abernathy and Jesse Jackson. He speaks movingly of the new memorial to Franklin Delano Roosevelt in Washington, D.C. "It's a place where you can really meditate," he said. He has lobbied on Capitol Hill for a plethora of environmental measures, from bison protection to the removal of underground oil tanks. He appears to be—appears, that is—the classic elite, liberal environmentalist whom right-wingers love to hate, who with one phone call got me onto Ted Turner's ranch.

"We here at the Greater Yellowstone Coalition are fundamentally about place: love of climate, of geography, of the great white North." Clark said that about 98 percent of the area was white. "The Indians are pretty much marginalized. Myth and symbolism are what we're about."

"In Los Angeles," I said, "a friend of mine derided the Pacific Northwest as 'the last wet dream of the white man, where upper-income liberals can live and posture about race relations without having to see blacks.' You could say the same thing about here, couldn't you?"

"There's some truth to that," Clark said. "In fact, the great white North is a doomed fortress unless we diversify. I know that we can't just have a buffalo commons empty of humans. We need to attract postindustrial growth that does not pollute and goes hand in hand with natural beauty. Because the beauty we have and seek to preserve will be the engine for an economy that can draw, for example, highly skilled nonwhites. I like the vision of a Polynesian-looking greater Yellowstone region with its capital in Bozeman, with a high-tech workforce but no new dams."

I appreciated Clark's blunt honesty about what he was and stood for. When I told him about a leaking underground oil tank that the seller of the property I had bought in Massachusetts had had to pay $48,000 to remediate—delaying the purchase for months and causing me much grief—Clark replied that he had helped write the federal cleanup legislation upon which the Massachusetts law is based.

Then Clark told me about the Gallatin II Land Exchange, which the Greater Yellowstone Coalition was supporting: "one of the largest and most complex land exchanges ever attempted in the West," in which Big Sky Lumber, an Oregon-based corporation involved in logging and ski resorts, will give back the land it owns north of Yellowstone National Park in return for land in the Bangtail Mountains northeast of Bozeman. The exchange would help consolidate all the land north of the park under National Forest Service protection, "so that the big herds can roam free."

He gave me a brochure that said:

If we don't acquire these lands, they will be lost forever. They are already subdivided on paper. With the intense real estate interest in Greater Yellowstone it is only a matter of time before elk and grizzlies give way to subdivisions and Suburbans.

But there was a catch: in order to save the elk and grizzlies (and bison, too), the homeowners in the Bangtails would have to pay a price. People who had paid premium rates for houses adjacent to scenic, "protected" national forests could find themselves looking out their windows at logging operations and cheap subdivisions that would follow behind the clear-cuts, land that has been denuded of trees. Clark, though he was supporting the exchange, wanted me to judge for myself, so one evening he took me to a public hearing in the Bangtails.

We stopped for dinner at an expensive restaurant, where over salmon and wine Clark and a friend talked about hiking in a part of northern Utah composed of "magnificent rosy uplifts." They mused about turning the area into a national park. Later, we got into Clark's car and drove to the Bangtails. In the glassy night air the ridgelines hovered just below a large, beautiful, oval yellow moon.

"The question is," Clark said in the car, "how much do we consume? The issue is sustainability. Human beings need to restrain themselves. There are about 250,000 people in the eighteen million acres of the greater Yellowstone region [one person for every seventy-two acres]. These are among the lowest density rates in the country, but it doesn't take that many more people to dramatically alter a landscape. I want small communities with a high quality of life, not a theme park or an airport bedroom that uses up water and erodes whatever natural treasure we have left."

The public hearing over the land swap was held in a ski lodge; the room was packed, and tension was high. Stress was apparent on the faces of the audience. The houses these people owned represented their biggest financial asset, on which loans for their children's higher education and much else depended. Now they faced the real possibility that the value of their homes could drop by . . . 5 percent, 10 percent, 30 percent . . . the truth was that nobody (including the proponents of the swap) knew.

At first the hearing went according to script. The environmentalists and Forest Service officials behind the deal explained why it was necessary to think in terms of "the long run." The audience was resigned but not unsympathetic: many of them were environmentalists, too. Then representatives of various home owners' groups in the Bangtails each presented his or her own alternative to the swap. Finally, a large woman with a shaky voice, after asking permission to speak, walked up from the back of the room to the podium. Awkwardly, she said what everybody, including me, was thinking: "What is happening is that a few people are getting very rich at the expense of many modest people. It's greed. . . . I do not want the Forest Service to subsidize a corporation."

For if the angry home owners and the environmentalists concerned about future bison herds had anything in common, it was a sense of helplessness: Big Sky Lumber—owned, as Clark told me, "by just a few guys who are already extremely wealthy"—was in control. Big Sky owned the land in the Gallatin Mountains north of the park,

and in exchange for keeping it pristine it was demanding the freedom to do what it wanted with the Bangtails: clear-cut, subdivide,
whatever. Big Sky would have to be satisfied, and there was little that
even the state or federal government might be able to do about that.

Clark hated Big Sky. After all, Big Sky, much more than the environmentalists, was forcing this miserable bargain, in which the interests of the home owners were being sacrificed for the well-being of
the bison.

But the problem is more complicated. Big Sky may be just a "few
rich guys," but they must have paid dearly for the land they acquired
and are looking to make a speculative profit as a reward for the risk
they took. The land itself is valuable, and this value cannot simply be
liquidated for the sake of elks and home owners: charity is noble, but
unfortunately it cannot be relied upon to solve the problems of a nation whose raison d'être has up until now been economic growth.

"SUSTAINABILITY" WAS THE word I kept hearing from western
environmentalists. It was the word Lou Gold was using now. Nearly
sixty with a short gray beard, Lou Gold had done Ph.D. work in political science at Columbia University and taught at Oberlin College
and the University of Illinois before "dropping out" in the turbulent
sixties to become a carpenter, eventually settling in the Siskiyou Forest region around Cave Junction, Oregon, near the California border.
It was Dennis Judd, the urbanist at the University of Missouri at St.
Louis, who had told me about Gold and how to reach him: Gold had
been Judd's "brilliant teacher-mentor" in urban studies at the University of Illinois before retreating to the forest like a latter-day John
Muir, the great nineteenth-century naturalist. So from the Yellowstone area, I drove due west, across the lunar-gray lava wastes and
potato and alfalfa fields of southern Idaho and the red, pottery-
colored buttes of eastern Oregon, to the moisture-lacquered, Scotch
green rain forest of the Cascade range, just to meet Gold: an unabashed, aging hippie tree hugger.

While the clean-cut Clark moved easily in Washington lobbyist
circles and with the likes of Ted Turner, Gold wore comical T-shirts,
carried a walking stick, and used worn sixties phrases like "the people," "the movement," and "living off the land." While Clark strate-
gized against logging firms behind closed doors, Gold and his band
of followers tied themselves to the trunks of Douglas firs and Port Orford cedars as loggers approached with chain saws. But Clark's and

Gold's environmental positions coincided. Indeed, Gold led me deeper into the philosophy of the environmental movement.

Gold's mission is to save the 700,000-acre Klamath-Siskiyou bioregion, which, according to ecologist Elliot Norse, is "biologically one of the richest temperate areas of the world" and according to Forest Service official Tom Atzet is "a storage disk for genetic information," since it was never glaciated and occupies the land bridge between the northern rain forests of the Pacific Northwest and the temperate redwood forests of California. "It's the forest furthest north from San Francisco and south from Portland, and it is the last to go: the most diverse conifer forest in the country, and corporations are logging it," Gold said in his Chicago accent as he led me through a dripping-wet realm of twelve-foot-wide Douglas firs and sugar pines, with understories of big-leaf maple trees draped in lichen. He knelt down to drink from a brook: "See, because there are no cattle here you can drink from the streams. But if more sand and sawdust from logging gets into the streams, they will no longer be safe to drink, and the salmon will die."

We walked for about a mile and reached a break in the forest about thirty feet wide and fifteen feet deep, extending along the hillside: a slurry mix of logs, stone, and other debris scoured to bedrock. "The loss of trees from logging led to floods, which caused the road here to collapse. This is how you get mudslides," Gold explained. "You think the forest is all around you, but what will be left is only a scenic belt of woods for tourists. If you let these companies off the hook, they'll log everything and sell the lumber for top dollar in the Pacific Rim."[3]

Gold and I were not alone. Tagging along were some of his friends, young people mainly, with long hair and bad complexions, who were taking turns protesting at a nearby site where the Rough & Ready Timber Company was logging. "The state sheriff's office," Gold said, "do not have the money to keep the protestors away from the site every day, so the logging firm is paying the salaries for extra sheriffs. In effect, these sheriffs are Pinkertons!" The protestors have had small victories, though, tying themselves to trees and being arrested and, thus, delaying lumber operations for a few hours. Gold reminisced about how twelve years ago he had saved a Douglas fir that a logging company thereafter left alone. "They made a wedge with a

[3]In 1988, for example, three quarters of the timber harvested in Oregon state forests went overseas, where it commanded a price 40 percent higher than logs sold domestically. Most of the logs went to Japan, South Korea, and China. See Carlos Arnaldo Schwantes, *The Pacific Northwest: An Interpretive History.*

chain saw, and I threw myself into the breach. The next day we went back to the tree and glued the wedge back with mud. I visit the tree now and then, it's doing fine. That, to me, is a great accomplishment of my life: I saved a beautiful, majestic living thing." The others gave their own stories. In each story the trees were like individuals, whose lives they saved or failed to save. They talked about the threat to this primeval forest as though they were relief workers warning against a humanitarian catastrophe in the Third World or human rights workers discussing genocide.

A generation ago, these people might have been marching for civil rights or for the War on Poverty. Now the plight of blacks in the inner cities did not stir their interest to the degree that primeval forests did. Thus, environmentalism at this extreme may be another form of alienation. Gold explained it in these terms as we sat together on the boulder overlooking the debris created by the clear-cut. Miles and Clark would probably have agreed: "Americans believe blindly in material and technological progress, it's their state religion. Just read what Henry Adams says about the dynamo: how Americans believed in it as much as the early Christians believed in the Cross. For Americans, technological progress is always good, even when it's bad. And it's bad now, it's destroying the most beautiful places. Environmentalists believe in making decisions based not on the welfare of this generation but on the seventh generation to come. That means that the seventh generation will occupy the same place that we will have preserved for them. So we're localists, because when you have no geography, not only do you have no accountability—like so many global corporations—but you have nothing to defend. But we can defend this watershed, this bioregion; we can't defend anything larger or something that's merely political, like a state or a country."

While Tocqueville's localism was inseparable from the commerce and material progress that has been the American secular religion for more than two hundred years, the localism of Gold and Miles spurned this materialism and thus Lawrence's "home-land . . . of the pocket," the same materialism that has attracted generations of immigrants here. The western environmental movement may foreshadow a new and subtle form of separatism as traditional patriotism becomes harder to sustain.

Later that day, Gold led me into a magnificent valley bordering the primeval forest, where a group of environmentalists had settled in the 1970s and 1980s, bought some do-it-yourself books, and built their own homes. One woman, a basket weaver, asked me what the book I was researching was about. I told her it was about whether or not many Americans would still be moved in fifty years when they heard John Philip Sousa music on Inauguration Day. She said that she can't imagine anyone feeling such an emotion even now.

That's where Miles and Clark—the latter of whom spoke movingly about the new FDR monument and is a frequent visitor to Washington—would part company with Gold and his friends. Still, these hippie environmentalists in southern Oregon might be onto something: what sounds extreme now may sound less so as the decades roll on. Here is Gold as he sat on the boulder: "You feel the power of the federal government most in the forests, where the National Forest Service rules, but most of us will increasingly inhabit sprawling cities, where the federal government will have little influence. The federal government, eventually, may be reduced to little more than the sheriff of Nottingham." The sheriff of Nottingham, of course, controlled more than a forest, but Gold's meaning was clear: the federal government, he suspects, will literally retreat to the periphery.

"And religion," he remarked offhandedly, "will become more place-centered, more influenced by the immediate environment," whether the environment is a primeval forest or a high-tech, byte-driven, posturban pod where a glitzy multimedia edifice such as the Crystal Cathedral will seem stark and pure compared to what such a church may become a few decades hence. And in such places as the Siskiyou Forest and the greater Yellowstone region, spiritual identity may become increasingly pagan: for the passion with which environmentalists approach the massive Port Orford cedar or the gray wolf is akin to worship.

I WILL PICK up my trail back in Bozeman, Montana, from which on another foray I headed northwest toward Canada, exploring this new localism further.

26

An Empire Wilderness?

I LEFT BOZEMAN, driving northwest to Missoula on Interstate 90. In Montana there is no daytime speed limit on the interstates. I stopped for gas at a Town Pump, a late-twentieth-century American caravansary serving caffé latte and sandwiches and offering a range of grocery products, where I could hear the electronic beeps of slot machines in an adjacent casino. At 10 A.M. the casino was half filled with truckers. For the next three hours I saw liberating vistas of meadows and grasslands that appeared to levitate, heaving up into hills that culminated in white-capped granite slopes. Here and there in this monumental landscape, split by rivers that sectioned it into separate, treeless mountain ranges, I saw a few horses breaking into a gallop behind a split-rail fence—yes, these images are real.

I drove into Missoula, a town of 50,000, which I had not seen for twenty-seven years, not since I had hitchhiked across America as a teenager. Now there was a strip mall several miles long that dwarfed the little town center I remembered. But the town with its art deco and redbrick early-twentieth-century buildings was still there, today with a Greek restaurant, Mexican and kosher food, Moose Drool and other beers from local microbreweries, espresso bars, good bookstores, various sportswear shops, antique furniture stores, gourmet food shops, and interesting lamps and wrought-iron flower baskets decorating streets and pedestrian walks. It was May 20, 1997. Two front-page stories in the *Missoulian* caught my attention.

The first reported that cooler, dryer days ahead meant that the danger of floods was receding. There was a picture of people laying sandbags along the Bitterroot River west of town. For the next few weeks of my journey through the Pacific Northwest, spring flooding would dominate the news. The second article reported that the New Jersey–based Robert Wood Johnson Foundation had selected Missoula as the headquarters for a $12 million "end-of-life care" network. This former Rocky Mountain backwater was now hooked into the global economy, with foreign newspapers as well as *The New York Times* and *The Wall Street Journal* on sale. The Aspen–Santa Fe phenomenon was spreading here, much to the dismay of western environmentalists, as people with money from both coasts as well as foreign countries discovered a spectacular new terrain.

Missoula was, however, in only a middling phase of gentrification. In the Dinosaur Café at "happy hour" I found a cross section of yuppies in blazers and expensive ties, unreconstructed hippies, and blue-collar types, young and old, male and female. Outside the café along the streets leading to the railroad station, I spotted a number of homeless, especially near Poverello's, a nondenominational shelter where the homeless can find free meals and a shower and do their laundry for twenty-five cents. Watching them, I thought of the August night in 1970 when I had slept in the park by the Clark Fork River, which runs through downtown Missoula. The park was now adjacent to a Holiday Inn, but the dark, brooding, olive-green hills, each with its own enfolding intimacy, brought back a sharp memory of summery stillness suffused with the kindness of a picnic supper offered by a group of teenagers my age after I had hitchhiked into town.

"Your experience in the park in 1970 and the number of homeless today have a common thread," explained Daniel Kemmis, a former mayor here. "Missoula has long been a journey breaker, known for its friendliness, a good place to stop for a day or so on the way somewhere else. It has the two things required for such a function: parks and a railroad. The Northern Pacific runs through here, and in the summer people sleep in the parks. It is still a stopping-off point for backpackers and the seasonal homeless, who hop the rails like earlier in the century."

Kemmis, fifty-one, with a serene expression, longish gray hair, an anorak, and a small blue hiking pack stuffed with books and papers, looked like still another member of the "liberal environmental elite," and, depending upon your politics, he may have been. But he would turn out to be more. We met for breakfast at seven-thirty, talked through the morning, then ate lunch together. By early afternoon, I thought I had a clearer vision of the future here.

A Harvard graduate, Kemmis served in the Montana State Legislature, rising to become the speaker of the House. "I was born way out in the bone-dry east, near North Dakota. It was painful to see the divisions between the eastern and western parts of the state acted out in the Capitol in Helena." From 1990 to 1996, Kemmis was Missoula's mayor. Now he is president of the Center for the Rocky Mountain West, a think tank that studies the relationship between the federal government and the Rocky Mountain region. Kemmis talked first about Missoula. Then, as we finished breakfast and walked around town, the discussion broadened.

"At the beginning of my mayorship I read Thucydides' *History of the Peloponnesian War*. It eased the burden on me considerably. You see, our natural tendency is to think that we master events. But Thucydides shows how we cannot control the basic forces of human nature, and that, because of the destructive power of competing self-interests, not to mention geographical and other limitations, our ability to affect events is limited. Moreover, each place has a life of its own that an individual mayor can influence but rarely alter.

"Lincoln, too, was a determinist," Kemmis added. "Had Machiavelli known about Lincoln, he would have used him rather than Cesare Borgia as a model of political realism. Lincoln was effective as a historical agent precisely because he knew that there were actually very few times when a national leader could act truly effectively. Lincoln knew that American geography *determined* that we would stay united, provided we were willing to pay the cost in blood."

Lincoln had written:

A nation may be said to consist of its territory, its people, and its laws. The territory is the only part that is of certain durability. . . . That portion of the earth's surface which is owned and inhabited by the people of the United States is well adapted to be the home of one national family, and it is not well adapted for two or more."

As for the Civil War, Lincoln said in his second annual message to Congress in December 1862 that "our strife pertains to ourselves, to the passing generations of men—and it can without convulsion be hushed forever with the passing of one generation of men." So in effect, only a few weeks after Antietam, a battle that cost 23,000 casualties in one day (to say nothing of those who had died already in other Civil War battles), Lincoln was telling his countrymen that because men were not permanent but geography was, the slaughter could be "hushed" over in twenty-five years or so. Such bleak realism would have impressed Machiavelli.

"When can you be most effective as a historical agent?" I asked.

"When you have the elite behind you," Kemmis said. "Society only follows a united elite. The elite got behind a downtown parking garage here. We built it, and shoppers returned."

Missoula, Kemmis said, had hit rock bottom in 1977, when the first regional mall had opened and downtown stores had been boarded up. Then the elite had united behind tax increment legislation, in which all additional tax revenues went to a downtown revitalization zone, similar to what I would soon see in Portland, Oregon. "For a hundred years garbage was thrown in the Clark Fork River. Not only did we clean the river, but we lined it with a park network. We commissioned stylish street lamps, too. These days, to make money and see your property values rise, you have to think in terms of aesthetics. In our case that meant removing the ugly facades from the 1950s and 1960s—the period of cheap, quick post–World War II growth—and putting up awnings to reveal the beauty of buildings erected in the 1930s and earlier."

Missoula has two things going for it that most places lack: a major university and magnificent scenery. The natural beauty of Missoula combines with the presence of the University of Montana to attract "highly skilled entrepreneurial types who excel at experimentation," Kemmis said. And not only are the elite well educated; so, too, are many of the other residents. "For example," Kemmis said, "one day in 1991 a guy named Chuck Kaparich dropped into the mayor's office. He told me that he was a cabinetmaker and also made wooden horses, and showed me several beautiful, hand-carved painted ponies. He said he had a plan for an entire handmade 1890s-style carousel. I sent him to the town's redevelopment agency. A collection campaign was organized, and the town got enthusiastically behind him. Kaparich then trained people to help him carve the ponies. Four years later the carousel opened. That level of individual inventiveness and communal efficiency is rare in most places"—places, that is, that lack the geographical and other circumstances with which Missoula is blessed. After Kemmis took me to see the carousel—a dazzling, intricate museum-quality piece under a pavilion near the Clark Fork River—it was easy to agree.

From the carousel Kemmis and I walked across the Clark Fork River bridge to his office. The Clark Fork is named for explorer William Clark, who passed through here on his return east after he and Meriwether Lewis had reached the Pacific. The river was now "bank full"—raging, that is—covering the bases of the cottonwood trees despite the wall of sandbags. Heavy snows had caused spring flooding. Kemmis pointed out an osprey nest and a flock of herons. Pointing at the snowcapped peaks, he said, "There is snow in sight eleven months a year here. Every day, from the city streets, we see the progress of winter as snow climbs down and then recedes up those peaks. The point is that the environment is not abstract in this region. Geography is absolutely present and critical in politics every second of the day."

Before he explained, he suggested that we have some coffee.

We had just entered his office in a renovated brick building along the river, owned by the Boone & Crockett Club, which Teddy Roosevelt had founded as a hunting club before it evolved into an environmental group to preserve animal habitats. Along with a cup of black coffee, Kemmis handed me a map entitled "Federal Government Lands in the West." The map, he told me, would explain much about militias, environmentalists, and "the new federalism," something in which he believed.

The map used different color codes to mark eighteen kinds of federal land: Forest Service land, Bureau of Reclamation land, Department of Defense and Department of Energy land, Fish and Wildlife Service land, national parks, and so on. The area from the Front Range of the Rockies westward to the Cascades was rich in color: it was largely "public land," while the Great Plains and Pacific Coast were overwhelmingly under private ownership. As for federal land east of the Mississippi River, Kemmis told me that there is so little of it that it wasn't worth putting on the map.

"For example, ninety percent of Nevada is public land, controlled mainly from Washington, D.C. Nobody can buy it, build on it, or do anything with it," Kemmis began. "Fifty percent of Montana is public land. The figure for the entire Rocky Mountains [from the Mexican to Canadian border] is over fifty percent. So there is a strong sense in the West of being owned and colonized. Out here, Washington, D.C., seems very much an imperial power. Conservatives want this land for development; they want to free up these vast federal acreages and subdivide them. It drives conservatives crazy that environmentalists want to prevent that, which accounts for much of the enmity between environmentalists and developers, and logging firms, too. Land may appear limitless in the West, but because so much of it is out of bounds and water is so scarce, the part that is actually available is at a premium, and therefore property is relatively expensive. This feeds class resentment. Gentrification of towns like Missoula and Bozeman and the consequent upward effect on real estate values make it worse for the blue-collar poor. Add to that the big in-migration of wealthy telecommuters and second-home owners from the two coasts, and you have a real conflict. When militia crazies say they want independence from the federal government, what they often mean is that they want an end to Washington's control of public lands.

"Therefore, I believe that for the West, the two hot-button concepts in the next century will be water and Thomas Jefferson. Increasingly scarce water will make the kind of development that conservatives demand that much more impractical, and they will wrap their rage in the cloak of Jefferson, who stood for a weak federal government. In the West, the city has always been the root of all evil, even if most of the West is urban. Still, this Jeffersonian ideal of rural purity runs strong."

Kemmis continued in his crisp western accent: "The liberals and environmentalists have latched onto the federal government, defending federal lands and so forth, while the conservatives have latched onto the sanctity of the states. But that, too, will lead to disaster because the states out here are no less impersonal and sometimes more irrelevant than the federal government. Boise, Idaho's capital, for instance, is becoming a world-class software city, but it has no control over Coeur d'Alene in the northern part of Idaho, which is an economic extension of Spokane, Washington. John Wesley Powell [the great surveyor of the arid West, who explored the Colorado River and the Grand Canyon] warned federal bureaucrats not to draw straight lines in setting political boundaries here; instead, he said, the lines should follow river valleys, drainage basins, and mountain ranges. Well, we ignored Powell, but the emerging economic reality is that of Billings and the Yellowstone drainage, Missoula and the Clark Fork drainage. . . . It is neither Washington, D.C., nor the state capitals that are determining reality here; rather, it is these urban areas that are spreading along the river drainages. Neither the state nor the federal government can make things work; it can only be the civic culture in each locale.

"Imperial pressure was imposed by Lincoln when Rocky Mountain settlement began during the Civil War, but that concept of nation building is antiquated, and Lincoln's model of one power dominating the east–west continent needs to be taken on. Yes, even Lincoln himself needs to be challenged, as Jefferson is being challenged now. The state system into which the Republicans have put so much faith is impeding the natural conglomeration of new urban units, whose borders will be geographical and not political."

During the period of western expansion we were an American empire long before we were a unified Atlantic-to-Pacific country. What Kemmis was suggesting, it seemed to me, is that we might eventually revert to being an empire once more: a subtle, ambiguous one of geographically determined, loosely connected posturban forms; a dry-land version of city-state Greece, in which ruthless economic competition replaces ancient wars. The phrase "an empire wilderness," from Hart Crane's poem of 1930, "The Bridge," occurred to me as a way of describing this new political arrangement.[1] Rather than rule these urban units, Washington, D.C., would, in effect, provide a protective shield against such hazards as global terrorists and computer hackers and supply aid such as specialized military units for floods and earthquakes. And as this transformation toward a system of mere imperial oversight proceeds, late-twentieth-century debates between liberals and conservatives regarding the balance of power between Washington and the fifty states will become increasingly irrelevant.

James Madison, in *The Federalist,* considered a comparable situation. Madison envisioned the settlement of the whole continental United States, but he did not foresee a modern transportation network that would allow Americans to inhabit one national community psychologically. His vision of our political future was of an enormous geographical space with governance but without patriotism, in which the federal government would be a mere "umpire," refereeing competing interests.[2] The concept went untested because a uniquely

[1] See Crane, *The Complete Poems of Hart Crane.*
[2] "Umpire" is also University of Tulsa scholar Paul A. Rahe's word for Madison's regime; see Rahe, *Republics Ancient and Modern.*

American identity and culture did take root. But as Americans enter a global community driven, in part, by gigantic corporations, many of which are based in—but not necessarily loyal to—America,[3] and as class and racial divisions within our borders prove intractable, Madison's concept may become relevant. America, ironically, will spread its material and mass cultural influence abroad through American-based corporations, even as federal and state governments become hollower here at home.

Kemmis did not go as far as I in speculating about the future, but he did say that, ultimately, disputes such as those between environmentalists and developers will be settled at the local level as urban regions become far more important in people's lives and as the federal-state superstructure diminishes—exactly what Lou Gold had told me.

"Manifest Destiny," Kemmis explained, "was merely the way continentalism played out in the nineteenth-century nation-state era," as America competed with Spain in the Southwest and with Great Britain in the Pacific Northwest. "Now continentalism could lead to a weakening of the nation itself. And because of the increasing importance of water, who or what controls the water-rich 'top of the continent' will define power relationships in the future North America.

"Canada can't hold together," he added. "Its breakup will amplify a north–south continental orientation at the expense of an east–west one. I can tell you that in the Great Plains of eastern Montana and North Dakota people are already oriented toward Calgary, Regina, and Winnipeg. Ethnically and racially, everybody is more or less the same on both sides of the U.S.-Canadian border in the West, and this will make for stronger north–south bonds."

Many Canadians I met later in British Columbia agreed with Kemmis that the breakup of Canada would not lead to an enlargement of the United States but would intensify localism and regionalism, particularly in the West. So far, most Americans have not thought much about the psychological effect of the peaceful disintegration of an entire Atlantic-to-Pacific middle-class nation on their northern border; an event that, at least in the northern United States, would lead Americans to see the world differently to a degree that not even the end of the Cold War has been able to do; which is why from Missoula I headed for British Columbia via Idaho and Washington.

[3]Of the world's 500 largest corporations, 153 are U.S.-based, according to *Statistical Abstract of the United States 1996*.

It occurred to me that Canada's demise might accelerate not only the melding of like-minded northern European farming and ranching communities in western Canada with those in the northern United States, but also that of the Hispanic-influenced Southwest with Mexico, bilingual south Florida with the Caribbean and Latin America, Quebec with New England, and so on, because it would destroy the myth of the permanent nation-state in North America into which we have all been indoctrinated and thus unleash cross-border energies everywhere on the continent. It has long been a truism that inhabitants of the forested East (in both the United States and Canada) have more in common with one another than with the inhabitants of the treeless West, which starts beyond the Missouri River. The breakup of Canada might turn this truism into a new and as-yet-undefined political reality: a Swiss-style North American confederacy based more on geography than on language.

DRIVING WEST FROM Missoula, I passed numerous ranches with brand-new split-rail fences, owned, I was told, by wealthy out-of-towners. The Lolo Pass, through which Lewis and Clark traveled in September 1805 on their way west, marked the Idaho state line. A few miles into Idaho I spotted the Bernard De Voto Forest and stopped. De Voto, a Mark Twain scholar and a midcentury columnist for *Harper's* magazine, won both the Pulitzer Prize in 1948 and the National Book Award in 1953 for his enchanting histories of the West. He also had a record of uncanny prescience. He was among the first to rail in print, in the early 1930s, against both Soviet communism and German Nazism, and, in a September 1949 column, he attacked Senator Joseph McCarthy's Red-baiting paranoia, which was then only beginning. Mike Miles, Mike Clark, and Dan Kemmis admired De Voto for his writings on the Rocky Mountains and for his record as a conservationist. De Voto's books are centerpieces of their lives, they told me. De Voto saw decades before anyone else that the integrity of the West's fragile, water-poor ecosystem was about to be challenged by unlimited development and that a battle over public lands was looming. A plaque "In Memory of Bernard De Voto, 1897–1955: Conservationist and Historian of the West," explained that his ashes had been scattered about this mossy primeval forest of lofty western red cedars, Pacific yews, and Engelmann spruces hundreds—in some cases thousands—of years old on the bank of the wild and noisy Lochsa River. Here, amid the scent of cedar in the electric high-altitude air, and surrounded by the windy roar of mountain water, De Voto had edited the journals of Lewis and Clark, who had passed nearby.

AT LOWELL, IDAHO, the Lochsa merges with the Clearwater, a hellish, wide, and arcing torrent, as clear as glass, which Lewis and Clark negotiated in dugouts. I stopped for an early lunch at a riverside café, where the proprietor and other guests were staring at a bowling tournament on television. A few miles further on, a garish casino heralded the Nez Percé reservation, home of what in the early nineteenth century had been, according to De Voto and other historians, a "charming" and "intelligent" tribe that had helped Lewis and Clark.

Then the Clearwater, now a cascade of slate-blue diamonds surrounded by white foam, met the Snake River, as a panoramic green gorge appeared near Lewiston. Beyond, as I drove into Washington the next day, was the Palouse, a magical, high-altitude stage of swirling hills shaped as if by the lazy movements of a giant planetary knife and coated with translucent green wheat fields. Spokane, like so many other cities I had seen, had an old downtown that you could pass in sixty seconds on the interstate and suburbs extending through some thirty miles of strip malls. I drove on, northwest.

AFTER ANOTHER HOUR of driving through a rippling tableland punctuated with buttes, I came upon a enormous, 151-mile-long, man-made lake rimmed by sharp drops, the result of mountainsides blasted away by dynamite. I felt the lash of a fresh wind off the water as I rolled down my car window. Franklin Delano Roosevelt Lake is formed by the Grand Coulee Dam, which loomed ahead as I rounded the next curve.

Unlike the Hoover Dam, which was carved out of a narrow rock amphitheater that magnifies it, the Grand Coulee straddles a vast, low valley that diminishes it. Even so, the mile-long, gray concrete span with its steep walls forty-six stories above the roaring white thunder of the Columbia River is stunning, like the first sight of the Rockies from the Great Plains: an icon of American power. Each of the innumerable concrete blocks from which the Grand Coulee is made weighs 2,300 tons and is held in place by its sheer weight, without adhesive.

As at the Pantex plant, I was overwhelmed by this exhibition of federal power.

In an era when minor road bypasses hang fire for years because of zoning and environmental problems, it is striking to contemplate this Pharaonic edifice, which drains an area the size of France, carries two and a half times as much water as the Nile from Canadian ice fields 650 miles to the north, and is the keystone of an elaborate dam network built by the federal government throughout the Pacific Northwest. In the 1930s, not just Grand Coulee, but the Hoover, Shasta, and Bonneville Dams, were under construction simultaneously. At the time, Grand Coulee was the largest building site in the world. The thousands of laborers working round the clock were best measured by the bars and brothels that stretched for miles in every direction.[4]

In a museum beside the dam, I saw the wooden wheelchair used by FDR on his October 2, 1937, visit to the site. A short, stirring film about the dam's construction ended with Woody Guthrie's zesty song "Roll On, Columbia, Roll On," commissioned by the Roosevelt administration to celebrate the dam: a song that in the words of writer Blaine Harden blended images of "Manifest Destiny" and "proletarian glory." Grand Coulee's reputation soared with America's entry into World War II, when its generators became part of the war effort, including the manufacture of plutonium for the atomic bomb. When President Harry S Truman visited here to dedicate FDR Lake after the war, forty-eight children with jugs of water from every state poured the water into the generators to start them up again.

Gil Nastrant, wearing a "U.S. Department of the Interior, Bureau of Reclamation" uniform, gave me a tour of the dam. His eyes closed and his hands opened as if in meditation, as he poured out statistics: "Twelve Westinghouse and General Electric pumps, each pumping enough water to fill the *Exxon Valdez* eighteen times per day. . . . There are only 285 employees, and all but 37 are maintenance workers: because of computerization, this whole thing requires just one operator per shift: the operator gets around the pumping stations and power plants by bicycle. . . . In the summer, the surplus electricity produced here is used to power air conditioners as far away as Los Angeles and San Diego."

I walked down to a park along the Columbia River at the base of the dam, from which I arched my neck to see the top of the sprawling

[4]See Marc Reisner, *Cadillac Desert: The American West and its Disappearing Water.*

concrete pylon as my ears filled with the boom of water. No structure built by previous empires equals this engineering feat. Roosevelt, Truman, and Eisenhower were the trio of imperial presidents who erected the greatest state of the Industrial Age: Roosevelt, who built these monumental dams; Truman, who triumphantly concluded the war that Roosevelt had begun, then assembled the greatest military alliance in the history of the West; and Eisenhower, who built the mammoth highway system that linked the continent, while through NATO Washington dominated this alliance for years. But now the Industrial Age characterized by such vast enterprises is waning: a computer runs this entire edifice with the help of a single operator. Already the dam has a yellowing, archaeological aura, and environmentalists and others now call Grand Coulee "just a big bed of silt" that does more harm than good. The sluggish irrigation canals it spawned have generated layers of soil-killing salts, while dams in general, by forcing more water through narrower channels, make rivers more likely to flood.

The age of imperial leaders such as Roosevelt, Truman, and Eisenhower is also over. Imperial golden ages rarely repeat themselves. But perhaps if the correct choices are made during a protracted period of transformation, a silver age will follow, in which the central government's main function will be to moderate the differences among its far-flung urban settlements.[5]

AS I DROVE north, the landscape of northeastern Washington became lunar, if the moon were covered in grass the dark color of seaweed. At Omak, fifty miles south of the Canadian border, I noticed that the shopping center signs were in both Spanish and English because Mexican immigrants had come this far north. Rivers had overrun their banks all around, and I overheard several conversations about sandbagging and basement damage. The border at Oroville was on a country road. The Canadian immigration official asked me about my work as a reporter and whether the work I was going to do in Canada "could not be done by a Canadian." Such hassles are typical at U.S.-Canadian border posts. Once an American immigration official told me that my driver's license was sufficient for re-entering only if he "decided to trust" me. When I replied that his attitude was

[5]The idea of an imperial silver age is a Chinese one and was related to me by Chas Freeman, a U.S. diplomat and China specialist.

not in the spirit of NAFTA, he shot back, "You think NAFTA will hold up? I doubt it." A Canadian I met later in Vancouver told me, "These immigration and customs officials are just petty functionaries from the two imperial capitals, worried that there may not be a border in the future and that they will be out of work."

2 7

Canada: The Wild Card

DISMISSING CANADA AS "irrelevant," "boring," or a "joke" comes easily to Americans, and occasionally to Canadians as well. The Canadian novelist Mordecai Richler writes that Canada "is not so much a country as a continental suburb, where Little Leaguers govern ineffectually, desperate for American approval." Canada's population is one ninth that of the United States (29 million as opposed to 261 million). Rather than struggle for independence, Canada had independence conferred upon it by the British in 1867, and that was only in order to contain the United States after the South's defeat and the ensuing consolidation of the Union. Rather than signifying, like the United States, the most daring political experiment since Athenian democracy—which would succeed beyond imagining—Canada has never had a clear-cut historical mission, except, perhaps, providing for its own survival. Polls show that Canada's identity rests heavily on its social service institutions, such as national health care, which are deteriorating. Canada, it has often been suggested, has distinguished itself from the United States through an unfocused fear of its larger neighbor, a vague and continuing British connection that is little beyond a "nostalgic heirloom," and a French community that accounts for nearly a quarter of all Canadians and is heavily disposed to secede.[1]

[1]See Conrad Black, "Canadian Capers."

(A majority of French Canadians voted for secession in 1995; the referendum failed narrowly because of the votes of immigrants and English-speaking Quebecers.)

Yet for Americans to ignore Canada's fate is to miss the point of North American history. Canada was formed from Britain's disparate North American provinces because of a perceived threat from the United States, and military events in Canada may have set the stage for American independence in the first place: had the French held on to Canada through the eighteenth century, they might well have forced the thirteen colonies to retain a protective bond to Britain.[2] The nineteenth-century historian Francis Parkman wrote, "So long as an active and enterprising enemy threatened their [the colonists'] borders, they could not break with the mother-country, because they needed her help. . . . [Then] there would have been no revolutionary war; and for a long time, no independence." But, as it happened, the French and Indian War in North America, part of the Seven Years' War, a struggle among the European powers, ended in 1759 with a British victory over French forces in Quebec, which, in turn, helped lead to France's withdrawal from North America, weakening the English-speaking colonies' dependence on Britain. In the War of 1812, New England actually debated secession to British North America. And it was this threat of regional secession northward that hastened the rise of American nationalism under President Andrew Jackson. The relationship between the United States and Canada is still symbiotic: if Canada dissolves, the effect on the United States will be very great.

Moreover, Canada, which along with Switzerland is already the most decentralized country in the postindustrial world, is split by a divisive, blood-and-soil linguistic nationalism that threatens to dismember it. When I asked the president of one of America's most powerful international corporations what important issue the Washington foreign policy elite was ignoring more than any other, he responded, "The eventual breakup of the Canadian federation and its effect" on our own nationalism.

Though Canada is the largest country in the Western Hemisphere, stretching to the polar ice cap, Canada is really like Chile laid on

---

[2]"A French Canada was a guarantee that the American colonies would be forced to remain British," writes Theodore Draper in *A Struggle for Power: The American Revolution*. This point is an important theme of Draper's book.

its side: almost all Canadians live within a hundred miles of the U.S. border, so their political merging with the rest of North America's temperate zone population is a reasonable prospect. In Canada's early days, before bridges and motorized boats, the St. Lawrence River and the Great Lakes formed enough of a natural barrier for an Atlantic-oriented nation to take root to the north of the United States. Even west of the Great Lakes, along the arbitrary frontier formed by the forty-ninth parallel, the fur trade, so much more important to the people north of that line than to those south of it, made for some semblance of an organic division. But with expressways and ferries now crossing seaways and the inexorable merging of the two countries' economies—four fifths of Canada's exports and two thirds of its imports have American addresses—geography is making Canada increasingly less distinctive from the northern states of the United States.

However, as the frigid tundra keeps Canada's population from spreading northward, America's loud materialism, unruly style, and social problems keep Canadians from straying south. Not only has that hundred-mile-wide belt of population from the Atlantic to the Pacific evolved as a subtly distinctive community, but while English and French Canadians may not mind separating from each other, immigrants from throughout the world—who already number more than 50 percent of the Canadian population and two thirds of Toronto's—may demand Canada's continued existence, since for them Canada provides unlimited freedom and economic opportunity while offering protection from the ruthless, laissez-faire capitalism of the United States.

The psychological importance for Canadians of their country's style and evolution should not be underestimated. Canadians' resentment of the United States is clear in the way they smugly disapprove of those who attempt great endeavors.[3] Indeed, writes Canadian writer Margaret Atwood, "Canadian rebellions have never become revolutions precisely because they have never received popular support. 'Prophets' here don't get very far against the Civil Service."[4] Canada never had a "Wild West" because the Royal Canadian Mounted Police got there first; Canadians love law and order—the policeman

---

[3]See Jack Hodgins's afterword to Canadian author Stephen Leacock's collection of stories, *Sunshine Sketches of a Little Town.*
[4]Margaret Atwood, *Survival: A Thematic Guide to Canadian Literature.*

is a national symbol; Canada's society prefers collective heroes, such as the builders of the transcontinental railroad, over individual ones.

It is not a stimulating place but one different enough that parts of English Canada are unlikely ever to merge with parts of the United States of their own accord. That would happen only if the Canadian federation fractured first. Thus, the character and timing of Canada's dissolution will affect America's own future in unpredictable ways. Because Quebec and its separatism are written about so often, I preferred to interpret Canada through a Pacific prism.

Take British Columbia, which, with its urban dynamo, Vancouver—linked more to the Pacific Rim than to most of Canada—is at the throbbing heart of North American regionalism. Strengthened by NAFTA, regionalism may yet undo the current divisions of sovereignty established by the 1763 Treaty of Paris.[5] Local historian Margaret Ormsby writes that "British Columbia was in, but not of, Canada." For Canada did not grow westward in the same organic manner as the United States did; British Columbia joined the Canadian federation only in 1871, four years after the British forced the other provinces to unite. Out here, Ormsby writes, the Canadian union "had not been based on sentiment" but on "material advantage": it was the economic benefits of the transcontinental railroad (the Canadian Pacific) that, in effect, bribed the inhabitants of British Columbia to join Canada. Even so, the "British" part of "Columbia" (which in 1846 split from the American part, which became the state of Washington) retained strong cultural and economic links to a San Francisco–based region; and now the air bridge across the Pacific and the highway to Seattle and Portland matter more than the links to the rest of Canada. British Columbia's economy is distinct. It exports an amazing 40 percent of its goods to the Pacific Rim and only 50 percent to the United States, compared to 75 percent for Canada as a whole. It is the only Canadian province that would surely do better, not worse, were the country to disintegrate. "Canada ends at the Rockies" is a phrase I heard here repeatedly.

NEVERTHELESS, WHEN I crossed the border, the distinctions between Canada and the United States were what I noticed first. Not

[5]See Charles F. Doran, "Building a North American Community," in which he quotes Francis Parkman on the significance of the Paris treaty.

only were the money, the measurement units, the shapes of the signs, the construction materials, and the flag—with the soft imagery of the maple leaf replacing the overtly political stars and stripes—different, so were the accents: sharper, vaguely British. "Schedule," I noticed, was pronounced without the *c*. But compared to the Third World–First World division along the Mexican border, these differences appeared trivial. Moreover, the news reports were exactly the same, dominated by spring flooding. The lakeside beach was almost gone in the border town of Osoyoos, where water was gaining on the trees near a luxury condominium development that advertised "gated underground entry" and "security alarm system" on its billboard (that, too, was the same as in the United States). The local radio station broadcast a plea for volunteers to lay sandbags. The looping Okanagan River was cutting new channels all over the valley, running down asphalt streets. Because of the far worse flooding in North Dakota and Manitoba at roughly the same time, the national media in both countries ignored these floods, which, in fact, are yearly occurrences. In the Pacific Northwest, the environment is truly everything, to a degree to which not even the greater Yellowstone region had prepared me. But this I would discover slowly.

I drove west toward Vancouver, a leisurely day's journey from Osoyoos. Halfway there I reached Manning Provincial Park, an extension of North Cascades National Park on the United States side in the state of Washington. For the westering traveler in Canada, Manning Park marks the beginning of the Cascade range, a north–south line of powdery white volcanoes and glaciers, tinted almost blue and garlanded by cold rain forests, which more than any other geographical feature—to say nothing of any state or national border—defines the Pacific Northwest. It is a magical frontier, breathtaking even when seen from the air. To fly, for instance, from the eastern United States to Portland, Oregon, and near the end of the journey, as the plane descends, to see the "Ring of Fire"—the glacier-mantled peaks of Mount Baker, Mount Rainier, Mount Hood, and Mount St. Helens soaring over brooding, cathedral-dark forests—is to arrive in a distinct place, or nation, almost. Even the geographical names—so matter of fact—on both sides of the United States–Canada border here suggest an icy clean, mathematical perfection: the Fraser, the Columbia, the Peace, and the False Rivers, Queen Charlotte Strait and the Strait of Georgia, Mount Baker . . .

I smelled dry, sneezy pine dust for the last time as I met Pacific mists, sparkling snow, moist and glistening spruce and fir forests, tumbling streams, and silvery lakes, beside one of which I met an Indian immigrant family fishing for rainbow trout: the parents spoke in the lilting accents of the subcontinent; the children the hard-edged English of Pacific Canada. Harlequin ducks and gray-and-white belted kingfishers flipped off the water.

Further west, close to Vancouver, the Fraser River was clogged with massive logs chained together—about to be dispatched to the Orient, perhaps. Vancouver came rather suddenly, a lesson in how compact and devoid of sprawl the cities of the Pacific Northwest are compared with others on the continent. For urbanites here, nature is close by.

28

Vancouver: Twenty-first-Century Patriotism

CLIFFS OF GLASS and polymer stood out against a background of ice-polished fjords. Geography, abetted by nineteenth-century politics, defends Vancouver against sprawl and keeps it an amphitheater from which to observe crystalline natural beauty. To the west is the Strait of Georgia, curving out into the Pacific; to the east are the 9,000-foot peaks of the Coast Range. Twenty miles to the south lies the forty-ninth parallel—the United States–Canada border—where the Americans and the British severed the Oregon Territory in the 1846 Treaty of Washington.

It was late afternoon when I arrived in Vancouver. Each street crossing in the residential neighborhood of flaming red hawthorn trees where I stayed in a bed-and-breakfast formed a traffic island, slowing cars. The cost of parking downtown was exorbitant, so I rode the bus. As in Portland, Oregon, and elsewhere in the Pacific Northwest, the nearby glaciers and volcanos, visible from many an urban street, have led to a preoccupation with conservation and penalties for automobile use.

The bus downtown was filled with well-dressed people and clamorous with conversation, so different from the United States, where bus riders are usually poor and silent (though Portland's buses would turn out to be like Vancouver's). Like the bus, the shiny, rose-bedecked stone benches on Robson Street, where I alighted, were filled not with the poor and homeless but with well-dressed people talking. The only cell phone I saw belonged to a man with a New York accent telling someone that he would be home in three days. There were many benches, as well as a profusion of cafés, all buzzing and crowded against a backdrop of glass, marble, interesting metals, and polymers. Corinthian pillars were set alongside dynamic, postmodern friezes blazing with tasteful pigments. As at the Fashion Island Mall in Orange County, architectural refinements and the maturation of trees and flowers planted beside new buildings in the 1970s and 1980s have made for some fine urban landscapes. But here, unlike in the Fashion Island Mall, there was true urban life amid the decor. Even in newspaper and candy stores, knots of people were talking by the counters.

Many of the faces were Oriental. A third of Vancouver's 1.81 million people are Asian, with Chinese alone making up nearly 20 percent of the city's population. Asian immigrants account for much of the city's 2.5 percent annual population growth.[1] According to a local joke, "The Japanese want to buy Vancouver, but the Chinese won't sell it." Mandarin is more popular than French—an official Canadian language—in the schools here. I saw many signs in Punjabi, Hindi, Farsi, Arabic, and Khmer but almost none in French. Vancouver, with its glitzy, visually stimulating high-rise condominiums, is becoming an Asianized city dedicated to global materialism on the Pacific Rim of North America: a real east–west hybrid culture is emerging here, reflected in the waters of False Creek during the annual Dragon Boat races.[2]

The next morning I visited Warren Gill, an urban geographer and the executive director of the Harbour Centre campus of Simon Fraser University, an institution founded in 1965 and named for an eighteenth-century Vermont-born explorer and fur trader in the Northwest. The campus consisted of a single building with green and blue glass interiors. Finished in 1989, for me it conjured up "the future"; that is to say, it made me aware of transition and change. Thinking of the Ringstrasse in turn-of-the-twentieth-century Vienna, I knew that social and economic change—often revealed through architecture—usually precedes political change. What the architec-

[1] These numbers come from statistical profiles prepared by the Greater Vancouver Regional District and the Cascadia Metropolitan Forum, among other sources.
[2] See Gordon Price's monograph, "The Deceptive City."

ture here revealed was the abstract, urban character of our collective future and the emergence of the city-state.

"There, you see it all, isn't it great?" asked Gill. He waved his hand toward his office window, showing me the panorama of the Burrard Inlet, a belt of blue water crowded with small seaplanes and set against the glacier-capped peaks of the Coast Range, with Vancouver's bustling harbor, a heliport, and a nexus of railroad tracks in the foreground. "This is all you need to be sovereign in the phase of history we are entering; a dynamic and highly educated population and strategic transport links. Cities and their environs already provide you with everything you need—garbage collection, schools, neighborhood, whatever—but they get the least of your taxes. The bulk of your tax money still goes to the state or province and the federal government, and what do they do for you: fuck all! Isn't it antiquated? But that will change. In the coming decades your tax money will increasingly go to the place that you really care about." Gill's tone was enthusiastic and self-consciously provocative. "Though I guess we should all pay taxes to that Information Age military you are creating in Washington, D.C. They'll in effect sell us the protection we will need against terrorists and other bad people. You see, we don't need *you* [he meant America], and we certainly don't need Canada. What we need is your military!"

I didn't try to interrupt.

"The miracle is that Canada has lasted as long as it has. It makes no sense. Oh, yes, I'm *fond* of Canada. Canada is something that you're fond of, like a drunken old uncle. And I'm proud to be a Canadian. We all are, in the sense that Canada is more aesthetically pleasing than the United States. It's cleaner and less unruly. But the nation-state is gone in Vancouver."

Gill called Vancouver "a beautiful setting in search of a city." As he explained, "Did you know that after L.A., Vancouver has the biggest entertainment industry in North America, a billion dollars a year in revenue? Hollywood makes *The X Files* here. The Canadian dollar is cheap, and we're in the same time zone as Los Angeles, so Hollywood finds us useful, especially as Vancouver looks like anywhere: it's a generic, modern-postmodern global place. But it's still not a real city in the sense of true creativity and economic dynamism yet. It's not L.A. or New York."

Vancouver, as Gill and others told me, had begun as a real estate venture in the 1880s on the heels of the Canadian Pacific Railroad, and it is still very much a boom-and-bust town, now riding a real estate bubble created by the Hong Kong Chinese, who in the 1980s and 1990s bought $2 billion worth of local real estate. Not only the Chinese but all the predominantly Asian immigrants will, it is estimated, pump $30,000 more per person into the Vancouver economy than they will ever use in the form of social services. In addition to real estate and immigration, there is the Hollywood-run movie industry, the cruise ship industry, and the closest air and sea links to Asia. Vancouver is one of the largest bulk ports on the continent, shipping out coal, sulfur, potash, natural gas, wheat, and timber products. But this fragile, real estate– and natural resource–driven economy lacks the self-sustaining entrepreneurial and creative spirit of Seattle and Portland, not to mention San Francisco or Los Angeles. There are, for instance, relatively few software or multimedia companies here.

The frontier, though, has always been about commerce and trade links rather than books and art. "The distinctive element of the West Coast, from Alaska to Baja, is newness," Gill said. "Many of these places have been built not to last. There are streets in my neighborhood of Kitsilano that have been three different things in my lifetime. The element of newness at the moment has to do with race. Interracialness is walking down the street, arm in arm. Without the Asians, we'd be a narrow-minded English town, like Portland. In Portland they look to Vancouver to see the outer, Pacific world; not to California or even to Seattle. The Asians," Gill explained, "are in the process of re-WASPing us: through their driven work ethic they are allowing us to rediscover our Calvinistic WASP roots. In the twenty-first century, hundreds of millions of Chinese and other Asians will become middle-class, tying themselves closer to North America. That will change Vancouver and the Pacific Northwest more than any development in North America itself." (In this view, the economic downturn in Asia in late 1997 modifies, but does not erase, the incredible growth there since the 1960s.)

GORDON PRICE, A member of the Vancouver City Council, picked up on that idea: "The Asian-British—that is to say, Asian-WASP—cultural mix is the most potent in the history of capitalism. Hong Kong and Singapore have represented the combination of British engineering, accounting, honest bureaucracy, and meritocratic government with Asian economic aggression. And it will work its magic here."

Here, we may be seeing something else, too: the erotization of race. As another Vancouverite told me, if you walk down the street and look at who's holding hands with whom, you'll observe that whites find Asians, particularly Asian women, with their small-boned symmetricality, highly desirable."

Price met me in his apartment in Vancouver's West End, then took me to the city library, designed by the world-renowned Israeli-Canadian architect Moshe Safdie. Here, amid a multistory maze of quartz and glass, where from designer shops and espresso cafés you could look in on the library and see people studying, I saw a panorama of Asian-Caucasian courtship. "Vancouver is attracting the young of the world's most dynamic middlemen minorities," Price told me. "If this happens across North America, the continent will rule the world's economy. The early-fifteenth-century Ming admiral Cheng Ho almost made it to the Pacific Northwest. Well, the Chinese finally got here anyway. Look at these Asian kids; many of them are sent here to study by their families in Hong Kong. For them, Vancouver must be like Paris in the twenties, an old and rooted capitalist culture compared to the overnight glitz of the Pacific Rim."

What struck me, too, was the urbanity, the roar of many conversations, and the crowded cafés and walkways. Safdie's glass-wall design, which encourages people to look at one another, certainly contributed to this, but the library also seemed to celebrate what was apparent everywhere in Vancouver. The city was a rebuke to Orange County, downtown St. Louis, and most other places I had seen in the United States, where the automobile ruled and often the only people sitting on sidewalk benches were homeless. The sea, the mountains, and the international border, which prevent sprawl, along with the high-tax Canadian social welfare system, which prevents widespread poverty (and also scares away software firms), are part of the explanation. The other part is a unified elite of investors and urban planners. Paraphrasing Jane Jacobs, the classic writer on urbanism, Price said, "People have confused overcrowding with high density. High density is actually desirable, because it means lively, safe, convenient, and interesting places in which to live."

Between 1956 and 1972, Price's West End neighborhood, for example, which had been overcrowded, transformed itself into a high-density area. Its population increased by about half, but the number of apartments grew fivefold: spacious one-bedroom apartments replaced teeming tenements. The West End now has the liveliness and sophisticated feel of Manhattan's Upper West Side. The ostensible reason for such success is that big businessmen took risks and built apartment blocks as small tradesmen opened shops. The Hong Kong Chinese culture, which is comfortable with high density, helped, too. But business and culture have both operated within a framework of deliberate planning choices. In 1956, the same year the West End was rezoned for taller apartment buildings, Eisenhower signed the Federal Highway Act, which created the interstates. Los Angeles consultants rushed to Vancouver, advising a freeway and tunnel system through the city. Vancouver planners rejected that advice, and the nineteenth-century grid pattern of narrow streets laid down by the British engineers has remained intact. The trolleys, the system of parks and benches, the profusion of cafés, and the explosion of tall residential buildings all followed. What Dan Kemmis in Missoula had told me about the power effect of a united elite holds true here. When Hong Kong billionaire Li Ka-shing bought 150 acres of downtown property from the provincial government, he worked with city planners to create such public amenities as several mixed-use, mixed-income communities. Vancouver is where Asian money, however reduced because of economic troubles, fits lock-and-key style with old-fashioned British planning.

"The automobile is the perfect metaphor for pure democracy," Gill had told me, "and pure individual freedom just does not work in an urban setting. The more urban the environment, the more controls you will need to make it work. Imagine how much more vibrant and crime-free Washington, D.C., would be with more planning but without the beltway? Imagine how if Washington prohibited a beltway, it would have had to build a whole new layer of public transport within the city, keeping many more people on the streets at all hours?"

"The automobile argument, the Orange County argument, let's say, is good only for another decade or so," Price told me back in his West End apartment. "The auto depends on cheap oil, cheap water for expanding suburbs, cheap land—which is tied to available water—cheap money, and government largesse to build, improve, and maintain freeways. You and I can argue about oil, but the rest, especially government money, will run dry. You are going to see the privatization of highways in the twenty-first century; great roads in some places and Third World collapsing infrastructure in many others. And you will have no loyalty, no patriotism of any kind, if you have no sense of a bound community tied to a specific place." That had been

Lou Gold's argument, and, indeed, it had been the erosion of communal commitment, leading to placelessness, that had cast a dark shadow over my otherwise positive impression of Orange County.

Vancouver, of course, is not perfect. With more and more affluence on display, there are more iron bars, break-ins, and private security. "You're in a gated community right now, though it doesn't look like one," Price said, referring to the electronic entry system of his apartment block. "Much of North America, metaphorically speaking, is becoming a privatized, gated community where the only urban reality that many well-off kids see is through the sensationalism of local TV news."

Still, Vancouver has something special, a cohesiveness evinced by the never-empty streets and interracial couples: people would fight for this, I thought. No one would fight for Orange County. Put another way, an America of Orange Counties might be a thriving continental archipelago of rising real estate values—for a time—but without the spirit of patriotism that arises from communal affection.

YET VANCOUVER IS governed less like a traditional city and more like an Orange County–style urban confederation. At dinner Ken Cameron, the chief strategic planner for the Greater Vancouver Regional District, told me that Vancouver is run as twenty municipalities. Each municipal council chooses people to represent it on the urban regional council, which, unlike city hall in downtown Vancouver, has the real power. "We have the most open economy in Canada," Cameron told me, "the most dependent on external trade—with the U.S., Japan, and other Asian countries. The Canadian government is irrelevant here. Vancouver, like Seattle and Portland, is just too far from the respective imperial capitals"—the word "imperial" is used a lot out here—"but unlike people in Washington and Oregon, we can't get decent representation in Ottawa because what qualified person would leave here to live there? It's too cold. You're in Canada's Sun Belt, remember."

Cameron went on in his dry English-Canadian accent, "The border is stupid. We've got plans for guards to wave you through with the appropriate sticker on your car. They don't stop you anymore at western European borders, and that will happen here. The city-state is a comer. Not only is our economy different from Canada's, it's different from the rest of British Columbia's. We have one percent of the land area of British Columbia but half the population. Eight hundred thousand of the province's next million residents will live in Vancouver. And it won't mean sprawl, either, since we've designated a green zone around the present city limits. Sustainable development is everything. The Fraser River is the last great salmon-bearing river in the world; we have to preserve it. This is a part of the world where people's loyalty is to the environment, both urban and natural."

As for the political future of the region, Cameron told me, "Oregon, Washington, and British Columbia are all part of British North America (the Oregon Territory). We all care for the environment. We have Asia and the Pacific in common. If the nation-state on your northern border comes apart, you in the U.S. are going to start thinking, too."

ALAN F. J. ARTIBISE is the founder of the Cascadia Planning Group, an organization that assumes, without formally admitting it, the eventual breakup of Canada. Artibise, from Canada's heartland province of Manitoba, is a former president of the Association of Canadian Studies and a planning professor at the University of British Columbia. He has served on numerous planning commissions. His short gray hair is receding, his voice is soft, his expensively furnished office overlooks the harbor. There is nothing radical or even vaguely counterestablishment about him.

For years Cascadia, formerly a geographical term for the Cascade Mountain region from central Oregon to British Columbia, has been a trendy political concept in the Pacific Northwest. A 1975 novel, *Ecotopia* by Ernest Callenbach, which envisioned an independent nation of the Pacific Northwest, sold 650,000 copies in the region.[3] The argument runs like this.

The area on both sides of the U.S.-Canada border once had a common Indian culture. The whole area was governed by the Hudson's Bay Company and later comprised the Oregon Territory, which was disputed by British and Americans. (In fact, the area of present-day Washington and Oregon was integrated with present-day Canada through the fur trade long before American missionaries arrived in the 1830s.) Most important, the region is united by its rather drowsy, wet climate—which may partly account for the profusion of coffee

[3]Joel Garreau's *The Nine Nations of North America* also helped popularize Cascadia.

bars and bookstores—and a unique topography, a northern rain forest boasting the world's largest firs, spruces, and hemlocks. Except for the Pacific Northwest, northern rain forests are found only in slivers of coastal terrain in Japan, Chile, southern Scandinavia, New Zealand, and a few other rare places. In 1989, sixty legislators from both sides of the border formed the Pacific Northwest Legislative Leadership Forum, and business leaders from both sides have formed a group called Pacific Corridor Enterprise.[4] More organizations, including Artibise's, have followed. What has emerged is nothing less than a strategic alliance of the business elite from Portland to Vancouver: an urban corridor linked by the "I-5 Main Street" (Interstate 5) and called "Portcouver," eventually to be connected by high-speed rail. (Passenger trains between Eugene, Oregon, and Vancouver are already 90 percent full.)

Ethan P. Seltzer, director of Portland State University's Metropolitan Studies Institute, told me later in Portland that Cascadia would constitute a giant high-tech trading bloc with major bulk ports in Portland and Vancouver and a container port in the Seattle-Tacoma area.

"Cascadia is more talked about in Oregon and Washington than it is here," Artibise said. "Because of the fragility of the Canadian federation, people are more sensitive on this side of the border because they know how possible Cascadia really is. If Quebec goes, all it would take is one skilled politician to take us out of the federation. It could happen very quickly. Cascadia is thus an economic escape scenario when Quebec leaves. Though they rarely admit it, many British Columbians would probably be relieved if Quebec seceded. [An unnerving one in three Canadians favors the use of force to seize Quebec's English and native areas should the province leave.[5]] All my students have been to Seattle and Portland, but never to Toronto. However, more sovereignty for British Columbia is not the answer. The province does even less for Vancouver than Ottawa does."

Artibise handed me a monograph, *Cascadian Adventures,* which contained the following information:

- Active plans are under way for a "Cascadian" Olympic Games in 2008. (Ethan Seltzer in Portland confirmed this.)

[4]See William Claiborne, "Cascadia: A Culture Evolves in Northwest."
[5]A story about the poll conducted by COMPASS Inc. for the *Southam News* appeared on the front page of the May 16, 1997, edition of *The Vancouver Sun.*

- Inhabitants of Vancouver and Portland are loyal to Seattle's professional sports teams. Discussions have been held to rename the Seattle Mariners baseball team the Cascadia Mariners.

- The border traffic between Washington and British Columbia, numbering 17 million crossings in 1996, is increasing at an exponential rate.

- Cascadia has been described as "so close to God and so far from Washington, D.C., and Ottawa."

Artibise, like everyone else with whom I spoke, hated the presence of the border and its officials. "I once told a guard that I was crossing to help a friend repair his house in Washington. He asked me if I had a work permit. Pretty soon we'll have 'smart cards' for fast clearances—if we don't bulldoze the checkpoints first."

I LEFT VANCOUVER to explore and think a bit about Cascadia.

From a low-flying commuter plane that took me fifty miles southwest from the city of Vancouver across the Strait of Georgia to Victoria on Vancouver Island, I gazed down upon a jigsaw pattern of moss-green islands embedded like hieroglyphs in the water. It was a seascape etched in crystal. Near the horizon, the glaciers on Washington's Olympic Mountains had carved shapes of the greatest clarity and nobility.

The Britishness of Victoria, the main city on Vancouver Island (and the official capital of British Columbia), seemed exaggerated to me. With its red phone booths, wrought-iron pavilions, pubs, Wax Museum, Crystal Garden, afternoon tea, and kilted bagpiper playing Christmas tunes out of season, Victoria was a Busch Gardens version of England. But the cloying atmosphere was not wholly invented; there were historical and social reasons for it. Though the Canadian Pacific had hoped to extend the transcontinental rail line to Vancouver Island, the railway had never gotten this far; it had terminated in the city of Vancouver, on the mainland. From that point onward, Vancouver projected itself into the future, as the rail bridge across the continent is now being reconceived as an air bridge across the Pacific. Meanwhile, Victoria, in its isolation, clung to the comfortable colonial past, redolent of the Hudson's Bay Company and the British Navy. By the turn of the twentieth century, Victoria was a

Bournemouth-on-the-Pacific, a clubby haven for "remittance men," the unemployable sons of wealthy English families.

Elizabeth Archibald, a medieval scholar from Cambridge, England, who teaches at the University of Victoria, told me that when she had been at Yale, "Everyone was enchanted by my English accent. In Victoria it's not even noticed. The flights between London and this part of Canada are full. Many Britons come here to live."

The abundance of Britons in Victoria, along with the nicely cadenced speech of English Canada, has produced a wonderfully clear local accent. The words slip from people's mouths like springwater vectored by rocks in a stream. This, at any rate, is what I thought when I met Douglas Homer-Dixon, who has spent his life as a forester on Vancouver Island. He escorted me for a walk along the coast in East Sooke Regional Park, pointing out the western cedars with their fanlike, matronly branches, the gnarled, sienna-hued arbutus trees, and the Pacific yews, whose coat of carbohydrate-rich lichen deer feed on. A gentle wind blew through the fog and ash-blue Strait of Juan de Fuca, connecting Puget Sound with the Pacific; it had been named for a Greek explorer who had sailed for Spain and adopted a Spanish name. Unlike the eastern fog, weighted with heat and humidity, the fog here is a silken lacework, draping the hillsides. I watched a Steller's jay, described by Meriwether Lewis, land silently on a branch, its fabulous midnight-blue color clashing with the green background. Each rain droplet seemed to have hardened in the cold air, as if millions of glass beads rested upon the leaves.

Homer-Dixon talked worriedly about the dispute between local environmentalists and loggers over the amount of old-growth forest to preserve. The Vancouver media were covering the same subject. The environment dwarfed other daily issues in the Pacific Northwest, and it was not just because of the beauty. With such a sparse history, I realized, nothing is more important than the struggle to preserve what already exists.

Of course, there is a past here, but it is one of heroic exploration rather than of ideological and cultural conflict. Historian Margaret Ormsby writes, "Distant from the travelled sea-lanes and girdled by mountains, British Columbia stood apart from the civilized world until late in the eighteenth century." The same goes for the American Pacific Northwest. Various native peoples have been here since time immemorial—and their breathtaking totem poles, weaving, and other art dominate the Royal British Columbia Museum in Victoria—

but unlike the Mayas and Aztecs in Mexico or the classical cultures of southern Europe, they produced no great urban civilization. The aborigines inhabited a thinly populated, unsullied landscape, which is why the area's environmentalists promote their artistic legacy. For most of its history, the region lay unexplored, the last coastline in the temperate zone to yield its secrets.[6] Only in 1793, not far from Vancouver Island, did Alexander Mackenzie become the first European to cross the Rockies to the Pacific. Twelve years later, Lewis and Clark repeated the feat further south, in what was to become the United States. From then on, there was a generally peaceful competition between the American authorities and the Hudson's Bay Company to determine the frontier between American and British (later Canadian) territory. Generally peaceful, that is, because in the San Juan Islands near Vancouver Island, a pig belonging to a Hudson's Bay Company employee was killed by an American settler in 1859, touching off a comic-opera dispute between Britons and Americans.

After reading this history, I thought, no wonder the Pacific Northwest, particularly Seattle and Portland, is a haven for the overwhelmingly white and Asian software elite! Not only does the Pacific Northwest represent a naturally engineered landscape (with glaciers and rain forests, which, despite their frigid appearance, exist in a mild, sensuous climate), but even more than California, it lacks an encumbering, tragic past. Here is a boundless tabula rasa on which to create any future one wants.

Here is a landscape on which Western civilization is only beginning to write its myths: in this case, perhaps, the myth of a posthistoric land of leisure, in an age when there are no great ideas left to fight for and when the great Western religions are giving way ever so gradually to a spiritualism arising from a natural setting visible from many an urban street and strictly protected by an implicit social contract to which everyone subscribes voluntarily.

At Pacific Rim National Park, a six-hour drive north of Victoria on Vancouver Island, I encountered nature worship in its most technologically advanced form. Almost all the cars were late-model four-wheel drives with kayaks, canoes, or surfboards strapped to their roofs and mountain bikes attached to their rear bumpers; some of the larger vans held, in addition to this equipment, tents and port-

[6]See Carlos Arnaldo Schwantes, *The Pacific Northwest: An Interpretive History.*

able cooking units, while the owners were arrayed in trekking shoes, wet suits, parkas, and so forth. Most of the license plates were local: from British Columbia, Washington, and Oregon—the borders of Cascadia.

I returned to Victoria, from which I took the ninety-minute car ferry across the Strait of Juan de Fuca to Washington. A school of black-and-white orcas accompanied the boat off its starboard side. "Nothing can exceed the beauty of these waters, and their safety," wrote Charles Wilkes, who from 1838 to 1842 explored the Puget Sound area for the United States. I love ferries. For me, nothing else provides such a pure sensation of travel. This ferryboat, partly filled with backpackers and other travelers, recalled the atmosphere of Greek island boats from the early 1970s, but here there were few smokers and many recycling receptacles for soft drink cans.

Port Angeles, the ferry terminal on the Washington side of the strait, is a clean-cut but unpretentious American town, far smaller and less developed than Victoria, with prefabricated dwellings, pickup trucks, and weedy lawns. This is a familiar U.S.-Canadian border phenomenon: because of Canada's cold climate, most Canadians live near the United States in Canada's most cosmopolitan cities, whereas the United States' border towns are usually remote. But Port Angeles, despite its prefabs and pickups, appeared up and coming. There was a new mall, an excellent bookstore with esoteric literary and policy journals, some restaurants with cosmopolitan menus, and engaging real estate advertisements. Nearby are excellent beaches and the Olympic Mountains, rising sheer from sealevel to almost 8,000 feet, with more than sixty glaciers. I could almost hear the rumble of moving vehicles in the years to come, as more professionals extend the limits of the already vast Seattle-Vancouver area.

What will these professionals be loyal to? Just as religion slowly gave way to nationalism as the Middle Ages ended, nationalism, it occurred to me as I drove south from Port Angeles, may slowly give way to a combination of traditional religion, various types of spiritualism, and loyalty to the planet rather than to a specific country. Not only does Cascadia, with its high-income professionals and growing Asian population, foreshadow greater loyalty to a region and its landscape than to a state or nation, it also suggests a place of resident expatriates, of "rooted cosmopolitans," living in one place but intellectually and professionally inhabiting a larger world—the one across the

Pacific and maybe beyond, as the old mass-production economy and the unified culture it spawned evolves into a customized production system loyal to no nation. Cascadia, in other words, gives concrete expression to what is already beginning to happen in many other parts of the continent.

29

Toward Cathay

I CONTINUED SOUTH along the shore of Washington's Olympic Peninsula. The glaciers of the Olympic Mountains and the Cascades were close by, silhouettes in the mist. In a few hours I reached the mouth of the Columbia River, where Lewis and Clark had ended their journey—a dreamy blue current clogged with logs bound for the Orient. I crossed the river to the town of Rainier, Oregon.

NO WORD IS so linked to Manifest Destiny as "Oregon": "the most valuable of all the unoccupied parts of the earth," according to Hall Jackson Kelley, an early advocate of white settlement, in an 1828 letter to Congress. When pioneers crossed the northern part of the Continental Divide in present-day Wyoming and Montana, they had entered "Oregon." The Oregon Country (later "Territory") was the basis of every state and Canadian province in the Pacific Northwest.[1]

[1] The distinction between the U.S. and Canadian sides of Oregon was subtle. For example, there were two Columbias, British and American. Only at the last moment was American Columbia's name changed to "Washington," in order to speed its approval as a new territory through Congress. I always preferred the name "Columbia" for the state.

The Oregon Trail, which split from the Sante Fe Trail at Fort Leaven-worth, brought many tens of thousands of settlers to the Pacific Northwest between the 1830s and 1870s. Frost, hunger, quicksand, rattlesnakes, Indian attacks, and disease made the two-thousand-mile-long trail "the longest graveyard in the world." Yet for many the ordeal was worth it, for it ended in "Eden."

"Eden" is what the early settlers called the Willamette Valley, a flat-land of rich magnesium soil and dark green vegetation lying between the white escarpments of the Cascades and the smaller Coast Range. The Willamette River meanders south of Portland for a hundred miles through the twenty-five-mile-wide valley. It is, arguably, the most richly endowed valley in the world for its size; here, between 1840 and 1860, 53,000 settlers laid out a gridwork of roads and towns. After the rigors of the desert-scarred Oregon Trail, here was a refuge protected from winds, abounding in nuts and berries, and blessed with mild temperatures. The earth here is so rich that for thousands of years, native tribes had regularly burned the valley floor to keep it from being overrun by trees, thus further fortifying the soil. In an 1852 let-ter to his wife, then Captain Ulysses Grant, who was stationed on the Pacific coast, wrote that the soil in the valley "produces almost double it does any place I have been before."

The Willamette has not changed. Rather than drive directly south from Rainier to Portland, I made a wide, westering loop, out to the Pacific, south along Oregon's magnificent pine-clad coast, and then back over the Coast Range into the valley, carpeted with red clover and luxurious yellow Scotch broom and filled with farms and suburbs. Two thirds of Oregon's population lives in the Willamette Valley, making the Portland-Eugene urban corridor more important than the state as a whole. As in Vancouver, I heard much resent-ment about "tax dollars flowing to the state rather than to nearby municipalities."

Portland boasts, perhaps, the most architecturally pleasing and meticulously planned downtown of any major city in the United States—so much so that Portland has been lionized by liberal na-tional magazines, while its Metro 2040 Plan, designed to extend the development of the city center and prevent more suburbanization, has been attacked by conservative free-marketeers. For instance, in a long *Forbes* magazine article about Portland, former *Wall Street Journal* editorialist Tim Ferguson writes that Portland's "social-engineering zeal is not to everyone's taste" and that "the internal combustion genie will not go willingly back into its bottle."[2] In three visits to Portland, I realized that while the view of liberal urban planners here was the wiser one, the conservative vision of unlimited growth, which will triumph almost everywhere else on the continent, has been defeated by culture and geography more than by mere good design. The cities of the Pacific Northwest are more resistant to overdevelopment than local planners and others are willing to admit.

With its neat trolley lanes, geometric parks, rustic flowerpots beside polymer and glass buildings, crowded sidewalk benches, and cafés with modish awnings that hang from sandblasted stone and veiny marble fronts, Portland exudes a stagy perfection, as if it were not simply a city but a kind of open-air museum. "View corridors" regulated by municipal ordinances keep new construction from blocking downtown vistas of the Cascades and, in particular, Mount Hood. Even when there is no mist, drivers (usually in late-model foreign cars) often use headlights or dims during the day, as in Canada. People speak in clipped accents like those of British Columbia. I saw people wait in single file to cross a street at a red light. They don't often jaywalk. Eighty-nine percent of them are white: the minority population of the Portland metropolitan area is less than half the national average, though in the city of Portland the number of Asians is more than half the national average.[3] Portland, like Minneapolis, to which it is often compared, evinces the political-cultural atmosphere of a Scandinavian country, where almost everyone shares the same background and values and, for the sake of preserving them, trusts the centralizing, controlling force of local government.

Not only was Portland, unlike Los Angeles, formed before the car, it was a city of Florentine and gothic facades even before the arrival of the transcontinental railroad. Surrounding the city on three sides, the natural environment of mountains and rivers is ever present in Portland and essential to its economy. Maintaining this pristine landscape is politically acceptable. Carl Abbott, in a presentation to the Urban Affairs Association here, described the city's liberal environmental politics as, in fact, "status quo conservatism" because it seeks to preserve the past rather than create a future.

---

[2]The quote about "social-engineering zeal" is from the article's subheadline rather than from the text itself; see Ferguson, "Down with the Burbs! Back to the City!"
[3]These figures come from Portland State University's *Metropolitan Briefing Book*, among other sources.

"Cars for us are evil," said Michael Carnahan of the World Affairs Council, a group dedicated to improving Portland's already prodigious trade links with foreign countries. "The whole point of our development plan is not to screw up our pastoral landscape, which is central to local history and culture," Ethan Seltzer, the director of Portland State University's Urban Institute, told me. "We seek a mythic, native adaptation to place. The natives burnt the fields in the Willamette Valley once a year to keep the forest from encroaching; we must do something analogous to keep the suburbs from encroaching further on the natural environment. And the only way to preserve the Cascade landscape while making economic use of it is to shift the economy further from agriculture and logging to high tech."

The Cascade landscape keeps Portland's new high-tech economy competitive by providing cheap Columbia River waterpower for washing silicon; the natural beauty, meanwhile, attracts people with university degrees. High-technology products have already surpassed timber as Oregon's chief export. Twenty percent of Portland's economy is based on foreign trade, and that figure, along with both high-tech production and the population of the greater metropolitan area, is expected to rise dramatically.[4] By 2010, the three-county region that includes Portland and Vancouver, Washington, across the Columbia River (not to be confused with Vancouver, British Columbia), will have an estimated 2.5 million inhabitants compared with 1.6 million in 1997.

The policy mechanism by which this rapid population growth can be accommodated is "the urban growth boundary," which delineates a greenbelt around the metropolitan area and thus forces developers to build higher-density neighborhoods, as in Vancouver, British Columbia. But such a plan means having a regional government in place, composed of representatives of the twenty-four municipalities in greater Portland. "To preserve the environment," Seltzer told me, "we are making a transition away from city hall toward the urban region. In any case, very few urbanites in North America live their lives in one jurisdiction anymore. They live in one municipality, work in another; it's especially true with two-career couples"; which is another reason why, while the urban federation may be the future, traditional cities are fading. (Manhattan, for example, the twentieth century's premier urban location, has attracted strikingly little new

[4]See Gary Finseth, *Trade Stats Northwest: Export Analysis of Portland, Oregon.*

business investment despite an impressive drop in crime and a popular Republican mayor, Rudolph Giuliani. Corporations appear to prefer posturban pods such as western Omaha. It is unclear whether Manhattan has made an authentic comeback as a twenty-first-century global meeting place or is experiencing, according to a historian, a beautiful "Venetian sunset.")

But the fading of the traditional city is not necessarily a social disaster, since all it may mean, eventually, is that instead of one downtown there will be many within a sprawling urban region, each providing the same socially unifying functions as the old downtowns. Even Orange County real estate expert Dennis Macheski had said that despite the ability to work at home via the computer, most people will want social venues close by. It is our very humanity—our need for others—that will help us through these troubling transitions. (Denver, for instance, which I recently visited, now has three thriving downtowns—Cherry Creek, "LoDo," and downtown Denver—as it transforms itself into an urban confederation.)

Even if Metro 2040 succeeds—even if suburban sprawl in the Willamette to the south is contained and new, well-educated migrants live in upmarket, high-density town houses and "bungarows"— Portland, Seltzer and others told me, will change dramatically in other ways. "The early settlers here," Seltzer explained, "re-created the New England village. Since then, we've been good at space arrangement and streetscapes. Our next challenge is to get along with each other." The white population is aging, and twenty years from now Portland will be like greater L.A. in terms of ethnicity.

The Pacific Northwest is, statistically speaking, one of the last bastions of the white race in the United States. Even the city of Seattle, which elected a black mayor, Norm Rice, for a second term in 1993, has a minority population of only 15 percent, well below the national average of 25 percent. Washington and Oregon have among the lowest percentages of African Americans in the country (1.6 percent of the population in Oregon's case; 3.1 percent in Washington's). Racism has a rich legacy in Oregon, where black immigration was banned in 1849 to avoid the slavery question, and the northeastern part of Portland was redlined by realtors after World War II to keep blacks away from well-off whites. What is more likely to happen, given the emphasis on high tech—and what people here admit to only partly—is that few blacks will migrate to the Pacific Northwest, but many more Asians will. In effect, economic factors will enforce racial segregation here, turning Seattle and Portland into replicas of Vancouver as Seattle and Portland trade more with the Pacific Rim.

Not only will Portland become more Asian, its urban layout will more closely resemble that of Orange County, as Portland grows because of the semiconductor boom and decentralized workplaces and production centers in the area increase the role of the car. Moreover, a statewide tax revolt that has won support even in Portland limits what Metro 2040 can spend to ensure spatial purity. The revolt has also opened further the chasm between a generally conservative state and a liberal urban federation in the making. Similarly, the growing estrangement between Portland and Washington, D.C., is increasing, manifested by criticism of "HUD [Department of Housing and Urban Development] regulations designed for East Coast cities that are forced on us."

It seems to me we cannot ultimately control these social and economic forces. As one expert told me, the whole New World—all of the United States, certainly—has been just one big subdivision marketed for most of our history to white Europeans. American cities have rarely been humanized by idealists, but always by tacky carpetbaggers and get-rich-quick guys. The modification has been that in some places, like Portland, this greed has had to conform to existing cultural expectations. But in many other places in America the communal culture is too thin for that.

THE UNITED STATES of America, just one big subdivision: one big, barely regulated Oklahoma land dash. Without the Oregon gold rush of the early 1850s, Oregon might not have survived as a territory: just as the Clearwater gold rush of 1860, more than any other individual event, brought settlers into the interior of the northern Rockies, in present-day Idaho and Montana. It was the pursuit of wealth that made these former wildernesses into territories that eventually became states. Our elected officials have generally not created facts on the ground but reacted to them. The imperial reach of such gargantuan public works projects as the Grand Coulee Dam was a historical aberration, the result of the Great Depression followed by a world war. "Bigness"—the mass Rooseveltian state of the mid–twentieth century—triumphed in response to a particular stage in the history of science and technology. Even the most successful and long-standing political creations will eventually succumb to the sovereignty of geographical-cultural-climatic factors, according to *American Region-alism: A Cultural-Historical Approach to National Integration* by Howard Odum and Harry Estill Moore, a 1938 classic that Seltzer had on his desk. Thus, as the last embers of the Rooseveltian state flicker and die in the Republican Congresses of the mid- and late 1990s, the northern rain forest of the Pacific Northwest and its unique culture have begun to secede from a formerly uniform nation.

Comparing the United States with Rome, Henry Adams wrote in 1906, "The climax of empire could be seen approaching, year after year, as though Sulla were a President or McKinley a Consul. Nothing annoyed Americans more than to be told this simple and obvious—in no way unpleasant—truth." Adams was wrong in his timing but perhaps not in his reasoning. The climax of the American empire may come sometime in the early twenty-first century, a minor detail in the long span of history. Adams's belief that the end of American empire would be "in no way unpleasant" dovetails well with what I had been hearing everywhere beyond the gates of Fort Leavenworth: from Rick Reiff, the gregarious journalistic booster of Orange County, to Ethan Seltzer, who wanted to preserve Portland's New England qualities. They believed that federal power was waning, that the massive ministry buildings of Washington, D.C., with their oxen armies of bureaucrats, are the product of the Industrial Age, when society reached a level of sheer size and complexity that demanded such institutions, and are not necessarily characteristic of the decentralized American future. Somehow, this leaden federal colossus must slowly evolve into a new, light-frame structure of mere imperial oversight—for the sake of defense, conservation, and the rationing of water and other natural resources—allowing, as I have suggested, for a political silver age if not another golden one.

Will America transcend its historic self? The vision, suggested by two of our most nationalistic poets, Walt Whitman and Hart Crane, is "Cathay": less a transpacific country or the Asianization of the population than the idea of losing ourselves, peacefully and productively, in the wider world as we span the oceanic gap.[5] For America to calcify like Rome seems unlikely in any case. The north–south reorientation of the continent and the eclipse of our largely white, east–west middle-class hegemony seems more probable. Ishmael,

[5]In addition to Whitman's "Psalm of Cathay!" and Crane's "The Bridge," see Langdon Hammer, *Hart Crane and Allen Tate: Janus-faced Modernism*, p. 195.

who understood the fragility of human hopes, was the lone survivor of the wreck of the *Pequod,* while Captain Ahab, who shouted, "All ye nations before my prow," perished with his ship.

Perhaps, as new regional and urban forms alter its landscape, greater Portland may follow Vancouver's path as an influx of Asians introduces British bureaucratic traditions of control and good government. As I contemplated the future of Cascadia, I recalled again that New England had almost seceded from the United States during the War of 1812 to rejoin British North America. Future secessions of regions and posturban pods will be far more subtle and therefore more likely to succeed; for they will not have to be acknowledged. Our subtle new regionalism will be largely invisible. Meanwhile, the two forms of urban confederation under this refined continental imperialism, the Portland form and the Orange County form, will compete for ascendancy. Hybrid forms will emerge, perhaps even within Portland and Orange County themselves; but the Orange County model will, on the whole, dominate.

YET WHEN I went to dinner at the Portland home of an Iranian immigrant, Jim (Jamsheed) Ameri, it was as if Sousa's patriotic march music had jumped in volume, as if midcentury Industrial Age America had never receded. Jim is a real estate developer and lives with his wife, Goli, in Tigard, on the southwestern fringe of Portland, in an opulent home at the head of the Willamette Valley. From their impeccable lawn, punctuated with majestic Douglas firs in a fine, pellucid mist, the valley, its homes and its gardens, unfurled. This was the bountiful Pacific Northwest as seen by the first pioneers, now savored by this latest migration of Oregon settlers. Jim and Goli had invited a number of their Iranian friends to dinner to discuss their experiences as very successful immigrants in America.

Sipping drinks on the porch in the sunset, Farsheed Shomloo, an immigration lawyer, pointed to a book on the patio table and told Jim, "You should read this new book about Iran, it's really interesting." Jim replied:

"I don't want to read it. I know the outcome already. In Iran, there is beautiful poetry and everything turns out a disaster. Here the poetry is not so beautiful, but people are free to discover the best in themselves; that's why America has happy endings. Here it's a negative system: there is no entrenched depotism, no will to dominate. We immigrants can remake the whole country if we want to. It's ours for the taking, as if there is a perpetual clean slate where nobody is ever owed anything. I'll tell you, the Iranian revolution was a disaster for Iran and a success for America, because it brought a lot of talented, ambitious Iranians here. Every time there is a disaster in the Third World, it's a good thing for America, since the best of the middle class finds its way here."

Farsheed agreed. "What is this country that sucks you up and draws out the best in you, and allows you for the first time to be yourself?" he asked passionately. "Periodically I reread the Constitution. I am amazed. What is this incredible system built by pessimists, yet built so as to unleash the human spirit? You know why I chose to live in Oregon? I looked in a book and saw that there was no sales tax here. In Iran I was oppressed by taxes and everything else. At the University of Oregon in Eugene I used to participate in protests against the shah [in the 1970s]. Then I realized that nobody in Oregon gave a damn about the shah or about me protesting. I was free to criticize U.S. government policy, and nobody cared! You cannot imagine what a revelation that was for somebody from Iran. That's when I stopped focusing on Iran and truly became an American."

"Do you know what is the most amazing thing for me?" Jim interjected. "To know that an assembly line composed of Mexicans, blacks, whites, Asians, and so on is more efficient than an assembly line composed only of Japanese. With all their Shintoism and work ethic, we can beat the Japanese!"

When I mentioned that a woman I had met in Cave Junction feels nothing when she hears patriotic music played, Goli, Jim's wife, who grew up in Iran, said, "When I hear it, I feel a chill up my spine." Nobody at Jim and Goli's home had any complaints. Farsheed said, "Even the INS [U.S. Immigration and Naturalization Service] is not that bad, especially compared to the French immigration authorities. Europe is a bit like Iran, an oppressive state system."

"How did you afford this?" I asked Jim, eyeing his property of several acres.

"The wealth I came with, believe me, was my youth, which allowed me to make myself over as an American. There are old Iranians who came here with fortunes and lost all their money. They thought that business was a matter of whom you knew, having a connection. Because in Iran nothing is ever done straight, it's all deals and shortcuts," he said, moving his hand like a snake. "I came with enough money to support myself at Stanford Business School. I learned that in the U.S. there is no shortcut from A to B, that it's a straight playing field. I began small in San Francisco. In the mideighties I saw that the Portland real estate market was undervalued. I saw that Epson, Fujitsu, Nike, Intel wanted cheap water, high-tech workforces, and nice scenery. So I invested in a lot of downtown Portland property, before the boom." Jim, a Republican, had made his money from the liberal planning regulations, which had forced investment downtown.

The families at the table were either sending or planning to send their children to private schools, in some cases the French school. (Yes, Portland, a foreign trade center, now has a French school.) And as the Islamic regime in Iran softens, they all had plans to visit and re-establish links there, even to spend several months a year there. Like other immigrants I had met, these Iranian Americans were much less rooted to place and to the public schools than immigrants of earlier periods. They may love America, but they do not consider themselves dependent on it. They came here for the freedom to make the most of their lives, but they are citizens of the world in a way that previous immigrants were not. I realized as I said good-bye to them that while we insist upon the illusion of a permanent continental nation that has existed less than a third as long as the Moorish occupation of Spain, we may find that we have become instead the creators of its diluted successor, which may be the most we can hope for.

PART VII

THE

MEANING

OF

VICKSBURG

3 0

History in Three Dimensions

IN SPRING 1997, I returned to Fort Leavenworth to participate in a "staff ride" with fifty-four captains and majors from the School of Advanced Military Studies at Vicksburg, Mississippi. Two chartered Greyhound buses left Fort Leavenworth before dawn and took us south through Missouri, Arkansas, and Louisiana to Vicksburg, Mississippi, which we planned to reach after dark. In the nineteenth century, Vicksburg—a fortified town of 4,500 inhabitants overlooking a hairpin turn of the Mississippi River—had been a pivot of continental destiny, as much as the journey of Lewis and Clark. For the Union Army, which in 1863 controlled New Orleans to the south and Memphis to the north, the capture of Vicksburg meant opening the whole North American waterway system and thus permitting trade from the Ohio River Valley to the Gulf of Mexico. According to Union General Henry W. Halleck, Vicksburg's capture was "of more advantage than the capture of forty Richmonds."[1]

"Gettysburg changed the war less than Vicksburg did," explained Chris Gabel, a military historian at Fort Leavenworth, who led one of the four seminars into which the large group of captains and majors was divided. "Gettysburg was an accidental, set-piece battle. After

[1]Shelby Foote, *The Beleaguered City: The Vicksburg Campaign.*

Gettysburg, the Union field commander, [General George G.] Meade, kept doing what he had always been doing. The Confederate commander, [Robert E.] Lee, kept doing what he had always been doing. Little of strategic importance happened. But Vicksburg cut the South in two, and it *brought Grant east,* to take control of the Union Army."

Though situated in the Deep South, in 1863 Vicksburg was considered "the West," just as Leavenworth was during the later Indian Wars, and just as the Rockies and the Cascades are today. Grant, the Union commander at Vicksburg, was in every respect a westerner. He grew up in Ohio and lived in Illinois, both part of the original "Northwest," the first territorial possession of the young United States and in the early nineteenth century—the time of Grant's youth and early adulthood—a frontier, with its own Indian wars. Grant had also served in California and Oregon. This experience of the Pacific may have steeled his commitment to a united union, which he shared with Lincoln.

As a general, Grant was blunt and practical, lumbering ever forward, risking what he had achieved in the knowledge that standing still means failure. And because he considered himself no better than his men, he was the ideal democratic leader.[2] For Grant, war was never heroic: like everything else in America, it was business. Grant exemplified the serviceable engineering education at which West Point excelled: so American, so unlike the more theoretical "chessboard" curriculum of European war colleges. Grant's *Personal Memoirs,* written at the end of his life, is the archetypal American narrative, perhaps more so than Thoreau's *Walden* or Whitman's *Leaves of Grass,* to which Edmund Wilson favorably compares it. With rough austerity, it tells of its author's struggles, setbacks, and ultimate rise, through sheer practical application in the course of extraordinary events. If I could boil America down to a single, exemplary personality, it would be Grant. For me, Grant, in his rough-hewn, unsophisticated ambition, *was* America. I was taking this bus journey on a hunch that learning more about Grant and what he had accomplished at Vicksburg might allow me a final insight into this country.

At Vicksburg, Grant truly came into his own, pulling the Union and the coming Industrial Age nation along with him. Vicksburg is about *process:* the little-by-littleness of change. Though Grant's victory there

[2]See John Keegan, *The Mask of Command.*

gave Union forces strategic control of the settled part of the continent, the exact moment of that victory is obscure; for Vicksburg was not so much a battle as a complex campaign of several battles and skirmishes. The turning point in the dense malarial marshes of the lower Mississippi Valley occurred in the midst of bloody weeks of drudgery, between Grant's seventh, failed attempt in late March 1863 to cross to the east bank of the Mississippi (where the Confederate fortress was) and the Confederates' final surrender on Independence Day, the same July Fourth when the guns stilled at Gettysburg.

These officers' reverence for the landscape of the Vicksburg campaign, like reverence for all Civil War battlefields, revealed a blood-and-soil nationalism of the kind that I had seldom encountered on my journey through the western United States. Chris Gabel, with a scruffy beard, unfashionable black-frame glasses, a Pennsylvania Railroad gas station cap, and his hands busy with maps and field markers, talked about "hallowed ground" and how "interest in the Civil War shows how truly patriotic you are." Regarding Earth Day, he said, only partly in jest, "I personally celebrate it by soaking an old tire in oil and burning it in my front yard." Cheers followed from the captains and majors.

The Civil War left nearly half a million Americans dead, more than Word War II.[3] Sixty percent of the casualties were caused by disease. Subtract World War II, and more men died in the Civil War than in all other U.S. wars combined, from the Revolution through the Persian Gulf War.[4] The Civil War was fought upon a familiar American landscape. Though it was bitterly internecine, the "hard war" tactics of Sheridan in the Shenandoah Valley and Sherman in Georgia and the Carolinas, who burned fields and looted homesteads, were confined to the war's final phase and in all their savagery do not compare with the indiscriminate slaughter of civilians common to Europe from the Middle Ages through World War II.[5] While the United States may remain somewhat divided over the war, with a few southerners still stubbornly flying Confederate standards, for the U.S. military the Civil War is a binding memory, symbolizing a romantic time long ago

[3]Source: *The World Almanac and Book of Facts.*
[4]Source: U.S. Department of Defense.
[5]See Mark Grimsley, *The Hard Hand of War: Union Military Policy Toward Southern Civilians 1861–1865,* for a cool, brilliant analysis of why "hard war" was not only rare in the Civil War but incomparable to what European civilians have often experienced.

when Americans died in large numbers, loyal to their flags. I have met many a southern officer who venerates Grant. Yet the Civil War as well as this new centurion army seemed unconnected to the continent where I had just traveled, with its increasingly diverse, cosmopolitan loyalties. By being with army officers again at the close of my American odyssey, I hoped to clarify further my feelings about what I had seen.

The annual staff ride to Vicksburg is the culmination of the most advanced, scholarly program in world politics and military history that the U.S. Army offers its future generals. The elusive aim of the ride was to pin down the exact moment when the surrender of the Confederate fortress became inevitable.

THE OFFICERS, WITH their short barbershop cuts and farm-boy looks, reminded me of World War II photographs. As dawn broke against an immense prairie landscape and the bus left Leavenworth for Vicksburg, the discussion ranged from potential conflict in Russia to social upheaval in the Philippines to the "oligarchic, politically centralized" Chilean Army: "It's not an army, it's a social class," one officer suggested, unaware that the same might almost be said of his own army. Then someone mentioned Xenophon, whose account of a Greek army in the fourth century B.C. marching from Persia to the Black Sea "reads like the Korean War," another officer added. As usual there was much friendly talk about Germany. The occupation after World War II and the sheer number of U.S. troops stationed there since, learning German and marrying German women, has given these officers a decidedly pro-German bias.

By midmorning we passed Branson in southwestern Missouri, the "Ozark Disneyland" and the second most popular auto destination in the United States after Orlando, Florida, according to the American Automobile Association, with casinos, theme parks, and more than thirty country music venues. An unregulated forest of garish signs rose from the barren Ozark Plateau, advertising theaters where Glen Campbell, Andy Williams, and other once popular singers perform. Glen Campbell's spired theater looked indistinguishable from Branson's First Baptist Church. There was a scary temporariness to these billboards and prefabricated structures that clashed starkly with the permanent plateau rock. Yet again, I felt that there may be nothing at the American center beyond these bursts of economic activity, what immigrants and carpetbaggers alike have found so liberating: a quarter century ago, Branson barely existed, and it might not exist a quarter century hence. Walt Whitman's easy acceptance of such raging, unstable materialism soured him to the Hudson River painters, whose idyllic landscapes, he felt, ignored the nation's explosive dynamism.[6]

Budding apple trees, deep gulches, rusted car bodies, corrugated roofs, and a profusion of tattered mobile homes with plastic Virgin Mary statues and hand-scrawled announcements of "rocks for sale" and "yard ornaments" marked Arkansas. The landscape of northern Arkansas could sear your heart, with sublime forests and mountains the backdrop to rust-chewed pickups with raised suspensions, streams filled with garbage, and the usual old appliances on porches.

Like the bus station in Albuquerque, the Little Rock bus station— where we waited for ninety minutes to change buses and drivers for the second leg of our journey to Vicksburg—was crowded with poor and homeless people, their belongings in garbage bags. There were pinball machines but no newspapers for sale. Later, as we drove through downtown Little Rock, I saw a few glitzy high-rises—mainly banks and savings and loans—a prosperous neighborhood or two, then rows of dreary, low-end blue-collar habitations. Day rolled into evening as we passed through southern Arkansas and northeastern Louisiana, a flat landscape of reddish soil cluttered with small factories, gas stations, cheap stores, fast-food outlets, a few prisons and refineries, and scrappy private residences. After dark we crossed the Mississippi River into Vicksburg.

The bayou country around Vicksburg, which we explored over the next four days in the course of retracing Grant's path to victory, was even poorer: plywood and tar-paper shacks, lean-tos, and mobile homes with garbage in the yards and porches (when there were any) stacked with rusted appliances. Floodwater sometimes lapped at their steps. There were autos from the sixties and seventies painted red, orange, and other loud colors; a monotony of bait shops, pawnshops, and junkyards with faded stenciled signs; rusty old condom machines; bent metal road markers with the occasional hunter's bullet hole. . . . I was reminded of the grimmest parts of Mexico, except that amid this devastation, in the heart of some of the towns we passed, I noticed some magnificent, white-columned homes sur-

[6]See David S. Reynolds, *Walt Whitman's America: A Cultural Biography.*

rounded by meticulously tended gardens. Here the middle class seemed insignificant. Most of the homes I saw were either rich or poor. There was a slash-and-burn quality to most of the architecture, as if the abandonment of one feeble dwelling for another—the lot of black sharecroppers—had affected whites, too. And with no expectation of progress, every old refrigerator was an heirloom, and gambling, as I was soon to learn, was the only hope.

CHRIS GABEL'S LECTURES, delivered in a hardscrabble Appalachian accent, helped untangle for me one of the most subtle, complex campaigns in military history. Moreover, Gabel's narrative of Grant's persistent struggles made Grant seem akin to the frontiersmen I had read about and the immigrants I had encountered. On the first morning, as the bus headed north along the Mississippi to Haines Bluff, the site of one of Grant's early failures, Gabel explained that the Mississippi was the product of the last ice age, some eleven thousand years ago, and that the loess soil from that distant period— like the similar soil at Fort Leavenworth—forms bluffs where the South placed artillery positions that Grant had to circumvent. As we turned inland, I saw what looked like another stretch of the river, but telephone poles rising from the water indicated that it was a flooded plain.

At Haines Bluff, overlooking the Yazoo River, the Confederates defended the approaches to Vicksburg and Yazoo City to the north. Here Gabel unfurled the first of many maps covered with blue arrows for Union troops and red ones for Confederates. A mottled stone plaque revealed that the first white man to settle here was a French missionary in 1698. In the shade cast by walnut and red bud trees, Gabel told us, "Grant was a long way from the flagpole, and he had a pretty long leash. He had taken thirteen thousand casualties at Shiloh, and while he finally had a national reputation, he knew that if he failed here he would be cast aside."

So far, Grant's Civil War career had demonstrated how war, like the frontier, provides the opportunity for meritocratic advancement. Grant had exploited one narrow opening after another. Having failed at farming and real estate, Grant, who had finished in the unimpressive lower middle of his class at West Point, showed a knack for leadership once the war began: he volunteered for the army, then recruited, equipped, and drilled troops at Galena, Illinois. In late 1861, he captured Belmont, on the Mississippi River between St. Louis and Memphis, but this campaign had not been specifically ordered, and the press criticized Grant for an unnecessary engagement. Then, in February 1862, Grant won the first major Union victory of the war when he captured fifteen thousand Confederate troops at Fort Donelson, on the Cumberland River in Tennessee. In April at Shiloh Church, near Pittsburg Landing, Tennessee, Grant repulsed an unexpected Confederate offensive, but with such heavy losses that the press raged at him, though military historians now see Shiloh as a Union triumph. The captains and majors argued that had the interfering press then been more influential than it was, Grant and Sherman both might have been removed from command and the war prolonged for lack of aggressive Union generals. (Sherman celebrated with his aides when he learned that four reporters had been killed near Vicksburg.7)

As I had learned at Fort Leavenworth, the power of the media foreshadows the end of the heroic period in American military history. Great battles of the type fought by Grant and Eisenhower mean risk and blood and a wide berth for error. Thus the staff ride became an exercise in valediction and nostalgia.

Before the Civil War, the United States had been a continental nation. But the war made it a real community: Americans were uprooted from their villages and made to commingle with others as they all trekked to—and together experienced—other parts of the country. The great stone and marble monuments dedicated to the regiments from Missouri, Illinois, Indiana, and other states here at the Vicksburg National Military Park testify to such a melding. But now, as I had seen on my travels, for a large class of prosperous Americans, a new world community is beginning to shred the bonds of union the Civil War firmly established.

For three days we followed Grant's campaign in the bayous, hiking through ankle-deep mud and shivering in semicircles in the cold rain—our maps protected by transparent plastic—in places where America was made, yet that are virtually unmarked and uncommemorated because this campaign was fought over a large tract, while the National Military Park includes only the site of the final siege. From many a bluff I saw an unstable landscape where the Mississippi was cutting new channels. The places we saw echoed the mighty music of Indian names or the folksy language of the frontier: Haines Bluff,

---

7See Foote, *The Beleaguered City.*

Chickasaw Bayou, and rivers called the Mississippi, the Tallahatchie, the Yazoo, and the Big Black. Black cannons against a green vale near the fortress where Grant had refused to call a truce to collect the dead suggested how patriotic myth is established through violent death: the Vicksburg campaign saw 16,700 casualties.

Nations abide by virtue of their boundaries, by the belligerent acts against them, and by the continually replenished memory of heroic deeds. The seepage at the Mexican border, the potential dissolution of the Canadian border, and the limitations imposed on the military by an omnipresent media and a distrustful society, whose members have rarely served in uniform and are increasingly foreign citizens and dual nationals—made the Vicksburg experience an emotional one for me.

THE ANNUAL VICKSBURG staff ride is, as Gabel put it, "history in three dimensions": voluminous reading before the trip, firsthand experience of the terrain, and then a refighting of every battle, in which each captain and major is assigned a role to play.[8] Here, briefly, is what had happened.

In the late winter and early spring of 1863, Grant tried and failed seven times to cross from the Louisiana to the Mississippi side of the river to attack the enemy fortress from the rear. The defeats were costly and time-consuming. At the Battle of Chickasaw Bayou, north of Vicksburg, for instance, the Union suffered 1,776 casualties. Grant tried digging a canal to get his boats closer to the fortress. That failed, too, and many died of disease in the process. Finally, he ran boats loaded with troops past the fortress and, on April 30, landed men twenty-five miles south of Vicksburg, where he cut his army loose from its food supplies, leaving his men to live off the land. He then won a series of battles that brought him east of Vicksburg. But rather than turn and march west to capture the fortress, he continued east to capture Mississippi's capital at Jackson, where he and Sherman cut its rail lines and destroyed its factories, so that Confederate reinforcements could not come to Vicksburg's rescue once his anticipated siege there began. Only then did he march west to Vicksburg, where on May 19 he commenced his siege.

[8]See William G. Robertson, *The Staff Ride.*

Where and when was Vicksburg won? Did it happen when Grant, running his boats below the fortress and sustaining only minor losses, knew that he could now get behind the enemy? Or did it occur when his army actually crossed the Mississippi at Bruinsburg, a site Grant had selected partly on the basis of intelligence from a black slave? Was it at Port Gibson, the first battle Grant won after breaking loose from his supplies? Was it at Raymond, en route to Jackson, where we lowered our heads in the rain at a black-gated cemetery holding the graves of 130 rebel soldiers of the "Seventh Texas" killed by Grant's forces?[9] Was it at Jackson?

If we reached any conclusion, it was that the culmination probably occurred at Champion Hill, a seventy-five-foot-high, crescent-shaped ridge that controlled three converging roads: here Grant's 32,000 troops arrived on May 16 while marching west from Jackson to Vicksburg and encountered 23,000 troops of the Confederate commander, General John C. Pemberton. The size of this battle and the closeness of the outcome may have been pivotal: Champion Hill was the closest thing Vicksburg—which otherwise resembled a modern Third World counterinsurgency campaign—had to a Gettysburg-style engagement. But here there were no monuments: only a small sign by the road a quarter of a mile away, near some shacks.

We hiked up a muddy stream until we arrived at a clearing. I was struck by the silence and remoteness: here, except for the spread of the forest since 1863, nothing seemed to have changed in 134 years. There had been 6,200 casualties in a few hours of mostly hand-to-hand fighting with rifle butts and bayonets. After the battle, Union General Alvin P. Hovey said, "It was a hill of death. . . . I never saw fighting like this." Gabel had several maps showing different stages of the battle: a few small arrows on the first map indicating probes quickly evolved into a crowded canvas of bars pointing in all directions. "Gentlemen," Lieutenant Colonel Richard Rowe Jr. said, standing in a clearing that had been the heart of the battlefield, "you don't often have the opportunity of walking through a theoretical point: Could the Confederates have fought this engagement differently?" The captains and majors then spent an hour in animated technical discussion. A few bayonet thrusts executed differently might have

---

[9]More specifically, Union actions at Raymond were led by General James McPherson, "a young pup" in Chris Gabel's words, whom Grant liked but kept a close watch over.

affected the outcome of the battle, thus affecting the campaign and much else about American history.

Except for me, everyone on the hill that late morning (the same time of day as the battle) was an army officer in a special forces, tank, infantry, or signals brigade who had fought in the Persian Gulf or Somalia, or had been involved in antidrug and other operations in Latin America, Southeast Asia, or Haiti. "Decisiveness is only a word historians use in hindsight," Rowe said. "The trick is to turn it to foresight through war-gaming. We affect the outcome of history by figuring out in advance what is decisive." Rowe, a graduate of Phillips Exeter Academy, was typical of the new elite army, many of whose officers are drawn from the best schools. Later, back at the motor inn for an "integration session," he continued, "The Civil War was also American in the sense that it was a war of technical experimentation. The telegraph was introduced after the Mexican War, so here we have the use of telegraph and railroads for the first time in war. Now, Grant has this gut sense that the old rules of the academy no longer apply and he's making new rules as he goes along. He goes to Bruinsburg on a whim, he forages off the land, he cuts the rails to Jackson; he's a frontiersman who improvises within the barriers set by geography." Or, as Grant himself wrote in his *Personal Memoirs:* "By moving against Jackson, I uncovered my own communication. So I finally decided to have none—to cut loose altogether from my base."

By forever casting off what has gone before, Americans are free to try what they choose—that is the frontier. The very temporariness of American civilization, in other words, as indicated by the Bransons and Tucsons and Albuquerques and Orange Counties, with their overnight theater-prop development, is the image of our dynamism. Portland may be beautiful with its architectural accumulation and civility, but too many Portlands, too tightly held, might stultify us, turning us rigid and fragile and likely to crack apart someday, like Rome.

ON THE LAST night of our tour we visited the *Ameristar,* a casino boat on the Mississippi that provided a vision of America as apocalypse. The path leading to the boat is lined with pawnshops and signs offering to lend money against car titles to pay gambling debts. Inside, the ship resembled the interior of a video game machine, with pulsing neon and the ear-splitting beeping sounds of slots, exactly like the casino on the Acoma Indian reservation in New Mexico;

these places are all alike. There were some three thousand customers here on this weekday night and the same number aboard the four other gambling boats in Vicksburg. Private security guards were everywhere. Gamblers were handed plastic riverboat hats and popcorn buckets for their chips. Because tourists prefer casinos closer to New Orleans, the crowd consisted generally of locals who had driven here from throughout the region. Men who looked like gas station attendants stood at the slots next to women in sequined dresses. Blacks wearing gold neck chains stood beside unshaven whites with leather pants and tattoos: all stared at the machines as if into an abyss. Despite the electronic beeping, the hall seemed as still as an operating room: hardly anyone spoke. Even the winners looked unhappy as they tossed their chips back into the machines on another bet. I noticed one woman with an inch of ash on her cigarette, so absorbed was she in the activity. I saw many machines saying "Credit limit reached" as gamblers exhausted their credit card charge limits. Another woman told me she had been driving from Oklahoma to Florida and stopped here "to rest my eyes." She won several thousand dollars and told me she didn't know what she would do with the money. The gift shop had a single theme: Elvis, with T-shirts in ghastly purples.

Vicksburg was not unique. Two hours north along the river, in Tunica County, a $1-billion-a-year gambling industry has risen overnight; there, ten casinos go twenty-four hours a day. The facades of the boats resemble Tudor mansions and Greco-Roman temples, among other outlandish designs. The casinos in Vicksburg and in Tunica County belong to out-of-state corporations; the money flows to faraway treasuries.[10]

In Tunica County, too, there is widespread black poverty and a small white gentry whose children go to private schools. I thought of East St. Louis, where gambling, like foreign aid, had brought money but little change in the way of doing things. What is to become of such people—black and white—left behind in a global economy? Though history is full of disasters, it seems cruel for a society to consign such people to oblivion, however foolish some of them might be, gambling away what little they had.

One of the majors said cynically, eyeing the crowd, "And we risk our life for this. Kind of makes you go warm and fuzzy inside." He and

[10]See John Kifner, "An Oasis of Casinos Lifts a Poor Mississippi County."

others in the group returned early to the motor inn. At five the next morning I saw them jogging in the rain past the statues and other monuments in the national military park.

"TO GET AWAY. Away from what? In the long run, away from themselves," D. H. Lawrence wrote about the American urge to escape. Maybe so. Perhaps only after democracy slips away, silently replaced by the power of corporations and other great concentrations of wealth in a society whose basic instincts are tranquilized by pharmaceuticals, masturbatory gambling, and the voyeurism of colosseum sports, will the true destiny of America reveal itself.

This is not so much a dark vision as the darkest aspect of a much larger, neutral gray vision. For even as the culture of the European Enlightenment dissolves in the United States; as the outside world, especially Mexico, and a ruthless global economy encroaches upon it; and as wealthier Americans increasingly live their lives within protected communities, heavily zoned suburbs, defended corporate enclaves, private malls, and health clubs, the American ideal of a middle-class society is spreading throughout Asia, Latin America, and formerly Communist eastern Europe.

Reinhold Niebuhr counseled in *The Irony of American History* that our supracontinental power, purchased in part through the strength of our military, has, ironically, "interwoven our destiny with the destiny of many peoples and brought us into a vast web of history," which will "contradict" our most fervent hopes. There is no escaping the fact that as we change the world, the world changes us. But if we can pass out of our history slowly and gracefully, carrying on a global struggle for human rights and economic opportunity (backed up by military force) until an authentic planetary civil society emerges, America will have accomplished more than it ever did in the Homeric age of the Civil War, World War II, and the Cold War combined. But even if that is possible, it is a frustrating scenario for our military. While our defenders will not expire in defeat or rebellion like those of former empires, the military's gradual transition to the role of first among equals in a lean and mobile global strike force, in which blood-and-soil traditions have all but vanished, will be difficult and unsatisfying.

Before boarding a casino-chartered bus to take me back to the hotel, I stared out into the black night over the mile-wide Mississippi, now in full flood stage, and took solace in the fact that the casinos here were only a few years old, so perhaps they will be gone in a few years, too: just another turbulence on a landscape whose immensity and constant economic upheaval make much of it appear still virginal.

And I thought once more of Grant's seven failures before he began to succeed here, and of the lines from Stephen Vincent Benét's *John Brown's Body:*

> We can fail and fail,
> But deep against the failure, something wars,
> Something goes forward, something lights a match . . .[11]

The next passage will be our most difficult as a nation, and it will be our last.

[11]Benét, *John Brown's Body.*

ACKNOWLEDGMENTS

JASON EPSTEIN AT Random House is present throughout this book because of his painstaking editing and judgment. The flaws of this book are mine; the strengths, in part, his. For their support and editing and the excerpts they ran, I thank Bill Whitworth especially, and also Cullen Murphy, and Corby Kummer of *The Atlantic Monthly*. Close behind are Joy de Menil at Random House and the rest of the *Atlantic Monthly* staff, especially Barbara Wallraff and Sue Parilla. Thanks too to Lynn Anderson for copyediting.

My agent, Carl Brandt, has again been critical in bringing an idea to fruition and in stimulating my thinking about the American West. Thanks, too, to his associate, Marianne Merola. Financial assistance came from the John M. Olin Foundation in New York, administered through the Foreign Policy Research Institute in Philadelphia: I thank William Voegeli, Harvey Sicherman, Alan Luxenburg, and Harry Richlin. There is also Ken Jensen of the American Committee on Foreign Relations, who put me in touch with a few fascinating people in far-flung places across America.

For generous help, hospitality, and advice, I thank the following: Kathy Allen, Homero Aridjis and family, Robert Berlin and family, Fergus Bordewich, Charles Bowden, Colonel Al Bryant, Michael Carnahan, Magdalena Carral, Leigh Crane-Freeman, Bill

Donovan, Robert Epstein, Steve Ermine, John Ford, John Fox and family, Nathan Gardels (and his excellent *New Perspectives Quarterly*), Paul Glastris, Lou Gold, Elizabeth Gunn, Amy Hameroff, Stuart Hameroff, Marla Hingtgen, David Hinton, Lynn Holley, Hume Horan, Dennis Judd, Joel Kotkin, Wendy Laird, Rafael Ledesma, Diana Liverman, William A. MacNeil, Steve Marsden, Cecelia Mason, Molly McKasson, Yehuda Mirsky, Deborah Moore, Tony and Petra O'Brien, Paul A. Rahe, Tom Ricks, Anibal Romero, Robert Salisbury, John C. Scott, Tom Sharpe, Roger Spiller, David K. Taylor, Andrew J. Theising, and Bob Varady.

SELECTED BIBLIOGRAPHY

Adams, Henry. *The Education of Henry Adams*. Boston: Houghton Mifflin, 1961 (1906).

———. *The History of the United States During the Administrations of Thomas Jefferson*. New York: Library of America, 1986 (1889–1891).

Allen, H. C., and C. P. Hill. *British Essays in American History*. New York: St. Martin's Press, 1957.

Allen, James P., and Eugene Turner. *The Ethnic Quilt: Population Diversity in Southern California*. Northridge, California: Center for Geographic Studies, California State University, 1997.

Alvarez, A. "Learning from Las Vegas." *New York Review of Books,* Jan. 11, 1996.

Anderson, Sherwood. *Winesburg, Ohio*. New York: Viking, 1959 (1919).

———. *Poor White*. New York: B. W. Huebsch, 1920.

Aridjis, Homero, and Carlos Fuentes. "The Image of Our Future." *New Perspectives Quarterly,* Spring 1989.

Artibise, Alan F. J. *Cascadian Adventures: Shared Visions, Strategic Alliances, and Ingrained Barriers in a Transborder Region*. Vancouver: University of British Columbia, 1996.

Atwood, Margaret. *Survival: A Thematic Guide to Canadian Literature.* Concord, Ontario: Anansi Press, 1972.

Averille, Charles. *Kit Carson, Prince of the Gold Hunters.* 1849.

Bader, Robert Smith. *Hayseeds, Moralizers, and Methodists: The Twentieth-Century Image of Kansas.* Lawrence: University Press of Kansas, 1988.

Bakolas, Anastasia. *Human Nature in Thucydides.* Honors thesis, Wellesley College, Wellesley, Massachusetts, 1996.

Baldessare, Mark. *Trouble in Paradise: The Suburban Transformation in America.* New York: Columbia University Press, 1986.

Barman, Jean. *The West Beyond the West: A History of British Columbia.* Toronto: University of Toronto Press, 1996.

Bearss, Edwin Cole. *Unvexed to the Sea: The Campaign for Vicksburg.* Dayton, Ohio: Morningside Bookshop, 1995.

Beck, Warren A., and Ynez D. Haase. *Historical Atlas of the American West.* Norman: University of Oklahoma Press, 1989.

Bender, Mark C. *Watershed at Leavenworth: Dwight D. Eisenhower and the Command and General Staff School.* Leavenworth, Kansas: U.S. Army Command and General Staff College, 1990.

Benét, Stephen Vincent. *John Brown's Body.* New York: Henry Holt and Company, 1928.

Bercuson, David J. "Why Canada and Quebec Must Part." *Current History,* March 1995.

Bissinger, H. G. *Friday Night Lights: A Town, a Team, and a Dream.* Reading, Mass.: Addison-Wesley, 1990.

Black, Conrad. "Canadian Capers." *The National Interest,* Summer 1992.

Bolton, Herbert E. *Coronado: Knight of Pueblos and Plains.* Albuquerque: University of New Mexico Press, 1949.

Boorstin, Daniel J. *Hidden History: Exploring Our Secret Past.* New York: Harper & Row, 1987.

Borah, Leo A. "Nebraska: The Cornhusker State." *National Geographic,* May 1945.

Bordewich, Fergus M. *Killing the White Man's Indian: The Reinvention of Native Americans at the End of the Twentieth Century.* New York: Doubleday, 1996.

Bouvier, Leon F., and Lindsey Grant. *How Many Americans?: Population, Immigration, and the Environment.* San Francisco: Sierra Club, 1994.

Bowden, Charles. *Blood Orchid: An Unnatural History of America*. New York: Random House, 1995.

———. "Laughter, Gunfire, and Forgetting: An Elusive Tale of the Mexican Drug War." *Harper's*, September 1995.

———. "While You Were Sleeping: In Juarez, Mexico, Photographers Expose the Violent Realities of Free Trade." *Harper's*, December 1996.

Boyd, Julian P, ed. *The Papers of Thomas Jefferson*. Princeton, N.J.: Princeton University Press, 1950.

Brands, H. W. *The Reckless Decade: America in the 1890s*. New York: St. Martin's Press, 1995.

Braudel, Fernand. *The Mediterranean and the Mediterranean World in the Age of Philip II*. (Part One: About how geography determines human characteristics.) New York: Harper & Row, 1972.

Brooke, Rupert. *Letters from America*. New York: Scribner's, 1916.

Brosnahan, Tom, John Noble, Nancy Keller, Mark Balla, and Scott Wayne. *Mexico: A Travel Survival Kit*. Berkeley, Calif.: Lonely Planet Publications, 1992.

Brown, Kenneth A. *Four Corners: History, Land, and People of the Desert Southwest*. New York: HarperCollins, 1995.

Bryant, William Cullen. "The Prairies" (poem). In *The Treasury of American Poetry*. Selected by Nancy Sullivan. New York: Barnes & Noble, 1993.

Bryce, James. *The American Commonwealth*. 2 vols. New York: Macmillan, 1891.

Callenbach, Ernest. *Ecotopia*. Berkeley, Calif.: Banyan Tree, 1975.

Camus, Albert. *American Journals*. Translated by Hugh Levick. New York: Paragon House, 1987 (1946).

Carter, Paul A. *The Spiritual Crisis of the Gilded Age*. De Kalb: Northern Illinois University Press, 1971.

Casey, Robert L. *Journey to the High Southwest: A Traveler's Guide*. Old Saybrook, Conn.: Globe Pequot Press, 1983.

Cash, W. J. *The Mind of the South*. New York: Knopf, 1941.

Cather, Willa. *My Ántonia*. Boston: Houghton, 1918.

Chandler, A. Russell III. *The Last Olympics*. Franklin, Tenn.: Wessex House Publishing, 1996.

Chanes, Carlos Welti. *La Fecundidad en México*. Mexico City: Instituto Nacional de Estadística, Geografía e Informatica, 1994.

Churchill, Winston S. *The River War: An Historical Account of the Reconquest of the Soudan*. Two vols. London: Longmans, Green, 1899.

Claiborne, William. "Cascadia: A Culture Evolves in Northwest." *The Washington Post*, May 5, 1991.

Clendinnen, Inga. *Aztecs: An Interpretation*. New York: Cambridge University Press, 1991.

Codrescu, Andrei. *Road Scholar: Coast to Coast Late in the Century*. New York: Hyperion, 1993.

Cohen, Mitchell. "Rooted Cosmopolitanism." *Dissent*, Fall 1992.

A Comprehensive Program for Historic Preservation in Omaha. Omaha: Landmarks Heritage Preservation Commission, 1980.

Cook, Samantha, Jamie Jensen, Tim Perry, and Greg Ward. *USA: The Rough Guide*. London: Rough Guides, 1994.

Coontz, Stephanie. *The Way We Really Are: Coming to Terms with America's Changing Families*. New York: Basic Books, 1997.

Cooper, James Fenimore. *The Pathfinder*. New York: Penguin Books, 1989 (1840).

Crane, Hart. *The Complete Poems of Hart Crane*. Marc Simon, ed. New York: Liveright, 1986.

Creede, Constance. *Jean-Jacques Rousseau. Great Thinkers of the Western World*, edited by Ian P. McGreal. New York: HarperCollins, 1992.

Cummings, Joe. *Northern Mexico Handbook*. Chico, Calif.: Moon Publications, 1994.

Dahbour, Omar, and Micheline R. Ishay. *The Nationalism Reader*. Atlantic Highlands, N.J.: Humanities Press, 1995.

Davie, Michael. *In the Future Now: A Report from California*. London: Hamish Hamilton, 1972.

Davis, Mike. *City of Quartz: Excavating the Future in Los Angeles*. New York: Vintage, 1992.

Debo, Angie. *Oklahoma: Foot-Loose and Fancy-Free*. Norman: University of Oklahoma Press, 1949.

Degler, Carl N. *Out of Our Past: The Forces That Shaped Modern America*. New York: Harper & Row, 1959.

De Sahagun, Bernadino. *General History of the Things of New Spain.* Santa Fe: School of American Research, 1950–1963.

de Tocqueville, Alexis. *Democracy in America.* New York: Penguin Books, 1956 (1835).

De Voto, Bernard. *Across the Wide Missouri.* Boston: Houghton Mifflin, 1947.

————. *The Course of Empire.* Boston: Houghton Mifflin, 1952.

Díaz del Castillo, Bernal. *The Discovery and Conquest of Mexico: 1517–1521.* Translated with an introduction and notes by A. P. Maudslay. New York: Farrar, Straus and Cudahy, 1956.

Dickens, Charles. *American Notes.* New York: Collier, 1868.

Doran, Charles F. "Building a North American Community." *Current History,* March 1995.

Draper, Theodore. *A Struggle for Power: The American Revolution.* New York: Times Books, 1996.

Dutton, Clarence E. *Tertiary History.* 1882.

Egan, Timothy. "Urban Sprawl Strains Western States." *The New York Times,* Dec. 29, 1996.

Etzioni, Amitai. *The Community of Communities.* Washington, D.C.: The Communitarian Network, 1995.

Everhart, William C. *Vicksburg and the Opening of the Mississippi River, 1862–1863.* Washington, D.C.: National Park Service, 1986.

Farley, John E. "Race Still Matters: The Minimal Role of Income and Housing Cost as Causes of Housing Segregation in St. Louis, 1990." *Urban Affairs Review,* 1995.

Faulkner, William. *The Reivers.* New York: Random House, 1962.

Ferguson, Tim W. "Down with the Burbs! Back to the City!" *Forbes,* May 5, 1997.

Finseth, Gary. *Trade Stats Northwest: Export Analysis of Portland, Oregon.* Portland, 1996.

Fitzgerald, F. Scott. *The Great Gatsby.* New York: Scribner's, 1925.

Foote, Shelby. *The Beleaguered City: The Vicksburg Campaign.* New York: Modern Library, 1995 (1963).

Frazier, Ian. *Great Plains.* New York: Farrar, Straus & Giroux, 1989.

Frederickson, George M. "Land of Opportunity?" *New York Review of Books,* 1996.

Fuentes, Carlos. *The Buried Mirror: Reflections on Spain and the New World.* Boston: Houghton Mifflin, 1992.

———. *The Old Gringo.* New York: Farrar, Straus & Giroux, 1985.

———. "Why Damn a Great State Resource?" *Los Angeles Times,* Sept. 28, 1994.

Gardels, Nathan. "*La Raza Cosmica* in America." (Interview with Ryzsard Kapuscinski.) *New Perspectives Quarterly,* 1987.

Garland, Hamlin. *Prairie Songs.* Cambridge, Mass.: Stone & Kimball, 1903.

Garreau, Joel. *Edge Cities: Life on the New Urban Frontier.* New York: Doubleday, 1991.

———. *The Nine Nations of North America.* Boston: Houghton Mifflin, 1981.

Gayk, William F. "The Taxpayers' Revolt." In Rob Kling, Spencer Olin, and Mark Poster, eds., *Postsuburban California: The Transformation of Orange County Since World War II.* Berkeley: University of California Press, 1991.

Gibbon, Edward. *The History of the Decline and Fall of the Roman Empire.* New York: Knopf, 1993 (1776).

Gilbert, Bil. *Westering Man: The Life of Joseph Walker.* Norman: University of Oklahoma Press, 1985.

Gilbert, Felix. *The Historical Essays of Otto Hintze.* New York: Oxford University Press, 1975.

Gillenkirk, Jeff, and Mark Dowie. "The Great Indian Power Grab: Is Peter MacDonald the Moses of the Navajo Nation, Or Is He an Energy Baron Out for Himself and a Few Loyal Cronies?" *Mother Jones,* January 1982.

Gillerman, Margaret. "West to East: H. C. Milford Helps Boost East St. Louis." *St. Louis Post-Dispatch,* 1995.

Glastris, Paul. "Out of the Melting Pot, Into the Fire." *The Washington Monthly,* 1995.

Glastris, Paul, and Dorian Friedman. "A Tale of Two Suburbias: The Decline of Blue-Collar Suburbs and Growth of 'Edge Cities' Create a New Kind of Isolation." *U.S. News & World Report,* Nov. 9, 1992.

Goodman, Robert. *The Luck Business: The Devastating Consequences and*

Broken Promises of America's Gambling Explosion. New York: Free Press, 1995.

Gottberg, John. *Los Angeles: A Lonely Planet City Guide.* Oakland, Calif.: Lonely Planet Publications, 1996.

Grant, Campbell. *Canyon de Chelly: Its People and Rock Art.* Tucson: University of Arizona Press, 1978.

Grant, Michael. *The Fall of the Roman Empire.* London: Weidenfeld and Nicolson, 1990.

————. *Readings in the Classical Historians.* New York: Scribner's, 1992.

Grant, Ulysses S. *Memoirs and Selected Letters.* New York: Library of America, 1990 (1885).

Green, Donald E. *Panhandle Pioneer: Henry C. Hitch, His Ranch, and His Family.* Norman: University of Oklahoma Press, 1979.

Greene, Graham. *The Power and the Glory.* New York: Viking, 1946.

Grimsley, Mark. *The Hard Hand of War: Union Military Policy Toward Southern Civilians 1861–1865.* New York: Cambridge University Press, 1995.

"The Guardian Angel." *The Atlantic Monthly,* June 1867.

Gunther, John. *Inside U.S.A.* New York: Harper & Brothers, 1947.

Hacker, Andrew. "The War over the Family." *The New York Review of Books,* Dec. 4, 1997.

Hammer, Langdon. *Hart Crane and Allen Tate: Janus-faced Modernism.* Princeton, N.J.: Princeton University Press, 1993.

Harden, Blaine. *A River Lost: The Life and Death of the Columbia.* New York: Norton, 1996.

Harris, Marvin. *Cannibals and Kings: The Origins of Cultures.* New York: Random House, 1977.

Hawthorne, Nathaniel. *The Marble Faun.* 1860.

Hochschild, Arlie Russell. *The Time Bind: When Work Becomes Home and Home Becomes Work.* New York: Metropolitan Books, 1997.

Hochschild, Jennifer L. *Facing Up to the American Dream: Race, Class, and the Soul of the Nation.* Princeton, N.J.: Princeton University Press, 1996.

Hoffman, Alexander von. "Good News!: From Boston to San Francisco the Community-Based Housing Movement Is Transforming Bad Neighborhoods." *The Atlantic Monthly,* January 1997.

Hoffmann, Stanley. "Report of the Conference on Conditions of World

Order—June 12–19, 1965, Villa Serbelloni, Bellagio, Italy." *Daedalus,* Spring 1996.

Holbrook, Stewart H. *Wild Bill Hickok Tames the West.* New York: Random House, 1952.

Hopi Tribe. *A Brief History of the Hopi-Navajo Land Problem.* Kykotsmovi, Ariz.: Hopi Tribe.

Howard, Philip, and Thomas Homer-Dixon. *Environmental Scarcities and Violent Conflict: The Case of Chiapas, Mexico.* Toronto: University of Toronto, 1995.

Howells, William Dean. *The Rise of Silas Lapham.* New York: Norton, 1982 (1885).

Hume, David. *Essays Moral, Political, and Literary.* Edited by Eugene F. Miller. Indianapolis: Liberty Fund, 1985.

Hunt, Elvid, and Walter E. Lorence. *History of Fort Leavenworth 1827–1937.* Fort Leavenworth, Kans.: Command and General Staff School Press, 1937.

Hurtado, Aida, David E. Hayes-Bautista, R. Burciaga Valdez, and Anthony C. R. Hernandez. *Redefining California: Latino Social Engagement in a Multicultural Society.* Los Angeles: UCLA Chicano Studies Research Center, 1992.

Jackson, Kenneth T. "America's Rush to Suburbia." *The New York Times,* June 9, 1996.

Jacobs, Jane. *Cities and the Wealth of Nations.* New York: Random House, 1984.

———. *The Death and Life of Great American Cities.* New York: Random House, 1961.

James, Henry. *The American Scene.* New York: Penguin, 1994 (1907).

Judd, Dennis R. *Walled Enclaves and the Construction of Community.* Vol. 6 of *Research in Community Sociology.* Greenwich, Conn.: JAI Press, 1996.

Judd, Dennis R., and Todd Swanstrom. *City Politics: Private Power and Public Policy.* New York: HarperCollins, 1994.

Jung, Carl G. *Man and His Symbols.* New York: Dell, 1968.

Kazin, Alfred. *On Native Grounds: An Interpretation of Modern American Prose Literature.* New York: Reynal & Hitchcock, 1942.

Keegan, John. *Fields of Battle: The Wars for North America.* New York: Knopf, 1996.

———. *The Mask of Command.* New York: Viking, 1987.

———. *Six Armies in Normandy: From D-Day to the Liberation of Paris.* New York: Viking, 1982.

Kennedy, David M. "Can We Still Afford to Be a Nation of Immigrants?" *The Atlantic Monthly,* November 1996.

Kennedy, Paul. *The Rise and Fall of the Great Powers.* New York: Random House, 1987.

Kerouac, Jack. *On the Road.* New York: Viking, 1957.

Kifner, John. "An Oasis of Casinos Lifts a Poor Mississippi County." *The New York Times,* Oct. 4, 1996.

Kipling, Rudyard. *From Sea to Sea and Other Sketches.* Garden City, N.Y.: Doubleday, 1925.

Kling, Rob, Spencer Olin, and Mark Poster, eds. *Postsuburban California: The Transformation of Orange County Since World War II.* Berkeley: University of California Press, 1991.

Kotkin, Joel. "Make Way for the Urban Confederates." *The American Enterprise,* November–December 1996.

———. "Will the Chinese Save L.A.?" *The American Enterprise,* September–October 1996.

Kozol, Jonathan. *Savage Inequalities.* New York: Crown, 1991.

Krauss, Clifford. "Fighting the Drug War with Boomerangs." *The New York Times,* Mar. 30, 1997.

Kunstler, James Howard. *Home from Nowhere.* New York: Simon & Schuster, 1996.

Kuralt, Charles. *Charles Kuralt's America.* New York: Putnam, 1995.

Langewiesche, William. *Cutting for Sign.* New York: Pantheon, 1993.

Lawrence, D. H. *Mornings in Mexico.* London: Martin Secker, 1927.

———. *Studies in Classic American Literature.* New York: Viking, 1964 (1923).

Leacock, Stephen. *Sunshine Sketches of a Little Town.* Toronto: Bell & Cockburn, 1912.

Least Heat-Moon, William. *Blue Highways: A Journey into America.* Boston: Houghton Mifflin, 1983.

———. *PrairyErth (A Deep Map).* Boston: Houghton Mifflin, 1991.

Lemann, Nicholas. *The Promised Land: The Great Black Migration and How It Changed America.* New York: Knopf, 1991.

Leonard, Nancy Laughlin. *Images of a Past: No Man's Land.* Privately published, 1989.

Lévi-Strauss, Claude. *Tristes Tropiques,* translated by John and Doreen Weightman. New York: Atheneum, 1974.

Lewis, Sinclair. *Main Street.* New York: Harcourt Brace, 1920.

Lind, Michael. *The Next American Nation: The New Nationalism and the Fourth American Revolution.* New York: Free Press, 1995.

Linthicum, Leslie. "Surge of Violence on the Reservation." *The Sunday Journal* (Albuquerque), Feb. 4, 1996.

Lowe, Percival G. *Five Years a Dragoon.* Norman: University of Oklahoma Press, 1965 (1905).

Luhan, Mabel Dodge. *Edge of the Taos Desert: An Escape to Reality.* Vol. 4 of *Intimate Memories.* New York: Harcourt, Brace and Company, 1937.

Macheski, Dennis, and Shais Khan. *Demographic and Economic Trends: Their Implications for Real Estate in Orange County, California.* Price Waterhouse, 1994.

———. *Demographic and Economic Trends: Their Implications for Real Estate in the Pacific West.* Price Waterhouse, 1994.

Madison, James, Alexander Hamilton, and John Jay. *The Federalist.* 1787–1788.

Madrick, Jeffrey. *The End of Affluence: The Causes and Consequences of America's Economic Decline.* New York: Random House, 1995.

Malone, Michael P. *Montana: A Contemporary Profile.* Helena, Mont.: American Geographic World Publishers, 1996.

Marcuse, Peter. "What's So New About Divided Cities?" *International Journal of Urban and Regional Research,* September 1993.

Márquez, Gabriel García. *One Hundred Years of Solitude.* New York: Harper & Row, 1970.

Mather, Christine, and Sharon Woods. *Santa Fe Style.* New York: Rizzoli, 1986.

Maurois, André. *Chateaubriand.* Translated by Vera Fraser. London: Jonathan Cape, 1938.

McDougall, Walter A. *Let the Sea Make a Noise: A History of the North Pacific from Magellan to MacArthur.* New York: Basic Books, 1993.

McGann, Thomas F. *The Ordeal of Cabeza de Vaca*. Vol. 1 of *American Heritage Illustrated History of the United States*. New York: Dell, 1963.

McKasson, Molly, and Dave Devine. "The Growth of Tucson's Working Poor." *Tucson Weekly,* Sept. 12–18, 1996.

McKenzie, Evan. *Privatopia*. New Haven, Conn.: Yale University Press, 1994.

Meinig, D. W. *The Interpretations of Ordinary Landscapes*. New York: Oxford University Press, 1979.

Melville, Herman. *The Confidence Man*. New York: Penguin, 1990 (1857).

———. *Moby-Dick*. New York: Everyman's Library, 1991 (1851).

Millet, Allan R., and Peter Maslowski. *For the Common Defense: A Military History of the United States of America*. New York: Free Press, 1994.

Milosz, Czeslaw. *The Captive Mind*. Translated by Jane Zielonko. New York: Vintage Books, 1955.

Minks, Louise. *The Hudson River School*. Avenel, N.J.: Crescent Books, 1989.

Mojtabai, A. G. *Blessed Assurance: At Home with the Bomb in Amarillo, Texas*. Boston: Houghton Mifflin, 1986.

Musil, Robert. *The Man Without Qualities*. New York: Knopf, 1995 (1952).

Nairn, Tom. *The Break-Up of Britain: Crisis and Neo-Nationalism*. Atlantic Highlands, N.J.: Humanities Press, 1977.

"New Mexico: Flirting with the Future." *The Economist,* Jan. 4, 1997.

Niebuhr, Reinhold. *The Irony of American History*. New York: Charles Scribner's Sons, 1952.

———. *Moral Man and Immoral Society*. New York: Charles Scribner's Sons, 1932.

Norris, Kathleen. *Dakota: A Spiritual Geography*. Boston: Houghton Mifflin, 1993.

Norse, Elliott. *Ancient Forests of the Pacific Northwest*. 1989.

Nugent, Daniel. *Spent Cartridges of Revolution: An Anthropological History of Namiquipa, Chihuahua*. Chicago: University of Chicago Press, 1993.

Nugent, Walter. "Where Is the American West?" *Montana: The Magazine of Western History,* Summer 1992.

O'Donnell, Guillermo. "The Browning of Latin America." *New Perspectives Quarterly,* Fall 1993.

O'Donnell, Terence. *That Balance So Rare: The Story of Oregon.* Portland: Oregon Historical Society Press, 1988.

Odum, Howard W., and Harry Estill Moore. *American Regionalism: A Cultural-Historical Approach to National Integration.* New York: Holt, Rinehart and Winston, 1938.

Ormsby, Margaret A. *British Columbia: A History.* Toronto: Macmillan Canada, 1958.

Owen, Louis. *John Steinbeck's Re-Vision of America.* Athens: University of Georgia Press, 1985.

Pachter, Mark. *Abroad in America: Visitors to the New Nation 1776–1914.* Washington, D.C.: Smithsonian Institution, 1976.

Palmer, Dave R. *1794: America, Its Army, and the Birth of the Nation.* Novato, Calif.: Presidio, 1994.

Pareto, Vilfredo. *The Mind and Society.* Translated by Andrew Bongiorno and Arthur Livingston. New York: Harcourt, Brace, 1935.

Parkes, Henry Bamford. *A History of Mexico.* Boston: Houghton Mifflin, 1960.

Parkman, Francis. *Montcalm and Wolfe..* New York: Atheneum, 1984 (1884).

———. *The Oregon Trail.* Gansevoort, N.Y.: Corner House Publications, 1980.

Parrington, Vernon Louis. *Main Currents in American Thought.* New York: 1930.

Payne, Douglas. "Mexico and Its Discontents." *Harper's,* April 1995.

Paz, Octavio. Interviewed by Nathan Gardels. *New Perspectives Quarterly,* Winter 1991.

———. *The Labyrinth of Solitude.* Translated by Lysander Kemp, Yara Milos, and Rachel Phillips Belash. New York: Grove Press, 1985.

Pearson, Michael. *Imagined Places: Journeys into Literary America.* Jackson: University Press of Mississippi, 1991.

Peterson, Peter G. "Will America Grow Up Before It Grows Old?" *The Atlantic Monthly,* May 1996.

Phares, Donald. *Addressing Urban Needs in a Highly Fragmented Metropolitan Area: The On-Going Saga of St. Louis.* St. Louis: North American Institute for Comparative Urban Research, 1994.

The Poem of the Cid. Translated by Lesley Byrd Simpson. Berkeley: University of California Press, 1957.

Polybius. *The Rise of the Roman Empire.* Translated by Ian Scott-Kilvert. New York: Penguin Books, 1979.

Prescott, William H. *History of the Conquest of Mexico: With a Preliminary View of the Ancient Mexican Civilization, and the Life of the Conqueror, Hernando Cortez.* 3 vols. Philadelphia: J. B. Lippincott & Company, 1868 (1843).

Preston, Samuel H. "Children Will Pay: Demography's Crystal Ball Shows That 21st-Century America Will Be Older, Wiser and More Ethnically Diverse. But Its Kids Face Trouble." *The New York Times Magazine,* Sept. 29, 1996.

Price, Gordon. "The Deceptive City: How Vancouver Built a City for the 21st Century on the Foundations of the 19th." Speech delivered to Association of Bay Area Governments, San Francisco, April 18, 1997.

Primm, James Neal. *Lion of the Valley: St. Louis, Missouri.* Western Urban History Series. Boulder, Colorado: Pruett Publishing, 1981.

Pyle, Ernie. *Ernie Pyle's America: The Best of Ernie Pyle's 1930s Travel Dispatches.* Edited with an introduction by David Nichols. New York: Random House, 1989.

Raban, Jonathan. *Bad Land: An American Romance.* New York: Pantheon, 1996.

Rahe, Paul A. *Republics Ancient and Modern.* Chapel Hill: University of North Carolina Press, 1992.

Rathjen, Frederick W. *The Texas Panhandle Frontier.* Austin: University of Texas Press, 1973.

Reavis, Dick J. *Conversations with Moctezuma: Ancient Shadows over Modern Life in Mexico.* New York: William Morrow, 1990.

Reed, John. *Insurgent Mexico.* New York, 1914. Republished in *The Collected Works of John Reed.* New York: Modern Library, 1995.

Reed, John Shelton. *The Enduring South: Subcultural Persistence in Mass Society.* Chapel Hill: University of North Carolina Press, 1986.

Reeves, Richard. *American Journey: Traveling with Tocqueville in Search of Democracy in America.* New York: Simon and Schuster, 1982.

Reisner, Marc. *Cadillac Desert: The American West and Its Disappearing Water.* New York: Viking Penguin, 1986.

Reynolds, David S. *Walt Whitman's America: A Cultural Biography*. New York: Knopf, 1995.

Richler, Mordecai. *Oh Canada! Oh Quebec! Requiem for a Divided Country*. Toronto: Penguin Books Canada, 1992.

Ricks, Thomas E. "The Great Society in Camouflage." *The Atlantic Monthly*, December 1996.

Riding, Alan. *Distant Neighbors: A Portrait of the Mexicans*. New York: Knopf, 1984.

Robertson, William G. *The Staff Ride*. Washington, D.C.: U.S. Army Center of Military History, 1987.

Rodriguez, Gregory. *The Emerging Latino Middle Class*. Los Angeles: Pepperdine University Institute for Public Policy, 1996.

Rodriguez, Richard. *Days of Obligation: An Argument with My Mexican Father*. New York: Viking Penguin, 1992.

————. "*La Raza Cosmica*." Interview with Marilyn Berlin Snell. *New Perspectives Quarterly*, Winter 1991.

Rosenberry, Katherine. *Condominium and Homeowner Associations: Should They Be Treated like Mini-Governments?* Washington, D.C.: Advisory Commission on Intergovernmental Relations, 1989.

Rosenstone, Robert A. *Romantic Revolutionary: A Biography of John Reed*. New York: Knopf, 1975.

Rudnik, Lois Palken. *Mabel Dodge Luhan: New Woman, New Worlds*. Albuquerque: University of New Mexico Press, 1984.

Rudwick, Elliott. *Race Riot at East St. Louis, July 2, 1917*. Carbondale: University of Southern Illinois Press, 1964.

Rybczynski, Witold. *City Life: Urban Expectations in a New World*. New York: Scribner's, 1996.

Sassen, Saskia. *Cities in a World Economy*. Thousand Oaks, Calif.: Pine Forge Press, 1994.

Schama, Simon. *Landscape and Memory*. New York: Knopf, 1995.

Schor, Juliet B. *The Overworked American: The Unexpected Decline of Leisure*. New York: Basic Books, 1992.

Schwantes, Carlos Arnaldo. *The Pacific Northwest: An Interpretive History*. Lincoln: University of Nebraska Press, 1989.

Schwarz, John E., and Thomas J. Volgy. *The Forgotten Americans*. New York: Norton, 1992.

Sedgwick, Ellery. *A History of* The Atlantic Monthly *1857–1909: Yankee Humanism at High Tide and Ebb*. Amherst: University of Massachusetts Press, 1994.

Setterberg, Fred. *The Roads Taken: Travels Through America's Literary Landscapes*. Athens: University of Georgia Press, 1993.

"Silicon Valley: The Valley of Money's Delight." *The Economist,* Mar. 29, 1997.

Silko, Leslie Marmon. *Almanac of the Dead*. New York: Simon & Schuster, 1991.

Simpson, James H. *Report of an Expedition into the Navajo Country in 1849*. Washington, D.C.: Senate Document 64, 1850.

Skerry, Peter. *Mexican Americans: The Ambivalent Minority*. New York: Free Press, 1993.

Skinner, Quentin. *The Return of Grand Theory in the Human Sciences*. New York: Cambridge University Press, 1985.

Smith, Anthony D. *National Identity*. Reno: University of Nevada Press, 1991.

Snow, Anita. "Smugglers Are Saints in Culiacan's Drug Culture." Associated Press. Published in *The Mexico News* (Mexico City), Sept. 4, 1995.

Snyder, Gary. *Turtle Island*. New York: New Directions, 1969.

Snyder, Louis L. *The New Nationalism*. Ithaca, N.Y.: Cornell University Press, 1968.

Solnit, Rebecca. *Savage Dreams: A Journey into the Landscape Wars of the American West*. San Francisco: Sierra Club Books, 1994.

Sorkin, Michael. *Variations on a Theme Park: The New American City and the End of Space*. New York: Noonday Press, 1992.

Statistical Abstract of the United States 1996. Washington, D.C.: U.S. Department of Commerce, 1996.

Stegner, Wallace. *Beyond the Hundredth Meridian: John Wesley Powell and the Second Opening of the West*. Boston: Houghton Mifflin, 1954.

———. *The Uneasy Chair: A Biography of Bernard De Voto*. Garden City, N.Y.: Doubleday, 1974.

Steinbeck, John. *The Grapes of Wrath*. New York: Viking, 1939.

———. *Travels with Charley: In Search of America*. New York: Viking, 1962.

Tarkington, Booth. *The Magnificent Ambersons.* New York: Bantam Books, 1994 (1918).

Theising, Andrew J. *Profitable Boundaries: Incorporating the Industrial Suburb.* St. Louis: University of Missouri, 1996.

Thompson, Jerry. *Diverting Interests.* New York: Equinox, 1993.

Thucydides. *The Peloponnesian War.* Translated by Thomas Hobbes. Chicago: University of Chicago Press, 1989 (1628).

Trueheart, Charles. "The Next Church." *The Atlantic Monthly,* August 1996.

Trueheart, Charles, and Dennis McAuliffe Jr. "Indians Demand Power, Economic Benefits as Free Market Sweeps the Hemisphere." *The Washington Post,* Sept. 11, 1995.

Tucson: The People and the Place: Highlights from the 1990 Census. Tucson: City of Tucson, 1992.

Udall, Stewart L. *To the Inland Empire: Coronado and Our Spanish Legacy.* Garden City, N.Y.: Doubleday, 1987.

Valle, Eduardo. "Narco-Power and the Subterranean NAFTA." *New Perspectives Quarterly,* Winter 1995.

Varady, Robert G., Helen Ingram, and Leonard Milich. "The Sonoran Pimeria Alta: Shared Environmental Problems and Challenges." *Journal of the Southwest,* Spring 1995.

Varady, Robert G., and Maura D. Mack. "Transboundary Water Resources and Public Health in the U.S.-Mexico Border Region." *Journal of Environmental Health,* April 1995.

Vlahos, Michael. *A Magna Carta for the Knowledge Age.* Washington, D.C.: Progress and Freedom Foundation, 1994.

———. "The War After Byte City." *The Washington Quarterly,* Spring 1997.

Walker, Captain J. G., and Major O. L. Shepherd. *The Navajo Reconnaissance: A Military Exploration of the Navajo Country in 1859.* Los Angeles: Westernlore Press, 1964.

Watkins, T. H. "The Laughing Prophet of Balk Mountain." *Orion,* Winter 1990.

Webb, Walter Prescott. *The Great Plains.* Boston: Ginn and Company, 1931.

Weir, Bill, and Robert Blake. *Arizona: Traveler's Handbook.* Chico, Calif.: Moon Publications, 1995.

Weiss, Stanley A. "Mexico's Ruling Party Would Do Better to Lose." *International Herald Tribune,* Aug. 18, 1994.

Williams, Jack. "The Gadsden Purchase: It Was Really a Bargain." *Nogales* (Ariz.) *International,* Oct. 31, 1995.

Wilson, Edmund. *Patriotic Gore: Studies in the Literature of the American Civil War.* New York: Farrar, Straus & Giroux, 1962.

Wilson, Elizabeth. *Hallucinations: Life in the Post-Modern City.* London: Hutchinson, 1989.

Winckler, Suzanne. "I-80's Exits to History in Nebraska." *The New York Times,* July 22, 1990.

Winship, George Parker. *The Coronado Expedition, 1540–1542.* Washington, D.C.: U.S. Government Printing Office, 1896.

Woodward, C. Vann. "The Irony of Southern History." Originally published in 1952 and republished in *The Burden of Southern History.* Baton Rouge: Louisiana State University Press, 1968.

Young, Norma Gene Butterbaugh. *Not a Stoplight in the County.* Boise City, Okla.: Boise City News Consultants, 1986.

Zukin, Sharon. *Landscapes of Power: From Detroit to Disney World.* Berkeley: University of California Press, 1991.

Zwingle, Erla. "Ogallala Aquifer: Wellspring of the High Plains." *National Geographic,* March 1993.

INDEX

ABOUT THE AUTHOR

ROBERT D. KAPLAN is a contributing editor of *The Atlantic Monthly* and the author of five previous books on travel and foreign affairs, translated into a dozen languages. One book, *Balkan Ghosts,* was chosen by *The New York Times Book Review* as one of the nine best nonfiction books of 1993. Two others, *The Ends of the Earth* and *The Arabists,* were chosen by *The New York Times* as "notable books" of the year in 1996 and 1993. He lives with his wife and son in the Berkshires, in western Massachusetts.

ABOUT THE TYPE

This book was set in Baskerville, a typeface designed by John Baskerville, an amateur printer and typefounder, and cut for him by John Handy in 1750. The type became popular again when The Lanston Monotype Corporation of London revived the classic roman face in 1923. The Merganthaler Linotype Company in England and the United States cut a version of Baskerville in 1931, making it one of the most widely used faces today.